PLATO'S POLITICAL PHILOSOPHY

PLATO'S POLITICAL PHILOSOPHY

PRUDENCE IN THE *REPUBLIC* AND THE *LAWS*

ZDRAVKO PLANINC

UNIVERSITY OF MISSOURI PRESS

Columbia and London

5 4 3 2 1   95 94 93 92 91

Library of Congress Cataloging-in-Publication Data

Planinc, Zdravko, 1953–
    Plato's political philosophy : prudence in the Republic and the Laws /
Zdravko Planinc.
        p. cm.
    Includes bibliographical references and index.
    ISBN 0-8262-0798-7 (alk. paper)
    1. Plato.   2. Prudence—History.   3. Political science—Philosophy—
History.   I. Title.
B395.P515   1991
320′.092—dc20   91–14637
                                                                      CIP

♾™ This paper meets the minimum requirements of
the American National Standard for Permanence of Paper
for Printed Library Materials, Z39.48, 1984.

Designer: Elizabeth K. Fett
Typesetter: Connell-Zeko Type & Graphics
Printer: Thomson-Shore, Inc.
Binder: Thomson-Shore, Inc.
Typeface: Aster

For Leah Bradshaw
Emma Planinc
Jacob Planinc

CONTENTS

PREFACE

PLATO AND ARISTOTLE STAND together in Raphael's *School of Athens*. Raphael deliberately contravened the iconography of his time to paint the *concordantia Platonis et Aristotelis*. Traditional iconography was based on Boethius's understanding of philosophy. It separated the figures of Plato and Aristotle and placed Aristotle in a lower station to represent the superiority of theory to practice. Raphael understood philosophy differently, placing theory and practice together. The aspiration to their concordance is the very heart of the school of Athens. Raphael depicts that aspiration not only in the central place he gives to Plato and Aristotle, but also in the manner of his self-portrait as a member of the school. Raphael stands to one side in the painting. A group of three figures stands close to him: an elderly man, a mature man, and a youth. Individually, they are thought to represent memory, intelligence, and providence. As Carl Gustaf Stridbeck has pointed out, the group taken as a whole represents prudence. Raphael stands below Plato and Aristotle, but his position demonstrates his willingness to ascend the steps toward them. For Raphael, the philosophic aspiration to the concordance of theory and practice is an aspiration to prudence.

Boethius's Christianity led him to distinguish the ascent to prudence from the ascent to philosophic theory and practice: prudence is a consequence of the love of God, not of philosophy. Boethius's fate led him to separate theory from practice. After many years as a successful politician, he wrote the *Consolation of Philosophy* in prison while awaiting execution at the hands of his enemies. Nevertheless, Boethius may be said to be a member of the school of Athens. He aspired to its end even though he only recognized the aspiration dimly in the writings of Plato and Aristotle.

Modern philosophy is a new school. Although it appropriates the language of Boethius's account of theory and practice, it rejects the aspiration Boethius shared with Plato and Aristotle. This is what makes it new. However, like all new schools, modern philosophy claims that it is not entirely new. It discovers its origins in

the old school, more specifically in Aristotle. For modern philosophy, there is no concord in the school of Athens: Plato and Aristotle stand apart, and Plato is placed in a lower station. The reasons
given for Plato's position in the new iconography are often paradoxical. Plato, the lover of myths, is insufficiently rational to
stand with Aristotle, the theorist; Plato, the idealist, is insufficiently reasonable to stand with Aristotle, the realist; Plato, the
theorist, is too rationalistic to stand with Aristotle, the practical
man. Paradoxical formulations of this sort are a direct consequence of the modern attempt to give new meaning to the pre-
modern language of theory and practice. The underlying reason
for Plato's low station, however, is constant: Plato, the divine, is
too much like Boethius to stand with Aristotle, the first modern
philosopher.

Plato and Aristotle do not stand together in most modern classical scholarship because most modern classicists either belong
to the new school, despite their professions of faith in scholarly
neutrality, or they advance its cause unwittingly by using the os-
tensibly neutral methods of analysis it has developed. It is possible to study classical texts without participating in the quarrel
between the Christian and modern (not to say anti-Christian) interpretations of them, but not if the study proceeds from ignorance of the full extent of the quarrel. It is possible to study Plato
and Aristotle directly, but not if one evades engagement with their
writings in the name of scholarly distance. Proper scholarship
requires both knowledge of the traditions of interpretation and
direct engagement.

In the past several decades, the study of Plato and Aristotle has
been transformed by the scholarship of Eric Voegelin, Hans-Georg
Gadamer, Leo Strauss, and Stanley Rosen. They have refused to
succumb to the philodoxy of the age, they have allowed themselves
to be addressed by the texts, and despite their other differences,
they have all recognized the simple truth that Plato and Aristotle
stand together. My work is based on theirs. It is intended to contrib-
ute to Plato's restoration. More specifically, it is an analysis of
Plato's account of prudence in the *Republic* and *Laws*. It is based on
the analyses of Plato's moral and political philosophy by Gadamer
and Voegelin, and it uses the techniques of textual commentary
developed by Strauss and Rosen, among others.

The best way to describe the substance of my work briefly is
with the assistance of Raphael's imagery. Modern classical schol-

arship does not see the *concordantia Platonis et Aristotelis* in the *School of Athens*. The painting is understood as a study in opposites. Plato's right hand is raised, a single finger pointing to heaven; the text indicating the significance of his gesture, the *Timaeus*, is held vertically in his left. Aristotle's right hand is extended in front of him, his fingers revealing the multiplicity of the world; the *Ethics*, the text indicating the significance of his gesture, is held horizontally in his left. The one is opposed to the many, the otherworldly is opposed to the world, and cosmogonic speculation is opposed to moral philosophy—hence, Plato is opposed to Aristotle. But this cannot have been Raphael's intention. It is an interpretation of the painting that simply restates the traditional iconography Raphael rejected. It does no justice to the manner in which Raphael presents Plato and Aristotle together.

The figures of the two philosophers are framed by a vaulted archway through which the vault of heaven can be seen. Where they are closest to one another, Aristotle's outstretched right hand is beside the *Timaeus* in Plato's left. The *Timaeus* describes the demiurgic genesis of the multiplicity of things in the cosmos from the One; the multiplicity of things itself is more fully described in Aristotle's writings. As Aristotle's right hand is associated with Plato's left, so too Plato's right hand is associated with Aristotle's left. The vaulted archway joins them. The line of the vault ascends toward heaven, following Plato's pointing finger, reaches its apogee above the vault of heaven, and then descends to the book Aristotle holds. The *Ethics* describes the worldly consequences of the soul's ascent toward what lies beyond the cosmos; the ascent itself is more fully described in Plato's dialogues. But Plato's dialogues also describe the worldly consequences of the ascent. The *concordantia Platonis et Aristotelis* is best seen in the account of prudence given in the *Republic* and *Laws*.

Without the patience and encouragement of my family, friends, colleagues, and teachers, this book could not have been written. All deserve my thanks, and several deserve public recognition. Leah Bradshaw and Leon Craig, in their different ways, improved my work by challenging me with difficult questions. Barry Cooper, though he may not want it on the record, taught me almost everything I know about Plato. Christian Lenhardt and Harvey Mansfield were charged, at different times, with supervising my studies; both did so with the liberality that identifies a true gentleman.

PLATO'S POLITICAL PHILOSOPHY

INTRODUCTION

Plato's Political Idealism

Plato is generally thought to be a political idealist. The most important feature of his idealism is said by his critics to be its lack of prudence or *phronesis*. There is no evidence that Plato had any understanding of prudence in either his words or his deeds, it is claimed. He neither possessed nor understood the good of possessing prudential political judgment. Plato's critics usually argue that his most political dialogues, the *Republic* and the *Laws*, describe ideal societies, or societies drawn up in accordance with abstract first principles, which Plato imprudently believed were practically realizable. The abstract character of these cities in speech is said to be most evident in his failure to describe prudence, or practical wisdom in the Aristotelian sense, as one of the first principles of their organization. Furthermore, Plato's critics usually claim that his own imprudence is apparent in the futile attempt he made to realize the political ideals of the *Republic* by means of an association with the younger Dionysius, a Sicilian tyrant. The disastrous consequences of this attempt led Plato to temper his idealism somewhat in his later years. But this does not mean that he came to understand the nature of *phronesis*, or that he came to possess good political judgment. It only indicates that his political idealism became less vigorous or more cautious. Most of Plato's critics would agree that traces of the totalitarianism inherent in his idealism can be found even in the political program of the *Laws*, his last dialogue.

This brief summary of several criticisms commonly made of Plato's political and personal imprudence is something of a hybrid. Its main themes reappear time and again in modern discussions of Plato's political philosophy. Consider, for example, the works of Ronald Beiner, Hannah Arendt, and Karl Popper.

Ronald Beiner's book, *Political Judgment*, contains a historical survey of various philosophical understandings of prudence and a lengthy discussion of the opposed accounts of political prudence

1

given by Aristotle and Kant. Concerning the ancient Greeks, Beiner argues that Aristotle was the first philosopher to comprehend the distinctive nature of *phronesis* as a dianoetic virtue or quality of the deliberative mind, and hence the first to describe adequately the specific characteristics of prudential judgment and political prudence. There is no such comprehension to be found in Plato's writings; if anything, there is a rejection of pre-Socratic understandings of practical judgment. Beiner writes: "the first recognition of a human faculty of judging particulars without the benefit of a universal rule goes back to Plato's dialogue, the *Statesman*."[1] In other words, the first recognition of the faculty of *phronesis* is to be found in the Eleatic philosophy presented in the *Statesman*. Platonism itself stands in opposition to it; the Eleatic insight is first developed by Aristotle.

Beiner does not discuss Plato's *Republic* and *Laws* explicitly, but he does make two criticisms of the Platonic understanding of *phronesis* that bear some relation to these dialogues. Beiner cites Hans-Georg Gadamer's account of Aristotelian ethics in claiming that "a universalist theory of the good, such as Plato provided with his 'idea of the good,' lessens the need for judgment (or Aristotelian *phronesis*), and diminishes the status of judgment. It is precisely because we do not have access to an absolute universal under which we need only subsume particulars that [we must seek] instruction from Aristotelian ethics." Plato's universalist theory of the good leads him to confuse *sophia* and *phronesis*, that is, theoretical and practical wisdom, and to consider *phronesis* as a mere knowledge of means. Beiner criticizes Plato's understanding of political judgment explicitly when he contends: "Platonic *politike techne*, in direct contrast to Aristotelian *politike phronesis*, renders ethics unproblematic by oversimplifying the dialectical relationship between universal and particular."[2] Not only does Plato not distinguish properly between *sophia* and *phronesis*; he also mistakes *phronesis* for a *techne* (art) in the political realm. Consequently, he cannot adequately distinguish between political action on the one hand and technical production or the realization of theoretical political goals on the other. The *Republic* and the *Laws*, Beiner would argue, contain just such abstract political ideals.

Plato is a political idealist for Beiner. His political idealism is a necessary consequence of the subsumption of practical wisdom to theoretical wisdom. If political matters are understood by way of the universals of theoretical wisdom and not by way of the formation of prudent political judgments, then political action becomes a *techne,* an application of abstract universals to particular circumstances. Like all imprudent idealists, then, Plato judged political matters by abstract universals and acted in the political realm by attempting to apply these universals in a technical way.

Hannah Arendt discusses Plato's political idealism similarly in an essay comparing Plato's attempts to educate the tyrant Dionysius and Martin Heidegger's association with Hitler's National Socialist Party. Arendt claims that Plato and Heidegger, because they are philosophers, are both "passionate thinkers." This is why they both lack prudence and sound political judgment. Passionate thinking does not lead to *phronesis;* indeed, it is inherently imprudent. Passionate thinking also is not the pursuit of theoretical wisdom. It is thinking as "pure activity—and this means impelled neither by the thirst for knowledge nor the drive for cognition."[3] Arendt would agree with Beiner that a philosopher's thought ought not be guided by, nor directed toward absolutes such as the Platonic idea of the good. Philosophic thought is identifiable by its passionate nature alone.

Arendt claims the first passionate thinker was neither Plato nor Socrates, but Thales. Thales is described in Plato's *Theaetetus* (174a–75d) as having been so intent upon observing the stars that he tumbled into a well, much to the delight of a farm girl, who thought him an imprudent fool. All human beings have this ability to wonder at things, but what sets the true philosopher apart, according to Arendt, is the "taking up and accepting [of] this wondering as one's abode." Arendt also writes that it would be best if philosophers did not leave their proper abode and "get involved in the world of human affairs," though Thales did so with some success (cf. Aristotle, *Politics* 1259a5–23). She finds it "exasperating" that Plato and Heidegger, "when they entered into human affairs, turned to tyrants and Fuhrers." Plato's trips to Sicily were, for Arendt, part of a "fantastic undertaking." He intended to realize his political ideals by turning Dionysius into a philosopher-king. He began by teaching Dionysius mathematics, since mathematics is "the indispensable introduction to philosophy and hence to the art of ruling as a philosopher-king." Arendt would agree with Beiner that the Platonic art of ruling is closer to the abstractions of mathematics than it is to Aristotelian *phronesis.* A Platonic philosopher-king rules by applying his knowledge of theoretical or abstract universals to particular circumstances. Plato encouraged Dionysius to do the same in Sicilian politics. The abstract universal to be applied was the ideal city of the *Republic*. For Arendt, the entire enterprise was folly. Plato's misunderstanding of the nature of politics led him to participate in "human affairs" in an imprudent way. He did not even notice that his political activity, "if seen from the peasant girl's perspective, looks considerably more comical than Thales' mishap."[4]

Arendt claims that Heidegger, like Plato, succumbed to the temptation to leave his proper abode when he supported the Nazi Party. In 1935 Heidegger wrote that the German nation had a "historical mission" to warn the Western world of the peril that would befall it if "the question of being" was not properly addressed. The National Socialists could make possible a global "awakening of the spirit" because they represented Germany's historical "relation to being." National Socialism possessed an "inner truth and greatness" that even many of its supporters could not fully understand.[5] Heidegger eventually withdrew from political affairs. Arendt claims that Heidegger, unlike Plato, learned from his political imprudence. In apologizing for his actions, she writes: "He was still young enough to learn from the shock of the collision, which . . . drove him back to his residence, and to settle in his thinking what he had experienced."[6]

Although they appear to be quite different in significance and consequence, Arendt believes that Plato's attempt to give Dionysius an education and Heidegger's active support of the truth of National Socialism are both examples of the *déformation professionnelle* of passionate philosophical thinking: the attraction to the tyrannical. Arendt writes that most philosophers ("Kant is the great exception") are attracted to the tyrannical as a direct result of their willingness to accept wondering as their abode.[7] When they leave their proper home behind for the world of human affairs, they do not leave behind the desire for perfection that is part of passionate thinking. And the imprudent aspiration to perfection in politics necessarily leads to tyranny or totalitarianism.

In comparing his political idealism unfavorably with the more prudent political philosophies of Aristotle and Kant, Beiner and Arendt criticize what they take to be Plato's failure to understand the distinctive nature of *phronesis* as a dianoetic virtue. Although Arendt excuses what she believes to be Plato's own lack of political judgment as part of her ambitious attempt to excuse Heidegger's support of a totalitarian movement, others are less willing to do so. Karl Popper is far less tolerant of Plato than are Beiner and Arendt. For him, Plato's lack of political judgment is inexcusable. Plato's attraction to the tyrannical is not an unintentional consequence of his passion for thought. It is rather the intentional goal of his political philosophy. Plato was the first theorist of totalitarianism. According to Popper, "Plato's political program, far from being morally superior to totalitarianism, is fundamentally identical with it."[8] If Beiner and Arendt are correct in their assumptions about Plato, there may be no justifiable way of avoiding Popper's conclusion.

Popper admits that his criticism of Plato originates in an impression that there is a "similarity between the Platonic theory of justice and the theory and practice of modern totalitarianism." It does not originate from an openness to the arguments found in Plato's dialogues. At one point Popper asserts: "Does 'justice' perhaps mean what [Plato] says? I do not intend to discuss such a question." The initial impression that led Popper to dismiss the theory and practice of Plato's political philosophy arises from Popper's distinction between open and closed societies. Closed societies are characterized by the belief in irrational or "magical" taboos, whereas open societies are those in which men have learned, to some extent, to be independently rational and critical of taboos. The ideal societies described in the *Republic* and *Laws* are closed societies. The Platonic ideas of "Justice, Wisdom, Truth and Beauty" upon which they are based cannot be questioned. They are irrational or magical taboos. This alone suffices to make Plato a theorist of totalitarianism.[9]

In order to substantiate his broader claim that Plato was also an advocate of totalitarian practices, Popper refers to a distinction between piecemeal and wholesale, or Utopian, social engineering. Piecemeal social engineering is rational, pragmatic and empirical. It attempts to overcome the problems encountered in a society as they occur by means of modest reform proposals drawn up primarily from the store of practical knowledge that has accumulated in the society from similar practices in the past. This is the method of reform best suited to open societies. In contrast, wholesale social engineering is irrational and idealistic. An advocate of this method of reform would argue that, if a society is to overcome any of the problems it faces, it must be completely reconstructed on the pattern of a detailed blueprint drawn up to embody abstract first principles of justice and truth. No practical knowledge guides the reformer. His blueprint is invariably one of a closed society. All advocates of wholesale reform are necessarily totalitarians because their abstract political ideals can only be realized in one way: through the "terroristic police control" of society.[10]

There is thus no essential difference for Popper between the political ideals drawn up by Plato in the *Republic* and *Laws* and the political ideals that motivated the National Socialists. The only difference of practical importance between Plato and Hitler is that Plato was less successful in persuading others to assist him in realizing his political goals.

The arguments made by Beiner, Arendt, and Popper are representative of the wide range of criticisms made by modern scholars who agree that there is no evidence of *phronesis* or political judgment in Plato, even though they do not agree among themselves on what good political judgment is. Plato's political thought is based on abstractions, they say, and all such abstract or idealistic thought about politics must lead to an understanding of political action as *techne* that is inherently tyrannical or totalitarian.

I argue, on the contrary, that Plato is not a political idealist. The common claim that there is no evidence of any understanding of *phronesis* in Plato is wrong. This criticism of Plato is generally directed against both his words and his deeds: there is no understanding of *phronesis* evident in his writings, it is said, and there is historical evidence of its absence in his political activities. The two aspects of the criticism are related. Those who argue the former often place a great deal of importance on the latter, even though the only substantive evidence we have concerning Plato's Sicilian voyages is given in his *Seventh Letter*—itself a written work requiring interpretation. I will limit my study to an examination of the understanding of *phronesis* presented in the *Republic* and the *Laws*. One need not indulge in idle speculation about Plato's character or historical circumstances in order to understand these dialogues. I will argue, rather, by means of a textual analysis of important parts of the *Republic* and the *Laws*, that Plato's political philosophy is founded on an understanding of *phronesis* comparable to the account of it given by Aristotle. The generally accepted view that there is a fundamental opposition between the imprudent, idealistic, and inherently totalitarian political theory of Plato and the prudent, realistic, and more moderate political theory of Aristotle is wrong. There will be no attempt made in this study to reach any comprehensive conclusions about the relation between the political philosophies of Plato and Aristotle. An account of Plato's understanding of *phronesis* or political judgment will suffice to demonstrate that the claims commonly made by those who oppose Plato and Aristotle are unfounded.

The works of Hans-Georg Gadamer and Eric Voegelin are especially relevant to my study of the *Republic* and the *Laws*. Neither accepts the view that Plato and Aristotle have fundamentally opposed understandings of *phronesis*, and neither accepts the criticisms commonly made of Plato's political idealism. However, Gadamer and Voegelin both tend to discuss Plato in the context of their broader concerns: hermeneutics, the philosophy of history and the philosophy of consciousness. Despite appearances, they spend relatively little time discussing Plato's political philosophy by means of exegetical analyses of the dialogues themselves. Their insights into Plato's account of *phronesis* are consequently often said to lack sufficient basis in the texts. My hermeneutic technique, such as it is, differs from theirs in two ways: I seem to require more sustained textual exegesis in order to reach comparable, but often less ambitious conclusions, and I tend to linger over puzzling details awhile. In these matters, I will confess to having been influenced by the interpretive method of Leo Strauss as it was developed by his colleagues and students, particularly by the most intrepid of his students, Stanley Rosen.

Before returning to the consideration of modern accounts of Plato's political idealism, it would be best to discuss two questions that have been raised by the preceding remarks: What is the understanding of *phronesis* shared by Plato and Aristotle? And how should Plato's dialogues be read?

Phronesis **and the Good in Plato and Aristotle**

In his most famous work, *Truth and Method*, Gadamer accepts without qualification the conventional view that "the distinction between the ideas of *sophia* and *phronesis* was first elaborated by Aristotle" in his criticism of Plato's account of the idea of the good. Gadamer writes that Aristotle's critique of Plato is "the root of the whole of his own philosophy. It contains . . . a radical revision of the relation between the universal and the particular, as it is implied in the Platonic doctrine of the idea of the good—at least as it is presented in the Platonic dialogues." The doctrine was for Aristotle "an empty generality." The relationship of universal and particular that typifies *sophia*, or theoretical wisdom, is one of simple subsumption. However, an answer to "the question of the humanly good, what is good in terms of human action," will not be meaningful if it is premised on such a subsumption. Knowledge of the human good is prudential or practical. Thus, Gadamer claims, by placing "limits to the intellectualism of Socrates and Plato," Aristotle became "the founder of ethics as a discipline independent of metaphysics."[11]

It would seem that Beiner is largely correct in citing *Truth and Method* in support of his own argument that Plato and Aristotle have fundamentally different understandings of *phronesis* and political judgment. The grounds of their agreement are seen most clearly in Gadamer's criticism of Leo Strauss's work. Gadamer claims that the most surprising aspect of Strauss's defence of classical philosophy is "the degree to which he seeks to understand it as a *unity*, so that the *extreme contrast* that exists between Plato and Aristotle in the nature and significance of their question concerning the good does not seem to cause him any trouble" (my italics).[12] This rather polemical criticism is disingenuous. It is seriously undermined by Gadamer's own ambiguity concerning the "extreme contrast" between Plato and Aristotle, an ambiguity not shared by Beiner. Gadamer concludes *Truth and Method* with the claim: "It might well be that Aristotle's critique, like so many critiques, is right in what it says, but not in that against whom it says it."[13] His subsequent work on Plato and Aristotle has attempted to demonstrate the unity of classical philosophy that underlies its apparent disunity.

Gadamer's most recent book is a lengthy discussion of what he calls "the Platonic-Aristotelian unitary effect." He claims that "the dominant 'historical' interpretive schema" of modern classical scholarship has led many to neglect or misrepresent the substantial agreement between Plato and Aristotle concerning the nature of the good and the virtue of *phronesis*. The schema is "derived from Hegel"; it "construes its subject matter in terms of antithetical relationships."[14] Consequently, Aristotle's often puzzling criticisms of Plato are made to serve as a thin textual basis for various starkly antithetical interpretations of their relation in the history of philosophy. However, not all suspect classical scholarship is founded on Hegelian dialectic. Some of it is founded on the attempt to discover the foundations of modern empiricism and rationalism in Aristotle's critique of Plato. Gadamer does not discuss these generally English traditions of interpretation in any detail.

Gadamer argues that Plato's dialogues are a celebration of Socrates' prudence and judgment: "The virtue of practical knowledge, of *phronesis*, appears as the epitome of everything that Socrates' exemplary life displays."[15] The foundation of Socrates' *phronesis* was his aspiration to know the good. When the descriptions of Socrates' *phronesis* in Plato's dialogues are compared with the distinctions made in Aristotle's ethical writings between theoretical, practical, and technical knowledge, the similarity between the Socratic aspiration to the good and Aristotelian *phronesis* is evident. Both Socrates and Plato were aware that knowledge of the good cannot be understood on the model of *techne*. The dialogues are full of Socrates' criticisms of the sophists' attempts to do so. Both were also aware that the good cannot be understood as the end of *sophia* alone, defined narrowly as theoretical knowledge. The dialogues contain criticisms of the Eleatic philosophers' attempts to establish this point, most notably in the discussion of "the doctrine of the ideas" found in the *Parmenides*. Finally, both Socrates and Plato were aware of the distinction between virtue (*arete*) and knowledge (*episteme*). Gadamer writes: "Socrates' statement that *arete* is knowledge ... proves to be a provocation." Indeed, it is "absurd" to believe, as many scholars do, that neither Socrates nor Plato understood "the role of habituation and character molding as these are implied in Aristotle's concept of *ethos*."[16]

Gadamer claims modern scholars have not seen the essential agreement between Plato and Aristotle because they do not read with sufficient hermeneutical sensitivity. There are different difficulties involved in reading Plato and Aristotle well that lead to misunderstandings. In Plato's dialogues, terms such as *phronesis, sophia, arete,* and *episteme* are used both in their traditional or customary sense and in their more precise philosophical or technical sense, depending upon the dramatic context. Confusion results when a reader does not perceive their two distinct usages. For instance, the cardinal virtues listed in book 4 of the *Republic* are often called the Platonic virtues when "in truth they are not Platonic but traditional." By giving theoretical status to this traditional list of virtues, which does not mention *phronesis,* a reader then tends to misunderstand the theoretical discussion of *phronesis* and its relation to the good in the later books. Turning to Aristotle's works, the most misleading feature of his criticisms of Plato is his manner of "taking statements not as they were intended, but literally, and then demonstrating their one-sidedness." In doing so, Aristotle deliberately contrives "dialectical perplexities [*aporiai*]" where there are none.[17] Two examples of this odd tendency are Aristotle's literal interpretation of Socrates' provocative equation of virtue and knowledge and his denial that Plato's understanding of the idea of the good has any practical utility or prudential content. Why would Aristotle introduce *aporiai* where there are none? Gadamer argues that they were intended to enable Aristotle to introduce solutions to them, with great rhetorical effect, as if they were his own discoveries. In doing so, however, Aristotle obscures his own "Platonic inheritance."[18]

Gadamer concludes his study of "the Platonic-Aristotelian unitary effect" by claiming that there is a fundamental agreement between the "Socratic Plato" and the "Platonic Aristotle" that underlies their apparent disagreement. They agree about two "basic truths." First, the good of human actions—that for the sake of which they are done—is "defined only by our practical reason—in the *euboulia* (well-advised-ness) of *phronesis.*" Second, "every existing thing is 'good' when it fulfills its *telos* (purpose, goal)."[19] And these two truths are one in the understanding that the *euboulia* of *phronesis* depends upon the forming and informing of reason by the good.

Eric Voegelin would agree with Gadamer's evaluation of the substantial agreement between Plato and Aristotle. He would also agree that one of the reasons the relation between Plato and Aristotle is presently misunderstood is that modern scholars generally do not perceive the critical clarification of philosophical categories from traditional usages in their writings. This is particularly true of their readings of Plato's dialogues.

In a study of the Socratics that predates Gadamer's recent book, Voegelin discusses the notion that a "great break" separates Plato and Aristotle. Those who defend the notion usually oppose "Platonic transcendentalism and idealism" to "Aristotelian immanentism and realism," claiming that Plato and Aristotle "developed two entirely different metaphysical systems." For Voegelin the break is "imaginary." Neither Plato nor Aristotle developed systems, and their thought cannot be characterized accurately in any antithetical manner. Philosophy was above all a way of life for Plato and Aristotle. They were "far too much engrossed" with the constant inquiry and reflection required by this way of life to become system-builders. Constant inquiry leads to the discovery of new problems. Although Plato and Aristotle were "in agreement on the presence of [transcendent] form in empirical reality," they turned their attention to different problems arising from an inquiry into this presence, and thus can be assumed mistakenly to be in fundamental disagreement. Misunderstandings of this sort occur when the analytic terms developed in philosophical inquiry are "torn out of their experiential context" and treated as if they are abstractions. The writings of any philosopher can be reduced in this manner to a collection of hypothetical assertions or "positions." Plato thus becomes an idealist and Aristotle a realist.[20]

Voegelin gives his account of the agreement between Plato and Aristotle concerning *phronesis* in an essay entitled "What Is Right by Nature?" Voegelin agrees with Gadamer that Plato's understanding of *phronesis* becomes evident in comparing the discussion of the cardinal virtues in book 4 of the *Republic* with the dialogue's subsequent discussion of the soul's ascent toward the good. *Phronesis* is "that virtue that is activated in man when he attains the *opsis*, the vision of the good." It is a virtue that results from the opening of the soul to the transcendent good. The four cardinal virtues with specified functions within the order of the soul—courage (*andreia*), moderation (*sophrosyne*), wisdom (*sophia*), and justice (*dikaiosyne*)—all find their place within the formation of the soul by *phronesis* after it has attained a vision of the good. Aristotle's understanding of *phronesis* is similar, although the similarity is somewhat obscured by the detailed differentiation and classification of the virtues undertaken in his writings on ethics. For Aristotle *phronesis* is a virtue of "deliberation about that which is good and useful for man," that is, about "the good life [*eu zen*]." It is concerned with changeable human affairs, but it is also guided by deliberation about the unchangeable good itself. *Phronesis* is distinct from both *techne* and *sophia*. *Techne* is production, or action within the changeable human realm which does not carry its end within itself or aspire to the highest end. *Sophia* is "a knowledge about the most eminent things [*timoitata*]." *Phronesis* and *sophia* are not identical, but they have *noesis* (intellection) in common. *Noesis* is the virtue of the soul's proper apprehension of the highest things, and particularly its apprehension of the good. Without *noesis, sophia* would be *episteme,* or demonstrable scientific knowledge, and *phronesis* would be simple cleverness (*deinoteta*).[21]

For Plato and Aristotle, then, the highest end, the end toward which all things aim, is the good. The soul's aspiration to attain a vision of the good gives order to the dianoetic or intellectual virtues. Without such an aspiration, a man cannot rightly be said to possess the good understanding and judgment of *phronesis.*

Reading the Platonic Dialogues

Gadamer and Voegelin agree that the hermeneutic difficulties involved in reading the Platonic dialogues prevent many modern scholars from coming to an understanding of the essential agreement between Plato and Aristotle concerning the nature of *phronesis* and its relation to the soul's aspiration to the good. It is only necessary to summarize the generally accepted premises of modern Plato scholarship to demonstrate that misunderstandings about the nature of the dialogues as written works can and do lead to mistaken conclusions about Plato's ethical and political philosophy.

Most modern scholars agree that the various philological techniques now used in analyzing the formal characteristics of Plato's dialogues provide useful guidelines for coming to an understanding of their philosophical content. It is generally accepted that the dialogues can be grouped according to their relative dates of composition by means of stylometric analysis, and that the actual or historical dates at which they were written reveal more about them than do the dramatic dates assigned to the dialogues by Plato.[22] There are said to be three groups of dialogues: the early, the middle, and the late works. The early works are also known as the Socratic or aporetic dialogues. George Klosko claims their most characteristic feature is coming to an end "without any satisfactory conclusions being reached." It is assumed that Plato's purpose in writing them was to describe the "historical" Socrates and his method of inquiry. The middle group of dialogues includes the *Republic, Symposium, Phaedrus,* and several others. In these works Socrates is made to defend arguments that are not his own; that is, he appears as an authoritative spokesman for Plato's philosophical and theological views. In the late dialogues,

Socrates no longer has this role. He is often present but silent throughout discussions. In these dialogues Plato speaks more or less directly to the reader through a variety of characters: the Eleatic of the *Sophist* and *Statesman,* the Pythagorean of the *Timaeus,* and the Athenian of the *Laws.*

It is evident from this brief summary that the simplest conclusions drawn by scholars concerning the philosophical content of the three groups of dialogues are based on something more than the philological analysis of their formal or stylistic features. They are also based on the assumption that the dialogues reveal "the steps that led [Plato] from Socraticism to Platonism," as Klosko puts it, and even the steps that led him from one form of Platonism to another. The grouping of the dialogues illustrates Plato's development as a thinker. There are scholarly disputes about whether the middle or the late dialogues are his most mature works, but these disputes do not call into question the basic assumption that it is possible to trace Plato's intellectual development in his writings.

The strongest evidence cited in support of this assumption is not philological. It is biographical and historical. Philological evidence alone proves nothing. The three groups of dialogues are dated in accordance with the dates of the three trips made by Plato to Sicily, described in the *Seventh Letter.* The first trip was made about 387 B.C., a dozen years after the execution of Socrates. While there Plato befriended Dion, the brother-in-law of the elder Dionysius, tyrant of Syracuse. He is also said to have become familiar with Pythagorean doctrines at this time. The early dialogues are thought to have been written in the period between Socrates' execution and the first trip, for the Platonism of the middle dialogues is believed to have been influenced by Pythagoreanism. Plato did not return to Sicily for two decades. During that time he founded the Academy and developed the political theory of the *Republic.* On the death of the elder Dionysius, Dion urged Plato to return to Syracuse and supervise the education of his nephew the younger Dionysius, who was the new tyrant. Plato thought this was a chance for philosophy and political power to act together for the betterment of mankind—in other words, a chance to realize the political ideal of the *Republic.* Plato's second and third trips (c. 367 and 361 B.C.) proved to be failures. Not only was Dionysius a poor student, but the factional battles that nearly cost Plato his life eventually led to the assassination of Dion

(c. 353 B.C.). The late dialogues are thought to have been written in the period after Plato's second trip, when it became increasingly obvious to him that the political idealism of the *Republic* was impracticable. Some commentators consider the late dialogues to be works of Plato's maturity: he appears to be a political realist in the *Statesman* and *Laws,* and his philosophical analyses are most sophisticated in dialogues such as the *Parmenides, Sophist,* and *Timaeus.*

There are many substantive problems raised by the generally accepted account of the grouping of Plato's dialogues. It is not possible to address them all, and for the purposes of this study, it is not necessary to do so. However, it is necessary to say something about the basic premise shared by most scholars that Plato's thought can be seen to change over time in the dialogues. Gadamer cites a simple fact he says is "more or less fatal" for all attempts to catalogue the dialogues by means of "historical-genetic" analysis: there are no reports of any changes in Plato's views in the ancient doxographic tradition. The tradition tends to be ignored because modern scholars are persuaded by a "dominant 'historical' interpretative schema" that leads them to assume that there must be some form of development or progress evident over time, no matter whether they are analyzing Aristotle's relation to Plato or Plato's dialogues alone.[23] I have no need of this assumption for my interpretation of the *Republic* and *Laws.*

The hermeneutic problems raised by the standard reading of the dialogues appear to stem from a naive view that there are no hermeneutic problems to be faced, only philological ones. The dialogue form is simply a poetic presentation of Plato's own views, it is said. Poetry, dialogue, and drama aside, Plato's views may be found in the mouths of his main characters. Their utterances need only be catalogued by topic and dated by stylometric analysis for Plato's "position" on any question at any time to be known. In opposition to this way of reading Plato, Gadamer writes that the distinct character of the dialogue form is "half-way between the variety of characters of dramatic writing and the authenticity of the pedagogical work." The proper hermeneutical method of reading a dialogue requires "our own relation to the actual problems that Plato is concerned with." As readers we must enter into the drama in order to understand what Plato teaches about problems that are "our own," or that we are willing to make our own. And in order to do this, we must be able to judge the characters properly from their words and deeds. Reading a Platonic dialogue is thus an exercise in *phronesis*. Perhaps it would be better to say it is an education in *phronesis,* a way of educating a reader to make *phronesis* his own. The truth of any prudential judgment cannot be exhibited "objectively" in a strictly empirical or method- ical way, and this is particularly true of judgments formed about the dialogues. A reader's "deciphering interpretation" must remain to some extent uncertain, since the dialogues are not simple state- ments of Plato's various "positions" on abstract and impersonal problems.[24]

A similar understanding of how the Platonic dialogues ought to be read can be found in methodological remarks made by sev- eral of the colleagues and students of Leo Strauss who have writ- ten commentaries on Plato's works. Strauss's own remarks on the proper way to read Plato are difficult to summarize.[25] But one need not enter into the contentious debates about Strauss's true meaning from this topic because Jacob Klein, Allan Bloom and Stanley Rosen have each given a more than adequate account of Strauss's hermeneutic principles. Jacob Klein writes that any "meaningful interpretation" of any Platonic dialogue has to rest on the following premises: (1) A dialogue is not a scholarly treatise or the text of a lecture, and ought not to be read as one. (2) It ought to be read "most carefully," since its purpose is as serious as that of a scholarly treatise, but with the awareness that "its serious- ness is permeated by playfulness." (3) No single dialogue and no single character within a dialogue represent Plato's "doctrine." (4) Each dialogue must be taken as a whole, on its own terms; and each character's dramatic part within the whole must be appreci- ated. (5) Plato's thinking on the questions he addresses can only be understood if readers participate as "silent partners" in the dis- cussion presented: "we must weigh and then accept or reject the solutions offered and must comment, as well as we can, on what is at stake." In short, the reader must exercise his judgment pru- dently in order to understand how "every word counts."[26]

In the preface to his translation of the *Republic,* Allan Bloom writes that many modern interpreters of Plato make a "fatal error" in attempting to separate the form and substance of the dialogues. It is wrong to believe that Plato's teachings can be discovered by stripping away and discarding a didactic or artistic wrapping. This reveals "a lack of clarity about the purposes of the dialogue form." A dialogue is "neither poetry nor philosophy," nor is it merely a combination of the two. It is an organic unity: "Every argument must be interpreted dramatically. . . . And every dramatic detail must be interpreted philosophically." The demands placed on the reader by the dialogue form are intended to "prepare the way for philosophizing." The dialogue compels him to think as Plato would wish him to think, to exercise the faculties and virtues of a philosopher. Furthermore, it does not allow him to develop the complacent belief that philosophy is the discovery of abstract principles. Bloom writes: "Any teaching which gives only the principles remains abstract and is mere dogma." The reader must also understand what such principles explain. He must "know enough of the world" to understand their relevance. A Platonic dialogue insists upon a "rich consciousness of the phenomena."[27] This is possible only when the reader has acquired good judgment or *phronesis*.

Stanley Rosen has claimed that Gadamer's phenomenological method of interpretation "is . . . not altogether dissimilar to that of the Straussian school, although the results are quite disparate" when their readings of particular dialogues are compared. Gadamer would agree with Klein and Bloom that Plato can only be understood if a reader takes upon himself "the essentially neutral task of getting Plato to speak for himself," that is, of reading the written text "as accurately as possible." And Klein and Bloom, following Strauss, would agree with Gadamer that this alone is insufficient. A reader must move beyond the text of a dialogue "to a genuine philosophical struggle with the results of [his] readings."[28] It remains to determine, then, whether the disparity of results mentioned by Rosen in itself presents any hermeneutic or philosophical problems.

A difference in interpretations of a text does not necessarily pose hermeneutical problems. It is not necessarily the sign of a conflict between different methods of interpretation. One of the goals of all competent and empathetic readings of the dialogues—a complete understanding of Plato's thoughts and intentions in writing them—is impossible to attain. It would be wrong to expect to attain it. And the dialogues themselves give no grounds for such an expectation. Indeed, their dramatic form actively discourages it. Disagreements in interpretation are thus unavoidable, even between readers with similar hermeneutic methods. Furthermore, a difference in interpretations does not necessarily pose a philosophical problem. The most important goal of reading the dialogues is an attainable one: the active participation of the reader in philosophical inquiry, as Plato understands it. *Philosophia*, the love of wisdom, never fully attains its end. The philosopher can be said to possess the dianoetic virtues of *sophia* and *phronesis*, but he cannot be said to possess wisdom. The philosopher is neither a *sophos*, a wise man or sage, nor a sophist, one who professes to be a sage. Thus, a reader compelled to participate in philosophizing by the dialogic form Plato deliberately gave to his works ought not be surprised to discover that the results of his reading and reflection are incomplete.

In his study of the *Sophist*, Rosen presents a helpful classification of the various ways in which modern scholars read the dialogues. He distinguishes between "two more or less contrasting perspectives": the dramatic and the technical or ontological perspectives. The dramatic perspective regards the dialogue as a unity and a work of art. Scholars who accept this perspective do not believe it possible to divide a dialogue into fragments some of which can be said to contain discussions of a "technical" or philosophical nature and others to contain those of an "artistic" or poetic nature. In contrast, the many scholars who accept the technical perspective believe that this is possible. They all agree that the technical content of Plato's writings is isolable from its essentially irrelevant poetic presentation, no matter whether their interest lies in his ethics, politics, or epistemology. Rosen's main criticism of the latter perspective is that its distinction between philosophy and poetry is based on the unsound conviction "that philosophy is a science, or . . . that philosophy is scientific." Philosophic inquiry does not lead to demonstrable knowledge in the way that empirical or mathematical inquiry does.[29]

Rosen's term for the most preferable way of reading Plato is "dramatic phenomenology." This requires some explanation. The dramatic approach, he argues in its defence, does not lead to the suppression of any "narrowly technical themes" in the dialogues: "On the contrary, it requires their meticulous analysis, both in themselves and as elements in a comprehensive dramatic structure." Unlike the technical perspective, it has an awareness that while the dialogues are not dramas proper, their dramatic structure or form is the whole in which all parts or aspects of the dialogue have their place. A Platonic dialogue is an "interpretation of human life," and especially of philosophical life, in dramatic form. This is admittedly not the same as a phenomenological description. Rosen claims, however, that anyone reading Plato must be content to practice dramatic phenomenology. The reader is compelled "to give a phenomenological *description* of a philosophical dialogue," even while recognizing that the dialogue itself is not such a description. The reader's "artistic reformulation" of a dialogue's descriptions of speeches and deeds, even though they are given "within the context of a unified statement about the good or philosophical life," is neither the formulation of an interpretation of human life nor the living of a philosophical life, although it may lead the reader to these higher activities.[30]

In a critique of Jacques Derrida's understanding of Plato, Rosen argues that the movement from reading the dialogues phenomenologically to living the philosophical life described in them is an exercise in "erotic hermeneutics." Hermeneutics is the interpretation or judgment of things. Interpreting the dialogues ought to lead to an understanding of the interpretation of human life, and of the best life possible, given in the dialogues. Plato understands the philosophical life as one "guided by a vision of the good," and the good "is said by Socrates to be 'beyond being' [*epekeina tes ousias*]" (*Republic* 509b). This leads Rosen to claim that the philosopher's aspiration to a vision of the good is itself both erotic and hermeneutical. He cites in evidence Diotima's statement to Socrates (*Symposium* 202d–e) that the power of Eros is "to interpret [*hermeneuon*] and convey" things between gods and humans, or between the realm of the divine and transcendent and the realm of the mortal and immanent. The point of Rosen's description of the philosophic life in this manner emerges in a bold claim: "an erotic hermeneutics of the Platonic dialogues shows that all doctrines are exoteric. There is no esoteric doctrine in Plato."[31]

In other words, the dialogues do not conceal anything, and no "technical" analysis of any kind is required to render them intelligible. Those who accept the technical perspective, Rosen argues, are best called "esotericists," for they are the ones who "attribute a secret teaching to Plato." Derrida's esotericism is of a unique type, but it shares one basic feature with all technical readings of the dialogues. The attribution of an esoteric doctrine to Plato stems from the inability of the technical perspective to "distinguish between the text and life."[32]

Rosen's discussion of the inherent esotericism of the technical perspective illuminates the failings of the standard scholarly analysis of the dialogues. The standard reading seems far removed from esotericism to those who accept it. Indeed, they say that its techniques of philological analysis are intended to prevent the esotericism of subjective interpretation. Yet, no matter how commonsensical it may seem, the purpose of such analysis is to discover Plato's esoteric doctrines. This does not imply that Plato deliberately hid his thoughts. The doctrines attributed to Plato by the generally accepted analysis of the dialogues are esoteric because anyone reading the dialogues with some sensitivity to their dramatic form could not assume that such doctrines were those of the author. Unless certain assumptions are made that have no basis in the dialogues themselves, it is not possible to defend the view that an objective analysis of the technical content of the dialogues reveals not only Plato's own thoughts but also the development of his thought throughout his life. The simplest such assumption is that Plato speaks directly to the reader through the main characters of the dialogues; the boldest is that historical and biographical information is the ultimate criterion for explaining Plato's doctrines. Both assumptions confuse text and life. Any conclusions concerning Plato's doctrines based on such assumptions are thus as esoteric as the assumptions themselves.

The standard scholarly analysis of the dialogues attempts to separate their form and content, or their poetic and philosophic aspects. In doing so, it understands neither the one nor the other, nor the relation between them. The technical perspective underlying the standard reading prevents it from appreciating the nature of Plato's "erotic hermeneutics." It cannot appreciate the dialogue form as a work of art or poetry. It cannot appreciate Plato's writings as one of the highest expressions of Greek culture or *paideia*. It cannot understand the philosophical life as one guided by the soul's vision of the good. At best, it might recognize this abstractly as a "position" held by Plato in his middle period. Thus, the standard reading cannot perceive how the dialogue form was intended to draw a reader toward the philosophic life and inspire him to acquire the highest virtues, *sophia* and *phronesis*. The insensitivity to the beauty of Plato's dialogues that typifies the standard reading, and indeed all technical analyses of the dialogues, is not surprising. Plato understood beauty as the image, in the world, of the good.

Ideal and Paradigm

Those who criticize Plato for his political idealism, or more generally for a lack of prudence, often claim to read the *Republic* and

Laws "literally," by which they mean as explicit statements of Plato's opinions on political matters at the time the dialogues were written. There is nothing literal about this procedure. The traditional dramatic interpretation of the dialogues is more properly called literal because it pays attention to the manner in which the dialogues were written and does not introduce criteria external to the dialogues in order to understand them. Despite their appeals to apparently commonsensical beliefs, the critics of Plato's idealism read the dialogues esoterically. In other words, the premises of their account are not, and cannot be drawn from what is given in the dialogues themselves. The most basic premise of such criticism is the most obviously esoteric: there is literally nothing written in either the *Republic* or the *Laws* about "ideal" cities and their realization. It makes no difference which of the cities in the dialogues is believed to be a realizable ideal, for neither dialogue describes its city as an "ideal," and the city of the *Laws* is described as "second best" according to a standard that is not itself said to be an ideal.

Plato does not write of "ideals." There is no word either in normal Greek usage or in his own analytic vocabulary that corresponds to what is meant by "ideal" as the term is used by modern scholars. Plato does write of ideas or forms (*ideai; eidoi*), but neither of his cities in speech is ever said to be an *idea* or *eidos*. It is said in the *Republic* (472d–e) that the city constructed in speech aspires to be "a pattern [*paradeigma*] in speech of a good city [*agathes poleos*]." The same is true of the city constructed in speech in the *Laws*. It is a *paradeigma*, a pattern or model. The meaning and significance of the term *paradeigma* for Plato can be determined by considering the relatively few passages in the *Republic* in which it appears.

The term first appears in the context of a discussion of the good man. Socrates says that the man who has a good soul (*psychen agathen*) is good (*agathos*). In contrast to the good man, the clever and suspicious criminal who has done many unjust things takes his bearings from the patterns (*paradeigmata*) within himself; he does not take his bearings from good and just men, and he lacks the *paradeigma* of such men within himself (409c–d). How does a soul become good? And what is the *paradeigma* from which the good and just man takes his bearings? In describing the highest point in the education of the best guardians of the city in speech, the ones who will become its philosopher-kings, Socrates says they must be compelled to turn the vision of their souls toward "the good itself [*to agathon auto*]," and having seen it, they must use it as a *paradeigma* for ordering not only their own lives but also the city in which they will rule (540a–b). Socrates had previously said that those guardians with no clear *paradeigma* in their souls would be unable "to give laws about the beautiful (*kalon*), the just (*dikaion*), and the good (*agathon*), if any need to be given" (484c–d). It is evident, therefore, that the best guardians are good and just men because they have good souls, and that their souls are good because they take the good itself as their *paradeigma*. It is also evident that the goodness and justice of the city they rule depends upon the manner in which they rule it, and that it will be a good and just city only if its rulers take the good itself as their *paradeigma*.

Does it make any difference whether this "*paradeigma* in speech of a good city" exists, did exist, or might exist? It does not. The city is intended to be a *paradeigma* "laid up in heaven [*en ouranoi*] for whomever wants to see, and seeing it, to found it within himself" (592a–b; cf. 472d–e). Why does Plato have Socrates refer to a city "in heaven" when the city founded in the dialogue is only a city "in speech"? He wishes to emphasize that the truth of the *paradeigma* does not depend upon the existence of such a city "on earth." But that is not his only reason. Plato is also providing the readers of the *Republic* with a warning. A reader may take the *paradeigma* of the city as a *paradeigma* for his own soul, and thereby become a good and just man. However, the city's *paradeigma* is not its institutional arrangement; it is rather "the good itself," the vision of which governs the souls of its rulers. The city's institutions, laws and customs are only an image of the good itself. And images must not be mistaken for originals. In discussing the education of the guardians Socrates says explicitly that the appearances of the heaven (*ton ouranon*) must be used as *paradeigmata* to aid in the study of things that cannot be seen with the eyes (529c–d). Therefore, a reader of the *Republic* must use the appearances of the city as *paradeigmata* to aid him in attaining the proper end of his study—the vision of the good itself, which can only be seen with "the eye of the soul" (533d, 540a–b).

If a reader of the *Republic* is open to the drama of the dialogue, he may be led toward the philosophic life. The philosophic life is dedicated to acquiring the virtues of *sophia* and *phronesis*, and these virtues are most fully formed when the soul takes the good

itself as its *paradeigma*. A reader open to the dialogue's drama
may also be led away from unwise and imprudent things. It would
be a grave error to believe that Socrates is lying when he says the
city in speech should not be founded on earth. Those who read the
Republic in this way confuse appearances and truth, or mistakenly believe appearances to be the only truth. They might say that
the city described in the dialogue cannot be founded within the
soul, for invisible things have no truth; so if there is any truth in
the city in speech, it will be evident only when the city comes to
exist visibly by being founded on earth. When the truth of the
Republic's city as a *paradeigma* for the soul is denied in this manner, the city becomes an appearance and its institutional order is
mistaken as a *paradeigma* for political action by the unwise and
imprudent. It will appear to them as an ideal intended to be realized through the exercise of political power. The realization of ideals has little to do with *sophia* and *phronesis*. It is a technical
activity, or rather it is political activity that imitates the *techne* of
production by attempting to enforce an abstract form on matter.

At one point in the *Republic*, Socrates says the city in speech is
a *kallipolis*, a beautiful city (527c). Its beauty depends upon its
goodness, for the beautiful is an image or appearance of the good.
The city is intended to be the *paradeigma* of a good city (472d–e). It
may be said to be a good city because the philosophers who rule it
take the good itself as the *paradeigma* of their souls and are thereby able to rule it with *phronesis*. It might even be said to be a
beautiful city because its institutional order is in some way an
image of the order of the good soul and because those who are
capable of seeing its beauty may make its *paradeigma* their own
by founding it within themselves. The beauty of the city's institutional order is an appearance. In the realm of appearances, however, all things must change. For this reason, the philosophers
who rule the city are not bound by its appearance. They may alter
the institutions of the apparently beautiful city in order that it
might remain the good city. Its true beauty depends upon its goodness, and not upon its unchanging appearance. An unchanging
appearance is an illusion of goodness; it is a false beauty, lacking
substance or a true *paradeigma*. The beauty of abstract ideals is of
this type.

The city in speech of the *Laws* is as much a *paradeigma* as the
city in speech of the *Republic*. However, both Magnesia and the
kallipolis are commonly said to be nothing but political ideals or

blueprints for political action. Few of Plato's critics agree about the character of his political idealism, though they all seem certain that this is how his political thought should be characterized. They generally agree that his idealism is imprudent. Beyond that, everything is subject to debate. Some find him consistently idealistic in the *Republic* and the *Laws;* others inconsistently so. Some find the *Republic* to be more idealistic than the *Laws;* others the opposite. Some criticize his consistency and others his inconsistency. Some find the imprudence of his idealism intolerable, some find it harmless, and some even find Plato's idealism praiseworthy precisely because of its imprudence. It would be impractical, if not impossible, to discuss all the various interpretations of Plato's political idealism in any detail. Suffice it to say they all share the assumption that the realization of an ideal is a technical problem. It does not require *phronesis* unless *phronesis* is understood as the knowledge of means for the realization of ideals, and it does not require *sophia,* unless *sophia* is understood as the source of theoretical or abstract ends for the formulation of ideals. Above all, it does not require a *paradeigma* of the good itself in the soul. Indeed, it is the very absence of any such *paradeigma* that leads to idealism. An idealist mistakes the theoretical and practical wisdom of a philosopher for the mere knowledge of ends and means necessary for the realization of political ideals. This is undoubtedly why so many of Plato's modern readers mistake him for an idealist.

In traditional readings of Plato's political dialogues, beginning with Aristotle's discussion of the *Republic* and *Laws* in the *Politics,* there is no discussion of the realization of ideal cities. This should be sufficient evidence that such terms are simply inappropriate. It is fitting to consider whether or not the *kallipolis* and Magnesia are possible cities, and by what standard they can be said to be the best possible or second best cities. These are questions raised in the dialogues themselves, expressed in the terms in which they are raised. It is also fitting to consider what purposes Plato might have had in leading the readers of the dialogues to consider such questions. In traditional interpretations there is no assumption made that the mere possibility of Plato's cities indicates anything about his intentions in writing the dialogues. When Plato's modern critics engage in disputes about the realizability of his political ideals, they make the unfounded assumption that the possibility of his cities explains everything about his inten-

tions. No matter how they might characterize his political idealism, they are thereby prevented from understanding the philosophic significance of the dialogues.

Scholarly disputes about whether one or both of Plato's cities
is a realizable ideal are necessarily inconclusive because their
underlying assumptions are never questioned explicitly. Those
who contend that both are realizable assume that because both
are possible, Plato intended them to be founded; or conversely,
they assume that because Plato intended to bring such cities into
being, they are possible, if only by use of tyrannical force. Those
who contend that only Magnesia is realizable can reach no agreement about whether or not it was Plato's intention to construct
only one practical ideal, and they can make no persuasive and
consistent argument explaining why the *kallipolis* is unrealizable.
When the possibility of Plato's cities is considered independently
of his purposes in writing the dialogues, the various disputes
among the critics of his political idealism seem rather misguided.
According to tradition, Plato wrote the dialogues with the intent
of drawing his reader toward the philosophic life. He intended to
inspire his reader to acquire the highest virtues, *sophia* and *phronesis*. Coming to a judgment as to whether the cities in the dialogues are possible cities and to a further judgment of the consequences of their possibility or impossibility is thus, above all, an
exercise of the reader's intellectual virtue.

Plato's cities are not forms to be applied to matter. The simple
imposition of form on matter is a *techne*, the *techne* of production
or manufacture. For Plato, the *techne* of politics is fundamentally
different. In the *Laws*, the Athenian calls it "the art of caring for
souls" (650b; cf. *Gorgias* 464b). The application of the *techne* of production to politics is a modern phenomenon. In the terms of Aristotle's account of the four primary causes (*Metaphysics* 983a24–b4),
it is quite common for moderns—ideologues and intellectuals
alike—to believe that societies are comprised of formal and material causes alone. It is equally common for them to be suspicious
of anyone who says otherwise. Those who claim that Plato is a
political idealist generally understand politics in this manner.
They find Plato's cities in speech suspect because Plato would
argue that all societies have efficient and final causes as well as
material and formal ones. Their suspicions are evident in the
reductive character of their criticisms: the efficient cause of Plato's
cities is Plato himself, they say, and the final cause of the cities is

not the pursuit of a philosophic life, but rather Plato's pursuit of the tyrannical power to impose his political ideals on others.

The best brief reply to all such criticisms is given in Aristotle's *Politics*. As an introduction to the section of the *Politics* in which the *Republic* and *Laws* are discussed, Aristotle develops a classification of cities as political partnerships intended to be applicable both to existing cities and to cities in speech. The basis of the classification is straightforward: "It is necessary that all citizens be partners either in everything, or in nothing, or in some things but not in others" (*Politics* 1260b36). Partnership in everything or in nothing is impossible, and there are only some things in which partnership is possible. Of the things in which there can be partnership, is it better for a city to participate in all of them or in some but not others? Aristotle claims that this is the question disputed by the defenders of existing regimes, by the defenders of regimes said to be well managed, and by Plato in the *Republic* and the *Laws* (1260b36–61a2). The *kallipolis* and Magnesia are the same type of partnership. Both are partnerships in many things in which partnership is possible. Existing regimes are partnerships in fewer things. Neither the *kallipolis* nor Magnesia is a partnership in everything, but both aspire to this end. It is not their character as cities in speech that sets them apart from existing cities, but the nature of their aspiration.

Neither the *kallipolis* nor Magnesia is, for Aristotle, an impossible or unattainable city. In one of his more general remarks on the relationship between Plato's two cities, Aristotle writes: "The *Laws* deals for the most part with laws, and little is said about the regime. As to this, although he wishes to make it more attainable by cities, he gradually brings it around again toward the other regime" (1264b43–65a4). The "other regime" mentioned is the *kallipolis*. Both Magnesia and the *kallipolis* are "attainable by cities" to some degree. By this Aristotle means that existing cities may emulate them, not necessarily by copying the details of their organization and offices, but by coming to aspire to their end. In particular, they may aspire to what is highest in both cities—education (*paideia*). And in both cities, Aristotle writes, "education is the same" (1265a6).

Aristotle implies that the difference between the *kallipolis* and Magnesia is not that one is less attainable than the other, but that one is apparently less attainable. Aristotle does not discuss this implication at any length. It is evident, however, that Magnesia's appearance of being more attainable is owed primarily to the drama of the *Laws*, in which a city is founded in speech in order that one of the characters, Kleinias, may take what has been said into consideration when he participates in the founding of a new Cretan colony (*Laws* 702b–e; cf. 968b–c, 969c–d). This simple drama allows the reader of the dialogue to be persuaded more readily by the arguments of the Athenian than he might be by the arguments made by Socrates in the *Republic*. The Athenian gradually brings both Kleinias and the reader of the *Laws* around to recognizing and accepting the need for men to attain an end that is difficult, but not impossible to attain: an education in the moral and dianoetic virtues. This is also Socrates' goal in the *Republic*. And for Aristotle the *Laws* is one of "the discourses of Socrates" (*Politics* 1265a10). The education in the virtues provided by the unnamed Athenian who participates in the founding of Magnesia is thus only apparently different than the education provided by the named Athenian who participates in the founding of the *kallipolis*.

As political partnerships the cities in speech of the *Republic* and the *Laws* both have as their end "that it is best for the city to be as far as possible entirely one." Aristotle has a criticism of this shared end: "it is evident that as [a city] becomes increasingly one it will no longer be a city. For the city is in its nature a sort of multitude, and as it becomes more a unity it will be a household instead of a city, and a human being instead of a household" (1261a14–19). The closer that the *kallipolis* and Magnesia approach their end, the worse they are as cities, for cities are multitudes, compounds or partnerships in only a few things; and being such compounds, cities "must be made one and common through education [*paideia*]" (1263b35). But the closer that they approach their end, the better they are as descriptions of a human being. The human being they describe is Socrates, whom Aristotle says is present in both dialogues. The closer they approach their end, the better they are as accounts of a proper education. Both the *Republic* and the *Laws*, therefore, can be said to provide a Socratic education for men and cities as they are, in order that they might aspire to the highest ends of which they are capable. Aristotle, however, would caution readers of the dialogues not to mistake the highest ends of human beings for those of cities.

To summarize Aristotle's discussion: the *kallipolis* and Magnesia are political partnerships in many of the things in which partnerships are possible. Both cities in speech are possible, although perhaps unlikely cities. Despite their particular differences, both the *kallipolis* and Magnesia aspire to what Aristotle considers an end impossible to attain: political partnership in everything, or in all things in which partnership is possible. This paradigmatic end is described in a Pythagorean proverb as a condition in which friends have all things in common (*Republic* 424a; *Laws* 739c). Neither the *Republic* nor the *Laws* describes a city in which this end is attained. Again, despite their particular differences, the *kallipolis* and Magnesia are identical in the one thing that is capable of making cities one and common—education. Both the *Republic* and the *Laws* can be said to provide an education in how cities may approach the unattainable end of political partnership. The dialogues are addressed both to cities that are partnerships in far fewer of the things in which partnership is possible than is the case in either the *kallipolis* or Magnesia, and to the men who live in such cities. Neither dialogue describes an abstract ideal. Rather, both dialogues attempt to persuade their readers of the truth of their arguments; and the dramatic form of the *Laws*, which describes a city in speech apparently more attainable than the *kallipolis*, is intended to be a means by which readers may be more easily persuaded, or educated, about such matters.

I PHRONESIS AND THE GOOD IN THE REPUBLIC

1 THE CAVE AND THE IDEAS

ALMOST ALL READINGS of the *Republic* that take it to be the work of a political idealist refer to the part of the dialogue that has come to be known as the cave allegory as the best evidence available in support of such an interpretation. It is often claimed that the cave allegory illuminates both the nature of the rule of philosophers in the *kallipolis* and the manner in which Plato believed the *kallipolis* could be realized if philosophers came to rule in existing cities. The cave allegory is part of Socrates' account of the "longer way [*makrotera . . . periodos*]" leading to the "most beautiful [*kallista*]" look at things (504a–21b; cf. 435c–d). It is generally said to describe the possible political consequences of the theory of ideas that Plato presents as the end or goal of the "longer way." The political idealism of the cave allegory complements the metaphysical idealism of the rest of the account. It is also argued that the cave is central to understanding how true philosophers will rule the *kallipolis*, since the description of the guardians' higher education—given immediately following the account of the longer way—concludes with Socrates' remark that they must descend into the cave to rule (521c–40c; cf. 520a–d). This in turn is followed by a brief description of the surprising manner in which Platonic idealists would descend into cavelike existing cities in order to realize their political ideals (540d–41a).

This summary of the cave allegory's importance is, as it were, an ideal type. There are a great many interpretations of the cave. There are also a great many interpretations of the longer way as a whole and of the higher education provided for the guardian class. In general, modern scholars have been unable to reach any agreement in their understandings of even the most basic things discussed in these passages of the *Republic*. More specifically, the commentators who are certain that Plato is a political idealist find the cave perpetually puzzling despite its significance for their interpretation. The difficulties encountered in attempting to understand what is said in the account of the longer way are commonly attributed to the

31

unnecessarily allegorical style used by Plato to present his political theory and its epistemological or metaphysical grounding. However, most Plato scholars believe such difficulties are secondary matters: it is possible to discern Plato's idealism and political idealism well enough.

That those who see Plato as a political idealist of some sort disagree widely in their interpretations of the *Republic* is, of course, no proof that Plato was not a political idealist, and even less proof that he was critical of political idealism. In this part of my study, I will discuss Socrates' account of the longer way, especially the ascent from the cave and its consequences, as well as his subsequent description of the guardians' education, in order to demonstrate that the sections of the *Republic* usually cited as the best evidence of Plato's political idealism are best understood as a dramatic presentation of his criticisms of idealism and political imprudence. However, before undertaking this task, a review of some of the issues that have been raised and disputed recently by scholars is in order. In the survey to follow I will summarize the main disagreements in currently popular readings of the longer way; in particular, I will discuss the interpretations of the cave allegory that have been presented recently by Dale Hall, Allan Bloom, Hans-Georg Gadamer, and Eric Voegelin.

It is not uncommon for scholars attempting to make sense of what they take to be Plato's cloudy symbolism to claim that their analyses will be literal. For example, J. E. Raven prefaces an article on the longer way with the assertion that, unlike other contemporary interpretations, his will be based "on what Plato himself actually wrote."[1] His analysis, however, is founded on several esoteric interpretive criteria. The most basic of these assumptions is a convention that is almost universally accepted among Plato scholars. Although Raven is aware that the discussion of the longer way should be seen as "an organic and indivisible whole," he divides it into several sections, each of which he reconstructs as an independently meaningful part of a theory being presented allegorically by Plato. He refers to each of these sections according to a central image: the Sun (507a–9c), the Divided Line (509d–11e), and the Cave (514a–17a). Raven does not explain why the ongoing discussion between Socrates and Glaucon is best understood in this manner. The esoteric character of this sort of analysis is evident in its immediate consequence. The dialogic relation of Socrates and Glaucon is what makes everything said in the account of the longer way "an organic and indivisible whole." When an analysis of the text does not recognize that it is a dialogue, the organic unity is lost and some esoteric interpretive criterion must be found in order to restore it. This is usually done by selecting one of the subsections as the most important. Raven stands with the majority of scholars in claiming that the divided line is the source of the organic unity of everything said in the discussion. The line is Plato's allegorical presentation of his epistemology. The sun and the cave are simply two analogies or allegories for the line. Raven even claims that any attempt to find "any wider significance whatever" in the sun and the cave allegories is "to destroy the whole analogy."

A properly literal reading of the text would discover far wider significance in what is said by Socrates and Glaucon than Raven suspects. In the preface to his translation of the *Republic*, Allan Bloom asserts: "In the discussion of the divided line, for example, the particular illustrations are chosen to fit the nature of Socrates' interlocutor; in order to see the whole problem, the reader must ponder not only the distinction of the kinds of knowing and being but its particular effect on Glaucon and what Socrates might have said to another man."[2] The same is true of Socrates' entire account of the longer way and the education of the guardians. Glaucon is the interlocutor throughout the discussion. Socrates chooses his words in order to have a particular effect on him. Glaucon is clever and politically ambitious. Socrates' purpose in speaking with him is to cure him of his imprudence. Indeed, according to Xenophon, Socrates only agreed to speak with Glaucon as a favor to Plato, Glaucon's brother (*Memorabilia* 3.6). Earlier in the *Republic*, Socrates describes Glaucon to the reader as "always most courageous in everything," even in arguments (357a). He has a very spirited nature and hence is honor-loving and victory-loving (cf. 545a, 550b, 581b). This makes him something of a geometrical thinker and an eristic in discussion. At times he honors the hypotheses of his thought unquestioningly, like a geometrical thinker, and is convinced that victory in discussion comes by way of strict demonstration from them; at times he pursues victory in discussion at any cost, honoring no hypotheses, like an eristic youth (cf. 454a-b, 511b-d, 527b, 539b-c).[3] Glaucon is consequently something of a political idealist, and a vigorous or courageous one at that. Throughout their discussion Socrates chooses his words and illustrations in order to lead him away from imprudent idealism toward a way of life that would enable him always to practice "justice with *phronesis* in every way" (621c; cf. 620c–d). The drama of their dialogue is the reader's guide to understanding the criticisms being made of Glaucon's imprudence.

Socrates' account of the longer way is his answer to the question, What is the good itself? While describing it, Socrates is attempting to lead Glaucon toward a vision of the good in order that he might become wise and prudent. Socrates' subsequent account of the guardians' education concludes with a description of how the best of them must see the good itself if they are to become wise and prudent and hence fit to rule justly. During this discussion as well, Socrates is attempting to lead Glaucon toward the good. His repeated attempts to lead Glaucon away from imprudent idealism, and Glaucon's repeated inability to ascend with Socrates beyond a certain point, are the main dramatic features of their dialogue. They are what makes the entire discussion, in Raven's words, "an organic and indivisible whole." And any interpretation that ignores the drama of their dialogue to reconstruct the text according to esoteric criteria will be unable to determine its "wider significance."

As was mentioned, most Plato scholars study the details of the images Socrates uses in speaking with Glaucon in analyzing Socrates' account of the longer way. They consider the proper understanding of the three images' interrelation as the hermeneutic key to unlocking the meaning of what is said. Their most fundamental disagreements, therefore, are about which image provides unity for the whole account. By far the most popular view is the one accepted by Raven: the imagery of the divided line is central and explains the allegories of the sun and the cave. Yet all those who accept this seemingly straightforward view can reach no consensus in their interpretations of the detailed interrelation of the three images.[4] In the last of a series of articles that often serve as a touchstone for modern analyses of the longer way, A. S. Ferguson writes: "The similes of the Sun, Line and Cave in the *Republic* remain a reproach to Plato scholarship because there is no agreement about them, though they are meant to illustrate."[5] This is as true today as when it was written. If anything, scholarly disagreements have increased in number and intensity. In particular, the popular convention of using the line as the key to reading the text has been subjected to strong criticism by a number of scholars who argue that the attempt to reconstruct an idealistic epistemology from the divided line in isolation from its significance within Socrates' whole account leads to misrepresentations of the meaning of the sun and cave images. They argue instead that the imagery of the sun as an offspring of the good is central. It should be used as the basis for understanding the account of knowledge in the image of the divided line and the account of education in the image of the cave.[6]

The dispute about whether the sun or the line is the central image of the longer way often leads to questions of textual interpretation that appear insignificant but are actually of fundamental importance for any attempt to understand Socrates' account of the good. The most basic question can be stated simply: Are the terms "the good itself [*agathon auto*]" and "the idea of the good [*tou agathou idea*]" strictly synonymous or not? It is almost universally the case that idealistic interpretations of the longer way take all references to the good as references to the idea of the good, and that all those critical of such interpretations attempt to distinguish between them. Another way of bringing out the fundamental disagreement underlying disputes about the relative importance of the sun and the line would be to consider what is meant by Socrates' statement that the good is "beyond being [*epekeina tes ousias*]," transcending it in dignity (*presbeia*) and power (*dynamis*). Those who read the *Republic* as the work of an idealist either agree with Glaucon, who dismisses it as "daimonic hyperbole [*daimonias hyperboles*]" (504b–c), or understand this passage as a reference to the idea of the good, demonstrating generally that the ideas themselves are different from being.[7] Most of those who consider the sun image to be of central importance in Socrates' account believe that such idealistic epistemological reconstructions misrepresent the transcendent nature of the good itself. Socrates' description of the power and dignity of the good cannot be taken to refer to the idea of the good, they claim. The idea of the good is the noetic apperception of the good itself.

In my exegesis of the text, I will attempt to demonstrate that this last reading is correct. It is in accord with the drama of the dialogue and the substance of what is being said. Socrates' description of the good beyond being is not a reference to the idea of the good. If it were, Glaucon would have little reason to object to it as he does. It is meant seriously, and should not be dismissed as daimonic hyperbole. Plato makes this clear to readers of the *Republic* by having Socrates speak directly to them, not to Glaucon, when responding to Glaucon's dismissal. Socrates says explicitly that Glaucon's remark is very laughable or absurd (*mala geloios;* 509b–c). Plato scholars should take Socrates at his word about this. They should be wary of interpreting Socrates' description of the good in ways that would not provoke a very laughable response from Glaucon. But this is what they do when they explain it as part of a Platonic theory of ideas or a Platonic account of dialectical thought. Neither such explanation does justice to the text and the drama it presents.

It remains to consider readings of the cave allegory in more detail. What is meant by Socrates' description of the cave and the ascent from it? This is probably the most disputed question in commentaries on the *Republic*. As was mentioned, most scholars accept the view that the cave is an allegorical restatement of the divided line, and even though there are many opinions about the proper way to correlate the details described in the line and the cave, most would agree that the relation between the line and the cave demonstrates the relation between Plato's idealism and political idealism. The authors who take the sun as the central image of the longer way are generally critical of this understanding. They claim instead that the significance of the cave is primarily pedagogical. It describes the *paideia* of the philosopher in society and perhaps also the *paideia* provided by the philosopher within society. Unfortunately, they offer little textual exegesis and dialogic interpretation to support either their criticisms or their own explanations of the cave.[8] However, one conclusion can be drawn from their work. If it is true, as Gadamer and Voegelin in particular argue, that the philosophic *paideia* of the cave image is crowned by *phronesis,* then it is evident that in describing the ascent from the cave Socrates counsels Glaucon in prudent political judgment and not political idealism. Most Plato scholars, then, misinterpret Socrates' account as evidence of Plato's political idealism because they, like Glaucon, cannot follow the dialogic pedagogy intended to lead Glaucon, and the reader of the dialogue, to understand the significance of *phronesis.*

Before discussing further the wide variety of disagreements between those who analyze the cave by means of the divided line and those who do not, and between those who consider the cave as evidence of Plato's political idealism and those who do not, it is important to call attention to an apparently minor point of textual interpretation that such disputes do not call into question. It is generally accepted—indeed, axiomatic—that Socrates' remarks from the beginning of his description of the cave (514a) to the time he mentions the possibility that "the man who attempts to release and lead up" might be killed by the cave's "perpetual prisoners" (517a) may be condensed into a summary description of a cave, which in turn may be analyzed as an allegorical image. It is equally axiomatic to consider all subsequent references to a cave, or to the way up and the way down, or even to light and darkness in general, in reference to this summary description. The cave is a particular and concrete place or thing, albeit an imagined one. As John Wright points out, "The figure of *a* Cave is Orphic, [but] that of *the* Cave is distinctly Platonic." In his own search for the meaning of Plato's cave, Wright makes the farfetched psychoanalytic claim that a trip to the cave of Vari on Mount Hymettus during Plato's infancy "crowded in on his mind and shaped and colored his development of the simile."9 Other scholars are less imaginative, but nonetheless equally convinced of the concreteness of the cave in their attempts to determine its hidden allegorical meaning. However, the axioms on which its concreteness is founded are not self-evident. My exegesis of what has come to be called the cave allegory will call these axioms into question by considering Socrates' remarks in the context of his dialogue with Glaucon. Socrates repeatedly attempts to lead Glaucon toward the good in his account of the longer way, and his various descriptions of a cave are best understood in this context. His references to a cave, to ascent and descent, and to light and darkness are not all references to an invariable, single thing. They are evocative and persuasive statements whose meaning varies according to the drama of the discussion. And their meaning is more Orphic than it is "distinctly Platonic," as Platonic idealism is presently understood.

The interpretations of the *Republic* that assume the divided line is the key to understanding Socrates' discussion of the good can be classified according to a useful schema developed by Dale Hall.10 Almost all idealistic interpretations of the "allegory of the Cave assume that its meaning is either exclusively epistemological or political," Hall claims. The more widely accepted and hence more "orthodox" epistemological interpretation is typified by arguments emphasizing the "one-to-one correspondence" between the four segments of the line and the four stages of ascent in the cave allegory. It claims the cave allegory has no particular political content. The cave's only purpose is "to contrast the philoso-

pher's understanding with the relative ignorance of ordinary men."
In contrast, the less widely accepted political interpretation is
typified by arguments emphasizing the discontinuities between
the line and the cave. It claims the cave has "a purely political
meaning." The allegory "contrasts the philosophic enterprise
with the life of political practice in existing *poleis;* it symbolizes
the opposition between the philosopher and the corruption of
[the] prevailing political condition." The epistemological interpretation emphasizes the intellectual differences among men,
using an account of Platonic idealism as a measure, without deriv-
ing any political consequences from such differences. The political interpretation emphasizes the differences between the philosophic life—understood in essentially the same way as in the
epistemological interpretation—and the political life possible in
contemporary Greek *poleis,* but without attempting to determine
if Plato's idealism is capable of overcoming what, for Hall, is "the
unnatural divorce of philosophy and political authority."[11]

Hall considers both of these readings of the cave "one-sided."
He argues instead that the cave is Plato's account of the relation
between epistemology and politics. Hall accepts the epistemological reading of Platonic idealism and the political reading of the
"cave-system" as a representation of the political realm, but he
combines them uniquely in an interpretation of the cave as an
allegory for a Platonic doctrine of political idealism. The cave is
not simply a representation of corrupt existing *poleis,* but of the
political realm *per se* when it is "deprived of philosophic rule."
The rule of philosopher-kings can best be described as the rule of
Platonic idealists in the "cave-system." They would be required to
rule by means of "an apparatus of political control through which
men are manipulated." For Hall the political apparatus is a neutral means that idealists can use for their own ends. On the basis
of this distinctly modern understanding of politics, Hall concludes that the *kallipolis* is a realizable ideal and that the cave
allegory is a description of the manner in which Plato believed it
could be realized in existing *poleis* or, indeed, in any society. In all
societies most men must remain at the lowest level of the "cave-
world," but when the Platonic idealists who are capable of leaving
it return to assume positions of political authority at the cave's
upper level, "communal enlightenment" will result. In Plato's
"ideal community," therefore, nonphilosophers would be able to
"participate in the perfection of the political whole" without having to leave the cave.

The enthusiastic optimism of Hall's account of the cave allegory has been criticized by Allan Bloom. Bloom claims that Hall "does not pay sufficient attention to the text," making factual errors in his exegesis. In particular, he is wrong to suggest that philosophers rule in the cave. Hall is right, Bloom says, in comparing the cave both to the requirement that philosophers rule the *kallipolis* and to the political realm *per se;* however, he adds that Hall is wrong in his understanding of what philosophers do when they return to the cave, and hence wrong in the political conclusions he reaches concerning the entire comparison: "It is true, as [Hall] says, that the potential philosophers must be compelled to leave the cave as well as to return to it. But once out, they recognize how good it is to be out. They never see a reason to go back. . . . It is only by going out that they become aware that the *kallipolis* is a cave, nay Hades, and to be in it is as to be a shade." As well, Hall is insufficiently attentive to the dialogic character of the text and thus does not bear in mind that Socrates discusses these things for Glaucon's benefit. When Glaucon learns about philosophy from Socrates, he also learns that the philosophic life is "essentially independent" of political life: "From the point of view of philosophy . . . the city looks like a cave or a prison." Glaucon's education liberates him "from the desire to rule." He would thus neither imagine that a philosopher would have reason to return to the cave or the *kallipolis* nor believe that the *kallipolis* was a political program to be implemented according to Socrates' description of the cave.[12]

For Bloom, Plato describes the philosophic life as one lived after "the ascent from the cave to the region of the ideas." Plato was no political idealist—those who live in the region of the ideas and those incapable of ascending from the cave have nothing to do with one another. The difference between the philosopher and the nonphilosopher is absolute. All those who are not philosophers cannot turn away from the cave's shadows: "they believe the shadows are real things and are passionately committed to that belief." Bloom states categorically:

> That is what cave-dwelling means. The cave must always remain the cave, so the philosopher is the enemy of the prisoners since he cannot take the nonphilosopher's most cherished beliefs seriously. Similarly, Socrates does not care for other men, but only to the extent that they, too, are capable of philosophy, which only a few are. This is an essential and qualitative difference, one that cannot be bridged.

Only those capable of ascending to the ideas are capable of "true virtue." In Bloom's interpretation of the *Republic,* true virtue is intellectual virtue: "The only authentic virtue [for Plato] is that of the mind contemplating its proper objects. . . . The *Republic* is not the *Ethics;* there are no moral virtues in it." By this Bloom also means that there is no Aristotelian understanding of *phronesis* in it. He claims that in Plato's psychology the "philosophic part of the soul has no use for action, and deliberation is not part of its function. . . . *Logismos* is for action; *nous* is for itself."[13] Plato is thus an idealist, though not a political idealist. The philosophic life, consequently, is one that has no use for *phronesis* because it is dedicated to contemplating the ideas; or perhaps it might be better to say that *phronesis* is the politic use of *logismos* (calculation) in the preservation of the philosophic life.

The disagreements between Hall and Bloom are fundamental and irreconcilable. Bloom is certainly right when he says the *Republic* is "the greatest critique of political idealism ever written." Socrates' construction of the city in speech does demonstrate that "political idealism is the most destructive of human passions."[14] Hall's optimistic political idealism prevents him from being able to accept the former statement as a proper interpretation of the *Republic* and the latter as true in itself. However, Hall and Bloom do not disagree about everything. The assumptions on which they base their readings of the longer way are often identical even though the political conclusions they reach are diametrically opposed. For example, they both consider the divided line as the hermeneutical key to unlocking the meaning of Socrates' account of the sun and the cave. They agree that Plato was an idealist about the good and the good life. As well, Bloom and Hall both consider the epistemological and political interpretations of the cave to be one-sided and incomplete. They agree that the cave represents both the intellectual differences among men and the nature of politics *per se.* It represents the relation between epistemology and politics or, more accurately, between knowledge and power. The fundamental disagreement between Hall and Bloom concerns the nature of this relation, and not the nature of the things related.

Bloom's most extensive analysis of the idealism he finds in Socrates' account of the longer way is given in the "Interpretive Essay" accompanying his translation of the *Republic.*[15] He agrees with the majority of Plato scholars in assuming there is no difference in meaning between Socrates' references to the good itself and the idea of the good: "the good in itself [is] an *idea* of the good in which the good things participate." This is not to say that the idea of the good is only a generalization from the many particular good things: "The good . . . must also be a super *idea*, an *idea* of *ideas*. . . . [T]hese other *ideas*, the many *ideas*, are participations in the one *idea* of the good."[16] Socrates never describes the good as "an *idea* of *ideas*." What might this mean? And what of Socrates' description of the good itself as beyond being in dignity and power (509b)? Bloom answers such questions by interpreting the text idealistically. He asserts that "the *ideas are*." In other words, the ideas and being or *ousia* are somehow the same. The good, therefore, as the idea of ideas, is beyond being or the ideas in that it is "the transcendent principle of the whole."[17] However, Socrates never describes the good in this way. He does once suggest that dialectic leads toward the good, which is the cause or beginning of all (*ten tou pantos archen*), but he does not define the good by reference to the whole (*to holon;* 511b). Indeed, in the *Theaetetus* (204b) Socrates explicitly differentiates between the whole (*to holon*) and the all (*to pan*).[18] For Bloom, then, the good is the unity of all ideas. As such it is the cause of the being of things. By this, he means that it is the cause of the idea of things, or the cause of things being known. However, in Socrates' account, the good is described as the cause of the being of all things as existents, not simply as things known to the knower. Glaucon dismisses the former account of the good itself as daimonic hyperbole. He would not dismiss the latter in the same way.

In Bloom's interpretation, wisdom is "knowledge of the true whole or the first causes," or even "knowing everything there is to know." It is the perfection of the mind's true virtue and the end toward which the soul of the philosopher aspires. The process of epistemological clarification leading to this end is described by the divided line. The soul's "progress from its lowest level of cognition, imagination, to . . . intellection, its highest level" is the path it must travel if it is ever to satisfy its "longing for completeness, . . . to know everything which *is*." The images of the divided line and the sun as the offspring of the good are perfectly consistent. The *Republic* does not demonstrate "that any man can convert himself from a lover of wisdom into a wise man."[19] It only describes the philosophical life devoted to the pursuit of the end of intellectual completeness. The philosophic life, Bloom writes, is one devoted to the perfection of the theoretical virtues: "The practical virtues can only be justified if they are understood to be the means to the theoretical virtues."[20] By referring to theoretical virtues in the plural, however, Bloom does not mean that the *Republic* contains an account of *sophia* and *phronesis* comparable to the one found in Aristotle's *Ethics*. Instead, it would be fair to assume that Bloom understands the Platonic theoretical virtues as theoretical knowledge about theoretical and practical things.

Bloom interprets the cave as Plato's allegorical presentation of his theoretical knowledge about practical things. He finds nothing resembling Aristotelian *phronesis* in the account. The cave can be understood "[o]nly by constant reference back to the divided line." The line shows "that reality extends far beyond anything the practical man ever dreams and that to know it one must use faculties never recognized by the practical man." The correspondence between the line and the cave is perfect: "the cave is the city," and the city is inhabited by practical men who never dream of any other reality than the "authoritative opinions about things" presented to them "by legislators and poets." The darkness of the cave in which men are imprisoned represents the practical power of such authoritative opinions. Only a few human beings can emerge from the cave and escape from the practical life—the few who have "a great contempt for the cave, its shadows and its inhabitants." They are the true philosophers. For Bloom, a true philosopher "wants always to live out in the light; the others do not know they are slaves, so they are content; but he knows it and cannot bear to live among them." The core of the philosopher's theoretical knowledge of practical things is simple. The non-philosophers who are enslaved within the cave or city are unselfconscious slaves. He wants nothing to do with them and their city: "Nothing in the city contributes to his specific pleasures, and he wants nothing from it."[21] He will not descend into the cave to engage in practical activities that compel him, unnecessarily, to have any dealings with slavish nonphilosophers.

Why then does Socrates build a city in speech with Glaucon and Adeimantus? Bloom would answer that his purpose is to demonstrate to his interlocutors that philosophers should have nothing to do with the city. The guardians who are capable of ascending to the region of the ideas and seeing the idea of the good must be compelled to return to the *kallipolis,* just as the souls capable of dwelling outside the cave must be compelled to return to its darkness. For Bloom, the rule of true philosophers makes the *kallipolis* the "perfectly just city," the "perfect city," and the "good city." But this requires compulsion. The cave allegory, therefore, reveals that philosophers would not come to rule even in the *kallipolis*. The ruled would not compel philosophers to rule them, and the philosophers, who want nothing to do with the ruled, would not ask to be compelled by them. The city in speech is thus a "perfect impossibility." Socrates constructs it in order to persuade his interlocutors, and especially Glaucon, that although all men have some duty to the city, true philosophers are "always at war with it."[22]

Bloom's understanding of the relation between knowledge and power in the *Republic* has been criticized by Gadamer for being one-sided or undialectical. Gadamer argues instead that the city in speech was not constructed in order to reveal "the irreconcilability of theoretical and civil life." If that had been "the whole point of Plato's invention," it would have been a wasteful "expenditure of intelligence and wit." Gadamer does not deny that the *Republic* describes a conflict between "an existence devoted to *theoria*" and one spent in "the world of social power structures," nor does he deny that there is an idealistic resolution of the conflict in "Plato's state in the clouds," which is intended to "prove to the thinking reader that the conflict is real." He finds, however, that if the *Republic* is read as "one grand dialectical myth," it gives some indication of how the conflict may be resolved. Plato's reasonable understanding of practical matters becomes evident when the institutions of his ideal city are understood "*e contrario*"; by this, Gadamer means that when the "utopian" institutions and structures of the city are compared "dialectically" with their opposites, "what is really meant" by them will emerge "somewhere in between."[23] Gadamer's point against Bloom is well taken, but it is not evident that the argument he makes in support of it is sound. He does not demonstrate how his method of dialectical interpretation can be derived from what is said in the *Republic* itself. More specifically, his understanding of Platonic dialectic may not do justice to Socrates' own discussion of dialectic in the *Republic*.

Gadamer agrees with much of Bloom's analysis of the cave allegory and its relevance for understanding the rule of philosophers in the *kallipolis*. The cave allegory, he claims, is intended to explain "nothing other than the life of the *polis*." It establishes "the superiority of those who know the good over those who remain caught in moral, political conventions." The way to "knowledge of the good" is through the sciences to dialectic. Indeed, this is the significance of the longer way as a whole: "the allegory of the cave [is] a curriculum of education leading through mathematics and dialectic. And the 'hyperbolic' position of the good, represented by the simile of the sun, is not really explained. . . . When it comes right down to it, the 'ascent' to the noetic dimension is the single theme." The scientific and dialectic knowledge of those who live the life of *theoria* has little to do with practical matters: "nothing is said [in Socrates' account] about the application of such theory to human practice." This makes the rule of philosophers in the *kallipolis* problematic and apparently even paradoxical.[24] Gadamer and Bloom agree this far. But Gadamer does not agree that nothing more can be said.

How then does Plato understand the application of *theoria* to practice? The answer to this question, Gadamer writes, has nothing to do with "the realm that Aristotle calls *techne*." The relationship "between ends and means in practical or political action" is not a productive activity for Plato. This is true enough, but Gadamer is hesitant to explain what the relationship is for Plato. He writes at length about Plato's sensitivity to "the hermeneutical problem which is entailed in every use of rules, that is, in their correct application," even though he must admit that such a general hermeneutical problem "has no bearing on the relation between politics and philosophy or on the tension between the political and theoretical ideals of life." Gadamer claims the similarity of the political and theoretical ideals can be seen by means of an *e contrario* interpretation of the paradox of the philosopher-ruler: "both aiming at the good and knowing reality pertain to the political actions of the true statesman as well as to the true theoretical life."[25] But how do the true philosopher and the true statesman similarly apply *theoria* to practice?

An answer to this question should be based on the discussion of *phronesis* and the good in Socrates' account of the longer way. Socrates neither discusses nor even mentions *theoria;* he does discuss *phronesis*. Although Gadamer is aware that Socrates' references to *phronesis* have dramatic significance in the dialogue, he does not refer to them in his own account of the Platonic understanding of *theoria* and practice. His silence is explained by a philological claim he makes concerning the relation of *phronesis* and dialectic: "In Plato's language reason [*logos*] and reasonableness [*phronesis*] are called dialectic." Gadamer bases his argument on this claim, even though there is no textual foundation for it. Dialectic is the truth and substance of Platonic theoretical and practical wisdom alike: "As a matter of fact, the connection between the logical and ethical aspects of true dialectic runs through the whole of Plato's work."[26] It is not immediately evident how the ethical aspect of dialectic can be anything other than the clarification of *logos;* nor is it evident that the ethical aspect of dialectic, however understood, is in any way comparable to the virtue of *phronesis,* which governs judgment and practical and political action.

Bloom claims that the only authentic Platonic virtue is associated with the mind's contemplation of the ideas. The philosophic life is dedicated to perfecting this virtue by pursuing knowledge of the idea of the good, the unity of all ideas. Insofar as Plato discusses practical and political matters at all, his intent is to explain the fundamental difference between those who are capable of possessing the mind's authentic virtue and those who are not. Gadamer's account of these things differs in that he explains the mind's contemplation of the ideas as a dialectical activity and alludes to the prudence of Plato's political judgment without being able to account for it adequately. Gadamer and Bloom have similar understandings of the ideas. For Gadamer the *ideai* or *eide* (forms) are equivalent to *noumena* (objects of intellection) and the *ontas onta* (things that are); all of these, he claims, may be called "[t]rue being," which itself "appears in thinking" in some way. Gadamer also agrees with Bloom and the majority of Plato scholars in considering Socrates' remarks about the good itself and the idea of the good to be synonymous. He explains Socrates' description of the good, beyond being in dignity and power (509b), as an indication that the idea of the good is "the 'cause' of the being of the many ideas," and Socrates' description of the good as the beginning of all (*ten tou pantos archen;* 511b) is explained as an indication that "the multiplicity of the ideas that make up the noetic realm" originates in the idea of the good.[27] Bloom's understanding of these passages is similar. Gadamer's most important difference with Bloom, then, is his insistence that knowledge of the idea of the good is necessarily dialectical, or incomplete, and not absolute. His criticism of Bloom's understanding of Plato's political judgment is founded on this fundamental point of disagreement. However, Gadamer's criticism is undermined by his failure to demonstrate that the virtue of *phronesis* is the result of the mind's dialectical knowledge of the idea of the good.

Gadamer takes Bloom to task for not reading the *Republic* dialectically. Bloom might reply that Gadamer does not read it as a dialogue, paying close attention to what is actually said. This is certainly true of Gadamer's textual proof that dialectic is the best name for "knowledge of the good" in the *Republic*. Gadamer claims that Plato speaks of such knowledge using several names: "a *dynamis tou dialegesthai* (ability to distinguish dialectically) (532d), a *methodos* (method), and an *episteme*" (see 533b–e).[28] There are several difficulties with this claim. Gadamer gives no indication that Socrates or either of his main interlocutors ever uses the phrase "knowledge of the good," and the terms he cites as names for such knowledge are taken from a discussion in which no reference is made to the good. His three names are taken from Socrates' discussion with Glaucon of the role of dialectic in the education of the guardians. The first phrase is spoken by Glaucon, the following two terms by Socrates. When Glaucon speaks using the phrase *dynamis tou dialegesthai*, he demonstrates that he has not understood Socrates' preceding account of dialectic. Indeed, Socrates is critical of Glaucon's remarks in his immediate response (533a). There is therefore little reason to believe that the phrase adequately describes dialectic and none to believe that it proves that dialectic is Plato's name for knowledge of the good. The terms spoken by Socrates give equally little support to Gadamer's argument. Socrates does describe dialectic as a way of inquiry (*methodos*), but he does not describe it as a type of knowledge at all. It is certainly not synonymous with *episteme*. *Episteme* is not the highest type of knowledge in Socrates' account. It is an aspect of *noesis*, which has to do with *ousia* (533e–34a; cf. 508e–9a). And not even *noesis* may be called "knowledge of the good," since the good is beyond *ousia*. There is simply no technical name given for "knowledge of the good" or "knowing the good" in the *Republic*. There is also no immediately evident reason to assume, as Gadamer does, that dialectic is a type of knowledge. Perhaps the most that can be said of dialectic is that it is a way or passage (*poreia*) by which intellection (*noesis*) may come to the end of the intelligible realm and the soul may come to see the good itself (532a–b, 539d–40a).

Gadamer's attempt to prove that dialectic is knowledge of the good and that it is therefore the truth and substance of Platonic theoretical and practical wisdom leads him to overlook not only the dialogic subtlety of Socrates' account of the longer way and the guardians' education, but also its most important point. Eric Voegelin states the point succinctly: "Concerning the content of the Agathon nothing can be said at all. This is the fundamental insight of Platonic ethics. The transcendence of the Agathon makes immanent propositions concerning its content impossible. The vision of the Agathon does not render a material rule of conduct, but forms the soul through an experience of transcendence." Socrates' discussion of the longer way attempts to form Glaucon's soul by leading him toward such an experience, just as his account of the guardians' education culminates in his description of how their souls will be formed in the same way. Voegelin also writes: "The excellence created by the Agathon in the soul is not identical with any of the four virtues in the model [*sophia, andreia, sophrosyne* and *dikaiosyne*] (518d); Plato's preferred term for its designation is *phronesis* (518e)."[29] *Phronesis* is not an aspect of dialectic, as Gadamer argues; it is the virtue of the soul's relation to the good. The philosophic life is not one typified by the mind's contemplation of the ideas, as Bloom argues; it is one dedicated to acquiring *sophia, phronesis,* and the moral virtues as well. Socrates' dialogue with Glaucon, therefore, is an attempt to persuade him to abandon his imprudent idealism and live the philosophic life that would enable him always to practice justice with *phronesis* in every way (621c).

Voegelin's own account of the longer way in the *Republic* is exceptionally insightful. However, his discussion of the text is often too brief and summary. He provides little exegesis and commentary, and equally little discussion of the drama of the dialogue between Socrates and Glaucon. This is particularly evident in his account of the cave: "The meaning of the Parable in general is clear and needs no elaboration. It is an allegory of the philosopher's education, as well as of his fate in the corrupt society, with a concluding allusion to the death of Socrates."[30] This raises a question. Since the importance of *phronesis* is discussed in Socrates' description of the ascent from the cave, how is it possible to reach a general understanding of the manner in which *phronesis* reconciles theoretical and practical matters, or even the philosophic life and the practical and political concerns that all men have as human beings, if Socrates' account is to be understood exclusively in the context of his own life and death? In other words, is any general understanding of *phronesis* presented in the text, or is it only possible to generalize the particulars of Socrates' life and death? In order to answer this question, a more detailed study of the text is required than is provided by Voegelin.

When confronted with the difficulties inherent in attempting to understand the *Republic*, particularly with the difficulties of attempting to understand the many scholarly interpretations of it available, D. W. Hamlyn was compelled to lament that "an inordinate amount of attention" has been paid to the sun, the divided line, and the cave. He favored discussions of "the general picture" Plato was painting in the dialogue, since it seemed obvious to him that the "great attention to detail" in such analyses had "blinded scholars."[31] However, more and not less attention must be paid to the details of Socrates' account of the longer way if "the general picture" being painted in the *Republic* is to be fully appreciated.

In my reading of the *Republic* (504b–41a), I will attempt to avoid the hermeneutic and analytic difficulties examined in the preceding discussion. The basic assumptions of my reading may be summarized as follows. The main feature of Socrates' lengthy discussion with Glaucon is the dialogic character of his repeated attempts to educate Glaucon about the good. The first part of the discussion, the account of the longer way, is a dramatic and direct attempt to lead Glaucon toward the good; the second part, the account of the guardians' education, is a somewhat more indirect attempt to do the same thing by having Glaucon imagine how it is possible for others to be led toward the good. The details of Socrates' account of the guardians' education derive their significance from what is said about the longer way. The longer way serves to complete the *Republic's* ongoing discussion of the just soul by clarifying the relation of justice and the good through Socrates' account of *phronesis*. The education provided for the guardians is intended to make them truly just and prudent. Socrates' account of it, therefore, serves to make possible a completion of the *Republic's* ongoing discussion of the just city. The rulers of the city in speech will be those capable of practicing "justice with *phronesis* in every way" (621c), but the manner in which truly just and prudent guardians will rule the *kallipolis* is not described in the dialogue. The only evidence of *phronesis* in the *kallipolis* is to be found in the souls of the best of its guardians, but it is a *phronesis* that is not described as being exercised in any way. The *kallipolis* is only potentially a truly just city. As it is described, there are injustices to be found within it, injustices that the guardians' practice of justice with *phronesis* could correct. In order to understand the true nature of the *kallipolis*, therefore, Glaucon must first come to understand how *phronesis* should be exercised, and this in turn requires him to understand Socrates' account of the longer way.

Socrates' account of the longer way is understandable only if its dialogic and dramatic character is recognized. No one image is of central importance. If anything, the entire account may be considered as a single complex image used by Socrates to answer the question, What is the good? The careful study of how the various aspects of Socrates' answer—commonly described as the sun, line, and cave images or allegories—are interrelated is an important hermeneutical key to unlocking the meaning of the whole account, but the nature of their interrelation cannot be determined by treating them exclusively as visual images independently of their status as images presented in speech. They are images spoken in a dialogue between two men for a reason. Their meaning and purpose does not depend on the details of their interrelation alone, but on the purpose and meaning of the whole discussion of which they are illustrative parts. Socrates' discussion of the longer way begins when he asks Adeimantus and Glaucon to recall that the greatest studies concern not justice, but rather *phronesis* and the good (504a–5b), and it ends when he asks Glaucon if he would like to hear how the guardians of the city in speech will undertake such studies (521c). The relation of justice, prudence, and the good is described in the latter part of the longer way, beginning with Socrates' first reference to a cave (514a). The political consequences of the longer way are not explicable by reference to a cave reconstructed from various things suggested in Socrates' remarks between 514a and 517a. They emerge only if the entire discussion (514a–21c) is understood in the context of Socrates' extended account of the good.

It is wrong to consider the cave as a single and concrete, albeit imaginary, place or thing. Socrates' various references to caves cannot be condensed into a summary description of *the* cave. They are evocative and persuasive statements the meaning of which varies according to the drama of his dialogue with Glaucon. Furthermore, Socrates' various references to light and darkness, and to the way up and the way down, cannot be incorporated into such a summary reconstruction of the cave, nor can any such reconstruction be used to explain them adequately. The paired symbols of light and darkness, and the ways up and down, are far more variable in meaning than scholarly analyses of the cave allegory suggest. If it is wrong to consider the cave as a single thing, then it is doubly wrong to consider the cave as Plato's allegorical description of politics, no matter whether it is believed to represent the political realm in general or the political circumstances of contemporary Athens in particular. The cave is neither an allegory for the relation between philosophy and the city nor an allegory for Socrates' fate. It is not an allegory at all. And the prudent political consequences of Socrates' account of the good, explained to Glaucon explicitly as well as by means of evocative references to caves, darkness and light, ascent and descent, are more far-reaching than most scholars suggest in their attempts to uncover *the* cave's allegorical significance.

If it is necessary to have a single definition for everything that might be meant by the darkness of a cave in Socrates' account, then I would suggest the following one, intended to capture something of the Orphic character of the longer way: anything from which it is possible for the soul to turn around toward a more brilliantly illuminated thing, or even toward the source of illumination itself, may be said to be enveloped in the darkness of a cave. All things short of the soul's illumination by the good beyond being, the goal of its ascent, are part of one cave or another. However, all caves are not thereby the same, and their darknesses are not all thereby the proverbial night in which all cows are black. There are caves with and without public or political substance and consequence in Socrates' account. The body is a cave or a darkness for the soul. The realm of becoming is a cave. So too is the visible realm. But the body, the realm of becoming, and the visible realm are not thereby the same thing. Nor is any of them strictly equatable with the several caves or darknesses named and described by Socrates in the latter part of the longer way that have public or political significance. Socrates mentions four: the "first home [*tes protes oikeseos*]" (516c), from which it is possible to ascend by nature; the cave resembling Hades, inhabited by "perpetual prisoners [*tois aei desmotais*]" (516e–17a) who refuse to ascend; the "common home [*sunoikesin*]" (520c) to which the philosopher descends with *phronesis* following his soul's ascent to the good; and finally, the dream world of factional political conflict within the "common home."

Most of this part of my study will be concerned with analyzing the subtleties of the longer way (504a–21b). In particular, I will be concerned with examining the differences between Socrates' several public or political caves in order to determine the relation of justice, *phronesis*, and the good in Socrates' account and to understand how the account as a whole illuminates the nature of politics in "every city" (520e). Before I undertake this analysis, however, I will briefly consider how Socrates and Glaucon come to take the longer way—along with the silent Adeimantus—after setting out to understand justice in itself. Once my exegesis and analysis of the longer way is complete, it will be possible for me to turn to Socrates' discussion of the education of the guardians with Glaucon (521c–40c). I will then conclude with a discussion of the dramatic significance of Socrates' amusing suggestion concerning the practicability of the *kallipolis* (540d–41a). By this point in the dialogue, enough has been said explicitly and indirectly about the practice of justice with *phronesis* for a reader to recognize that Socrates' suggestion that everyone above the age of ten except the best guardians be sent out of the city is intended to expose the comic imprudence of Glaucon's youthful political idealism.

2 THE SEARCH FOR JUSTICE
AND THE GOOD

IN THE *REPUBLIC* SOCRATES leads Glaucon and Adeimantus toward the philosophic life because he judges them to be capable of following him some distance along the way. Their willingness to do so is evident in the manner in which they ask Socrates to lead a serious discussion of justice and injustice. Glaucon and Adeimantus set the terms of the discussion, not Socrates. Although they are not philosophers when the dialogue begins, Socrates takes up their opinions and leads the two of them toward an end that seems to attract them. In particular, he undertakes the building of a city in speech as a way of discussing justice and injustice with them. They say they would like to be truly (*alethos*) persuaded that it is in every way better to be just than unjust. And the manner in which they initiate the discussion indicates they understand that the inquiry should lead them to consider the relation of justice and the good.

Glaucon asks Socrates what kind or form of good is justice. Socrates replies that it belongs to the finest kind, the one chosen both for its own sake and for its consequences. Glaucon then asks to hear about justice in a somewhat different way. He would like to know what power (*dynamis*) it has in and of itself in the soul, dismissing its consequences (357a–58b). It is not immediately evident why he prefers to speak of justice as a power in itself instead of as a type of good, especially since it is questionable whether anything can be a power without having consequences. Perhaps he would prefer to hear about justice as the type of good he described as worthy of choice for its own sake—the type to which pleasure (*hedone*) belongs. Before Socrates can answer, Adeimantus says that he would like to hear about justice without also having to hear about the appearance and reputation of justice that the unjust draw around themselves to seem just while they pursue unjust things (362d–63a, 365b–66e). The appearance and reputation of justice are not consequences of having a just soul and may be the consequences of having an unjust one. Adeimantus is more forthright than Glaucon in his description of justice. He asks Socrates to praise justice as one among the greatest goods— goods such as sight, hearing, and intelligence (*phronein*), which are all worth having both for their consequences and more so for their own sake. Leaving aside reputations and wages, he asks what benefit justice is to the one who has a just soul (367c–d).

Socrates replies that the investigation they propose is suited to someone who sees sharply. It would be best if they began by recognizing their limited vision. In other words, it would be best if they recognized the limits placed on the investigation by the manner in which it begins. He says that since small letters at a distance are more difficult to read than larger ones on a larger and presumably closer surface, he will first describe justice in a bigger thing, a city, in order that justice in a smaller thing, a soul, might be seen more easily afterwards. The city he founds and discusses at length with Glaucon and Adeimantus is intended to be the likeness (*homoiotes*) of a just soul, and nothing more (368c–69b).

Why does Socrates describe the city in this way? Not because he has been asked to give an account of political justice, but because he would like the discussion to be appropriate both to the natures of Glaucon and Adeimantus and to the "not bad" beginning they have made of it (367e–68a). Socrates' decision to describe a city seems to present an account of justice comparable to Glaucon's understanding of it as a power. Although Glaucon may find it attractive for this reason, Socrates does not claim that the regime of the just city describes the political consequences of having a just soul. The consequences of justice in the soul are evident in another way. Socrates' decision to describe a likeness of justice also seems to present an account of it as an appearance contrary to Adeimantus's warnings about injustice. Reputation and wages play no part in the city, but its status as a likeness of justice may suggest to Adeimantus, if he wonders about such things, that appearances are not necessarily false. Socrates' building of a city in speech is thus a discussion of justice and injustice that receives its form from both the beginning made by Glaucon and Adeimantus and the end to which Socrates would lead them. Any interpretation of the discussion as the presentation of an ideal of political justice is the result of misreading the larger letters of Socrates' account as a "literal" description of the political consequences of justice understood as a power in the soul. The smaller letters indicate that the larger are intended to represent the likeness of a soul that is just and that recognizes justice as one of the greatest goods.

Before the discussion begins, Socrates warns Glaucon and Adeimantus that there may be problems with the likeness he will present. He reminds them that larger letters aid in the reading of smaller ones only if they are the same (368d). The similarity of the two sets of letters should raise several questions. For example: Why read the smaller letters if the larger are the same? And what does the similarity of the larger and the smaller mean? In a word, the similarity in itself means nothing. It is not an aid to understanding what either set of letters means. As well, their similarity can only be determined once both the larger and the smaller letters have been read properly. And a proper reading is one that searches for the meaning of what is written, not one that sees only letters and words. Thus, any similarity between the order of the just city and the order of the just soul in the subsequent discussion may mean nothing in itself. It may not be an aid in understanding what justice is in either a soul or a city. But this remains to be seen as the discussion proceeds. For now, Socrates gives Glaucon and Adeimantus a specific warning. His remark that larger letters are an aid in reading smaller ones only if they are the same suggests that the order of the just city he will describe will differ in some way from that of a truly just soul. Glaucon and Adeimantus should be on their guard, for Socrates is testing how sharply they see and how well they listen.

Before large or small letters can be read properly, they must first be visible, and this requires an adequate light. The light appropriate to any attempt to see likenesses of justice is the light of the good. This helps to explain why the difficulties Socrates anticipates in presenting a true likeness of a just soul are caused in part by the manner in which the discussion begins—Socrates is asked to give an account of justice without first giving an account of the good, even though justice has been recognized as a kind or form of good. It also helps to explain the significance of the differences between Socrates' descriptions of the just soul and the city that resembles it, since these differences are often signs of his attempt to persuade Glaucon and Adeimantus that they should follow him beyond the boundaries of the discussion toward the good itself. They will not be truly persuaded of the superiority of justice to injustice unless they are persuaded that justice is ultimately a consequence of the soul's vision of the good. What is more, they will not be truly persuaded unless they themselves become just. In order that they might become just, Socrates attempts to lead them toward the good. This is the truest answer he can give to the questions they have asked him.

Socrates describes one of the consequences of the soul's vision of the good in the concluding words of the *Republic* (621c). He says that anyone who has been persuaded or guided by him will always keep to the upward way (*ano hodou*) and will always practice justice with prudence (*dikaiosyne meta phroneseos*). Justice is not truly justice unless it is practiced with *phronesis,* and a soul cannot be said to possess the virtue of justice unless it is ordered by *phronesis.* Socrates suggests this many times throughout the *Republic.* Early in the dialogue he says that a soul is in its best condition when it is most courageous and most prudent (*phronimotaten;* 380e–81a). A soul becomes most prudent by setting out courageously on the "longer way around [*makrotera . . . periodos*]" toward the good itself (504b; cf. 540a). Socrates also explains that the greatest study, the study of the good, makes all things useful and beneficial. Without the good, nothing is of any benefit, not even justice (505a–b). By aspiring to see the good, a soul may acquire the *phronesis* necessary for it to be truly just. Only a prudent soul deliberates, judges, and acts finely or properly (582a–d, 604c–e). A soul cannot rightly be said to be just unless it deliberates, judges, acts finely or properly, but these are essential features of *phronesis* and not *dikaiosyne.* Those who truly desire to be just, therefore, will always keep to the upward way by which *phronesis* is acquired.

In the *Republic,* Socrates' account of justice in the soul is more complete than his account of the city that is presented as a likeness of a just soul. This is the most important difference between what is said by the smaller and the larger letters. A soul must follow the longer way and take the good itself as its *paradeigma* if it is to be just and prudent. The account of the longer way is set apart from the building of the city in speech. The justice of the city depends primarily on its status as a likeness of the order of a just soul. However, it is a likeness of the soul thought to be just before Socrates gives his account of the longer way. As it stands, therefore, the city cannot be completely just. It appears to lack all *phronesis.* Socrates' account of the genesis of a just city is incomplete, not because the city is a mere likeness nor because it cannot be completed, but because Socrates does not complete it after describing the longer way and the education of those courageous enough to follow him to its end. And he does not complete it simply because he is not asked to complete it.

Socrates does give Glaucon and Adeimantus some indication of how his account of the just city can be made more complete. He tells them that they are engaged in "making a *paradeigma* in speech of a good city [*agathes poleos*]" (472d–e). The soul that takes the good itself as its *paradeigma* comes to possess justice with *phronesis*. The city they are building must also somehow take the good itself as its *paradeigma* if it is to be truly just. As it is described, the city is a distant likeness of the truly just soul, and this only because it is said to be ruled by those philosophers whose souls have attained a vision of the good (540a–b). Their rule should be a just rule, for they will possess *phronesis*, and this should make the city a good city. However, Socrates goes no further than saying that only those philosophers who have followed the longer way to its end ought to rule the city in speech. He does not describe a city in which they actually rule. If they practiced justice with *phronesis* in the city as it is described, they would find themselves compelled to change those laws and features of the regime that can be seen to be unjust and imprudent in the light of the good. The rule of philosophers in the *Republic*'s city in speech thus represents only the possibility that the city might become a *paradeigma* of a good city.

Socrates initially undertakes the discussion of justice and injustice with Glaucon and Adeimantus in order to lead them toward the philosophic life, or at least as far toward it as they are willing to follow. He would undoubtedly like them to acquire enough good judgment to be able to recognize the difficulties that just and prudent philosophers would encounter in ruling the city in speech, and perhaps even enough to be able to complete the account of the genesis of a just and good city themselves. This would be a sign that they were well on their way to acquiring the intellectual virtues and learning to practice justice with *phronesis*. If they were to reconsider their discussion with Socrates after acquiring the good judgment that is evidence of *phronesis*, they would recognize the significance of the difficulties inherent in the methods they and Socrates agreed upon for the discussion as well as the significance of the difficulties encountered along the way as they attempted to apply those methods. Socrates gives them fair warning at the outset. And throughout the building of the city in speech he patiently points them toward the upward way while bringing to light injustices they have not seen in the city. Nowhere in the dialogue is this more evident than in Socrates' search with Glaucon for the justice and injustice of the city after its founding is said to be complete.

When Socrates claims to have completed the account of the genesis of the city, he says that the only thing remaining to be done is to find an adequate light somewhere and begin searching for justice and injustice. He then tells Glaucon that the city, "if it has been correctly founded, is perfectly good [*teleos agathen*]" (427c–e). Glaucon raises no objections to this remark; neither does Adeimantus, though he is listening closely. Perhaps this indicates that they both believe their city to be a just and good one. It cannot be assumed, however, that this is what Socrates believes. He has said that the city requires illumination; that is, the city, as it has been described, is not illuminated sufficiently by the light of the good. It cannot be said to be a perfectly good city. And neither can it be said to be a just city, for Socrates has also said that it will be possible to see injustice in it once the proper light is found. This should lead Glaucon and Adeimantus to search for the necessary light, and once they find it, they should be able to conclude that the city has not been correctly founded.

Socrates begins the search for justice and injustice in the city by saying that the city, if it is perfectly good, will also be wise (*sophe*), courageous (*andreia*), moderate (*sophron*), and just (*dikaia*). Glaucon agrees without question. The four virtues listed are the ones traditionally said to be good. Is the list exhaustive? There is no reason given for this to be assumed. The only remark Socrates makes about the virtues is that they happen to be four.[1] He then proposes a very strange method of searching for the last on the list, justice. If someone is searching for any four things, Socrates claims, he will discover the fourth easily if he recognizes the first three, since the fourth is simply what is left over (427e–28a). This is obviously false for a number of reasons. Socrates does not say why any list of four things should be thought to be exhaustive and comprehensive, he does not say why such a list should comprise only four things, and he does not explain why what is left over after three things have been discovered is nothing but the fourth thing. Socrates' proposed method obviously leads to the false conclusion that the fourth thing on a list is the same as all that *is* minus the first three things on the list. Glaucon sees nothing wrong with Socrates' proposal; he accepts the method as a correct one. Adeimantus also raises no objections. Both Glaucon and Adeimantus therefore commit themselves to a method of searching for the fourth virtue of their city that, if they hold to it, will lead them mistakenly to equate *dikaiosyne* with all that *is* minus *sophia*, *andreia* and *sophrosyne*. What of the light with which they should be searching for justice in their city, the light of the good? They will assume that the city's justice and the good are the same. And what of the injustices of their city that would be revealed if it were illuminated by the light of the good? They will not see them in the darkness, or worse, they will conclude that the injustices are just.

Socrates now begins the search for *sophia* in the city (428a–29a). He says immediately that something about it appears strange (*atopon*). The city they have described can be said to be wise (*sophe*) if it is well advised (*euboulos*). Those who advise it well must themselves possess *euboulia*, the well-advisedness of prudence. The search has begun strangely because some account must be given of a virtue necessary for the city to be just and good, and that virtue was not on the list. Glaucon does not notice anything strange. He readily agrees with a suggestion made that *euboulia* is a kind of *episteme*, since good counsel cannot be given from ignorance (*amathia*). Perhaps Glaucon believes that all knowledge is a type of *episteme*, and that all men are either knowledgeable in this way or ignorant. However, by giving examples Socrates reminds him that *episteme* is generally the technical sort of knowledge evident in productive activities. The *euboulia* of the city thus differs from *episteme* in the same way that *phronesis* differs from *techne*. But Glaucon believes the city's *euboulia* to be the product of the art of the guardians, the ones called the most perfect (*teleous*) and true (*alethinous*) guardians. He believes their *episteme* to be the most perfect and true knowledge. It is not concerned with producing goods. Even though it is similar in form to productive knowledge, it differs from the *episteme* of carpenters, blacksmiths and farmers because it is the art exercised by the few who rule over the many inhabitants of the city. The *episteme* of such rulers makes the city both wise (*sophe*) and well advised (*euboulos*). Glaucon is satisfied that *sophia* has been discovered—Socrates is not. Neither *sophia* nor *euboulia* have been clarified sufficiently, but he lets it pass.

Socrates takes up the point later in the dialogue (474c–75c), shortly after reminding Glaucon that they are engaged in making a *paradeigma* in speech of a good city and suggesting, to Glaucon's great surprise, that the most perfect and truest guardians of the city must be true philosophers if it is to be such a *paradeigma* (472d–e, 473c–74a). Glaucon admits that he scarcely understands what Socrates means by the statement that if a man loves a thing he must love all of it and not only one part of it. Socrates reminds him of what this might mean by giving several examples and obtains his agreement that it is true. It then follows that the true philosopher or lover of wisdom loves all of wisdom and not only a part of it, and that the lover of learning (*philomathes*) who undertakes every kind of learning (*pantos mathematos*) with delight and who is insatiable is properly called a philosopher.

The relevance of these remarks for understanding the strangeness of *sophia* in the earlier search for justice is straightforward. The guardians must love all of wisdom, not only a part of it, if the city is to be *sophe* and *euboulos*. The wisdom they love cannot be an *episteme*. Their rule over others is not strictly comparable to a productive activity; it demonstrates their *euboulia*, their practical wisdom. If they are to become true philosophers and guardians, therefore, they must undertake every kind of learning necessary for them to acquire the virtues of *sophia* and *phronesis*. They will be required to undertake the greatest study, the study of the good itself. If they are not insatiable in this study, they will be unable to rule the city justly. The strangeness of *sophia* in Socrates' earlier discussion with Glaucon is thus the result of a strange method of inquiry that makes it difficult to account for the *euboulia* of *phronesis*, which is necessary for truly just rule and is a consequence of the soul's vision of the good itself. In the absence of such an account, the rule of the guardians will seem like a productive *episteme* requiring no true wisdom. Perhaps this is why Glaucon did not find it strange.

As Socrates continues going through the list of the city's four virtues, he hesitates when he comes to *sophrosyne* and asks Glaucon an odd question: How can we find justice so we won't have to bother about moderation? He hesitates because an adequate account of moderation will require him to discuss *phronesis* explicitly. This will not only call into question what Glaucon understands about the wisdom of the guardian class, it will also lead the discussion well beyond the strict comparison that Glaucon expects between the virtues of the city in speech and the just soul. Glaucon does not agree to any change in the order of the discussion, as if it were a matter of justice which virtue comes last on the list (430d–e).

In order to explain the city's *sophrosyne*, Socrates is compelled to abandon the order of the discussion agreed upon and discuss it in a soul first (431b–d). Immoderate souls have many diverse desires, pleasures, and pains. Moderate souls have a few simple ones, and those they have are guided by calculative reasoning (*logismos*), in turn aided by *nous* and right opinion (*ortha doxa*). Such souls are best by nature and education, and *sophrosyne* is thus a virtue of maturity. What of the city in speech? Socrates now calls it a young city, suggesting that it must still grow and be educated properly if it is to be truly moderate. But he also suggests that it is moderate in some way. He tells Glaucon that the desires of the many are mastered by the desires and *phronesis* of the few. Glaucon may believe that the city's *sophrosyne* is a consequence of the effectiveness of the guardians' rule alone. Socrates reminds him, however, that *sophrosyne* is unlike *sophia* and *andreia*, each of which have been said to reside solely in a part of the city; it must extend throughout the whole of the city, residing in the souls of the rulers and ruled alike (431d–32a). The souls of the rulers must therefore possess *phronesis* as well as *sophia*. *Sophia* alone cannot rule the soul in which it is present. Such a soul would be extremely immoderate; its wisdom would be simple cleverness in the service of the desires. *Phronesis* orders the soul and makes it moderate. This does not mean, however, that *phronesis* is simply moral virtue. Both *phronesis* and *sophia* are virtues of the *nous*. When the guardians are themselves governed by *nous,* they will be able to rule the city justly with the aid of right opinion. Without *phronesis* they would rule it like tyrants.

Socrates now comes to the last item, justice. If the methods used in the investigation were sound, it would be a simple matter to determine what justice is in the city. But there are immediate difficulties. Socrates tells Glaucon they must hunt for justice among the shadows in the twilight (432b–c). Glaucon seems to be captivated by the image of hunting and capturing prey, since he does not think to search for a light to dispel the darkness. Before he and Socrates initially undertook their search, Socrates had said it was necessary only to find an adequate light in order to see the justice and injustice of the city (427c–d). Glaucon does not remember this, and consequently cannot catch sight of justice. He admits that he is only able to see such things if they are shown to him.

There is now a dramatic break in the dialogue. Socrates directly addresses the man to whom he has been recounting the previous evening's discussion with Glaucon, Adeimantus, and the others. He tells him, "I caught sight of it." Socrates does not tell Glaucon that he caught sight of justice itself. Instead, he tells Glaucon only that he found a track that might have been left by justice. Socrates also tells him that he found it like someone searching in the distance for something he is already holding in his hand (432d–e). This is an ambiguous remark. It may mean that his own sighting of justice was made possible by what he was holding in his hand—the light of the good. It may also mean that the track possibly left by justice is as different from justice itself as something seen in the distance differs from something held in the hand. Both meanings are probably intended. In any event, the track possibly left by justice is the common opinion that justice is the minding of one's own business. This is the rule upon which the city in speech was founded initially: each one in the city must practice only one of the city's functions, the one for which he is most fit by nature. It may appear to Glaucon that the two of them have finally stumbled upon justice in the dark (432d–33b; cf. 479d).

Socrates decides to test Glaucon, with whom he has been speaking since he declared the city to have been founded (433b–d). He asks him if he knows how the discovery of this thing, which in a certain sense appears to be justice, was inferred. Glaucon does not recall the strange method of inference with which they set out to discover justice. Socrates then suggests that his discovery of a possible track of *dikaiosyne* in the city is what is left over after considering its *sophrosyne, andreia,* and *phronesis.* In recounting the list of four virtues backwards, he replaces *sophia* with *phronesis.* Glaucon does not notice the difference. He neither wonders what the relation is between *sophia* and *phronesis,* nor wonders what Socrates' change to the list might mean for understanding the significance of *dikaiosyne.* Socrates then asks Glaucon to exercise his judgment. He tests Glaucon's *phronesis* by questioning him about what is good. He asks him which would do the city the most good: the unity of opinion among rulers and ruled, an aspect of *sophrosyne* when the rulers possess *phronesis;* the preservation of lawful opinion by the soldiers, an aspect of *andreia* when the soldiers are themselves moderate; or the *phronesis* and guardianship that acquire substance (*enousa*) in the rulers, the aspects of their wisdom that enable them to rule justly. He then very deliberately adds one more thing to the list, emphasizing its difference from the three preceding manifestations of *phronesis:* the founding rule that each must mind his own business in the city. Glaucon does not question how Socrates presents the list of the city's four virtues in the light of the good. He questions neither the predominant role of *phronesis* in the presentation nor the relative insignificance of the understanding of justice upon which the city was founded. What is more, he does not come to a judgment. Instead of asserting that justice as it has been defined does the city the most good, his only reply to Socrates' question is that it would be a difficult judgment to make.

Socrates does not pursue the matter any further. He simply reminds Glaucon of the original list of virtues, obtains his agreement that justice is a rival to *sophia, andreia,* and *sophrosyne* in contributing to the city's virtue, and tentatively defines injustice as meddling among the city's various class relations (433d–34d). This is more to Glaucon's liking. Socrates is no longer speaking of *phronesis* and the good. Glaucon eagerly accepts the opinion that justice is each of the city's classes minding its own business: "that is my opinion and no other." However, Socrates does not accept it. Instead, he proposes to test Glaucon's city (434d–35a). If the form of the city in speech, when applied to a single human being, is acceptable as the form of a just soul, Socrates will concede to Glaucon that the city is just; if not, he will not make that concession. He then recalls what was said when he first proposed to found a city in speech by saying that it is now time to turn away from the larger thing to catch sight of justice in the smaller. More precisely, he had compared large letters to small ones, mentioning in passing that the larger are an aid in reading the smaller only if they are the same (368c–d). A city was to be founded in speech in order to serve as a helpful likeness of the just soul for those with poor vision.

Why does Socrates now suggest that a soul must be constructed as a likeness of the likeness in order to test whether or not the likeness is itself just? How can the abstract application of the form of the city in speech to a human being be a test of the justice and injustice of the city? This can be valid only if some understanding of the just soul has already been attained against which the application of the city's form will appear to be unjust. Enough evidence of the just and prudent soul has already come to light for this to be possible.

If there are differences between the bigger and the smaller thing, where does the error lie? If the city is understood as an aid to the sight of someone searching for justice in the soul, then differences between the likeness and the original of which it is a likeness reveal that the city in speech somehow is not a true likeness. The larger and smaller letters are not the same. But if it is obvious that they are different, it is equally obvious that both sets of letters have been read and compared. There has already been sufficient sight of the smaller letters to show that the larger are misrepresentative. Socrates had previously mentioned that skilled readers can make out any combination of letters in large or small writing and can recognize unusual images of writing because they already have knowledge of the originals of such images (402a–c). This helps to explain the significance of his proposal to test the city by applying its form to a soul and determining whether or not the result is just. The application of the form will produce an unusual image—the likeness of a likeness of the original. When the likeness of the likeness is compared to the original, it will be evident that the likeness itself is an untrue one. Therefore, the city in speech said to be just because it appears to possess the virtues of *sophia, andreia, sophrosyne,* and *dikaiosyne* is not a true likeness of the just soul. A soul ordered to resemble or mirror the order of such a city is obviously an artifice or a manufactured reflection of an untrue appearance when compared to the original. And the original is a soul that is just because it aspires to see the good itself and thus comes to possess *phronesis* and *nous.*

If there are differences between the bigger and the smaller thing in the test Socrates proposes, knowing its outcome, then both are in error. Neither is a form of the good. The soul resembling the city said to be just is not just, and the city is neither just nor a true likeness of justice. Socrates compares the form or order of the city in speech and the order of the soul resembling it to two sticks held in his hands (434e–35a). The two images ordered according to a track possibly left by justice—that is, according to the opinion of justice as minding one's own business—are as different from justice itself as something seen in the distance differs from things held in one's hands. Both are sticks grasped in the twilight while hunting in the thicket for justice (cf. 432b–d). In order to catch sight of justice itself, a light is required: the light of the good. Socrates suggests to Glaucon that they rub the two sticks together. Justice would then burst into flame. The flame would eventually consume the sticks, but it would provide sufficient light to aid in the search. Once justice has come to light in this manner, Socrates says they could confirm it for themselves by comparing the things they see to the original (cf. *Seventh Letter* 344a–b).

Socrates now begins to apply the form of the city to a single soul so that the two images may be considered side by side and tested against each other. He undertakes the task to assist Glaucon in realizing that both of the images are misrepresentative in different ways. Once Glaucon recognizes this, he may be able to see that a just and good soul possesses *phronesis* and *sophia*, and that a just and good city is one in which these virtues govern in some reasonable and moderate way. Since Socrates knows the images to be misrepresentative before he begins, it is not surprising that he becomes impatient shortly after they set out on what he anticipates will be a lengthy and tiring discussion. He says, "Know well Glaucon that in my opinion we will never apprehend this matter precisely on the basis of methods [*methodoi*] such as we are now using in discussion. There is another far-reaching and greater way [*makrotera kai pleion hodos*] leading to it" (435c–d). Glaucon's ways are many (*methodoi*, from *meta hodoi*); Socrates' way is one. Glaucon's methods are less demanding than Socrates' way, but if he truly desires to apprehend what justice is, he has no choice. He must follow Socrates on the other, longer way around the proposed test (*makrotera . . . periodos*) to the most beautiful (*kallista*) look at such things (504a–b). And if he always keeps to the upward way (*ano hodou*), he himself will be able to practice justice with *phronesis* (621c). Glaucon, however, is satisfied with the methods proposed for the discussion, even though Socrates has warned him explicitly that they will *never* prove effective. He asks Socrates not to grow weary, but to go ahead with the inquiry (435d).

3 EDUCATING GLAUCON
ABOUT THE GOOD

Images of the Good

AFTER SOCRATES CONCLUDES the inquiry according to Glaucon's methods he begins the account of the longer way. It appears initially to be a digression, but it is a necessary discussion. Socrates, Glaucon, and Adeimantus have constructed a just soul in the likeness of the city in speech, which itself is thought to be the likeness of a truly just soul. It is now necessary to compare this likeness with the original.

Glaucon and Adeimantus seem satisfied that the virtues of *dikaiosyne, sophrosyne, andreia,* and *sophia* have been described well enough for them to understand the nature of the greatest studies (*mathemata megista*) necessary for the guardians to become philosophers, or the "most perfect guardians." There are no objections from Glaucon, or anyone else listening to the discussion, when Adeimantus tells Socrates that they found the account satisfactory within measure (*metrios*). Socrates must remind them that "nothing imperfect is the measure of anything." The discussion prompted by Glaucon's methods is imperfect. It has produced only a sketch (*hypographe*) of the virtues or a description of them in something less than "their most perfect elaboration." What is more, it has led to the odd assumption that there is nothing greater than *dikaiosyne*. In order to get the "most beautiful [*kallista*]" look at things and come to the end of the single greatest study (*megiston mathema*), Glaucon and Adeimantus must follow Socrates on the longer way toward the good. The good itself is the measure. It is "what every soul pursues and for the sake of which it does everything." There is no profit in possessing anything in the absence of the good, Socrates says. This would be true of the virtues described in the imperfect sketch that Glaucon and Adeimantus find satisfying (503b–6e).

What is the good? How is it the measure of the virtues? And how would the four virtues described appear if they were to become useful and beneficial to the soul? Socrates suggests an answer to these questions when he says that it is of no advantage to be prudent (*phronein*) about everything apart from the good (*aneu tou agathou*) while being prudent (*phronein*) about nothing beautiful and good (*kalon de kai agathon*). There is some relation between *phronesis* and the good that is not described in the sketch of the virtues. Furthermore, disputes about the good are more numerous and more violent than those about what is just and honorable. Justice, therefore, cannot be the greatest virtue. But before discussing the good and the relation of *phronesis* to the virtues of the imperfect sketch, Socrates first explains what the good is not. He does this by summarizing the dispute about it between the many and the few. The many believe that pleasure (*hedone*), that is, their own pleasure, is the good; the few believe that prudence, that is, their own prudence, is the good. Neither of these opinions grasps the good itself, though both are confused attempts to do so. Neither the many nor the few know true pleasure and *phronesis*, though both wish to do so. Adeimantus and Glaucon, however, are unlike the many and the few. They would like to know if knowledge (*episteme*) or something else besides is the good. Adeimantus urges Socrates not to question others, but to give his own account of it, and Glaucon is particularly insistent to have an explicit answer, swearing at Socrates in the name of Zeus. As Socrates takes up the discussion, Adeimantus falls into silence. He listens as Socrates educates Glaucon about *phronesis* and the good (505a–6d).

Socrates uses imagery in his discussion of the good with Glaucon. The entire account is a series of images, known to Plato scholars generally as the sun, the line, and the cave. When Socrates begins his description of the ascent from the cave that is later called the "first home," he tells Glaucon explicitly that he will present an image or ikon (*eikon;* 514a). The descriptions of the sun and the line may also rightly be called ikons. Indeed, Socrates' whole answer to the question, What is the good? may be considered one ikon. However, it might be asked, Why does he answer with images? Why does he not answer unambiguously, as Glaucon and Adeimantus had requested? Are his images not merely allegories? In other words, are they not evidence that Plato is presenting an esoteric doctrine about the good in exoteric terms?

It should be noted first of all that Socrates does not answer ambiguously because of the nature or intelligence of his interlocutors, or because of the circumstances in which the discussion is being held. Adeimantus and Glaucon both desire to know the good itself, and Socrates judges them more worthy than most to undertake such a difficult study. Although Socrates does have reservations about Glaucon's ability to follow him to the end of the longer way, he is not being disingenuous, cautious, or ironic in telling Glaucon he wishes both that he were able to give a complete account of the good and that his audience would be able to understand such an account if it were possible (506e–7a; cf. 509c). These remarks should also give some evidence that Plato did not write ambiguously because he suspected the nature or intelligence of his readers, or because of the circumstances in which the *Republic* was distributed.

Socrates uses imagery in part for its evocative power. He begins the description of the ascent from the first home by asking Glaucon to compare his understanding of "our nature [*physis*] in its education [*paideia*] and lack of education [*apaideusia*]" with the understanding he will hear in the *eikon*. In particular, Socrates asks Glaucon to participate in the experience (*pathos*) that the *eikon* is intended to evoke (514a). All readers of the dialogue are also members of his audience. The intention of Socrates' account will be evident to us only if we engage in the imaginative participation and reflection that it demands of us.

Aristotle begins *On Interpretation* by asserting: "Words spoken are symbols [*symbola*] of affections [*pathemata*] of the soul [*psyche*]; written words are the signs of words spoken" (16a). In order to interpret Plato's written work properly, it must be understood in this manner. The dialogue consists of signs of words spoken that are themselves symbols of the *pathemata* of the speakers' souls as they are engaged in dialogue. Socrates attempts to educate Glaucon and the rest of his audience about the soul's true nature by describing its various *pathemata* evocatively. The end that guides him is the good itself. Plato attempts to educate his audience in the same way. Readers of the dialogue will be able to recognize the ikons if they know their originals beforehand, or if they are open to the persuasion of someone who does (cf. 402b).

The account of the longer way is not allegorical. An allegory is an account of something that disguises or misrepresents a truer account of the same thing. Plato scholars often reconstruct the imagery of the longer way with the intention of determining the truer esoteric doctrine that they believe is being presented exoterically. It is common, for instance, to consider the cave and the sun as allegories for the line, and the line itself as an allegory for Plato's metaphysical, epistemological, or ontological doctrine, with complete disregard for the dialogic character of the statements used in such a reconstruction. But Socrates' ikons are not allegories. His concern in discussing the good with Glaucon is, above all, whether or not his account represents the good adequately and in a manner that Glaucon will understand. The truthfulness of what he says, in the final analysis, depends on the relation between the account as a whole and the thing it describes, not on the relation of one part of the account to another, and certainly not on the relation of some part of the account to an unknown esoteric doctrine.

The ascent from the first home is called an *eikon*. This gives some indication that Socrates' use of imagery is intended to provide a truthful account of the good for Glaucon. The simple word for image is *eidolon* (idol). An *eikon* is a certain kind of image or idol; so too is a *phantasma* (phantasm). Plato uses these terms with care in the dialogues. It is said in the *Sophist* that all images have the properties of appearing and of seeming, but not of being what they copy. It is also said that there is a distinction between an ikon and a phantasm: the former is an accurate image, which represents things truly, and the latter is an inaccurate one, which distorts them. The property of seeming, common to *all* images, is not the same as the misrepresentation specific to phantasms (*Sophist* 235b–37a). Just as a visual image is not the thing it represents, so a name is not the thing it names. A name is a "shadow," a sound transmitted through the sensible realm representing something. The thing represented is not necessarily a sensible or visible thing. Aristotle goes so far as to say that a name is a symbol of an affection of the soul. Speech itself never loses the property of seeming most evident in names. Even true accounts of things are images, both of the things represented and of the soul providing the account. An account of something in speech may be an ikon or a phantasm. In order to determine the truthfulness of any particular account, it is necessary to engage in some form of investigation, introspection, and discourse. This is also what should be done in interpreting Socrates' account of the good. It is what he asks of Glaucon. It is also what Plato asks of his readers.

Socrates' use of imagery is partly the result of his recognition of the nature and limitations of speech. However, the most important reason he speaks in ikons is because he has been asked to give an account of something that is transcendent or "beyond [*epekeina*]" (509b). The good, by its nature, is something of which it is impossible to give a complete and unambiguous account. The good itself cannot be discussed in the same way that particular good and useful things are discussed. All accounts of it are necessarily incomplete and ambiguous. Speaking of it in ikons is perhaps the truest possible speech, and attempting to give a complete account of it is therefore misrepresentative. The one time Socrates refers to his own discussion of the good, he says, "The god knows whether it is true" (517b). There is no need to suspect him of irony in this remark. It shows that he recognizes the limitations inherent in speaking about a transcendent good. Glaucon does not believe that it is impossible to give a complete account of the good. It seems he believes that the good is *episteme*. He dismisses Socrates' description of the good, beyond being in dignity and power, as daimonic hyperbole (*daimonias hyperboles*) and comes close to treating Socrates as a laughingstock (509c-d; cf. 506d-e). In order to emphasize that Glaucon's dismissal is absurd, Plato has Socrates speak directly to the reader and not to Glaucon in describing it as very laughable (*mala geloios*).

The transcendent good is the measure of all things. It is also the measure by which to judge the affections and virtues of men's souls. It is therefore a measure of men's public and political associations as well. *Phronesis* is the virtue of a soul able to judge and act according to the measure. *Phronesis* is not the good, as some believe. However, the illumination of the soul by the good provides human beings with the *phronesis* necessary both for them to distinguish properly among the many different types and degrees of light and darkness in souls, and for them to act properly on their own account or in public (517c). Without a longing to see the good, a soul is unable to judge what is good, just, and honorable and to act accordingly.

Socrates' ikon of the sun and the good (507a–9c) describes the transcendent nature of the measure of all things. He begins by saying that the sun appears (*phainetai*) as an offspring or descendant of the good and that it is most like the good. In the realm of the visible, objects of sight are visible to those who exercise their faculty of sight, with the assistance of the medium of light. Light is the bond that yokes together sight and the capacity to be seen; it is therefore "precious or honorable." Sight is not the sun, just as it is neither the thing seen nor the light. But the power of sight has its cause (*aitia*) in the sun. It is sunlike or sun-formed (*helioei-destaton*) and is capable of seeing its cause in some way. The sun not only makes things visible; it is also responsible for their generation, growth, and nourishment, though it is not itself generation (*genesis*). Although it is somehow beyond it, the sun both generates and illuminates the realm of coming into being and passing away, in which the things seen and the thing seeing are found. It is thus the cause of sight. It would be an obvious error, therefore, to think that sight possesses all of the sun's powers simply because it is sunlike and capable of seeing the sun.

The good begets or is the cause of the sun. Both the realm of coming into being and passing away and the realm of the visible are thus its descendants. Its relation to the intelligible or noetic realm is thus similar to, but not the same as, the sun's relation to its own immediate offspring. What is intellected (*ta noomena*) is intelligible to those who exercise their intellect (*nous*), with the assistance of the medium of truth (*aletheia*). The result is knowledge (*episteme*). Truth is the illumination or the precious and honorable bond that yokes together the intelligible and the intellect. The intellect is not the good, just as it is neither what is intellected nor the truth. But the power of intellection has its cause in the good. It is formed or informed by the good and is capable of "seeing" its cause in some way. When the intellect looks toward its cause, it ascends toward the idea of the good. Insofar as the idea of the good is the cause of knowledge and truth, it can be understood as something known (*gignoskomenes men dianoou*), but it is not itself an object of knowledge or intellection. Knowledge (*episteme*) and truth are like the *agathoeide* (form of the good), "but to think that either of them is the good [*agathon*] is not right" (509a).[1] The idea of the good is the manifestation of the good itself in the realm of the intelligible. The same things cannot be said of the idea of the good and the good itself. The idea of the good can be said to be the source of illumination for the intelligible realm. However, it cannot be said to be the cause of the existence of the intelligible realm, just as it is not said to be the cause of the sun. The sun as a source of light differs from the sun as the source of the generation, growth, and nourishment of things illuminated, and the sun itself is neither of these things. So too, the good as a source of truth and knowledge differs from the good as the source of the intelligible realm's being or existence, and the good itself is neither of these things. The good itself is "beyond." It transcends *ousia* in dignity and power, and it is of overwhelming beauty.

Glaucon is willing to believe that the good might be of overwhelming beauty while he imagines that it might be pleasure. But when Socrates makes it clear that the good is neither pleasure nor knowledge (*episteme*), Glaucon accuses him of daimonic hyperbole, swearing by Apollo (509a, c). Since Socrates does not wish to seem to be playing the sophist, he provides Glaucon with another, more Apollonian image—the mathematical or geometrical image of the divided line (509c–11e). The line seems to follow naturally from Socrates' initial remark that the good begat the sun to stand in a proportion (*analogia*) with itself (508b–c). However, Socrates now discusses the visible and intelligible realms only by means of ratios or proportions, representing degrees of clarity and participation in truth.

There is no mention of the good itself in the divided line image. The realm of what appears to sight and the realm of the ideas are discussed without reference to what illuminates them. Consequently, it is tempting to say that the image of the sun as an offspring of the good is a more complete account. However, the image of the divided line concludes by describing various affections (*pathemata*) of the soul, though it does not begin that way, and there is no mention of souls in the sun image, except in the context of establishing the transcendence of the good (508d–9a). It is also tempting to say that the divided line is, therefore, a more comprehensive account. But it is best to resist both temptations. Taken together, both images attempt to explain how the nature of the soul's relation to the good affects its relation to the realms of the visible and the intelligible. By the conclusion of Socrates' description of the divided line image, a distinction has evidently been made between the joint aspiration of the soul (*psyche*) and intellect (*nous*) to the good, and the aspiration of the intellect, in the possible absence of a similar aspiration of the soul, to grasp the idea of the good as knowledge (*episteme*). Socrates then addresses the question of what consequences might follow from a separation between the aspirations of the intellect and the soul in his subsequent account of the ascent from the cave.

Socrates begins his description of the line by saying that it is cut into two unequal segments, one representing the visible, and the other the intelligible realm. He does not mention a proportion for the cut. Like Glaucon, the reader of the dialogue must make an assumption about which of the segments is longer or represents the greatest clarity and fullest participation in or illumination by truth, and proceed on the basis of his hypothesis. It would be incorrect to assume that only one segment participates in the truth or that the truthfulness of one segment depends, in some way, on its participation in the truthfulness of the other. Both participate in the truth to some degree, since the realms they represent both originate in the good in some way. Each of the two segments is then cut in the same proportion according to the same criterion. The two middle subsegments of the line are always of the same length; it makes no difference which proportion is used for the cuts or even which major segment has been assumed to be longer. It would be a fair assumption that Socrates takes the intelligible segment to be longer than the visible. However, we cannot know by how much. In any event, it would seem that the proportion of the cuts is not fixed but depends on the soul's variable *pathemata*.

Socrates then says that the shorter subdivision of the visible segment represents images made by light. These shadows and reflections of things are said to be ikons, not phantasms. The longer subsegment represents the things themselves of which the images are images, including living things and all man-made objects. Human beings are not listed explicitly among the living things. Socrates, therefore, is not required to discuss the difference between accurate and inaccurate images of them at this point in his account. He then subdivides the intelligible segment in a different manner, using *pathemata* of the soul as his criteria. He describes two ways of thinking and not two objects of thought. The shorter subsegment corresponds to what is described as the habitual exercise of "geometrical" thinking by a soul. Like the souls that might be said to correspond to the equivalent subsegment of the first division of the line—the ones that assume the visible to participate in the truth somewhat more fully than the intelligible—the souls that engage in geometrical thinking trust in the truth of what they see. Unlike the former, however, the latter think about things by means of hypotheses, using them in the same manner that geometers use axioms. The origins and nature of these hypotheses are not discussed.

The longer subsegment of the line representing the intelligible corresponds with a soul's dialectical investigation of hypotheses.

It can be assumed that dialectical inquiry concerns either particular hypotheses accepted trustingly or the hypotheses necessary for thought itself. The end toward which such inquiry aspires is that which is "without hypotheses and is the beginning of all." This cannot be a description of the idea of the good. It describes the good beyond being. Socrates goes on to say that dialectic not only ascends but descends through the intelligible realm as well. Dialectical descent begins not from the end to which its ascent aspires, but from that which itself depends upon the end. In other words, there is a descent to the intelligible realm from a "beyond" that is not within it. The highest point of dialectical ascent is thus best understood as the state (*pathos*) of the soul's ascent in which it is illuminated by the good. Without attaining this state or affection, it is possible for the descent through the intelligible realm from the things that depend on the end to have the character of geometrical thinking. Thought in the absence of the soul's illumination by the good—even if it is a descent from the things that depend on the good, understood as hypotheses—is an image of the philosopher's love of wisdom. Whether or not such thinking is a sophistic *phantasma* of the philosopher's dialectical activity ultimately depends on the openness or closure of a man's soul to the transcendent good.

Socrates concludes his account of the divided line by persuading Glaucon to agree to list four *pathemata* of the soul in relation to the four segments of the line as he understands it. Affections of the soul are now the only criteria for the subdivisions of the line. Glaucon does not notice or comment upon this fact.

The four *pathemata* in descending order are *noesis* (intellection), *dianoia* (thought), *pistis* (trust, belief), and *eikasia* (image making).[2] No explicit statement is made about how the four are related to each other, nor is the manner in which they are related to the four previous correlates of the line segments explained. *Noesis* and *dianoia* do not correspond to dialectical and geometrical thought respectively. *Dianoia* is simply thought, and all thought requires trust (*pistis*) in some hypotheses. *Noesis* directs thought toward an end and is the affection of the *psyche* when the *nous* is formed or informed by the good, ascends toward it, and is capable of "seeing" its cause in some way. This illuminates the hypotheses of thought with the light of the good. Dialectical thinking is the way of thought associated with *noesis*. It ascends toward a vision of the good—which illuminates all that *is* as well as all that comes into being and passes away—and then descends from its vision toward conclusions which are themselves hypotheses of thought. Geometrical thinking, on the other hand, is a type of *dianoia* in the absence of *noesis*. Since *noesis* is the foundation of the intellectual virtues, geometrical thinking seems not to be a virtuous way of thinking. At its best, it may be founded on demonstrative knowledge (*episteme*). This sort of knowledge has its place in mathematics and the sciences. At its worst, however, it is a refusal to question at all any hypothesis of thought accepted trustingly. It originates in a refusal of the soul to ascend and a longing to descend. This sort of thinking has no place even in mathematics and the sciences, as they are properly understood.

It would be evidence of geometrical thinking to believe that the geometry of the line itself should be the basis for interpreting everything Socrates says about it and the various things its segments represent. Those who interpret the line in this way usually arrange the things corresponding to the line's four segments into an esoteric epistemology, ontology, or metaphysics. Such reconstructions generally disregard Socrates' accounts of the medium of sunlight between the eye and the things seen, of the medium of truth between the intellect and what is intellected, and of the ultimate dependence of sunlight and truth on the good. All that can be said about the line is what Socrates himself suggests: the relative lengths of the line segments represent assumptions about the degrees of clarity and participation in truth of the intelligible and visible realms. The only thing that can be inferred directly from the line's geometry is that the two middle segments are always of the same length. This implies that *dianoia* and *pistis* are equal in clarity and participation in truth, no matter what assumptions are made about the relation of the intelligible and the visible. It also might imply that all thought requires beliefs or hypotheses and that the dialectical investigation of particular hypotheses can never completely transcend the hypotheses of thought itself.

What is to be made of Socrates' concluding use of the soul's affections and hypotheses as ordering criteria for the line? The list of the four affections he gives is not a list of types of souls, but it does imply that the various souls discussed in his account can be compared according to the criteria mentioned and that there ought to be at least four types. It does not follow from this, however, that such a comparison would result in either an exhaustive account of the soul or even a complete list of types.

An initial comparison of souls is possible on the basis of assumptions made concerning the visible and the intelligible realms. There are two main types of souls, those that believe the intelligible participates more fully in truth than the visible and those that believe the opposite. The first type can be subdivided according to the manner in which a soul deals with the hypotheses of its thought: there are those that engage in dialectical inquiry and those that engage in geometrical thinking. Are these the only two possibilities? Is it not possible for a soul to consider the visible as participating in truth more fully than the intelligible and still be more open to examining the hypotheses of its thought than the soul that engages in geometrical thinking? This may best be described as the common-sense understanding of things.[3] It is one possible subdivision of the second main type of soul, a subdivision that is implied by Socrates' account but is not carried out. Following up the implication, a fourth type of soul could be described as one that both considers the visible to be more fully true than the intelligible and engages in something similar to geometrical thinking. An indication of the nature of this soul is given in the list of the four *pathemata* Socrates uses to end his account of the line. The last is *eikasia,* or "image making." The fourth type of soul has something to do with image making. However, it cannot simply be called the soul of the image maker since there are both accurate and inaccurate images.

This sketchy and incomplete typology of souls raises several questions. For example, is the first type the soul of the philosopher? What is the relation between the first type and the common-sense soul? And is the fourth type the soul of the sophist or the soul of the lover of spectacles (*philotheamones*)? These questions and others are taken up in Socrates' account of the ascent from the cave.

The Ascent toward the Good

Socrates' description of the ascent from the cave later called the first home begins with his reference to "our nature [*physis*] in its education [*paideia*] and lack of education [*apaideusia*]" (514a). The nature that is his primary concern is the nature of the soul. His description is intended to educate Glaucon about the soul by way of a dramatic use of imagery. Glaucon should be able to recognize the images since he undoubtedly has some knowledge of the original (402a–b). In particular, he should be able to recognize that the soul is educable. If it is well educated, it will become prudent and wise; if not, its natural *apaideusia* will be transformed into folly, or *aphrosyne*. The soul's natural *apaideusia* is simply a lack of education. It is not the ignorance of not knowing, of stupidity or of boorishness (*agnosia, amathia*). The soul's various possible ignorances are not the first things described by Socrates. They are suggested in his account as various follies to which the soul may succumb in the ascent from its natural *apaideusia* toward the good and *phronesis*. As will be seen, the most fundamental of such follies is the result of the soul's unwillingness or refusal to ascend toward the good after its initial ascent, by nature, toward the fire in the cave.

Within the cave, some human beings are bound by their legs and necks so that they are unable to see anything but the play of shadows on a cave wall directly in front of them and are unable to hear anything but sounds echoing from it. This seems to be a bodily image, but its primary concern is what the soul sees, hears, and understands. These human beings see shadows of various things, projected by the light of a fire behind a wall that is above and behind them; they see the unmoving shadows which they themselves cast and the moving shadows of objects carried, in a random and meaningless sequence, by other human beings behind the wall. The objects carried are all manufactured. They are either simple artifacts or copies of living things—men or animals—made from every kind of material. The "carriers" cast no shadows themselves. The humans in bonds hear the random sounds uttered by the carriers, which have no necessary relation to the objects carried, and they hear the echoes of their own unimpaired voices, which they do not recognize as being their own. All sounds are thought to emanate from the moving shadows on the cave wall. In such circumstances, the prisoners would have a limited understanding. They would believe that "the truth is nothing other than the shadows of artificial things" (514a–15c).[4]

The prisoners are freer than they seem at first. They are physically free in that their hands are not bound and they have no prison-keepers preventing them from attempting to escape. They are intellectually free in that their eyes, ears, and voices are unimpaired and there is real light in the cave. Why is it that they are imprisoned? Or perhaps it is better to ask by what their souls are imprisoned. The answer to this question lies in the shadows. The prisoners believe that only the moving shadows are true or real things. They pay no attention to the relatively undefined and unmoving shadows they themselves cast. More important, the cave wall is lit well enough to be seen, but they consider it to be an unreal or untrue thing. The presence of an unimpaired faculty of sight, an object capable of being seen, and the medium of light ought to result in the perception of the thing, but the prisoners mistake the moving shadows for existing things and an existing thing for nothing. In the cave a sharply defined shadow is completely dark, the absence of light; it can be understood to represent not-being, or that which *is not*. The prisoners thus mistake what *is* for what *is not*, and what *is not* for what *is*.

Why do they make this mistake? Partly because of the apparent movement of the shadows, but mostly because they are prevented from naming things properly. The prisoners have the natural ability and the desire to name the things they see before them, but they are unable to do so. The clarification of names requires discussion, and there are two reasons discussion is impossible in such circumstances: the random sounds uttered by the carriers prevent the development of a common language, and the prisoners' bonds prevent them from being able to attribute utterances to other human beings. The echoes of all utterances are thought to be sounds emanating from the shadows that seem capable of movement. The shadows come to life, as it were, because they are thought to move and speak.

In a word, the prisoners are imprisoned by sophistry, and the actions of the carriers are a description of the effects of sophistry writ large. The carriers never appear in the cave; they always remain in the darkness and utter their nonsense from it. In the *Sophist* (254a–b), the Eleatic stranger describes the sophist as someone who "takes refuge in the darkness of not-being, where he is at home and has the knack of feeling his way." This is in stark contrast to the description of the philosopher, at home in the light of the divine, whose thoughts are said to dwell constantly upon the nature of what *is*, or at least as constantly as is possible for a human being. The sophist creates a false image, a phantasm of what *is*, in a "shadow-play of words" (268c–d); the philosopher speaks of it in ikons. When the differentiation between ikons and phantasms is made in the *Sophist*, its immediate context is again a definition of the difference between philosophers and sophists. A sophist is a wonder-worker, a trickster, and an imitator of what *is*, and he requires the darkness of not-being to produce his phantasms (235a–36c; cf. 268c–d). With his shadow-play, he attempts to persuade others that he not only knows all things but also possesses the power "to produce all things in actual fact by a single form of skill" (233a–d; cf. *Republic* 596c–e). The sophist claims to be able to produce all that *is* with his phantasm-making; the philosopher attempts in his speech only to account for all that *is* and is illuminated by the good.

This description explains why only artificial things are used by the carriers to make shadows in the cave. In the divided line image, the last segment of the line was said to represent shadows and reflections of things, made by the sun, with the exception of human beings. The shadows in the cave are made by the carriers from manufactured copies of things, including human beings. They manufacture copies of living things by imposing forms taken from the appearances of these things onto any kind of matter, and they then give movement to the shadows of these copies as they will, not in accordance with the manner in which the souls of living things move by nature. The entire process demonstrates no knowledge of the nature of the things themselves. All is appearance—or perhaps it is better to say that all is as the carriers' sophistry wills it to appear.[5] This brings to light the carriers' sophistic understanding of human nature, best summarized by the opening sentence of Protagoras's work *Truth* (*Aletheia*): "Man is the measure of all things; of that which *is*, that it *is*, and of that which *is not*, that it *is not*" (frag. 1 D–K; cf. *Laws* 716c).

Socrates now turns to considering what it would be like for such imprisoned men to be released from their bonds, using one prisoner as an example (515c–e). Once again his bodily or physical description is significant primarily because it is an image of events in the soul; the release of the body from its bonds is also the release and healing of the soul from its folly (*aphrosyne*). A prisoner is released and compelled to stand up, turn his head around, and approach the light of the fire. He is described, in the passive voice, as suffering the events. It is not said that the prisoner is released and compelled to ascend through the agency of another man. The events are said to occur "by nature [*physei*]." The prisoner's own nature is the agent, the nature that all human beings possess. Even though they might be imprisoned by sophistry from birth, all prisoners are, by nature, able to free themselves from their bonds. However, this is not to say that all of them will do so. Some will and some will not. It is not possible to determine initially which of them will. The consequences of the release are also said to be suffered. The ascending man experiences physical pain and sensual confusion. He is also spiritually confused when the temporary blindness caused by the light of the fire subsides and he is able to make out the artifacts whose shadows he had previously believed to be the truth. His previous beliefs conflict with what is now evidently true. His perception of the artifacts is not so much an empirical observation as an immediate understanding of the nature of the things before him. He requires no tutoring to reach this understanding, for it exists by nature and was already present in the lowest depths of the cave even though it had been denied or suppressed by the sophistry of the carriers.

In this state of confusion, the ascending man is compelled to ascend further, this time by "someone," an unnamed human agent. It is possible to say that the agent has the soul of a philosopher and not a sophist, for he immediately exposes the lie upon which the power of sophistry is founded. He says that the shadows in the cave are *phluaria*, which can be understood as "nonsense," "foolish talk," or even "silly nothings," thus capturing the nature of the shadows in a single word. The ascending man recognizes the things used to create shadows when he is shown them, and he understands what is said about the things and their shadows. He is now described both as being able to understand what he is told and as being able to speak in reply to the agent, who has not yet compelled him to ascend further than he has already by nature. These are apparently natural abilities. His further ascent occurs when he is compelled to look at the light itself, that is, when the agent questions his assumptions or hypotheses about what the things before him are in themselves, intending to lead his soul toward higher things.

Later in his account, Socrates explicitly compares the light of the fire with the sun's power (517b). The fire is in the cave, but not of the cave. Its light is much weaker than that of the sun, but it is a true light by which to see. So too, the questions posed to the ascending man are initially simple, but they are comparable in nature to the dialectical questioning that is capable of leading the soul toward the good. This makes a strict comparison of the stages of the ascent from the cave and the geometry of the divided line impossible. The higher things represented by the various line segments are all present at this level of the ascent. The unquestioned hypotheses about things evident at this level have been brought into the light of dialectical inquiry.

Socrates now asks Glaucon about the ascending man's reaction to looking directly at the fire, that is, to being compelled to participate in a dialogue with a Socratic interlocutor. Glaucon believes that, because his eyes would hurt, he would flee from the fire, "turning away" to the things he is able to discern. He also believes that the man would be at a loss to answer the questions put to him and would thus also turn away from his interlocutor by refusing to question the hypotheses of his thinking (515e). The ascending man represents all men, and since Glaucon does not intend to class himself with those who would turn away, he intends in his answer to distinguish between those whom he considers the knowledgeable few—men such as Socrates and himself, no doubt—and the unreflective or ignorant many. We need not assume that Socrates agrees with Glaucon's answer, nor need we answer Socrates' question as Glaucon does.

The ascending man is confronted with a choice: he may either follow the ascent further, overcoming his initial discomfort and disorientation, or he may refuse. He is made aware of the choice by a human agent, but he is able to understand the choice by means of the initial agent of his ascent, that is, by nature. Since the ascending man represents all men, all are, by nature, capable of ascent. Some will refuse to do so. But those who refuse know what it is they have refused. They turn away from something they have seen. It is thus possible to conclude that there are two basic types of souls, those who are willing to ascend toward the good and those who refuse to do so. In other words, there are those who are open to the transcendent good and those who resist transcendence. This stands in contrast to Glaucon's apparent classification of souls into those who are able and those who are unable to ascend to the highest things and grasp them as knowledge.

Only those who have turned their backs to the fire, the souls who resist transcendence, can now rightfully be called the inhabitants of the cave. Socrates will soon describe them to Glaucon as "perpetual prisoners" (516e). He does not apply this term to all men, nor even to all except philosophers. At this point in the account, the *eikon* of the cave has begun to change its meaning. Some will leave the cave and others will remain, and a cave inhabited only by those who refuse to leave it will differ fundamentally from the cave as it was first described. The consequences of this differentiation of the cave *eikon* will appear as Socrates' account proceeds.

What more can be said about the perpetual prisoners who refuse to leave? Not all of them will be content to return to their bonds and watch the shadow-play on the cave wall. Some will turn away from the fire in order to become carriers. In the initial account of the release of a prisoner from his bonds, the carriers were not mentioned. The prisoner did not see them as he walked around the wall and toward the light, even though he could see the objects they had manufactured. This oddity is due in large part to the difficulty of accounting for the carriers before establishing the nature of the choice between ascent and refusal. It is also intended as an indication that there is no one to prevent the prisoners from leaving the cave and that even firelight has sufficient power to dispel the sophistic darkness the carriers inhabit. But what of those who do not become carriers, those who return to their bonds voluntarily? They must know the shadow-play to be a fabrication. They agree to believe in the truth of the shadow-play, even though they also know something about the techniques or tricks used by the carriers to deceive them and even though they know the shadows to be phantastic images of what is true.

Socrates does not accept Glaucon's implication that all men except the truly knowledgeable would turn away from the fire. In order to continue his account of the long ascent, he overcomes the resistance to it evident in Glaucon's answer by describing the forcible removal of a prisoner from the cave and his trip along the rough and steep path leading to the mouth of the cave and the light of the sun beyond (515e–16a). This is an uncharacteristic use of physical force by Socrates, even in an image. Glaucon's imagination might be stirred by such imagery, but it is unlikely that anyone can be forced to ascend in the manner described. The upward path can only be taken voluntarily (cf. 536e). This does not mean that it is not difficult or that it requires no assistance. Its roughness and steepness represent the difficulty of the soul's attempt to move from being open to the questioning of some of its hypotheses to being completely open to the ascent toward the good. The need for assistance along the way implies that dialectical ascent is not possible without dialogue with others. And this may even be true for the philosophic agent of the prisoner's ascent.

Once the ascending man is completely outside the cave, it is no longer necessary to use any form of compulsion to assist in his ascent. He is free to discover the things of the world on his own. Socrates now gives an account of how the man's eyes become accustomed to the light illuminating all things (516a–c). The account of this process, again, cannot be explained by reference to the geometry of the divided line alone. It is a constant clarification of the nature of things in which the movement of the soul from darkness to light is repeatedly renewed. Within the cave there had been a movement of the soul from the complete darkness of the shadows, progressing through the recognition of manufactured things and the things of which they are copies, toward the light of the fire. Outside the cave there are several similar movements toward the light.

The first begins in the initial ability of the man free to ascend on his own to discern shadows. Shadows are now understood not as the absence of light, but as a dim light that allows him to see things in the shade. He then discerns the reflections of men and other things in water, then these things themselves, and finally he turns toward the source of the light. This begins the description of a second movement toward the light. The man does not look directly at the sun. Socrates says he must contemplate the heavens first, not only their appearances but "heaven itself." The progression from darkness to light is described by means of an image based on the distance and intensity of sources of light. The man contemplates the heavens, first by looking at the light of distant stars at night and then by looking at the sunlight reflected from the moon. During the day, the heavens are obscured by sunlight. He is finally able to look at the sun and its light—first at its reflection in water and then directly. From his observations of the appearances of the stars and sun over a long period of time, he would be able to make conclusions about natural phenomena, such as the course of the seasons and the years.

At this point, Socrates reminds the ascending man—and Glaucon as well—that he has had companions all the while. He had hinted that there were other human beings outside the cave by referring to their reflections in water, implying that it is possible for human beings to dwell outside the cave at this point in the ascent. Socrates now refers explicitly to conclusions drawn by the ascending man from all of the things "they" had seen together (516c). The ascent would not have been possible for the man free to discover the illuminated things of the world and the source of all light if he did not have companions with whom to name things and develop a common language. The ascent itself, at least in the stages so far described, is not possible without the company of and dialogue with others willing to ascend.

There remains one final movement of the soul from darkness to light: it must be recalled that the sun is the child of the good. Socrates does not mention the final step of this movement explicitly. Once again, he draws back as he approaches the end that guides his account, perhaps risking that Glaucon will think him a laughingstock (cf. 506d). However, Socrates does expect Glaucon to recall what had just been said about the sun and the good; it was, after all, the basis of his answer to the question Glaucon insisted he address. Socrates allows Glaucon, indeed, each of the members of his audience, to complete the ascent on his own. To remind them of the transcendent end guiding his whole account, he gives an incomplete description of the final movement from darkness to light. The ascending man must first look at reflections of the sun's light in water, reflections that Socrates describes as *phantasmata* for the first time (516b).[6] He may then look at things that cannot be seen with the eyes: the sun's light and then the sun itself in its own realm. What remains for his soul's ascent to attain its highest point is the insight that the sun is the child of good. In comparison to the soul's illumination by the good itself, even the light of the sun is a *phantasma*.

All attempts to establish a strict correspondence between the long ascent from the cave and the divided line obscure the subtleties of Socrates' account. One significant point is always lost in such attempts: the stages of the ascent within the cave resemble the stages of ascent outside the cave. Both begin with shadows, but the shadows in the cave are the complete absence of light, whereas the shadows created by sunlight are simply areas of dimmer light in which things can be seen more clearly. Both then move to images of various things, including human beings, but the images made in the cave are made by the carriers from appearances for the purpose of creating shadows, whereas the images created by sunlight are simply the various appearances of things themselves. Both have a source of light, but the fire in the cave is man-made and the sun is not. The ascent within the cave stops with the belief that the fire is man-made. The ascent outside the cave begins with the recognition that even the light of a man-made fire may illuminate some things, and it continues toward the brightest light: the transcendent good, the cause and illumination of all that *is*. The cave inhabited by perpetual prisoners is therefore a sophistic phantasm of all that *is*, in which some human beings claim for themselves the powers of the good itself.

It is possible to imagine several types of souls, each of which experiences profoundly a movement described in one of the four stages of the ascent. This recalls the classification of souls implied at the conclusion of the account of the divided line. The two accounts are directly related to one another. There were two ordering criteria given in Socrates' earlier account: the soul's initial hypotheses concerning the relative clarity and participation in truth of the visible and intelligible realms, and the soul's openness or closure to the questioning of its hypotheses. There are also two ordering criteria implied by his account of the ascent: the soul's openness or closure to the transcendent good, and the degree of its openness or closure. The latter criteria are the more fundamental. The lowest type of soul is that of the perpetual prisoners. This type of soul assumes the visual realm to participate more fully in truth than the intelligible and is closed to the questioning of its hypotheses. Even in combination these two characteristics seem to be simple human frailties. Why does Socrates describe this type of soul so critically? Because its extreme closure to the transcendent good is its most significant quality. This is the psychic state that transforms the two seemingly harmless characteristics into aspects of a pathological condition. There are at least two sorts of perpetual prisoners, depending on the degree of their resistance to transcendence. The worst is the sophistical soul of the carrier, or lover of false image making. It is far more resistant to ascent than the soul of a cave dweller who is simply too weak to resist the charm of the illusions made by the carriers.

The remaining three types of souls are all open to transcendence in various degrees. Because openness or closure to transcendence is the most significant criterion for classifying souls, the basic similarity of these souls is more important than their differences. The first type encountered in Socrates' account of the ascent is that of the man of common sense. Such a man believes that the visible participates in truth more fully than the intelligible. He trusts what he sees in the clear light of the sun, and not without reason. Consequently, it is not surprising that he is somewhat open to the questioning of his hypotheses. The next type of soul encountered in the ascent ranks the intelligible higher than the visible. A man with such a soul might prefer to spend his time contemplating the movements of the stars, moon, and sun, that is, the appearances of the heavens. He does this in order to be able to determine their mathematical regularities and draw the appropriate inferences from his hypotheses. This is the soul of the geometrical thinker, who is less open to the questioning of his hypotheses, even when they do not concern the heavens, than is the man of common sense. The final type of soul is, of course, that of the philosopher. The philosopher's openness to the transcendent good guides all that he does. It especially guides his dialectical questioning of all hypotheses, no matter whether they are his own or those of some other man. Without this openness, the philosopher might be indistinguishable from a geometrical thinker or perhaps even from a sophist.

This typology of souls, all originating in the ascent from the first home, is less sketchy than the one implied at the conclusion of Socrates' account of the divided line. Nonetheless, it remains a sketchy and incomplete typology. Some of the questions it raises are taken up in the following discussion of how the first home should be recalled.

Recalling the First Home

If there can be said to be one, this is the point of highest ascent in the *Republic*. Socrates has now given an adequate, if not a complete and unambiguous answer to the question, What is the good?[7] The images of the sun, the line, and the ascent toward the sun given in his answer form one coherent *eikon* of the good, though it requires some imagination and some knowledge of the originals to understand how the images are interrelated. Socrates seems to leave his answer incomplete by not stating explicitly that the soul's ascent toward the sun must be an ascent toward the good. Perhaps he dislikes "telling again a well-told tale," just as Odysseus found it hateful to retell to the Phaiakians the story of how he came from Kalypso's island to their land (*Odyssey* 12.450–53). The incompleteness and ambiguity of Socrates' account suggests the difficulty of speaking of the highest things without leading those who listen to reject what is said out of hand or to accept it dogmatically in the manner of geometrical thinkers. It also suggests that the best way to tell others of the highest things is to evoke the proper *pathemata* in their souls and require them to go beyond merely listening to what is said. If Glaucon wishes to know the good itself, he must complete Socrates' account of it himself, using the *pathemata* Socrates' words were intended to evoke as the basis of his understanding. In particular, he must recall that the sun is the offspring of the good beyond being, even though he previously thought this to be daimonic hyperbole. If Glaucon has been attentive, he should now be better able to form prudent judgments on the basis of an understanding of human nature in its education and lack of education and in its aspiration to the good.

Socrates now asks Glaucon a question about happiness (*eudaimonia*) to test his judgment. If Glaucon's judgment has not been informed by the good, he will most likely misunderstand happiness, and particularly the happiness of others. By asking him the question, Socrates demonstrates his openness to the possibility that Glaucon has understood what he has been told about the good. The manner in which Socrates asks it, however, reveals that he has his doubts. It might even be described as a leading question. Perhaps Socrates has a score to settle with Glaucon. In any event, Glaucon's answer determines the subsequent course of their discussion.

Socrates asks Glaucon, while he is imagining himself as the ascending man at the highest point of the ascent, to recall his "first home." Glaucon's understanding of the highest point in the ascent will determine how he recalls the lowest. If he has attained the insight that the end guiding the ascent is the soul's illumination by the good, he will recall the cave as the first home of all men, from which all are able to ascend by nature, despite their bonds and the charm of sophistic illusions, although some will refuse to do so. He will also recall that those who refuse to ascend inhabit a cave of their own construction, a second home, as it were, which they refuse to leave. If Glaucon has not attained the insight Socrates hoped to evoke in him, he will recall the cave as he imagined it when Socrates asked him implicitly if all men would refuse to leave it. He will believe that the cave is a perpetual prison for all men, except those whose end is to attain certain knowledge of things, and that all perpetual prisoners are indistinguishable from each other in their ignorance. It is most likely that Glaucon imagines the highest point of the ascent to be the contemplation of the movements of heavenly bodies, for this appears to lead from perception to undoubtable hypotheses about the nature of things from which to draw conclusions by reason alone. In other words, it appears to lead to certain knowledge. But perhaps he has come to understand the difference between dialectical and geometrical thinking and the differing ends to which these two kinds of thought move.

Socrates asks whether, when the ascending man recalls his first home and the wisdom (*sophia*) there, he would consider himself happy for the change (*metabole*) and pity his fellow prisoners. Glaucon answers that he would indeed (516c). The enthusiastic tone of Glaucon's reply gives away its meaning more readily than his words do.

The question is intended, in part, to reveal how Glaucon judges other men. Does he consider it possible for there to be nonphilosophers whose souls are open to the good, or does he assume that all nonphilosophers are vulgar souls? Socrates had given a few hints in the question itself. He suggested that there is wisdom of some sort in the first home. Glaucon most likely took this as irony. He also suggested by his use of the term *metabole* that the change from the manner in which it is possible to love wisdom in the first home to the manner in which the philosopher loves wisdom is not a change between two absolutely distinct states. Glaucon no doubt understood the ascent as a *metastasis*, a fundamental change in the nature of the ascending man. He may even have believed that the entire account was intended ironically. His answer reveals that he understands the difference between those who inhabit the cave and those who do not as absolute and impossible to bridge. It is the difference between the souls of the philosopher and the nonphilosopher as he understands them, the difference between the knowledgeable and the ignorant man. The souls within the cave are pitiable, both for their ignorance and for their natural inability to ascend from the cave, while those outside the cave consider themselves happy because they are not pitiable by nature. In Glaucon's mind, there are no other types of souls.

We need not answer as Glaucon does. The simplest thing learned about human nature from Socrates' account of the good is summarized at the beginning of Aristotle's *Metaphysics:* "All human beings by nature desire to know. An indication of this is our esteem for the senses; . . . and most of all the sense of sight. . . . [S]ight best helps us to know things, and reveals many distinctions" (980a22–27). Human beings by nature have a sense of wonder that the world is as it is, and this wonder is the basis of the desire to know. They esteem sight in their desire to know because the wonderful sight of things is, in part, the intellect's recognition of the intelligibility of what *is*, as well as the soul's simple awareness of the illumination of all that *is* by the good.

Socrates' discussion of wonder (*thauma*) in the *Theaetetus* (155c–56a) also summarizes an important feature of the ascent. He says the sense (*pathos*) of wonder is the mark of the philosopher: "Philosophy, indeed, has no other origin [*arche*]." The experience of wonder that compels the philosopher's soul to ascend is similar to and originates in the wonder that all souls experience by nature. Both are evidence of the soul's openness to the good. The philosopher's soul aspires to attain a vision of the good itself, to which the wondering soul is open, but which it perhaps might not attain on its own.[8] Socrates also suggests in the *Theaetetus* that some souls are closed to even the simplest experience of wonder. He speaks of those "who believe that nothing is real except what they can grasp with their hands" and who do not believe "that actions or processes or anything invisible can count as real." Theaetetus calls such people hard and repellent (*sklerous kai antitupous anthropous*); Socrates calls them remarkably crude or vulgar (*euamoutoi*). The typology of souls implicit in Socrates' image of the divided line makes no reference to those who admit nothing to participate in truth except what they can grasp with their hands.[9] This repellent vulgarity occurs only in those souls whose closure to the transcendent good takes the form of a refusal to ascend from matters of the body.

If Socrates' ikons had succeeded in evoking the proper affections in Glaucon's soul, he might not have been so quick to judge the souls of those who are not philosophers as pitiable. If he had stopped to think, he might have recalled a similar discussion he had had with Socrates earlier that night (*Republic* 475b–80a). Glaucon had insisted that Socrates give a precise definition of the philosopher. He favored the suggestion made by Socrates that the philosopher is one who desires all of wisdom, not only a part of it, without stopping to consider whether or not it would be possible to attain such an end. When Socrates went on to say the desire was insatiable, Glaucon paid no attention. He responded instead by asking if he would class, among others, the lovers of sights or spectacles (*philotheamones*) with the true (*alethinoi*) philosophers. Socrates replied that while they are not philosophers, they are like philosophers. The rest of the discussion was spent in clarifying the differences between true philosophers and others.

Socrates explained the nature of the similarity between the *philosophos* and the *philotheamones* by making a distinction between philosophers, who are able to approach beauty itself and see it by itself and appreciate the things that participate in it, and other men, who believe in beautiful things but who neither believe in beauty itself nor are able to follow another's guidance toward knowledge of it. Not all men can be classed in one or the other of these categories. Glaucon accepted the distinction as an exhaustive classification, but we need not do so. Lovers of sights or spectacles fall into the latter category because they are insatiable in their pursuit of particular beautiful things. Their only similarity with philosophers is the insatiability of their desire. However, not all nonphilosophers have such a pathological love of spectacles. Most men who love particular beautiful things are not closed to beauty itself. They may be led some way toward it by a philosopher. And the ascent need not result in an equally pathological loss of love for all particular beautiful things, since the particular participates in beauty itself. The true philosopher is also a true lover of beauty (*philokalos; Phaedrus* 248d).

Socrates then went on to contrast two conditions of the soul. The pathological closure to beauty itself of the *philotheamones,* indeed the whole life of such a man, is a dreaming state of the soul (*onar*). The whole life of the *philosophos,* on the other hand, because of his insatiable desire to attain a vision of beauty itself and to know the things that participate in beauty, is a waking or wakeful state of the soul (*hypar*). There are, of course, degrees of dreaming and wakefulness. Even the life of the philosopher can only be said to aspire to the end of the soul's perpetual wakefulness. Socrates then contrasted two conditions of the intellect. He called the thought of the *philosophos* knowledge, and that of the *philotheamones* opinion, not ignorance. Knowledge (*episteme*) depends on what *is,* he said, and ignorance (*agnosia*) depends on what *is not.* What then is opinion (*doxa*)? It is neither ignorance nor knowledge but something between them. Glaucon would prefer to believe that opinion is ignorance because it is not knowledge. Socrates attempts to persuade him that such a belief is wrong. Although opinion may be led toward ignorance and the total darkness of what *is not,* it may also be led away from such ignorance. The soul, by nature, forms opinions; and the soul, by nature, is educable. Opinions in themselves are not evidence of stupidity, boorishness or ineducability (*amathia*) simply because they are opinions. They may also be evidence of a simple lack of education (*apaideusia*). If a soul is open to persuasion, its opinions may be taken up toward *episteme* by dialectical inquiry.

If Glaucon had stopped to think before answering Socrates' question about the first home, he might also have recalled what Socrates had said, just before being charged with hyperbole, about light and darkness in the image of the sun and the good (508c–d; 509b). Socrates said that when the soul fixes itself on that which is illuminated by truth and which *is*, the soul intellects, knows, and "appears to possess intelligence [*noun echein phainetai*]." And when it fixes itself on the realm of coming into being and passing away—the realm in which light is mixed with darkness—the soul opines (*doxazei*) and "seems not to possess intelligence [*eoiken au noun ouk echonti*]." Just as the eye sees things less clearly at night in starlight or moonlight than it does in the sunlight, so the soul sees that which *is* less clearly in the dim light of the realm of coming into being and passing away than it does in the realm of being itself. That which *is* can be seen in that which comes into being and passes away. The two realms are not independent of each other. They both originate in and are illuminated by the good in some way. When the soul fixes itself on that which comes into being and passes away, it only appears not to possess knowledge. It may indeed possess it to some extent. When the soul fixes itself on that which *is*, again it only appears to possess knowledge. It may not possess it. The intellect's knowledge or lack of it ultimately depends on whether or not the soul is open to the good—in other words, whether or not the soul recognizes that the light illuminating both realms originates in the good beyond being. The knowledge of those who prefer starlight and moonlight to sunlight—geometrical thinkers—is only apparent knowledge. If in their search for certain knowledge they come to believe that the realm of being illuminates the realm of coming into being and passing away, or that the intellect illuminates what is perceivable, they are in error. The error may be a simple one, possibly due to youthful imprudence. But it may also be evidence of the soul's resistance to further ascent toward the good.

Socrates does not say that the soul can fix itself on what *is not*. What *is not* cannot be, at least not in the way that what *is* can be said to be. Its existence depends on a type of ignorance in the soul. In the particular instance of the soul's attempt to see what is true in what comes into being and passes away, it must see in dim light

and must not be misled by the movement of things. In such conditions it may err in intellection and believe that something *is* that *is
not*. This is simply evidence of the soul's confusion. The soul may
long for a more brilliant illumination or it may welcome such a
brighter light when it appears. If it does, the opinions it has formed
in confusion and error may be clarified. If it does not—that is, if
the soul is closed to the more brilliant illumination of the good—
its initial confusion and error will be led toward the ignorance of
sophistry. Such a soul will turn away from the light that blinds it
and claim that what *is* is best seen in darkness. It may even deny
that light is necessary for sight or that the good illuminates what
is. If so, such a soul will believe that the intellect's certain knowledge of things is possible only because of its closure to the good.
The sophistic soul, completely closed to the transcendent, is a
pathological type of soul that attempts to intellect what *is not* in
order to deny that what *is* is illuminated by the good. The type of
thinking that is associated with this state of the soul is not unlike
that of the geometrical thinker, who prefers observing the stars at
night to wondering at the world illuminated by the sun.

Glaucon might think it daimonic hyperbole, but the judgment
of whether someone is happy or pitiable depends, in the first
instance, upon the openness or closure of his soul to the good. In
other words, happiness (*eudaimonia*) depends upon having a good
daimon. The various manners in which a soul may direct itself
toward that which *is* and that which comes into being and passes
away are of less importance than the manners in which the soul
may aspire to or turn away from the good. The same is true of the
various manners in which a soul may decide the relative clarity
and participation in truth of the intelligible and visible realms.

Who then can be said to be pitiable and who happy? Those
souls are pitiable whose manner or degree of closure to the good
allows them to be led by sophistry. Those souls whose manner or
degree of openness to the good allows them to be led by philosophy are not pitiable, but are happy in their own way. All souls may
be said to be ranged between those of the sophist and the philosopher. Insofar as this conclusion can be used to judge any particular human being, however, it should be recalled that a typology of
souls is only a typology. As such, it is the imaginative result of
considering in what manners the things that are present in all
souls might possibly be arranged. It should not be accepted dogmatically and applied imprudently.

What can now be said about the soul's ascent from the first home? It has become evident that the soul may turn toward the good or away from it at any level of the ascent and that the turn toward or away from it may be partial or complete. This allows a reconsideration of the typology implicit in Socrates' account of the ascent.

Socrates' account did not begin with an explicit description of the vulgar soul, the one that believes nothing to be real except what can be grasped with the hands (*Theaetetus* 155c–56a). No doubt there are many people who refuse to ascend from bodily matters, and no doubt people with such souls are cave dwellers. But Socrates' account had as its primary concern the description of "our nature," particularly the nature of the soul in its education and lack of education. The soul does not originate in vulgarity, and the vulgar soul is not representative of the state of the soul "from childhood." Socrates implies that the soul is bound to the body from birth, but he insists that "by nature" the soul may release itself from such bonds and ascend. The prisoner in his description uses his hands to release himself, not to grasp things (514a–b; 515c–d). Children, by nature, have a sense of wonder about the world, and all men esteem the sense of sight for the assistance it provides their natural desire to know (*Metaphysics* 980a22). The vulgar soul, therefore, is one that refuses to ascend and perhaps can no longer ascend, but not one that cannot ascend by nature; the vulgar soul is a perpetual prisoner of the cave only because of its refusal. The same criterion was used in determining that the sophistic soul and those other souls too weak to resist the charms of sophistry are also perpetual prisoners.

All other souls dwell in the sunlight outside the cave of perpetual prisoners and are open to the good. That is not to say they are without bodies, but bodily matters are not important in understanding either their fundamental similarity or the differences between them. The soul of the common-sense man, free to discover the things of the world on his own and motivated by a sense of wonder, was described previously as believing that the visible participates in truth more fully than the intelligible, trusting what is evident in the clear light of the sun and being somewhat open to the questioning of its hypotheses. It is now possible to add that the common-sense soul loves the sight of beautiful things, for it recognizes that beautiful things are visible images, in the world, of the good. A soul of this type may err or fall into confusion and perhaps may even be deceived by sophistry on occasion, but it is fundamentally educable. It can be led to turn its attention to the things in the heavens so that it might appreciate their beauty and understand their movements and nature. It can also be led to see that the intelligible participates in truth more fully than the visible. The education of the common-sense soul need not result in the loss of its sense of wonder. It is possible that learning of the mathematical regularities in the movements of the stars, moon, and sun might make them seem less beautiful; it is also possible that learning of the order of the intelligible realm and the charm of drawing proper inferences might lead to an unwillingness to question certain hypotheses. However, the sense of wonder can be preserved throughout the ascent toward the good.

Wonder is necessary for philosophy's ascent. The philosophical soul wonders and questions without cynical doubt, the doubt that simply negates what is called into question in order to assert something else unquestioningly or even to enjoy the power that negation seems to bring. Its ascent need not result in either the loss or the intellectualization of the sense of the beautiful and wonderful. Indeed, Socrates says that "true [*alethinoi*]" philosophers are "lovers of the sight of the truth [*tous tes aletheias philotheamones*]" (475e). He does not say they are lovers of the intelligible realm. The truth is the illumination of the intelligible by the good. Philosophers are thus lovers of the light of the transcendent good, a light that illuminates both the intelligible and the visible realms in different ways.

What of the *philotheamones* and the geometrical thinker? There is something ambiguous about them. It seems that they ought to find a place in the range of all possible souls between the educable common-sense soul and the philosophical soul. It also seems, however, that their idiosyncrasies ought to lead them to descend to the cave ruled by sophistry. They are both products of the ascent from common sense, but they both demonstrate an unwillingness or refusal to continue the ascent. Socrates describes the *philotheamones* as one who neither believes in beauty itself nor is able to follow another's guidance toward it, though he is able to appreciate beautiful things. He cannot distinguish between things that are beautiful because they are ikons of the good and things that only appear to be beautiful because they are phantasms of the good. The charm of the visible realm misdirects his sense of wonder and blinds him to the good. The charm of the intelligible realm, on the other hand, misdirects the geometrical thinker's sense of wonder and blinds him to the good. His faith in the certain knowledge of unquestioned hypotheses and the certain procedures of drawing inferences from them prevents him from being led toward the beautiful or the good. He cannot distinguish between the meaningless utterances of the sophist and the dialectical reasoning of the philosopher because the former is apparently as consistent as the latter, if not more so. Will the *philotheamones* and the geometrical thinker be charmed by the sophist? It is difficult to say. The question of whether they will remain in the sunlight or descend to the cave of perpetual prisoners is determined only by the particular degree of their resistance to the good.

The sophist is both a *philotheamones* and a geometrical thinker whose soul is completely closed to the good. He is the lover of phantasms of his own making and the lover of the utter nonsense produced by his own "shadow-play of words" (*Sophist* 268c–d). This makes him charming to those who are too much like him for their own good. His charm also gives him a certain power over those too weak to resist him. He can be said to rule them in the cave. The sophist also rules over the vulgar. His power over them is not the result of his charm, which the vulgar might find suspicious, but the result of his skill in making phantasms and false beliefs from the darkness and ignorance of what *is not*. When all manifestations of the good are hidden by his skill and false images of all that *is* have been made to take its place, the vulgar then imagine they have complete freedom to place their souls in the service of their bodies.

The cave of perpetual prisoners is a false world of the sophist's creation in which he rules over the spiritually weak and the vulgar. The cave dwellers are "perpetual" prisoners as long as they refuse to ascend toward the good in any way. They live in a dream-world. All other men are awake. Because they are awake, they are justified in considering themselves happy and, along with the philosopher, in pitying the perpetual prisoners in their ignorance.

Healing Glaucon's *Aphrosyne*

In answering Socrates' question, Glaucon finds pitiable all men but those whom he believes to be true philosophers. He does not recall all of what Socrates said about the first home of all men from childhood and the possibility of ascent from it by nature. While imagining himself alone at the highest point in the ascent, as he understands it, Glaucon mistakes the dreamworld of the cave ruled by sophistry for the perpetual home of all nonphilosophers, even of those whose souls are open to the good. This is evidence of the imprudent folly (*aphrosyne*) of geometrical thinking. Socrates judges from Glaucon's reply that he is as reluctant now to ascend beyond geometrical thinking as he had been when he laughably dismissed the description of the good beyond being as daimonic hyperbole. Yet Socrates attempts once again to overcome Glaucon's resistance to the final stage of the ascent and to heal his soul of its *aphrosyne*. In his account of the ascent from the first home, Socrates overcame Glaucon's hesitations by means of the compelling image of a prisoner being dragged from the fire to the mouth of the cave. He now uses a far more compelling image to capture Glaucon's imagination. Socrates attempts to drag Glaucon, in speech, from the depths of the cave of perpetual prisoners along the entire length of the longer way. Before this can be attempted, however, Glaucon must be made to return to the cave's darkness.

Socrates begins by accepting Glaucon's hypothesis that the dreamworld of the cave is the first home of all men except philosophers. He then describes the sophist's dreamworld in more detail, to see if Glaucon will notice the differences between it and his previous description of the first home (516c–d). The prisoners do not merely watch the meaningless procession of phantasms created by the carriers passing before their eyes, he says, nor do they merely listen to the carriers' nonsensical utterances. They compete among themselves to determine who is quickest and cleverest in anticipating what the carriers will do or say next. The sophistic *techne* of the carriers produces meaningless results, but the *techne* itself is predictable and requires cleverness to learn and utilize efficiently. The perpetual prisoners are aware of the *techne;* they speak coherently among themselves about it and are more or less clever in their exercise of it as amateurs. Socrates also describes them as being able to compete among themselves for honor, praise, and prizes without hostilities.[10] None of them desire to leave the cave, as did the ascending man, even though they seem to have a great deal more freedom than did the prisoners of the first home. Only those who wish to remain in the cave take part in the competition.

Socrates now asks Glaucon, who is still imagining himself to be the ascending man at the highest point of his ascent, a difficult series of questions about his opinion. Would he desire such honor, praise, and prizes? Would he envy, emulate, or be jealous of those who are honored by and have power among the cave dwellers? Socrates distinguishes, as he did previously, between the prisoners and the sophistic carriers, but the latter are now said to have power among the perpetual prisoners. He also distinguishes between ordinary prisoners and those among them who are clever and are honored because they imitate or resemble the sophistic carriers—men such as the *philotheamones* and the geometrical thinker. When all this is brought to mind, will Glaucon be able to resist the appeal of the prisoners' competition? He is clever in the manner of a geometrical thinker and would easily take the prizes (cf. 520c). But more importantly, will he be able to resist the appeal of the power of sophistry? He is spirited as well as clever, and he believes that the clever deserve to have power over others. Who else is there to rule but the perpetual prisoners? And how else can they be ruled but by sophistry?

Socrates continues by contrasting the affections of the soul raised by these questions with a different affection evident in a quotation from Homer. He asks Glaucon if he would greatly prefer to be "on the earth, a hireling of another, of a landless or portionless man" and endure anything rather than live the life of a perpetual prisoner and opine as they do? A prisoner's life will obviously seem unattractive to a spirited and clever man. But this is not what Socrates wishes to discover. If Glaucon can recall the rest of the passage, he will understand the significance of what is being asked of him. He should be able to recall it, for Socrates cited it fully earlier in their discussion that night (386c).

Socrates quotes from the *Odyssey* (11.484–91). Odysseus has just consoled Achilleus in Hades by reminding him that even though he was honored as a god among the Argives while alive, he now "rules mightily among the dead." Achilleus replies that he would prefer a poor life on the earth as the hireling or serf of another to being "ruler over all the perished dead." By quoting this passage, Socrates compares the cave of perpetual prisoners to Hades and the refusal to leave the cave with the soul's living death. He asks Glaucon pointedly if he would like to be the sophistic master of all perpetual prisoners. Since Glaucon believes that all men except philosophers are prisoners, this is a great deal of power to turn down. The alternative is the life of a hireling or serf. But how is it that such a simple man is not one of the perpetual prisoners? Socrates reminds Glaucon with his quote from Homer that it is not only the philosopher who may leave the cave and live on the earth in the sunlight. Even a serf may be open to the good in his own way. For this reason alone his life is preferable to that of the sophist who is master of all the dead, even though the serf's is not the life of a philosopher.

Glaucon agrees with Socrates that the life of a perpetual prisoner is unattractive. He says nothing about the manner in which they opine, however, and he is equally silent about whether he thinks the life of a serf is preferable to the life of someone who has power among the prisoners. Socrates now compels Glaucon to leave the sunlit realm and descend to the cave in which he would place others who do not belong there (516e–17a). He says that Glaucon, as the ascending man, must return to his seat and participate in the prisoners' competition "once again." If he could recall the first home clearly, he would not be able to recall having competed previously.

Since Glaucon's ambitions are now limited to contests in judging shadows, there is no reason to doubt that he would take highest honors. He is far more knowledgeable than the prisoners about the *techne* of making shadows. And his spirited disdain for the prisoners would lead him to attempt to demonstrate his superior knowledge, perhaps to the point where he could claim that his cleverness in such things should entitle him to rule the cave. However, he fails badly. His failure is not said to be due to a reluctance to participate; it is due, rather, to circumstances completely beyond his control. He cannot satisfy whatever ambitions he might have because his eyes cannot adjust quickly enough to the cave's darkness for him to win the contests and because the prisoners discover him before his eyes have recovered fully. Glaucon becomes a laughingstock for the prisoners. The men he considers ignorant get the better of him in a simple game. They would probably dismiss anything he has to say in explanation of his failures as daimonic hyperbole.

At this point, Socrates reminds Glaucon once again that he is not in the first home. The other prisoners do not laugh at Glaucon's failure to win any prizes; they laugh at his poor vision. They say of him that he went up and came back with ruined eyes and that the ascent therefore is not worth the effort. The prisoners are obviously able to engage in quite sophisticated discussions among themselves, unlike those in the first home. They also demonstrate an understanding of what is beyond the cave—even while denying its truth—that would only be possible if they had ascended to the fire by nature and then turned away from it.

Socrates now asks something puzzling. If the prisoners could lay their hands on and kill the man who attempts to release and lead up, would they not kill him? Glaucon has no doubt they would. But Glaucon, who is imagining his own failure and ridicule, is not this man. Why has he been asked this? Glaucon should recall that the philosophic soul present in the first home has no place in the dreamworld of those who refuse his assistance. He should also recall that the philosopher does not release prisoners from their bonds in the first home; he assists those who have ascended, by nature, toward the fire and are willing to ascend further. Some refuse to ascend, but even though their hands are free they do not kill him. They might be tempted to kill him if he persisted, but he need not have any more dealings with them. However, those who turn away know about the ascent they have refused, and in order to remain perpetually imprisoned in their dreamworld, they feel compelled to ridicule all those whose poor vision betrays them as having returned to the cave from the sunlight. The vulgar, those who believe only in what they can grasp with their hands, prefer killing to ridicule. The vulgar cannot distinguish between a philosopher and a geometrical thinker, but they can distinguish between a sophist and anyone else. Glaucon has reason to fear them, especially if he is tempted to play the sophist. By questioning Glaucon about the fate of the philosopher entering the dreamworld, Socrates has given him greater cause to resist the charms of the sophist and his power. He has also graciously allowed Glaucon to imagine himself the philosopher.

By compelling Glaucon to imagine himself suffering humiliation at the hands of his inferiors, Socrates has playfully begun to settle an outstanding account with Glaucon (cf. 506d–e, 509c–d). However, his main reason for having Glaucon imagine himself a laughingstock, or even a murder victim, is to weaken his resistance to the final insight attained in the ascent toward the good. Socrates has used Glaucon's own phantasm of the first home as a sophistic dreamworld to evoke a powerful affection in his soul—shame. By experiencing shame in this way, Glaucon might come to understand that the *aphrosyne* of geometrical thinking leads it to be charmed by sophistry and that the imprudent geometrical thinker, if he is a spirited and ambitious man, may abandon the ascent toward the good in order to aspire to the sophist's power.

Socrates now descends into the deepest darkness of the sophistic dreamworld and forcibly drags Glaucon—shamed, but imagining himself a philosopher—along the entire length of the path toward the most brilliant light of the good without allowing him a chance to turn away (517a–c). He reminds Glaucon of the ascent from the first home in a few words. He says there is light in the prison home. The firelight should be likened to the sun's power; it is not man-made. The soul, not the intellect alone, ascends from the visible to the intelligible realm. Socrates then describes the phenomena (*phainomena*) of the intelligible realm as they appear to him (*phainetai*). He looks at the intelligible realm from without, that is, from the highest point of the soul's ascent, while describing it. This allows him the most beautiful look at things (504b). The last thing to be seen within the intelligible realm is the idea of the good. Its vision points to a conclusion. But in which direction does it point? Is the conclusion to be a deductive descent or an ascent toward the good itself? Socrates recalls the image of the sun as the offspring of the good while saying that "this" is the cause of all that is right (*orthon*) and beautiful (*kalon*) in everything. But once again Glaucon is left to draw his own conclusion from Socrates' account of the ascent. His response will reveal whether Socrates' hopes or fears will be fulfilled. Glaucon replies that he follows him, but only "so far as he is able." His soul, once again, does not aspire to the vision of the transcendent good.

Socrates begins his description of the soul's rapid journey from Hades to the good beyond being by referring to his own previous account of the ascent. He describes it as an *eikon* and tells Glaucon: "The god knows [*oiden*] whether it is true" (517b). In other words, the god both sees and knows perfectly (*oiden*) whether it is true. He is beyond the visible realm, the intelligible realm, and the truth. The god in Socrates' remark is the transcendent good. The soul's ascent toward the good is also an ascent toward the god, who knows whether any account of the ascent is true. It is possible, therefore, to speak of the affection of the soul engaged in the greatest study in two ways: as ascending toward the good beyond being or as ascending toward the god. This is in accord with the first of the models for speech about the gods (*hoi typoi peri theologias*) that Socrates had mentioned earlier in the dialogue: the god is good in reality (*agathos ho ge theos toi onti*) and nothing but good (379a-b). It is also in accord with what was said at the beginning of Socrates' discussion of the good with Glaucon and Adeimantus: "nothing imperfect is the measure of anything" (504c). The goal of the soul's ascent should be the perfect measure of all that *is*. In the *Laws*, the Athenian describes the goal in this way: "the god is the measure of all things in the highest degree, and far more so than is any man, as they say" (716c). "They" are the sophists who rule dreamworlds such as the one from which Glaucon has been dragged. They believe what Protagoras says: "Man is the measure of all things; of that which *is*, that it *is*, and of that which *is not*, that it *is not*" (frag. 1 D-K). The greatest study brings the lie of what they believe and say into the light.

Socrates is now explicit about the difference between the longer way taken by the philosopher and the way Glaucon seems to prefer. The longer way ascends through the intelligible realm, not without difficulty, and leads to the illumination of the philosopher's *psyche* and *nous* by the good. Glaucon seems to aspire only to know the highest idea within the intelligible realm, but even this end requires study and the illumination of truth. The failure of a soul to attain its proper end by coming to see the idea of the good and drawing the appropriate conclusion may indicate one of several things: an unwillingness or inability to undertake difficult study, even while recognizing that such study is guided by truth; the misguided intellectual aspiration to know the highest things without recognizing that they are illuminated by the good; or even the desire to possess knowledge of the highest things in the belief that, since the highest things are created and illuminated by *nous*, knowledge of them will provide great power. Which of these possibilities does Glaucon's failure to ascend indicate?

Socrates' description of the ascent from the first home began with the recognition that the soul must be healed from its *aphrosyne* (515c). Each part of the ascent is the healing of the *aphrosyne* that typifies the previous stage. Socrates describes the consequences of attaining the ascent's end when he says that a man's soul must see the good if he is to "act prudently on his own account or in public [*emphronos praxein e idiai e demosiai*]." *Phronesis* is the result of always keeping to the upward way (cf. 621c). Glaucon's aspiration to know the highest things without recognizing that they are illuminated by the good will not make him prudent and wise. It will lead him to the folly of geometrical thinking and perhaps to something worse. When the folly of geometrical thinking is accompanied by a refusal to heal the soul by ascending further, a pathological condition results. The soul becomes blind to the good even though it has turned away quite late in its ascent. And since the love of wisdom becomes misguided without the love of the good to direct it toward its end, the geometrical thinker's aspiration to be a philosopher may easily be transformed into sophistry, the greatest *aphrosyne* of the soul. Unless Glaucon attempts to acquire *phronesis*, his ways will lead him to be charmed by sophistry, and he will become closed to the philosopher's persuasion.

The *phronesis* of the true philosopher cannot be imitated by the geometrical thinker or the sophist. It is evidence that his soul has been healed from the temptations of great follies. Socrates speaks seriously of *phronesis* and the life of philosophy on the day of his own death, recounted in the *Phaedo*. He says that *andreia, sophrosyne, dikaiosyne*, and all true virtue (*alethes arete*) exist only with *phronesis*. Without *phronesis* even a virtue such as justice is merely a shadow-painting (*skiagraphia*) having nothing healthy or true in it. These virtues, truth, and *phronesis* itself are all a kind of cleansing or purification (*katharsis*), similar in some way to the purification of the soul practiced by the *bakchoi*, or initiates in the Bacchic celebrations (*teletai*). The philosopher's life has more in common with a Bacchic celebration than an Apollonian rite (69a–d). Unlike the Apollonians, the Bacchics attempt to purify their souls of bodily matters and ascend toward the god with the help of wine. Socrates differs from them only in that he does not attempt to do so without *nous*.

Socrates' last words of advice, just before preparing to drink the hemlock, reveal how a philosopher purifies his soul (114d–15a). A man ought to turn away from the pleasures and orders of the body, eagerly seek out those of learning, and order his soul in the proper and honorable way. The first of the soul's own raiments which Socrates lists are again the virtues of *andreia, sophrosyne*, and *dikaiosyne*. Again he does not complete the list with *sophia*. He suggests that *sophia* is attained with the assistance of learned men. The final things listed are evidence of the importance of *phronesis* in the soul. They are liberality and truth (*kai eleutheria kai aletheia*). *Aletheia* is the good's illumination of all that originates in it and is the soul's guide to the good. *Eleutheria* is not simply freedom, but the exercise of *phronesis*. It is liberality in actions.

But above all, it is liberality in judging others (cf. *Republic* 402b-d, 485a-87a). The manner in which *aletheia* and *eleutheria* adorned Socrates' soul led all those who knew him well to think of him as "the best and most prudent and most just man [*aristou kai allos phronimotaton kai dikaiotaton*]" (*Phaedo* 118a). The evident lack of these things in Glaucon's soul reveals that he will not live the life of a true philosopher, though he may possess many good and honorable virtues.

Phronesis and the Common Home

In Socrates' account of the ascent from the first home, the *eikon* of the cave began to change its meaning when it became clear that some will leave the cave to live in the realm illuminated by the sun and others will refuse to leave it even though there is nothing to prevent them from doing so. By compelling Glaucon to descend into the darkness of the sophists' dreamworld, Socrates shows how the cave inhabited only by those who refuse to leave it differs from the cave described as the first home. In order to continue the differentiation of the cave *eikon*, it remains to account for the life of those who prefer the realm illuminated by the sun to the cave of the perpetual prisoners, those who, like the philosopher, would rather be "on the earth, a hireling of another," than rule over "all the perished dead" (516d; *Odyssey* 11.484-91). They dwell in "the common home of the others [*ten ton allon xunoikesin*]" (520c). This is the term Socrates uses to describe the realm that is neither the first home nor the Hades ruled by sophists.

The "common home" is the realm inhabited by all those open to the good in some way. It is shared by all those who would leave the first home behind and the philosopher capable of guiding their ascent. It too is a cave, but only the philosopher recognizes it as one. The geometrical thinker believes it to be a cave as well, but his understanding of it is mistaken. The geometrical thinker might imagine that he is capable of leaving the common home. He might even imagine that he need never return to it from the heights of his ascent. And yet he never leaves it. The common home is a cave only to the true philosopher when he descends, as he must, after attaining the end of the ascent to which the others in the common home aspire in their various ways. Even though his eyes never become accustomed to the darkness of the perpetual prisoners' cave, they easily become accustomed to the darkness of this sunlit cave. When they do, it is evident to him that the common home is a realm in which a life of *phronesis* is possible.

When Socrates snatched Glaucon from the darkness of the sophistic dreamworld and dragged him quickly toward the most brilliant light of the good, hoping to instil *phronesis* in his soul, Glaucon disappointed him again by being unable to follow the ascent past a certain point. Socrates expresses his disappointment in the manner in which he continues the discussion (517c–e). He now asks Glaucon not to wonder (*me thaumaseis*) that those who have ascended to the good are not willing to engage in "human affairs [*ta tou anthropou prattein*]." The human affairs in which true philosophers are unwilling to participate after their descent are those of the common home. Socrates explains that the souls of philosophers ever feel the upward urge and yearning to live above. They long for divine contemplation (*theion theorion*), or the purifying contemplative ascent of the soul toward the divine good. It is nothing at which to wonder (*thaumaston*), he says again, that one such man, returning to human affairs from the heights of his ascent, would appear graceless and extremely laughable or absurd (*sphodra geloios*). Glaucon agrees, believing that he has understood Socrates. He neither wonders about it nor thinks it strange. But to what has he agreed? He has agreed that the true philosopher would be laughable because of his poor vision. Once again, he comes close to considering Socrates a laughingstock because he assumes, for some reason, that the philosopher's eyes can never become accustomed to the darkness of his human surroundings. Perhaps he assumes this because he believes that the contemplative thinker can only descend to the cave of ignorant perpetual prisoners; perhaps he assumes it because he is unwilling to accept that the philosopher is a better judge of things, especially of human affairs, than is the geometrical thinker. Socrates has something to say in reply to Glaucon's slight. Before considering his reply, however, it is necessary to discuss his initial remarks in greater detail.

Socrates says the human affairs to which the true philosopher returns from his divine contemplations are not disputes about the good, but disputes about justice (cf. 505d). How does the philosopher fare in such disputes? He has seen justice itself in his ascent to the good (cf. 432d), and justice, in its most complete sense, is the virtue that orders his soul and his actions. The philosopher is the most just man; his *phronesis* allows him to judge truthfully the justice and goodness of men and their political associations and to act justly in giving every man his due. But Socrates says the philosopher would appear graceless if he were compelled to contend, "in courts or elsewhere," about the images (*agalmaton*) and shadows of justice and that he would be thought ridiculous if he were compelled to dispute how these things are understood by those who have never seen justice itself.

Socrates implies that those who have never seen justice itself are the vulgar, who would also refuse to be led toward it in any way. The vulgar undoubtedly understand the images and shadows of justice defended in courts or elsewhere in a way different from those who are not vulgar. Furthermore, disputes about justice in which the vulgar participate are undoubtedly different from those in which they do not. Perhaps the philosopher might be able to lead others who are neither vulgar nor philosophers toward some understanding of justice itself if the vulgar could be prevented from disrupting or even ending the discussion. The philosopher can speak prudently and persuasively to the others about what is just and good. If they are open to his persuasion, they will overlook his apparent lack of grace. Socrates leaves open the question of how those who are neither vulgar nor philosophers understand the images of justice they see—for instance, in the *nomoi* of their *polis* and in the examples provided by just men. He speaks instead about the images and shadows themselves. The images are neither said to be phantasms nor ikons, but *agalmaton*, honored images or perhaps even gifts for the gods. The images and shadows are not justice itself; but then, they cannot be. However, some of them may be seen to represent justice well enough if judged with *phronesis*.

Socrates is compelled to discuss and dispute images of justice in a court in the *Apology*. If Glaucon had accompanied Adeimantus and Plato to the trial or if he had been one of those sitting in judgment, he would have seen that Socrates does not consider all 500 of the men of Athens trying him to be perpetual prisoners or vulgar men. Meletus, who brings the charges, is vulgar. He is said to be a very insolent and unrestrained man (*hybristes kai akolastos*). On his own he need not be feared because he is prevented by the greater strength of the law from laying hands on Socrates and killing him. Meletus will have his way, however, if the prejudice (*diabole*) and envy (*phthonos*) of the many allows it (26e–28b) or, more precisely, if the prejudice and envy of 250 other men allows it. Why would such men envy Socrates if not for the justice and goodness of his soul, evident even to them? Socrates is far from graceless and ridiculous in his own defense. And he is certain that if it were not for the requirement that capital trials be completed in one day, he would persuade most of the jury of his innocence (37a–b). As it is, a good many are persuaded. Although they may never have seen justice itself, these men are able to recognize an *eikon* of justice when it is shown to them by the philosopher.

Two votes are taken by the court, the first to decide guilt or innocence and the second to decide between the death penalty and a suitable fine. There are only three ways in which men might combine their two votes. Socrates addresses all three groups in his remarks. Those who voted for his guilt and his death have been led to their decision by his clever and sharp accusers (*deinoi kai oxeis;* 39b). This is hardly a description of Meletus. It is, however, a description suited to several men mentioned by Socrates who have formed the prejudices of the many and whom the vulgar favor over Socrates: Aristophanes, a *philotheamones* of sorts; and the sophists Gorgias, Prodicus and Hippias. Those who voted first for Socrates' acquittal and then for a fine are either 220 or 221 in number. Socrates speaks to them all as friends (*philoi*) and says without irony that only they are worthy to be called judges (*dikastes*), though none of them are philosophers or are likely to be found in the circle of those who listen to his discussions with others (39e–40a). There remain those who voted for his guilt and a fine. Since 279 or 280 considered him guilty and at least 251 voted for his death, those voting for his guilt and a fine number twenty-nine at most. These men probably voted against Socrates in anger because he did not behave shamefully in making pitiful appeals for mercy before the court (34b–35c). Perhaps many of those who voted for his death also did so because they were shamed or made resentful by his justice and goodness. The many who voted for his death are perpetual prisoners of a dreamworld. The many who did not are open to his persuasion, to various degrees. They were roused from their sleep by his sting (30e–31b) and in their wakefulness were liberal enough for Socrates to judge them his friends.[11]

In his remarks to Glaucon, Socrates also says the philosopher is prevented from ascending and compelled to discuss and dispute images of justice "elsewhere" than in courts. He is referring to the very discussion he is having with Glaucon and the others. By making such a reference while asking Glaucon if he agrees that the philosopher is graceless and even ridiculous when engaged in disputes about justice, Socrates indicates something of what he thinks about Glaucon. Glaucon is of two minds about philosophy and the philosophic life. He would compel Socrates to participate in a lengthy discussion about justice and injustice. This reveals that he is, to some extent, open to what Socrates has to say. And yet he would also compel Socrates not to exceed what he considers to be the proper boundaries of such a discussion. This reveals that, at times, he believes Socrates to be too graceless or laughable to participate in a serious discussion of important human affairs.

Glaucon has had many opportunities to hear what Socrates has to say about justice and the good. Socrates now settles accounts with Glaucon about who is truly graceless and laughable (518a-b). He tells Glaucon that if a man were intelligent (*noun*) he would remember that there are two "disturbances" or movements of the eyes that cause temporary blindness: the movement from light to darkness and the movement from darkness to light. Glaucon experienced both in the extreme when Socrates compelled him to descend into the sophists' dreamworld and then dragged him forcibly toward the good. And yet Socrates must remind him of what he should have learned from his experiences.

Socrates tells Glaucon that if a man were intelligent he would not laugh unthinkingly at a soul unable to discern things, as if its condition were necessarily perpetual and evidence of its ignorance and vulgarity; rather, he would first observe or determine which of the movements between darkness and light the soul had undergone before judging it happy or pitiable in its condition or its life. Socrates does not remind Glaucon explicitly of his imprudent judgment in considering all men except true philosophers, as he understood them, to be pitiable (516c). He also does not remind him explicitly of the many movements from darkness to light in the ascent from the first home. Socrates speaks of only two such movements, in order to compare himself to Glaucon.

Socrates says the anonymous intelligent man—perhaps the one to whom he is recounting the entire dialogue—sees one soul coming from a brighter life and unaccustomed to its surroundings, and another coming from the deeper dark of ignorance (*ex amathias pleionos*) into a greater brilliance. The intelligent man would understand the first soul described as an image of Socrates' return from his purifying ascent to Glaucon's company, and the second as an image of Glaucon's inability to attain a vision of the good after having been dragged toward it from the dream-world. Only if they are taken in this way do Socrates' next remarks become understandable, for he then says the first would be judged happy in its experience (*pathos*) and its life, while the second would be judged pitiable. If the intelligent man wanted to laugh, his laughter at the expense of the second soul would itself be less laughable than his laughter at the expense of the first. Socrates laughs at Glaucon and thinks him pitiable in his condition, though not without also making a joke at his own expense. He does not consider Glaucon ignorant, however, or merely clever, and speaks to him as a friend worthy of some degree of honor. Glaucon thinks Socrates' remarks a very fair or measured statement (*mala metrios legeis*), perhaps because both souls appear equally laughable to him. It is, in truth, measured and fair: Socrates and Glaucon have now laughed at each other twice each.

The discussion now takes a different turn. Socrates now begins an explicit account of some of the lessons of *phronesis* that Glaucon should have learned from the preceding discussion. Socrates' use of imagery seems to have been lost on him. By speaking plainly, Socrates almost manages to convince Glaucon of the truth of what he says. However, Glaucon again hesitates and resists Socrates' persuasion.

The first thing discussed is the nature of *paideia* (518b–19b). Socrates had begun his account of the ascent from the first home by asking Glaucon to compare his understanding of "our nature in its *paideia* and *apaideusia*" with the one he would present in an *eikon* (514a). He now states explicitly that *paideia* is not what sophists and geometrical thinkers—and perhaps even Glaucon—believe it to be, that is, the placing of demonstrable knowledge (*episteme*) into a soul that contains none. Socrates says the soul possesses an indwelling power. The soul of every human being is educable by nature, and may be led to see what is evident. The whole soul, including the instrument with which the soul learns, the *nous* (intellect) or *logon* (rational part), must be turned around (*periakteon*) from that which comes into being and passes away to that which *is* and to the brightest part of that which *is*. Glaucon accepts Socrates' suggestion that the brightest part is the good, but only because he has not been reminded that the good itself is beyond being (cf. 509b–c). Education is thus the art (*techne*) of "turning around" a soul (*periagoge*) or moving it from darkness to light until it reaches the end toward which it is being directed.

The proper exercise of this art requires that the educator possess the virtue of *phronesis*, not only because it is a *techne* and hence governed by *phronesis*, but also because the educator must attempt to lead souls toward the good in order that they might be healed of their *aphrosyne* and acquire *phronesis*.

Socrates next discusses *phronesis* explicitly. *Phronesis* is the most divine (*theioteros*) of the soul's virtues, he says. In comparison, the other virtues of the soul, as they are called, are like those of the body; that is, they are like those produced by habits (*ethoi*) and practice (*askesis*). Without *phronesis*, therefore, even virtues such as courage, moderation, and justice are like shadow-paintings (*Phaedo* 69a–c) or are akin to Aristotelian moral virtues (*Nichomachean Ethics* B).[12] Socrates then says that if the indwelling power of the soul to attain *phronesis* is turned away from the direction of its ascent in education, it is not lost but becomes something useless and harmful. It becomes cleverness. Men commonly said to be bad (*poneron*) but also wise or smart (*sophon*) do not have poor vision. Their "little souls" have a keen or shrewd vision that is compelled to serve vice. A proper education, beginning in childhood, would attempt to prevent the turning away of a soul toward things of the body by freeing the soul from the "leaden weights" of bodily pleasures (cf. *Laws* 644d–45c). Glaucon accepts the good of moral virtues. However, moral virtue alone cannot prevent the soul from refusing to ascend toward the good, and bodily vices cannot be said to be the cause of a soul's imprudent cleverness. Socrates passes over this without comment, but it is evident from what he has said already that a soul's intellectual cleverness will come to be ruled by bodily desires alone as a consequence of its turning away from what is necessary for it to attain prudence and good judgment.

The philosopher's *phronesis* is his measure of human affairs. Socrates now turns to discussing human affairs explicitly before returning with Glaucon to the city in speech. He describes how a *polis* ought to be ruled, and in particular how true philosophers ought to rule in *poleis* (519b–21a). Socrates first says that neither those without education (*apaideutous*) and experience in truth (*aletheias apeirous*) nor those with nothing but education or study to the end (*dia telous*) will ever govern a *polis* adequately. Neither is capable of ruling properly because neither has attained *phronesis* and consequently neither can judge things or act properly. The former have no single goal or aim (*skopon*) in living to direct all their actions "on their own account or in public"; they do not follow truth and aim at what would bring them *phronesis* (cf. 517c). The latter cannot recall the end that illuminates everything they study, and are in danger of becoming as blind to it as those who turn away from it. If they prefer study to all else, believing that enough of it will eventually bring them *sophia*, and do not recall that the end of their study is to acquire *phronesis* along with *sophia*, they will be unwilling, if not incapable, of engaging in actions of any kind. They will believe they have been transported to the Isles of the Blessed (*en makaron nesois*) while still alive.

Socrates says no more, and need not, about those lacking education. Instead, he tells Glaucon that the "best natures [*beltistas physeis*]" must be compelled to undertake the greatest study. Their souls must ascend to a vision of the good if they are to become true philosophers. Any of them who cannot attain this end may rightfully be called prisoners of a cave even if their prison seems as splendid to them as the Isles of the Blessed. The true philosopher does not imagine that he need not learn to judge things properly and act in the world, as if he were already dead. He ascends beyond the dark cavern inhabited by the perpetually studious in order to descend again and rejoin other men. Because the soul's vision of the good is not a permanent state and because the philosopher who ever experiences the upward urge remains a mortal, he must descend and continue to live among other men, "those prisoners" who cannot follow his ascent to its end. Philosophers are not gods. They must go down again among other men and share their labors and honors, no matter whether they are of lesser or of greater worth.

All things short of the good may be said to be part of one cave or another. But to which cave does the true philosopher descend? He goes down to the world illuminated by the light of the sun, the common-sense world, in which the labors and honors of others are not entirely pitiable and laughable. He spends his time among the others of the common-sense world attempting to educate them by turning their souls around toward the light and leading them as far as they are willing to follow. However, the philosopher lives not only in the common-sense world, but also in a particular city. He does so without being of that city entirely, but those with whom he shares labors and honors are also not entirely of their city. They too may be able to ascend from its particularity in some way. It would be imprudent of the philosopher to believe them all to be prisoners of their city because they cannot follow him along the entire way toward the good itself. Some of them live and work in the light of the sun; others live perpetually in a dreamworld ruled by sophists. No particular city is entirely a dreamworld. The vulgar and those they hold in honor may predominate in a city, but it is possible for someone born in that city to turn his back to them and leave the darkness of their cave. No city will be entirely a dreamworld in broad daylight unless the vulgar succeed in killing not only the philosopher, but everyone whose eyes have been corrupted in any way by the sun.[13]

Socrates tells Glaucon that if the best natures among the guardians of the city in speech are to become true philosophers, they must be compelled first to ascend to the end of the greatest study and then to go down again among "those prisoners" in the city (519c–20b, 539e–40c). Glaucon's immediate response to this is to consider the requirement that the guardians put aside their studies an injustice. Evidently, a life of study that never succeeds in turning the soul toward that which illuminates all objects of study is for Glaucon a better life than one in which the philosopher must prudently share in the labors and honors of others when his soul is not ascending in divine contemplation. In responding to Glaucon's objection, Socrates first speaks generally about *nomos*. *Nomos* is not concerned that any kind or class (*genos*) in the city should fare exceptionally well. It attempts to bring this about for the whole city by harmonizing and adapting the citizens to one another by means of persuasion and compulsion. *Nomos* attempts to produce a community (*to koinon*). The attempt may fail to attain its end unless a philosopher rules or somehow establishes the *nomoi* and the citizens and inhabitants are willing to follow his persuasion (cf. 473c–e, 499b–c, *Laws* 722d–23b). All particular cities fail to attain the end guiding *nomos*, but it would be imprudent to judge them all to be equally bad as a consequence of their failure. They do not fail because they are governed by regimes (*politeiai*). All cities require government. They fail because one *genos* comes to predominate in the *politeia* and rules the rest of the city in its own interest. Judging the failure of a particular city to attain the end of *nomos* requires a prudent look at the natures of the *genos* that rules and the *genoi* that are ruled. In accord with these general remarks about *nomos* in all cities, it is not unjust that the guardians of the city in speech not be allowed to live the life that seems best to Glaucon. They must become truly just and prudent in order that their city might fare well by becoming a harmonious community through their rule.

Socrates then tells Glaucon that the city in speech and all "other cities" have one other feature in common besides their aspiration to attain the end of *nomos* (520a–b). Philosophers in them are not eager to pay the debt for their upbringing to the regimes that rule them. They "grow up spontaneously [*automatoi emphyontai*]" against the will of regimes, and it is justice (*dike*) that a nature that grows by itself (*autophyes*) is not eager to pay off the price of its rearing to anyone. Philosophers do have some debts to pay off, however, and it would be an injustice for them to refuse. They do not become philosophers automatically and by themselves, though they may be said to do so by nature. Not even plants grow automatically and by themselves. They require nourishment and sunlight (cf. 509b, 510a, 516a, 532a–d). Philosophers are obligated in some way to their parents and families, their companions and friends, and their teachers. However, it is somehow not fitting for them to share in the "labors" of their city; in other words, it is not fitting for them to hold political office in the regime, even though they may be compelled to do so at some time. Philosophers are just; they have "seen" justice itself. The justice of any particular regime can only be an image or shadow of justice, and it may even be a *phantasma* held in honor by the vulgar. The philosopher does not disdain all political offices because the understanding of justice is equally a *phantasma* in all regimes. His soul is compelled to act with *phronesis* by its vision of the good. He must act with courage, moderation, justice, liberality, and truth (cf. 402b–d, 485a–87a, *Phaedo* 114a–15a). He may not be able to do so within the constraints of any political office. But there is no reason why he cannot do so with his parents, family, companions, friends, and teachers, and in general in all his actions on his own account or in public.

A substantial portion of Socrates' answer to the objection that the guardians will be done an injustice if they are compelled to live a life that does not seem best to Glaucon is addressed to the guardians themselves, and only indirectly to Glaucon (520b–21a). Socrates is compelled to address them, not Glaucon, about the descent from the good with *phronesis* because it can be assumed that they will attain the end of the greatest study (540a–b). However, he also addresses them rather than Glaucon because he has something to say to all philosophers in all cities. Socrates says:

"Down you must go [*katabateon*] . . . to the common home of the others [*ten ton allon xunoikesin*]" (520c; cf. 327a), the common home that is neither the first home nor the sophists' dreamworld. Each philosopher descends from the vision of the good with *phronesis* and is thus able to judge others in the common world, the world of experiences in common that all men inhabit. He has seen the truth of the beautiful (*kalon*), the just (*dikaion*), and the good (*agathon*). Once habituated to the light in the common home, he will be able to see far better than the others. The same would not be true if he had descended into the darkness of the sophists' dreamworld (cf. 516c–17a). He will know what each of the images (*ta eidola*) in the common home is and of what it is an image. He will be able to judge whether an image is an *eikon* or a *phantasma*, and how distant it is from the truth he has seen.[14]

The philosopher will be able to judge political things clearly as well. Socrates says that cities now are governed (*oikesetai*) as in a dream (*onar*) by men who fight one another over shadows and form factions for the sake of ruling, as if it were a great good and perhaps even the greatest good. Such men are vulgar and pitiable. Socrates calls them beggars, men starved of the good on their own account (*peinontes agathon idion*) who go to public things (*ta demosia*) thinking they will be able to grasp or seize it there. When rule becomes the object of war among such men, the war—a civil war within the *polis*—destroys these men themselves and the rest of the city as well (*kai ten allen polin*). But who comprises "the rest of the city"? Not the vulgar and the pitiable. The rest of the city is comprised of all who are not starved of the good on their own account and who can be said to despise the life of seeking political offices when it is a war for rule. They are those whose souls the philosopher judges to be open to the good in some way and thus those whose conditions and lives could be deemed happy if the war among the vulgar did not threaten to destroy the *polis* itself.

With this description of how cities now are governed, the differentiation of the cave *eikon* reaches its final stage and the most explicitly political of Socrates' caves appears. Cities are located in the realm called the common home, but Socrates does not describe the political realm *per se* as a unique type of cave within a cave. It is the dreamworld of factional political conflict threatening to destroy the *polis* itself that is a cave within the common home. Human beings do not live alone in the common home, they live in

common. They live together in cities, and cities require govern-
ments. It is possible for cities to be well governed and to aspire to
the end that guides *nomos*. Such cities are no more caves than is
the common home itself. However, when beggars starved of the
good come to predominate in a city and the war among such vulgar
and pitiable men threatens all other men and even the *polis* itself,
then the *polis* becomes a unique cave. It can best be described as
the cave that results when the perpetual prisoners who inhabit the
sophistic dreamworld come to predominate in a *polis* within the
common home.

When the cave called the first home in Socrates' account was
differentiated into the cave resembling Hades inhabited by perpetual prisoners and the common home that is a cave to the philosopher, it seemed that those who lived in the realm of sophistic
darkness and those who lived in the realm illuminated by the sun
had nothing to do with one another. Now it is clear that all human
beings, even the perpetual prisoners, dwell in the common home.
The perpetual prisoners are vulgar and pitiable precisely because
they deny that they see what is before their eyes and evident to all
human beings. They refuse to admit that they dwell in the common home. They turn their souls away from it and imagine instead
that they live happily in a world of their own construction. Their
souls are dead and the cave in which they imprison themselves is
Hades to all reasonable human beings. However, the spiritually
dead and the spiritually living continue to live together in the
same cities in the common home. They cannot live together in
peace. The spiritually dead cannot tolerate anyone whose eyes see
clearly, for they know what it is they refuse to see and they refuse
to be reminded of it in any way. They would compel everyone to
become a perpetual prisoner. If everyone lived in their cave, they
would be able to ridicule the ruined eyes of all those who have
come from the sunlight and to kill anyone who attempted to
return to it. In order to do this, the perpetual prisoners would rule
the *polis*. Their vulgar aspirations threaten all reasonable men
and even the life of the *polis* itself.

Socrates' final cave—the dreamworld of factional political conflict within the common home—and the first home most resemble
one another. The account of the first home and the ascent from it
can be understood as Socrates' description of *paideia* within contemporary Greek *poleis* governed as in a dream by the vulgar and
pitiable. Their predominance within and rule of Greek *poleis*

makes "strange prisoners" of all reasonable human beings "from childhood" (514a, 515a). They attempt to deny the truth of what is evident to all "by nature" in the common home (515c). They even attempt to deny that *paideia* is the *techne* of turning around a soul (*periagoge*) toward the light of the good, claiming instead that it is the sophistic skill of placing knowledge into a soul that contains none, comparable to a magical ability to put sight into blind eyes (518b–c). The first home is Socrates' final cave, as it appears "from childhood." The final cave is the first home brought into the light of the common home. Neither, however, is a description of the political realm *per se.*

Socrates does not summarize for Glaucon what may be learned by a prudent man about human affairs from the account of the longer way. He concludes this part of his discussion with Glaucon by stating a simple truth about political things. He says a city will be well governed (*eu oikoumene*) if those who hold office are not eager to do so, but rather take up their obligations dutifully or from necessity (*anagke*) even though they would prefer to be minding their own business. A city governed in this way would be free from faction. And the more those who held office disdained holding office, the freer from faction and better governed the city would be. Consequently, the more those who rule are eager to rule, that is, the more the vulgar look in public things to seize hold of the good they themselves lack, the worse a city will be. The truly rich must rule if a well-governed city is ever to come into being. They are the rich, not in gold, but in the wealth of a happy man—a good and prudent life (*zoes agathes te kai emphronos*). The man who least desires a life of political offices is the true philosopher. He prefers to live the greater part of the time—or as often as it is possible for a mortal to do so—in what Socrates calls the "purer realm [*en toi katharoi*]," the realm in which the soul is purified. The rule of philosophers would be best, if the others would accept them. The worst rule would be that of the man who is indistinguishably a sophist and a tyrant. He would believe himself to be the measure of all that *is* and would seek to be the sole master of all vulgar perpetual prisoners, whom he would have do his bidding in killing anyone whose eyes have been corrupted by the light of the sun. However, there are many others who are not philosophers, nor sophists or tyrants, nor vulgar.

Socrates now asks a few questions to determine whether or not Glaucon has learned anything from his more explicit discussion of the lessons of *phronesis* (521b). He asks Glaucon if he can name any life other than that of true philosophy (*ton tes alethines philo-sophias*) that disdains political offices. Glaucon replies that he cannot. Socrates reminds him that those who are not lovers of ruling—he does not say those who are philosophers—must be drawn to holding public office in order to prevent "rival lovers" from fighting (*hoi ge anterastai machountai*). Once again he asks Glaucon: Who would he compel to take office other than those who are most prudent (*phronimotatoi*) and have a life that is better than the political life? No one else, he answers. Glaucon believes that no one but the true philosopher, as he understands him, can be said to be happy or to live a good and prudent life. However, the most prudent man would not answer the question as Glaucon does. He would answer it with more liberality (*eleutheria*).

Cities and Caves

My interpretation of Socrates' account of the longer way has been intended, in part, to demonstrate that it is wrong to consider *the* cave as a single and concrete, albeit imaginary place or thing, and doubly wrong to consider it as an allegorical description of either the political realm *per se* or the political circumstances of Plato's Athens. When sufficient attention is paid to the drama of Socrates' discussion of the good with Glaucon, it becomes evident that anything from which it is possible for the soul to turn around toward a more brilliantly illuminated thing, or toward the source of illumination itself, may be said to be enveloped in the darkness of a cave. All things short of the soul's illumination by the good beyond being are part of one cave or another. However, all caves are not thereby the same. The caves without immediate public or political substance and consequence are described in Socrates' three ikons of the sun as the offspring of the good, the divided line, and the ascent from the first home toward the sun and the good. To the point in the discussion at which Socrates asks Glaucon to recall the first home, Socrates' primary concern is to account for the good as the perfect measure of all things. As the discussion proceeds, he explains how the good is the perfect measure of all human affairs through the *phronesis* of the true philosopher. This is done by means of a differentiation of the initial cave *eikon*. The account of the ascent from the first home is differentiated into the cave resembling Hades inhabited by perpetual prisoners and the sunlit common home that is a cave to the true philosopher. The final cave in Socrates' account with explicitly political substance and consequence is the dreamworld of factional political conflict within the common home. It explains how the first home is not a place apart from the realm illuminated by the sun and the good, but is a dreamworld of the spiritually dead who turn away from the common home without thereby being able to leave it.

The cave disputed by most Plato scholars is generally reconstructed from Socrates' descriptions of the first home and the Hades of perpetual prisoners (514a–17a). If the legitimacy of such an esoteric technique of reconstruction is accepted, then the drama of the dialogue is lost and with it any chance of understanding what Socrates' evocative references to caves, darkness, light, ascent, and descent are intended to reveal to Glaucon. The reconstructed cave then seems to be an allegory for the political realm composed by an idealist, if not a political idealist. In fact, the various caves of Socrates' account of the longer way are part of his criticism of idealism and political idealism and his defence of the *phronesis* of the true philosopher. The only textual basis scholars may have for confusing the first home and the cave of perpetual prisoners is Glaucon's tendency to do the same thing. However, Glaucon's imprudent judgment of Socrates' meaning cannot be cited as evidence of Plato's idealism. Plato had no intention of describing "every city" or the political realm *per se* as a Hades of perpetual prisoners. Had he wished to do so, he need not have written the account of the longer way with such subtle and difficult imagery. He need only have referred to the *Odyssey*. There are many caves and darknesses mentioned in the *Odyssey*. The one that would have best suited such a purpose is the darkness in which the Kimmerians lived. The Kimmerians were not dead souls. They were wretched mortals who lived and governed themselves in total darkness on the shores of Hades (*Odyssey* 11.14–19). The land and the city of the Kimmerians are never mentioned in any of Plato's dialogues.

The political consequences of Socrates' account of the longer way are not exhausted by his description of factional political conflict in the common home among beggars starved of the good. The prudent man who returns to the common home from the upward way has the ability to judge the justice and goodness of every city and man. It is Socrates' judgment that cities now are governed as in a dream by beggars starved of the good, but this is a judgment neither of all cities nor of all men. How then does he understand cities in which the vulgar and pitiable do not predominate or rule? There are a number of indications given throughout his account.

All human beings dwell in the common home, the realm of human affairs. They dwell together, sharing in each other's labors and honors in some way, and they are neither pitiable nor laughable for doing so. They are educable. They recognize, if their souls are open to the good in some way, that *paideia* is possible and necessary if human beings are to heal the *aphrosyne* of their souls. The basis of their education is a regimen of moral virtue that allows *phronesis* to develop. Since the common home is illuminated by the sun and the good in several ways, and since souls may move from darkness to light and light to darkness in several ways, human beings will engage in disputes about justice and the good. These disputes need not lead to war within or among societies or cities. Cities comprised of various *genoi* can be peaceful if they are governed in accord with *nomos*. *Nomos* attempts to produce a community (*to koinon*) by harmonizing and adapting human beings to one another by means of persuasion and compulsion. It prevents any *genos* from ruling in its own interest. Factions of "rival lovers" formed for the sake of seizing rule, therefore, need not come to predominance in cities. A city governed according to *nomos* would exclude such beggars from office. It need not be a victory-loving or honor-loving regime, an oligarchy, a democracy, or a tyranny (544c–d; cf. *Laws* 712d–13a). If those who shared in the wealth of a happy man—a good and prudent life—were compelled to take up offices even though they were reluctant to do so, their city would be, to some extent, well governed, just, and good. It would have as its ends friendship (*philia*), liberality (*eleutheria*), and *phronesis* (*Laws* 693c–e).

It remains to be determined how Socrates would judge the *kallipolis*. Is it a unique type of cave or is it no more a cave than any city in the common home? Is it the *paradeigma* of a just and good city or are there injustices to be found within it that make it a likeness of the dreamworld in the common home? Now that the account of the longer way and its political consequences has been concluded and the relation of justice, *phronesis* and the good has been clarified, these questions may be addressed explicitly.

4 EDUCATING THE GUARDIANS ABOUT THE GOOD

THE ACCOUNT OF THE LONGER WAY around to the most beautiful look at things is complete, and it is now evident why Glaucon's ways would never lead to this end (435c–d, 504a–b). The original has been seen, and it is now possible to determine whether images of it are ikons or phantasms.

The soul's vision of the original, the good itself, gives it *phronesis*. In comparison with the truly just soul, all other souls said to be just are but images. In particular, the image of a just soul constructed by Glaucon's methods of discussion is a phantasm. It is the likeness of a phantastic likeness, since its original is the city in speech that was assumed to be the likeness of a truly just soul before Socrates gave his account of the good. The city in speech is not perfectly good (*teleos agathen*). There is injustice to be found within it, more injustice than the practice of justice with *phronesis* would find acceptable. Thus, the city has not been properly founded (427c–e). The soul constructed as a true likeness of such a city would not take the good itself as its *paradeigma*. It would be unjust and unsound, a phantasm of the truly just soul. The city in speech is a phantasm of justice itself, but it is a true image of the common opinion that justice is the minding of one's own business. The just soul constructed with Glaucon's methods is a phantasm not simply because it is the likeness of a likeness, but because it is the true likeness of a true likeness of a false original. A city that was properly founded, well governed, just, and good would be a true likeness of the just and prudent soul that takes the true original as its *paradeigma*.

The tests proposed by Socrates for justice and injustice in Glaucon's city are now complete (427c–e, 434d–35a).[1] The city and the soul resembling it are as different from justice itself as something seen in the distance differs from something held in the hand. Both are founded on an opinion concerning justice that is itself unjust. To use Socrates' own metaphor, both are sticks grasped in the dark while hunting in the thicket for justice itself. The tests are complete, but the dialogue is not. The two sticks proved useful, for when rubbed together they burst into flame and illuminated the longer way. However, now that the *paradeigma* of the truly just soul has been described, the city in speech must be refounded in its light. It must become a *paradeigma* in speech of a good city (472d–e).

Socrates now returns to Glaucon's city and gives an account of the higher education of the guardians who will rule, showing Glaucon how they can be led toward the good. The guardians are not yet true philosophers. At best, their souls are ordered according to the sketch (*hypographe*) of *sophia, andreia, sophrosyne,* and *dikaiosyne* given by Socrates as part of his strange method of testing Glaucon's city (427e–28a). Their wisdom appears strange, for they do not possess the *euboulia* of *phronesis* (428a–29a). Such strange wisdom does not result in justice—not in justice as a virtue of one's own soul, nor in the ability to recognize justice and injustice in others, nor in the ability to act justly on one's own account or in public. Consequently, such wisdom is said to be governed by justice in the sketch of the virtues. Without subordinating their wisdom to justice, the guardians would be incapable of judging and acting justly at all. But the justice governing their souls has now been shown to be as strange as their wisdom and its subordination to a lesser virtue. In comparison with the truly just soul governed by *phronesis,* the souls of the guardians are unjust.

In order to lead the guardians away from injustice, Socrates describes a long and difficult course of study intended to make them both *sophe* and *euboulos.* If they wish to become true philosophers, they must undertake every kind of learning with insatiable *eros,* and love all of wisdom, practical as well as theoretical (474c–75c). But more than this, Socrates says at the conclusion of his account of their *paideia,* those who have proved themselves best, both in deed and in knowledge, must at last be brought to the end (*telos*) before they will be allowed to rule (540a–b). They must ascend where Glaucon would not ascend. They must be compelled to turn upward the light of their souls (*ten tes psyches augen*) and look toward the source of all light. The most sunlike part of the soul must look toward the sun that is its cause and of which it is a reflection. They must see the good itself (*to agathon auto*) from which the sun is descended. Those guardians capable of attaining it must use their vision of the good—not their studies—as the *paradeigma* for the right ordering of their souls and their city for the rest of their lives. Those who are incapable of attaining it will not be allowed to rule. They have no *phronesis* and consequently will not be able to rule others, or even themselves, justly and honorably. Only those capable of practicing justice with *phronesis* will be able to recognize the injustices in the city, as it has been founded, and act to eliminate them, refounding the city if necessary. Their rule would make the city *sophe* and *euboulos*, a *paradeigma* of a truly good city.

Socrates begins the discussion of the guardians' *paideia* cautiously. He initially avoids speaking explicitly to Glaucon about the good beyond being, but he brings the discussion around to it gradually. Socrates does this not to avoid Glaucon's ridicule (cf. 509b–c), but because he remains hopeful that Glaucon will be able to follow his persuasion. He begins by asking Glaucon if he would like to know how the guardians who will govern his city might come into being and how one can lead them up to the light just as some men are said to have gone from Hades up to the gods. Glaucon is most eager to know (521c). Glaucon evidently does not recall that he has already been told of these things several times. He could have learned of them through his own experience—the experience that Socrates' account of the longer way was intended to invoke in his soul—had he not sought to possess certain knowledge of such things. In particular, Glaucon seems to have learned nothing from his own recent journey from Hades to the gods, the journey he took when Socrates sent him down to the dreamworld of the perpetual prisoners and then dragged him quickly along the entire way leading to the divine good.

Socrates' use of imagery was lost on him. Indeed, Glaucon does not recognize that in his question Socrates alludes rather explicitly to the journeys of Odysseus, who traveled to Hades and returned to the world of mortals before coming to dwell with the goddess Kalypso on her island and almost becoming an immortal himself.[2] If he had caught the allusion, he might have understood that the entire account of the longer way, and particularly of the ascent from the first home, was an odyssey intended to capture his imagination. The entire account was a series of ikons of the good, and the imagery for the account was taken from the *Odyssey*. Socrates assumed that since Glaucon was spirited, clever, and a lover of honor (*philotimias*) like Odysseus, he would have more than a passing familiarity with the *Odyssey* and its interpretations. By using Homeric imagery of caves, light and darkness, ascent and descent, Socrates hoped to persuade Glaucon to follow him toward the good and see the journey through to its homecoming. In other words, Socrates hoped Glaucon would want to be as clever as Odysseus in avoiding the many follies that sent all of his companions to Hades, and therefore that he would be clever enough, if he followed the persuasion of the ikons, to see the good itself and return to the common home with *phronesis*. But Glaucon would not ascend beyond geometrical thinking. The *aphrosyne* of geometrical thinking is comparable to the *aphrosyne* Odysseus overcame on Kalypso's island. He became so enraptured by Kalypso that, at times, he imagined he might become an immortal on her island. And yet he wept because he longed for his homecoming. The Olympians then ordered Kalypso to release him from her dark and hollowed caverns. Like Odysseus, the true philosopher has his homecoming. He returns from the upward way to the common home with *phronesis*. The best guardians of the city in speech must also avoid the folly of geometrical thinking and have their homecoming. However, Glaucon is only eager to hear how they will ascend to what he believes are the divine heights of *paideia*.

Odysseus has his homecoming in the *Republic* as well as in the *Odyssey*. When Socrates recounts the story of Er's journey to the beyond for Glaucon at the conclusion of the dialogue (614b–21b), he tells him that each man must seek, even to the neglect of his other studies, the greatest study of learning how to distinguish the good life from the bad. He then describes for Glaucon a "pitiable, laughable and wonderful" sight: how each of the many souls in the beyond chooses a life for itself. The blame belongs to him who chooses; god is blameless, he says. In Er's story, Odysseus's soul was by some chance the last to choose. Its memory of former labors, endured both in the Trojan War and during the voyage home, enabled it to recover from its love of honor (*philotimias*), and it chose the life of a common man who minds his own affairs (*bion andros idiotou apragmonos*). It was as happy to choose this life last as it would have been to choose it first, for in this life it would always be able to keep to the upward way and practice justice with *phronesis* in every way.

The discussion of the guardians' *paideia* is not without the mythopoetic imagery of the longer way and Er's story. It seems to lack any such imagery as it begins, but it concludes with a reformulation of the ikons of the longer way, intended once again to educate Glaucon about the good and aid him in his homecoming.

The discussion begins with an explicit description of philosophy by Socrates (521c–d). He says philosophy is the turning around (*periagoge*) of the soul from a day that is like night to the true day. The day that is like night is the visible realm, illuminated by the sun. The true day is the intelligible realm, illuminated by truth, the light of the good. Socrates adds that philosophy is also the way up to the being or essence of things (*tou ontos ousa epanodos*), a journey the soul must undertake in response to its *periagoge*. He then asks Glaucon to consider which studies have the power (*dynamis*) to bring about the soul's *periagoge* by leading it from becoming (*tou gignomenou*) to being (*to on*). He does not mention the good in his question. The soul's movement from becoming to being, therefore, is not a complete description of the way of philosophical ascent, even though it does describe a necessary condition for the final *periagoge* of philosophy to occur. The realms of becoming and being both originate in the good, but in different ways. The realm of becoming does not originate in and is not illuminated by the realm of being, just as the visible realm does not originate in and is not illuminated by the intelligible realm. Studies that turn the soul from becoming to being or from the visible to the intelligible realm, revealing a greater clarity or illumination by truth to it, are intended to give the soul an insight from which it may recognize the transcendent source of all illumination. If a soul never attains this insight—if it, for example, never gives up the belief that it intellects the objects of intellection without the medium of truth originating in the good—it would not be a truly philosophical soul. It would be unable to turn around from a day that is like night to the true day.

Socrates also describes what philosophy is not. It is not the twirling of a shell, he says, referring to a warlike game in which a shell with black and white sides is spun to determine which of two groups of players will flee and which will give chase. This is an amusing reproach to Glaucon's belief that the difference between philosophers and nonphilosophers is absolute and unbridgeable. If his belief were true, only war or warlike games between the two groups would remain. However, the common home of all human beings, though often torn by wars between rival lovers, is not necessarily a home that is hostile to philosophy and to philosophers. Philosophers are neither at war with the common home itself nor with those common-sense souls who dwell in it without ever ascending to the heights attained by philosophers. And insofar as the common home may come to be dominated by rival lovers whose souls are closed to the good, philosophers are not the only ones who seek to prevent wars among such men from destroying the peace.

Socrates then says that the studies he and Glaucon are seeking to lead the guardians toward the life of philosophy "mustn't be useless to warlike men" (521d–e). Glaucon finds this suggestion attractive. He is not immediately aware of its significance. Socrates does not intend the guardians' studies to make them into greater and more efficient champions of war, but precisely the opposite. In the *Phaedo* Socrates says, "War and revolution and battles are due simply and solely to the body and its desires." As long as the soul is governed by the body it will be drawn toward war and battle, and it will have no chance of attaining its object, the truth, by way of philosophy (*Phaedo* 66b–e). The guardians' studies must turn them away from bodily things toward the truth, just as Odysseus's labors during his journey home turned him away from honor-loving and victory-loving (cf. *Republic* 545a, 550b, 581b). If the guardians are to have truly just souls, they must be as free as possible of the bodily compulsion to war and battle; if the city they rule is to be a truly just city, it must also be as free as possible of faction and warfare.

Earlier in the dialogue Socrates and Glaucon had agreed that there is no greater evil for any city than that which splits it apart and makes it many, and no greater good than that which binds it together and makes it one (462a–b). They had also agreed that the city in speech should be arranged according to the Pythagorean proverb that friends should have all things in common as far as possible (423e–24a; 449c–d). This would make the city one. Indeed, Socrates calls this proverb "the track of the good" in the city (462a). However, the city in speech has been founded according to the track possibly left by justice, that is, according to the opinion of justice as minding one's own business (432d–33b). This opinion cannot make the city one. It acts only to split it apart and make it many. In his discussion of the *Republic*, Aristotle goes so far as to say that the city in speech "must necessarily be two cities in the one, and these opposed to one another," because the guardians constitute "a sort of garrison" within the city (*Politics* 1264a24–27). The studies now described by Socrates as being useful for the warlike guardians are intended to rid them and their city of all evidence of the false track of justice. By becoming truly just themselves, they will be able to refound the city properly, making it as free as possible of faction and warfare. When the entire city, not merely a part of it, is ordered according to the proverb that friends should have all things in common as far as possible, the city will be as free as possible of injustice. It will no longer be split into parts and ruled by a faction. Instead, it will be well governed, just, good, and one.

The discussion between Socrates and Glaucon, though friendly, is not free of contention. Throughout the account of the guardians' education Socrates continues his attempt to persuade Glaucon that geometrical thinking prevents the ascent of the *psyche* and *nous* to the highest things. The way up of dialectic and the way down of geometrical thinking, as well as the consequences of the two ways, are contrasted at every opportunity.

There are several studies described by Socrates collectively as "a prelude to the song itself"—a prelude, in other words, to dialectic (521d). The first given in the discussion is the study of number, which is common to all sorts of arts (*technai*), thought (*dianoiai*) and sciences (*epistemai*). The next few studies concern number and things seen: geometry, both plane and solid, and astronomy. The last study of the prelude concerns number and things heard: harmonics. There is no epistemological argument to be made in explanation of the sequence of studies Socrates describes.[3] Each of them is shown in the discussion to be able to lead the soul upward or downward. Each of them may turn the soul toward becoming (*genesis*) or being (*ousia*). And if any one of them is successful in turning the soul around toward being, it may eventually lead the soul toward the highest and most eudaimonistic part of being.

Glaucon initially finds these studies attractive because they may be turned downward toward becoming and bodily matters. They are all useful for war and warlike pursuits. Calculation, plane geometry, and astronomy can all be of use in military campaigns (522c–e, 525b, 526c–d, 527d). Even harmony is described provocatively as the torturing of strings (530e–31c). Socrates is attracted to these studies only because they may serve as a prelude to dialectic by turning the soul upward, away from such bodily matters. If studied in this way, they have no usefulness for war (cf. 527a–b). In particular, he does not say that solid geometry is militarily useful, even though its further development as a field of inquiry depends on some city taking it up, honoring it, and being charmed by it (528a–c). As well, dialectic, the song itself, has no usefulness for war. Its only usefulness for a soul is as a means of ascent toward the good. Glaucon and Socrates are attracted to these studies for different reasons, but Socrates remains hopeful that Glaucon may be turned around as their discussion proceeds. When Socrates comes to discuss dialectic with Glaucon, he even risks ridicule by suggesting that the greatest tests of courage are not to be found on battlefields but in severe studies that are not concerned with bodily things (534b–c, 535b). If Glaucon were truly courageous in all things, he would be unafraid to turn away from the study of war and follow Socrates on the long and difficult upward path (cf. 357a).

The guardians' education begins with the seemingly lowly business of distinguishing the one, the two, and the three. Number and calculation, if studied rightly, may draw them toward being (*ousia*) and intellection (*noesis*). There are some objects of perception that summon the *nous* into activity by requiring it to judge whether the object is one or two or whether it can be both at once (522c, 523a–c, 524b). All human beings experience this summoning to *noesis* or wonder. Some are compelled by it to turn around toward the contemplation of what *is* (524e–25a). The guardians, therefore, must begin with calculation (*logistike*) and stay with it until they come to contemplate the nature of number by *noesis*. Socrates says that such study will turn their souls around from becoming (*genesis*) to being (*ousia*). But they must not rest content in the contemplation of *ousia*. Their studies must also compel them to use the *nous* itself on *aletheia* itself (525b–c, 526a–b). By saying this, Socrates once again suggests to Glaucon that *noesis* must ultimately be directed toward the *agathon* beyond being. The suggestion becomes clearer in the ensuing discussion of geometry.

Socrates tells Glaucon he is concerned only with the portion of geometry that enables the *nous* to distinguish the idea of the good and the *psyche* to see the most eudaimonistic part of what *is*. Again, he does not mention the good itself explicitly, but it is evident that the best part of geometry leads toward this end (526d–e). Socrates now asks Glaucon to agree that such study is for the sake of knowing what always *is*. Glaucon misunderstands Socrates' remark and answers with an assertion that geometrical knowledge *is* such knowledge (527b). He gives no indication in this assertion of any understanding or conviction that the study of geometry might be undertaken for the sake of something higher than acquiring geometrical knowledge. In order to determine if Glaucon is once again unable to ascend beyond geometrical thinking, Socrates asks him to clarify what he has said. Glaucon is emphatic in his reply, claiming that geometrical knowledge is, to the greatest extent possible, productive of philosophic understanding (*philosophou dianoias*). He believes that it directs upward what is turned downward and draws the soul toward truth.

Socrates does not accept Glaucon's equation of geometry and philosophy. He immediately draws out the consequence of this equation for the city in speech. It is at this point in the dialogue that Socrates names the city. He says: "to the greatest extent possible, the men in your *kallipolis* must be required never to neglect geometry" (527c). The city, as it has been founded, is Glaucon's city, not Socrates' city. It is his beautiful (*kalos*) *polis*, or rather a city that seems beautiful to him because its guardians and rulers will believe, as does he, that geometrical knowledge is the highest type of knowledge. The city is not beautiful to Socrates. He names it the *kallipolis* for a different reason. To Socrates, it is Kalypso's *polis:* a seemingly beautiful city that is, in truth, a cavernous prison from which all those who desire a homecoming must escape. Socrates descends to Glaucon's city in order to assist its guardians to escape. He enjoins them to study geometry not because he wishes them to become geometrical thinkers, but rather because such study may turn their souls around toward the *agathon*. If they cannot escape the type of thinking that is suited to the city as it has been founded, they will never become true philosophers and the city will never become a *paradeigma* of a good city.

Glaucon again agrees emphatically with Socrates that there is a complete difference between a man who is devoted to geometry and one who is not (527c). He does not hear the irony in Socrates' remark. Glaucon takes it to refer to an absolute difference between men who possess certain and demonstrable knowledge of all that *is*—as well as the power he believes such knowledge brings—and men who do not. The former are intelligent and honorable, the latter ignorant and vulgar. The former study geometry to perfect their intellect, but also because it is useful for war. Since the difference between the ignorant and the intelligent is absolute, they must be at war in every city—even in the *kallipolis*. But Socrates' remark refers to an absolute difference between the geometrical thinker and the true philosopher. The former's soul is turned downward, and the latter's soul upward. What is more, Socrates says he is amused by Glaucon's fear of the many. It is evidently difficult for Glaucon to realize that there is an instrument in everyone's soul with which the truth may be seen, an instrument that can be perfected through the study of number, geometry, and the like. If a soul has not been blinded or destroyed by other practices, it will undoubtedly benefit from such study (527d–e). The study of geometry for its usefulness in war is one of the practices that blinds a soul.

Socrates now forces Glaucon to retreat in the discussion. It seems there is something he does not know about geometry. He believes enough has been said about it and is now eager to discuss astronomy and its usefulness for war. Socrates points out that Glaucon has proceeded from the study of plane surfaces to that of solids in motion without considering the geometry of solids at rest (527d, 528a–b). Socrates' discussion of this study and its contemporary neglect is quite puzzling (528c). No city honors it, he says, for it is difficult. It cannot be undertaken without a good supervisor, but such a man is hard to come by. And when he is found, the geometers will not listen to him. To overcome the arrogance of such geometrical thinkers, the supervisor must persuade "a whole city" to join in supervising its study and in honoring it. The many at present would despise such a study, not because their understanding has been influenced by the geometers, but because no one yet has given them an adequate account of its usefulness. Socrates does not say that it is useful for war. Indeed, his silence about it suggests precisely the opposite. He concludes his account by saying that it would not be surprising if such a study came to light in a city, since its charm will cause it to grow despite the many obstacles it faces.

Where is the whole city that will take up and honor solid geometry under the guidance of a supervisor like Socrates, ignoring the arrogant opinions of geometrical thinkers and practicing it not for its military usefulness but for its ability to turn the soul around toward the highest things? Such a city is described in the *Laws*. By means of Socrates' odd account of solid geometry, Plato is explicitly contrasting Magnesia and Glaucon's *kallipolis*. Magnesia is the city Glaucon's *kallipolis* might become if its guardians succeed in escaping the bonds of geometrical thinking.

The following discussion of astronomy and harmony, the last two studies comprising the prelude to dialectic, is somewhat comic, which may be only fitting after such a serious and provocative suggestion. Socrates' reproach of Glaucon's initial vulgar praise of astronomy leads Glaucon to make amends by proposing, immodestly, to praise it as he believes Socrates would. He does poorly in acting the Socratic. Glaucon claims that "it's plain to everyone that astronomy compels the soul to see what's above and leads it there away from the things here" (529a). But looking up with the eyes is looking down with the soul. Glaucon is simply befuddled (529b–c; cf. *Theaetetus* 174a–b). Socrates explains to him that the visible heavens must be studied as *paradeigmata* of the true movements that are grasped by *logos* and *dianoia* alone. The true astronomer will be moved by how beautifully the craftsman of the heavens has fashioned his work. The proper study of astronomy, therefore, should aspire to this end. If it does, Socrates says, the soul's naturally indwelling *phronesis* will be converted from uselessness to usefulness (529c–30c).

Glaucon does not make the same mistake again when Socrates suggests they next speak of harmony. Instead, he has great fun ridiculing those who put "ears before intelligence." However, though the torturers of strings are laughable, Socrates must point out to Glaucon that he has erred in grouping the Pythagoreans with such men. He has confused the way up and the way down in a different way this time. The Pythagoreans are not guilty of studying sounds alone. They seek number in harmony. But they do not ascend beyond this study to consider problems in number (530d–31c). In other words, they do not study harmony in order to compel their souls to use the *nous* itself on *aletheia* itself (526a–b). Glaucon now calls a halt. He again accuses Socrates of speaking about something daimonic. Socrates replies: "Useful, rather . . . for seeking the beautiful [*kalos*] and the good [*agathos*], but useless pursued in any other way" (531c). The meaning of his reply is clear.

Socrates now performs the daimonic ascending song for which the discussion of the guardians' studies has been a prelude (531d–32d). The performance is intended to persuade Glaucon that dialectic, like harmony, is useful only in seeking the beautiful and the good. Dialectic's search is an upward journey or passage (*poreia*). In describing it, Socrates restates and reformulates two of the ikons presented in his account of the longer way: the sun as an offspring of the good (507b–9b) and the ascent from the first home (514a–16c). There is no mention of the divided line (509b–11e). Socrates spoke of dialectic in his account of the divided line without mentioning its relation to the good because Glaucon had objected to what he believed was daimonic hyperbole in Socrates' description of the good beyond being. Now Socrates speaks of dialectic without mentioning the divided line in order to explain what he had then been compelled to leave unstated. Unlike Socrates' initial account of the longer way, his performance of dialectic's song is not a dialogue with Glaucon. Glaucon must listen. And if he listens attentively, he will hear how the ascent from the cave toward the sun is completed by remembering that the sun is the offspring of the good.

The way up (*epanodos*) from the cave is a turning around from the cave's shadows to the idols (*eidola*) and light of the realm illuminated by the sun. The *eidola* of this realm are appearances of the things that *are*. In contrast, all things in the cave are shadows: the light of the fire, when judged in comparison with sunlight, is like a shadow cast by something else (*aposkiazomenas*); the manufactured artifacts used to cast shadows are themselves shadows of the *eidola* of the realm beyond the cave. Thus, the completely black shadows on the cave wall are shadows of shadows of a shadow. Someone who ascends to the realm illuminated by sunlight cannot immediately look at the animals and plants. These living things were not mentioned in Socrates' previous account, though human beings were. Here, human beings are not mentioned, though there is a human being attempting to see the flora and fauna. The shadows of existing things will be visible before their appearances can be seen directly. These appearances are themselves *eidola* of the things themselves, which cannot be seen with the eyes alone. The human being in the sunlight will first see the shadows of animals, then the animals, and finally the animals themselves. Before he may look at the stars themselves and the sun itself, and even before he may see the light of the sun, he must first see the divine phantasms (*phantasmata theia*) of these things in water. Sunlight reflected in water presents a distorted and thus phantasmic image of the sun. The sunlight itself is not distorted. Like the sun itself, it cannot be seen with the eyes. The image of the sun is a phantasm of it. The phantasm of the sun in water is divine, however, because it may lead the soul from the visible realm to the intelligible realm and eventually to the end of the intelligible realm (*toi tou noetou telei*). Sight attempts to see the animals themselves, the stars themselves and even the sun itself, but these things must be seen with the *nous*. The *nous* attempts to grasp each thing that *is* by *logos* and dialectic, which is the discourse of *logos* (*dialegesthai*). Discourse about the *ousia* of the things that *are* is not necessarily undertaken alone, but it may be if there are no companions available for such a dialogue. However, the soul's apprehension of the highest things requires a solitary or individual and silent ascent. Dialectic's ascent ends in the soul's apprehension of the *agathon* itself by *noesis* itself. The *agathon* itself, and not the *idea* of the *agathon*, is the *telos* of *noesis*. It is as distant an end for the *psyche* and *nous* ascending with dialectic as the sun itself is distant from all eyes turned upward attempting to see it.

Glaucon hears none of this; or rather, he hears the song but cannot follow it. He replies strangely, as if Socrates had said nothing, asking him to proceed now to the song itself and to discuss it as he had discussed the studies of the prelude. He asks, what are the power (*dynamis*), forms (*eide*), and ways (*hodoi*) of dialectic (532d–33a)? Evidently he would like dialectic to be as useful as he understood the studies of the prelude would be useful. For Glaucon, dialectic must be turned downward and have practical utility. It must be a power of applying forms in various ways. However, the practical end of dialectic's journey is not a utility that might appeal to a geometrical thinker; it is rather the virtue of *phronesis* that is a consequence of the soul's ascent. Socrates' reply to Glaucon's request is curt: "My dear Glaucon, you will not be able to follow me."

Socrates now turns to discuss the arts (*technai*) of the prelude again in order to show Glaucon that they too have the power (*dynamis*) to release and lead up what is best (*ariston*) in the soul to the contemplation of what is best (*ariston*) in the things that *are* (532d). Arts are generally directed downward to human opinions (*doxai*) and desires, to generation (*genesis*) and composition (*synthesis*), or to the care of growing and constructed things. Some arts, however, do dream about what *is*. Socrates explicitly names geometry and the arts following it in his previous account; he does not mention number and calculation, perhaps because they are found throughout all of the arts. Although these arts grasp something of what *is*, they dream about it because they use hypotheses without giving an account of them. All arts, if they are to be demonstrable, must use hypotheses, and all arts descend from hypotheses to practical ends. But there may be ascent from their hypotheses as well. Dialectical inquiry begins by taking up hypotheses (*tas hypotheseis anaipousa*) to the beginning (*arche*) itself.[4] The eye of the soul may be turned downward, and the soul may be buried in a bog of practical concerns governed by unreflective opinions and bodily desires. However, the arts of the prelude, along with dialectic, may turn the eye of the soul around and direct it upward. The soul would then no longer dream of what *is*, but see it with waking vision. Dialectic clarifies the hypotheses of the arts. Socrates proposes to use the term *doxa* (opinion) for the hypotheses of arts turned downward toward the barbaric bog. The hypotheses of the arts that assist dialectic should be called *dianoia* (thought). *Doxa* is darkest, *dianoia* is brighter, but brightest and most illuminated is knowledge (*episteme*). Socrates thus uses *episteme* to mean the dialectically clarified hypotheses of an art. Even the hypotheses of the arts of the prelude are not properly called *episteme* unless they have been taken up by dialectic (533b–e). The dialectical clarification of an art's hypotheses must affect its practice. The practice of a *techne* with *episteme* will obviously differ from the practice of it with *doxa*. The difference is that the former gives evidence of the practitioner's *phronesis*.

After giving a dialectical account of the soul's ascent from the first home toward the good and—in order that the arts would not thereby be misunderstood—a dialectical account of the role the arts may play in turning around a soul, Socrates now clarifies what he had previously discussed with Glaucon when he described the divided line. In the previous discussion Glaucon was asked to conceive of a line divided into segments representing the greater and lesser degrees in which the intelligible and the visible participate in or are illuminated by truth and subdivided according to the same proportion. The subdivisions of the segment representing the visible realm were said to correspond to certain objects of sight. Those of the intelligible segment, however, were said to correspond to two *pathemata* or affections of the soul: geometrical and dialectical thinking. At the conclusion of the account, Socrates persuaded Glaucon to list four affections of the soul in relation to the four line segments: *noesis, dianoia, pistis,* and *eikasia* (in descending order). The end of the account is at odds with what is said in the beginning and the middle. In particular, it reformulates the premises with which the account began in order to lead directly into Socrates' description of the ascent from the first home. Now Socrates takes up the previous conclusion and reformulates it again in order to emphasize the difference between geometrical and dialectical thinking (533e–34a).

Glaucon is persuaded to accept a new list of four *pathemata* corresponding to the line segments. *Episteme* replaces *noesis* as the first affection; the others remain the same. This is probably immediately attractive to Glaucon, since it seems to place the certain and demonstrable knowledge of highest things sought by geometrical thinkers in the highest position. However, this is not the significance of Socrates' change. He goes on to say that *episteme* and *dianoia* taken together are *noesis*, and *pistis* and *eikasia* taken together are *doxa*. The relation between the two aspects of *noesis* has been explained: the dialectically clarified hypotheses of *dianoia* are *episteme*. However, Socrates then says that *doxa* has to do with *genesis*, and *noesis* with *ousia*. In this simple statement, Socrates shows that the hypotheses of the initial division and subdivision of the line are unsound. The visible and intelligible realms do not correspond perfectly with the realms of *genesis* and *ousia*, even though both pairs of realms trace their origins to the good itself. The realm of *ousia* is not the realm of the ideas. *Ousia* is intelligible, but the ideas do not constitute the realm of *ousia*. So too, the realm of *genesis*, the opinionable realm, is not the visible realm. *Genesis* is visible, but the visible does not constitute the opinionable realm of *genesis*.

The nature of the soul's relation to *genesis*, *ousia*, and the *agathon* beyond *ousia* cannot be described adequately by referring to the relation of the eyes to objects of sight, or of the *nous* to objects of *noesis*, or even by referring to some speculative relation between vision and intellection. Socrates is no modern idealist. His discussions of the divided line provide no such epistemology, ontology, metaphysics, or phenomenology. What then are the ideas? Perhaps nothing more can be said about them than that they are the necessary hypotheses of *noesis* in the soul's relation to *ousia* and the *agathon*.

Socrates now tests Glaucon's geometry. He changes his description of the ratios or proportions of the divided line. If the main line segments are identified as A and B, in descending order, and the subsegments are A_1, A_2, B_1 and B_2, in descending order, then in Socrates' initial description of the line he says that A:B is the same as both A_1:A_2 and B_1:B_2. Socrates now says that A:B is the same as both A_1:B_1 and A_2:B_2. This demonstrates that he knows A_2 and B_1 to be equal for all possible ratios A:B where A and B are not equal to zero.[5] Glaucon does not notice the change in Socrates' description. He cannot go on, therefore, to consider what significance it might have beyond being a geometrical demonstration.

Why is the relation of *dianoia* and *pistis* constant? And what do the new pairings of *episteme* with *pistis* and *dianoia* with *eikasia* indicate about the soundness of the initial premises of the line's division? These obvious questions do not arise. Socrates even excuses Glaucon from considering the relative proportion of the segments corresponding to *noesis* and *doxa,* knowing that this would call into question Glaucon's assumption concerning the relative proportion of the main line segments in the initial division of the line. Socrates would like to be spared any more long arguments, especially since none of the arguments they have been through so far has succeeded in overcoming Glaucon's resistance to noetic ascent.

To conclude his reformulation of the longer way, Socrates briefly discusses *noesis* and dialectic (534b-d). A man has *nous* and is a dialectician if he grasps the *logos* of the *ousia* of a thing and can give a *logos* of it to himself and others. Insofar as a man is unable to do any of these things, he lacks *nous* in that proportion. A man may be said to know the good itself in a somewhat different way. He must be able to distinguish the idea of the good from all other things in a *logos,* and then he must go through the test of *ousia*— for the test of *doxa* is one of mere speech—coming through everything with the *logos* on its feet. Socrates gives no examples of how this might be done, but it serves as a good description of the manner in which he took the longer way with Glaucon. Socrates does not propose a name for coming to know the good in this way; nonetheless, Glaucon cannot deny that a man who comes through the test of *ousia* knows (*ouden*) the good itself. What of those who cannot be said to know the good itself as the true philosopher knows it, those who begin by grasping an *eidolon* of it? Since an *eidolon* may be an *eikon* or a *phantasma,* each of the various *eidola* grasped by men must be tested, with a philosopher's assistance, before this question can be answered. Socrates does not bother to discuss these things with Glaucon. He knows what Glaucon would say. He would say that all *eidola* of the good are *doxa* and not *episteme,* and that all those who hold them to be true dream throughout their lives and go to Hades before awakening. Glaucon agrees with Socrates, swearing by Zeus that this is indeed what he would say. He takes Socrates' playful remark too seriously and misses its humor.

This concludes Socrates' reformulation of the ikons of the longer way (531d-34d). The song itself, together with its prelude, will lead those guardians of Glaucon's *kallipolis* who are fit to be true philosophers toward the philosophic life. Throughout his account of their higher education Socrates has criticized the many ways in which geometrical thinking prevents the soul from turning around and ascending. The guardians must escape its bonds and leave the caverns of Kalypso's *polis* if they are ever to practice justice with *phronesis*. When they can be said to have *nous* and know the good itself because they have gone through the test of *ousia*, they will be able to return to Glaucon's city and rule it justly. They will then no longer be warlike men. They will have *sophia* and *phronesis*, and will therefore be truly just and courageous. Their prudent political judgment will enable them to recognize and correct the injustices of the city, as it has been founded. Their rule will "save the *polis* and the *politeia*" (536b).

It would now be a simple matter for Socrates to set down a law (*nomos*) outlining the education of the guardians, treating his discussion of the studies of the prelude and the song (*nomos*) itself as the law's prelude (cf. *Laws* 719e–20e, 722d–23d). However, there is more to be said before this may be done. Although everything he has said to this point is generalizable to all cities and regimes, if done with prudence, Socrates now explicitly discusses how philosophic studies ought to be taken up in any city. In doing so, he continues the discussion of *paideia* in a manner similar to his continuation of the account of the longer way. His reformulation of the three ikons is followed by a more explicit discussion of what Glaucon might have learned from them. The continuation of the account of the longer way was intended, in part, to explain to Glaucon how conflicts among the beggars starved of the good who now rule the *polis* threaten all reasonable human beings and even the *polis* itself. The continuation of the discussion of *paideia* is intended, in part, to explain to Glaucon how the manner in which philosophic studies are now taken up brings only dishonor, ridicule, and slander to philosophy "among the rest of men" (535c, 536a–c, 539b–d). Socrates says two things must be avoided: those who are unfit for philosophy should not take it up, and those who are fit for the philosophic life should not take up their studies improperly. If those fit for the life in all cities took up their studies properly, philosophy would be saved from disgrace. Moreover, the cities themselves would be saved if such just and prudent souls were somehow to come to rule them and if those who now rule as well as those now said to practice philosophy were somehow to be excluded from them (cf. 473c–e, 499a–c, and *Laws* 711d–12a).

Those who are not spiritually courageous and wholly lovers of the labor of difficult study are not fit for the philosophic life. True philosophers love all of wisdom, not just a part of it, and they have an insatiable *eros* for every kind of learning by which they might acquire wisdom (474c–75c). They will not be lame, therefore, in their love of the labor that comes with such learning, loving half of it while having no taste for the other half (535b–d). For example, a man is lame if he loves the labors of the body, such as gymnastic, hunting, and military training, but not the labors of the soul. He might also be lame if his love of labor were exclusively the opposite way. But since souls are far more likely to be cowardly in difficult studies than in gymnastic, it may be beneficial for those who love wisdom to be lame in bodily labors (cf. 496b–c). Above all, those who take up philosophy must not be lame when faced with the most difficult study, loving the half that descends but not the half that ascends, or loving the half that ascends while having no taste for the other half. A true philosopher is neither a geometrical thinker nor a contentious eristic.

Socrates also says that those with maimed souls should not take up philosophy (535d–e). A maimed soul is lame in a unique way. It is not lame concerning the labor necessary for philosophic study, but it is concerning *aletheia* and *pseudos*. A maimed soul will not approach *aletheia* because of its lameness in responding to lies in itself and in others. It seems to hate the willing lie because it becomes greatly angered when others lie in this way, but it finds its own willing lies merely difficult to bear. It is also content to receive the unwilling lie from others; it does not become angered when it is caught being ignorant in this way itself, but accommodates itself to its ignorance like a pig wallowing in mud. Such a soul is not a true lover of learning, listening, and inquiry. It cannot engage in serious dialogue, and so cannot participate in the dialectical ascent of philosophy guided by *aletheia*.

Those who are fit to take up philosophic studies should do so in the proper way (536d–37d). Calculation, geometry, and the like, the arts of the prelude, should be studied in childhood, but in a playful manner without compulsion. As they mature, some youths will demonstrate their dialectical natures by being able to integrate the studies they have undertaken without any particular order into an overview (*synopsis*). Any one of the arts of the prelude may lead a soul from becoming toward being and what illuminates being, enabling it to see how all of the arts are akin. As they become adults, some of the youths whose souls have been turned around will demonstrate, when tested with dialectic, that they are able to go to what *is* in itself (*auto to on*) in company with *aletheia*. They will take the test of *ousia*, which ultimately leads to the soul's vision of the good. The test begins with dialectical questioning. But the question arises, Who is fit to ask the questions? Only a true philosopher who knows both the way up and the way down and who has returned from the ascent on his feet would be suitable.

At present, those who are fit for the philosophic life and who would take it up in the proper way are questioned by sophists, not true philosophers. Sophists practice eristic, not dialectic. The youths they teach consequently become filled with lawlessness (*paranomia;* 537e; cf. 454a–b). To persuade Glaucon that such youths are deserving of sympathy or forgiveness (*suggnome*), Socrates tells him a story about an adopted child (537e–39d). A child taken from its parents and raised in another large, wealthy, and great family is more likely to honor and obey the parents and kin of this family—not neglecting their needs or saying or doing unlawful things to them—than he is likely to honor and obey the flatterers that are attracted by its wealth and greatness. If he comes to know the truth about his origins, and if he then cannot find his first parents, he will be more likely to honor and obey the flatterers than his family. But this need not always be the outcome. Socrates only says it is likely that he will be persuaded by flatterers and live by their ways, no longer caring for his adoptive family. If he is by nature kind and moderate (*epieikes*), however, this will not happen.

The story helps to explain the consequences of the improper and proper ways of practicing dialectic, and if Glaucon uses his imagination while listening to it, he might find that it also describes his own upbringing in Athens. Socrates explains that from childhood everyone is raised in certain convictions (*dogmata*) concerning the beautiful and the just that are honored and obeyed as one honors and obeys one's parents. These are a city's *nomoi*. If a city is large, wealthy, and great, flatterers will be drawn to it. Their flattery consists in presenting their knacks of giving pleasure to the body and soul as true arts (cf. *Gorgias* 462e–65e). The sensible and moderate man (*metrion*) will honor the ancestral things and will not be persuaded by such flattery. The convictions in which he was raised are more honorable. However, the sophists among the flatterers may question him about his convictions concerning the just, the beautiful, and the good, and they may refute with contentious eristic arguments any reply he might make. The sensible man then discovers that even the arguments given by the lawgiver of his city, the arguments upon which his convictions are founded, may be torn apart and destroyed by sophists. The parents who raised him no longer seem to be his true parents. But who are his true parents? If he cannot answer this question, if he cannot find his true home, he will most likely become dishonorable by living in the ways of the flatterers.

It is true that one's convictions concerning the highest things can be called into question as hypotheses. But in what way ought they be questioned and by whom? Eristic questioning destroys all hypotheses, no matter whether they are theoretical or practical, sound or unsound. Someone unaccustomed to such questioning will probably be unable to distinguish between the eristic destruction of all convictions and the dialectical questioning of theoretical or practical convictions to determine if they are sound or unsound in some degree. If he is unable to distinguish between them, he will abandon the convictions in which he was raised, after becoming convinced that no coherent account of them can be given. He will believe, wrongly, that he has no true home and will spend his time and money with the sophists he believes have enlightened him. But he does have a true home—two of them, in fact. The proper dialectical questioning of convictions about the highest things takes them up toward the things themselves. A true home can be found in the realm illuminated by *aletheia*, the light of the good, and anyone searching for it can find it easily with the assistance of a philosopher. On the way up, sound but previously unquestioned hypotheses can be given a proper foundation in speech, and unsound ones can be tested against sound ones. After returning home from the upward way, it will not be difficult to see what is truly worthy of honor and obedience, what is truly lawful and necessary. Someone who is by nature kind and moderate, and therefore open to the philosopher's persuasion, will not abandon his family. Instead, he will honor and obey his parents as it is fit for him to do, neither neglecting them nor treating them unlawfully. His parents gave him a true home by raising him to be sensible, moderate, and wise enough to see that the ways of the flatterers are dishonorable.

The study of dialectic does not produce lame or maimed souls incapable of honoring what is honorable—sophistry does. Those of the young whom the sophistic flatterers enchant with the power of eristic disputation seem at first to be like puppies. They enjoy pulling and tearing with words all those who approach them. However, their seeming play soon has serious consequences. They quickly fall into a profound disbelief of what they formerly believed. They become filled with *paranomia* and dishonor their true home. Socrates says sensible men will not be willing to participate in such madness (*mania*), and Glaucon agrees (539b–d).

Socrates concludes the account of the guardians' *paideia* by stating the law (*nomos*) for which the preceding discussion has been a prelude. He began the prelude to the law with a description of what philosophy is and how it can be useful to warlike men, that is, to lovers of honor and victory such as Glaucon (521c–d; cf. 545a, 550b, 581b). He ended the prelude with a description of what sophistry is and how it produces dishonorable eristics, or lovers of victory in argument, who consider themselves wise even though they participate in madness. And within the context provided by the contrast between philosophy and sophistry, he discussed the *technai* of the prelude to dialectic that, together with dialectic (the song [*nomos*] itself), will serve as the basis of the best guardians' *paideia*. The prelude and the *nomos* may serve as the basis for *paideia* in any city. In the city in speech, however, the prelude and the *nomos* will enable the guardians to escape the bonds of geometrical thinking without thereby participating in the madness of eristic disputation and suffering its dishonorable consequences. They must first escape the bonds of Glaucon's city if they are to become true philosophers and return to their home with *phronesis*. Indeed, the *nomos* will compel them to do so.

According to the *nomos*, the studies of the prelude are to be taken up by children in play and pursued without any particular order until they are twenty (536d–37b). Twenty-year-olds are then to be tested in order to determine which of them have dialectical natures. Those who do will be able to integrate their studies into an overview (*synopsis*). They will understand the kinship of their studies to one another and to the nature of things (*tes tou ontos physeos;* 537b–c). In other words, the souls of some will have been turned around (*periagoge*) from becoming (*tou gignomenou*) to being (*to on*) by their playful studies (521c–d). But this is far from enough for them to be considered true philosophers. They must be tested again by the power of dialectic (*tei tou dialegesthai dynamei*) when they are thirty to determine which of them is able to go to being itself (*auto to on*) in the company of truth (*aletheia*). The soul's *periagoge* must be continued as an ascent to *aletheia* (537c–d). Those who pass this test must then devote themselves exclusively to strenuous participation in argument (*epi logon metalepsei*) between the ages of thirty and thirty-five (539d–e). Each of them must learn how to grasp the *logos* of the *ousia* of a thing and how to give a *logos* of it to himself and others (534b–d). In other words, each must become a good butcher, one whose *logos* cuts at the joints of *ousia* (*Phaedrus* 265e; *Statesman* 287c). They will then be reasonable (*metrioteros*) and will not bring dishonor to the practice of discussion (539c–d; cf. 538d). But this also is far from enough for them to be considered true philosophers.

According to the *nomos*, fifteen years of testing by dialectic to determine if the students will stand firm in argument must be followed by fifteen years of testing by experience (*empeiria*) to determine if they will stand firm or give way in practical matters. Socrates tells Glaucon that the thirty-five-year-olds "will have to go down into that cave again for you, and they must be compelled to rule in the affairs of war and all other offices suitable to youth" (539e). Socrates is now explicit in calling Glaucon's city a cave. Perhaps Glaucon should wonder at this, since he believes that the city is a *kallipolis* because of the intelligence of its rulers and the manner in which they rule. What is more, Socrates suggests that Glaucon's city is a cave, not only to true philosophers, but even to the thirty-five-year-old guardians who might one day become true philosophers. It is not a cave to them simply because it is a *polis*. If they do not wish to be lame in any way, they will not consider fifteen years of service in political affairs as a barrier to the philosophic life (535d). They will love all the labor necessary to attain such a life and not merely half of it; they will also love all of wisdom, theoretical as well as practical, not merely half of it. They are required, therefore, to spend an equal amount of time being tested by dialectic and by experience in order to prove themselves "in every way best at everything, both in deed and in knowledge" (540a). The *nomos* requires it of them in order that they might eventually acquire both *sophia* and *phronesis*. Glaucon's city is a cave to the thirty-five-year-olds because their *paideia* has made them sufficiently reasonable to recognize that it has been founded according to the methods of geometrical thinking. It may seem to be a just city and the likeness of a just soul to Glaucon, but they do not find it beautiful. They must be compelled to return to it. Compulsion is necessary, not simply because the city is not beautiful to them, but especially because they must rule in the affairs of war. Their *paideia* has made them sufficiently reasonable to recognize that a city must be as free as possible from faction and warfare if it is to be truly just (462a–b). Glaucon's city is a cave because it has been founded on an opinion about justice that splits the city apart instead of binding it together and making it one. In this, it resembles the final cave described in Socrates' account of the longer way: the dreamworld of factional political conflict within the common home.

The fifty-year-olds who prove themselves "best at everything, both in deed [*en ergois*] and in knowledge [*epistemais*]," are not yet true philosophers. They have *episteme* because they have participated in the dialectical clarification of hypotheses for fifteen years, but *episteme* and skill in dialectic together are not enough. They also have *empeiria* because they have participated in political offices for fifteen years and have shown themselves to be as firm in withstanding being pulled in all directions by practical matters as they are in withstanding being pulled in all directions by eristic disputation. *Episteme* and *empeiria* together are not enough either. The fifty-year-olds are admirable. They are not lame or maimed in any way. But they must now ascend where Glaucon would not ascend. Socrates tells Glaucon that they "must at last be led to the end [*telos*]." They must be compelled to lift upward "the brilliant beams of their souls . . . [and] see the good itself [*to agathon auto*]." They will then be able to use the *agathon* as the *paradeigma* for ordering the city, other men and themselves for the rest of their lives (540a–b). Neither their *episteme* nor their *empeiria* nor both taken together is sufficient for this. Nor is their skill in dialectic the means of their ascent. Fifteen years separate their mastery of the practice of discussion and the ascent. Dialectic and *empeiria* both prepare them to come through "the test of *ousia*" with the *logos* on its feet (534b–c). However, the ascent to the good beyond *ousia* requires a further compulsion, and the ascent itself can only be described in an evocative image. Perhaps all that can be said is that there is no profit or usefulness in *episteme*, dialectic, and *empeiria* in the absence of the good (cf. 505a).

Socrates' description of the *nomos* compelling the best guardians to ascend and return emphasizes the differences between the preparations necessary for the ascent, the ascent itself, the *telos* toward which the *psyche* and *nous* ascend, and the consequences of the ascent and return for the *psyche* and *nous*. Only those guardians who are able to see the good and take it as their *paradeigma* in all things on their return home can be said to be wise and prudent human beings. Only the guardians who have acquired *sophia* and *phronesis* in this way will be true philosophers capable of ruling the city in speech, indeed any city, justly.

The guardians who will rule Glaucon's city are not like those who "spend their time in education continuously to the end" and who therefore are not "willing to act" because they believe they have "emigrated to a colony on the Isles of the Blessed while still alive" (519b–d; cf. 540b–c). But how will they rule? Socrates says that they must take the good as a *paradeigma* for ordering the city, other men, and themselves. This indicates that the city and all those who live in it are in need of reordering. The city has not been founded with the good as its *paradeigma;* it is not a just and good city. The rule of the best guardians, therefore, should be the means by which the city and all those who live in it will become just and good. But Socrates says little to describe the nature of their rule. He says only that they spend most of their time in philosophy, and that each drudges in politics, ruling for the city's sake, when his turn comes to do so. Drudging in politics, even in the highest political office, does not seem to be an effective means for reordering the city. Indeed, the *politeia* seems to place limitations on what may be done by the ruling guardians. Their rule is not absolute: they must rule for the city's sake, and they must act within the limitations of office. They are not similarly restricted, however, in how they may act when they are spending their time in philosophy. What is a philosophic life? It is not an emigration to the Isles of the Blessed while alive. It is a life lived with *sophia* and *phronesis* in the common home. The best guardians do not spend their time in continuous study when not in office. They live among other human beings, sharing in their labors and honors, and attempting to turn their souls toward the good. Their practice of justice with *phronesis* in every way is *paideia* for all other human beings. The good will therefore be a *paradeigma* for the city and other men when the best guardians rule and reorder the city through *paideia*.

Socrates says only one thing about *paideia* in Glaucon's city at this point in his account: the best guardians must always educate others like themselves to take their place as guardians of the *polis* (540b). They guard the *polis* with *paideia,* not by drudging in politics. Drudging in politics is a necessity, but it does not require a philosopher's wisdom to do it well. Indeed, anyone who is not starved of the good on his own account can do it well. A city will be well governed if all those who are not beggars can be compelled to hold office in turn, even though they would prefer to mind their own business (520d–21a). *Paideia* is another matter. It should be entrusted only to the wise and prudent. The well-educated are the only ones capable of guarding the *polis* in this way. The well-born cannot guard the *polis* properly unless they become well educated.

How should *paideia* be administered in Glaucon's city to ensure that the well-educated will always rule it? There is a difficulty in the *nomos* describing the guardians' education that Socrates identifies explicitly—the distribution (*dianome*). He reminds Glaucon that older men were selected as rulers of the city in the discussion preceding the account of the longer way (535a–c). However, the subsequent discussion of how the guardians will be led to see the good compels them to adopt a different selection. Socrates says all the great and numerous labors belong to the young, not the old. The studies described as part of the prelude to dialectic must therefore be put before children, not adults. When calculation, geometry, and the like are taught without compulsion to children in their play, it is not difficult to discern "what each is naturally directed toward" (536c–37a). But this suggests that the difficulty in the administration of *paideia* pointed out by Socrates is not restricted to the education of the guardian class alone. There is no reason that the *nomos* describing the guardians' education cannot be extended to all children in the city. The only thing to prevent it is the belief that the city, as it has been founded, is perfectly just and good and that any change will make it less just. But Glaucon's city is not just. It may be changed for the better. Furthermore, the guardians who have become true philosophers must reorder the city, using the good as their *paradeigma.* They rule the city through *paideia,* and the most important purpose of *paideia* in the city is the proper formation of children to ensure that true philosophers will always be guardians of the *polis.* The reordering of Glaucon's city, therefore, may be brought about by means of a redistribution of the guardians' *paideia* to all children in the city. *Paideia*—not eugenics—would then determine the order of the city.

What would such a city be like? It would have the same *paideia* as Glaucon's city, but it would not be "two cities in the one, and these opposed to one another," with the guardian class constituting a "garrison" within it. This is how Aristotle describes the most important similarity and difference between the *kallipolis* and Magnesia (*Politics* 1264a24–27, 1265a6).

Glaucon says that Socrates' account of the guardians' *paideia* has produced ruling men who are wholly beautiful (*pagkalous;* 540c). They seem beautiful to Glaucon either because he imagines them to be men who live together on the Isles of the Blessed or because he imagines their rule in the city to be something more than drudging in politics. Perhaps they are beautiful to him because their knowledge and power both appear to be absolute. Socrates' account has produced guardians who are wholly beautiful, but not for the reasons Glaucon imagines. They are beautiful because they are true images of the good. The *psyche* and *nous* of each are turned toward *ousia* and *aletheia*, and they are open to the *agathon* beyond *ousia*. Each of them is truly *sophe* and *euboulos*, for each always keeps to the upward way and practices justice with *phronesis* in every way. Glaucon does not understand all that Socrates has said about *paideia*. If he did, Socrates would not have to remind him that his account applies equally to women and men—in other words, to all human beings. If Glaucon cannot recall this simple fact, then he probably cannot recall what Socrates said about the education of children. But Socrates does not remind him of the best manner of discerning what any child is naturally directed toward. Instead, he humors Glaucon's understanding of *paideia* by having him consider if all the things they have discussed are possible "in no other way than the one stated" (540d).

5 THE *TELOS* OF THE CITY

SOCRATES' LENGTHY DISCUSSION of the good and the guardians' *paideia* with Glaucon has reached an end, but Socrates and Glaucon understand the end of the discussion differently. Glaucon believes that Socrates has finally brought his account of the just city and the just soul resembling it to an end. As far as he has understood all that has been said, the discussion is complete (541b). In contrast, Socrates has taken the discussion toward an end by suggesting far more than Glaucon has understood about the manner in which a truly just soul and city would be ordered by the good. The discussion is not complete for Socrates. There remains more to be said, though perhaps not to Glaucon. The account of the longer way was given to show that the discussion of the just soul according to Glaucon's methods had produced nothing but an incomplete and misrepresentative sketch. The city constructed in speech according to the same methods is also nothing but an incomplete and misrepresentative sketch of a truly just city. It remains for Socrates to present an ikon that would reveal it to be a phantasm in the same way that the ikons of the longer way revealed the sketch of the just soul to be a phantasm.

Socrates suggests how the discussion might proceed toward its proper end when he tells Glaucon that the best guardians must be compelled to see the good itself and return to their city. Glaucon's city should be reordered in accordance with what has been said about the homecoming of true philosophers in the account of the longer way. But Socrates is reluctant to continue the dialogue. Glaucon has repeatedly shown himself unwilling to follow Socrates' persuasion, and he is now certain that the discussion of justice is over. Indeed, Glaucon is now so certain of his own understanding of justice that he readily agrees—only moments after Socrates had admonished him for being unable to recall that his account of justice in the soul applies to men and women alike—with Socrates' rather humorous suggestion that enough has been said about the city and the man (*andros*) like it (540c, 541b). Socrates is satisfied to bring their discussion to an end by raising the question of whether all the things they have discussed are possible in no other way than the one stated. The manner in which the question is presented and discussed with Glaucon is wonderfully ironic. In a few words, Socrates brings out the comic imprudence of Glaucon's political idealism without having Glaucon take offence at anything that is said, at the same time suggesting also how the discussion of justice in the city might proceed with someone more prudent and open to persuasion than Glaucon.

Have the things said about the *polis* and *politeia* been entirely daydreams (*hemas euchas*)? Are they not hard, but possible in a way? And are they possible in no other way than the one stated? When Socrates asks these questions (540d), Glaucon says he does not believe that the *kallipolis* is a daydream. It is both a perfectly just city and a possible city. If any existing city is to be perfectly just, the *kallipolis* must be founded within it. This would be hard to do, but there is no other way. To Socrates, Glaucon's city is a daydream. Like many daydreams, however, it can be seen to express a truth if it is not taken too seriously. It is a dreamlike *paradeigma* "laid up in heaven for whoever wants to see, and seeing it, to found it within himself" (592a–b; cf. 472d–e). Its foundation within the soul is hard, but possible, and it requires that its founder must want to see the *paradeigma* that the city's best guardians also want to see in order to become truly just (540a–b). Founding the *kallipolis* as a city on earth is another matter entirely. Earlier in the dialogue Socrates warned Glaucon that even if the city's possibility were granted, it might still be doubted that the city would be what is best (*ariston*). He said that the argument about the city's possibility thus seems a daydream (*euche dokei;* 450c–d). Glaucon never questions whether the city in speech is best. Its possibility and its goodness are identical for him (471c). Glaucon is daydreaming, therefore, even while he believes that he is thinking seriously about the question of the city's possibility. His daydreaming is not idle or harmless. Socrates understands its consequences because he knows why the *kallipolis* is not best: in its main features, it resembles the dreamworld of factional political conflict within the common home. If what has been said about the *polis* and *politeia* is ever to assist existing cities in becoming just and good, it will not be by way of founding the *kallipolis* within them. Any attempt to do so would be a great folly.

The way to justice begins when true philosophers (*alethos phi-*

losophoi), many or one, come to rule (*dynastai*) in a *polis* (540d). Glaucon believes that the best geometrical thinkers are true philosophers because they possess knowledge to the greatest extent possible of what *is*. He also believes that proficiency in geometry is not the only criterion for determining who is best among geometrical thinkers. Spiritedness and skill in warfare are also necessary (527b–c). The *kallipolis* is perfectly just because its *politeia* is the image of such a man, and because such men will always rule in it. In order for any existing city to become perfectly just, such men need only come to rule it as they might rule the *kallipolis*. This will undoubtedly require them to engage in war and battle with those now ruling the city. For Socrates, however, the true philosopher is not the most warlike geometrical thinker. He is the wise and prudent man whose soul is open to the good. His ability to practice justice with *phronesis* in every way makes him truly courageous. Such a man is the salvation of both the *polis* and the *politeia* (536b). What is more, he is the salvation of both existing cities and Glaucon's city. Socrates ends his account of how Glaucon's city will become truly just and good with the description of how true philosophers will come to rule it. He suggests how the account may proceed when he indicates that they will rule and transform the city through *paideia* and not through the *politeia*. Their *paideia* will even be the salvation of the *politeia* of Glaucon's city. The same is true of how true philosophers may come to rule in any existing city. They will not engage in factional political conflict. If they are to lead a city toward justice, they will rule it and its *politeia* through their *paideia*.

Socrates now describes what a philosopher or philosophers will do when they come to rule in a city. He says first that they will disdain (*kataphronesosin*) current honors and regard them as illiberal (*aneleutheros*) and worthless (540d). This should remind Glaucon that the true philosopher's judgment is governed by *phronesis* and that his judgments of what is honorable will therefore be tempered by liberality (*eleutheria*). It should also remind him of something else. The last time Socrates had used similar words, he asked Glaucon if he could name any life other than the philosophic life that disdains (*kataphronounta*) political offices. Glaucon had replied illiberally that he could not (521b). Glaucon has not changed his mind since then. He has not understood that Socrates' disdain for the factional political conflict and war fought among those who are beggars starved of the good does not extend to "the rest of the city" (520c–21a). All current honors in cities may be illiberal and worthless because the cities are ruled by those who believe that political power is the greatest good, but the lives of all those who inhabit the cities are not thereby equally worthless and pitiable. Some want no part of rule and are truly happy in their lives and conditions (cf. 516c–e). Glaucon continues to believe that the only worthwhile life is the one lived by the men who rule the *kallipolis*. All others are equally worthless to him. He cannot imagine that a true philosopher, as Socrates has described him, would disdain the life he holds most precious and consider it to be illiberal and worthless.

Socrates now turns from what philosophers disdain to what they judge to be honorable and worthy. They place the right (*to orthon*) and the honors coming from it above all else; they consider the just (*to dikaion*) to be greatest (*megiston*) and most necessary (*anagkaiotaton*); and they set their own city in order (*diaskeuoresoutai ten heauton polin;* 540d–e). The philosopher must have *phronesis* both in order to determine what is right and just and in order to place the right above all and make the just most necessary in all he does. He acquires *phronesis* by setting his own city in order, that is, by founding the city perhaps laid up in heaven within himself. Glaucon understands Socrates' remarks differently. Since he believes the *kallipolis* to be a perfectly just city, he takes Socrates to mean that philosophers make the just most necessary and set their own city in order by founding the *kallipolis* in existing cities.

The illiberal, imprudent, and even tyrannical nature of the seemingly harmless type of thinking that Glaucon associates with philosophy is readily apparent when consideration is given to how geometrical thinkers would rule a city. Such men say they disdain political office, but if they somehow get a free hand, they overcome their reluctance and rule over others with disdain. Their idealism quickly becomes political idealism. They assume that an abstract *paradeigma* of a perfectly just city can be derived from first principles and can then be established in a city by applying the methods of the productive *technai* to politics. In particular, Glaucon's guardians assume, as does Glaucon, that the order of the *kallipolis* is the perfect form to which the worthless matter of existing cities must be made to conform if they are to be just. If it were possible, this would be the greatest tyranny. Glaucon's geometrical thinkers are not true philosophers: they have no *phro-*

nesis or political *episteme*. Such men are unfit for political office because they are tempted by tyranny. They will not be allowed to rule in the city in speech. Socrates' remark about what philosophers do when they come to rule may have caught Glaucon's imagination; had he understood its implication for the *kallipolis*, however, he would not have found it attractive. When the best guardians return from their ascent with *phronesis*, they must "set their own city in order." In other words, the *kallipolis* is not in order and must be reordered if it is to become a *paradeigma* of a just and good city.

Glaucon would like to know how philosophers will set their city in order. Socrates replies to his question in a surprising way: all those in the city older than ten must be sent out to the country (540e–41c). Socrates had said previously that there will be no rest from ills for cities, indeed for mankind, until philosophers rule the cities or rulers adequately philosophize, and all those now pursuing one apart from the other are excluded from them (473c–d). It is necessary to exclude the political factions that fight for rule in cities and the sophists currently said to philosophize, but not all those older than ten in a city are either part of a political faction or members of a sophist's following. All "rival lovers" must be excluded, but "the rest of the city" need not be (520c–21b). All sophistic flatterers who corrupt the youth and bring dishonor to philosophy must be excluded, but "the rest of men," particularly those "who are at all sensible," need not be (537e–39d). Why does Glaucon accept Socrates' surprising reply without question? Perhaps he believes that all those older than ten, except philosophers, are equally worthless. Perhaps he imagines that the guardians of his city are sufficiently spirited and skillful in war for this to be possible as well as desirable. Perhaps he does not find the image of a few or even one man among many children displeasing (cf. 474d–75a). In any event, he takes Socrates seriously.

Socrates' remark is both playful and serious in ways that Glaucon does not understand. It is a playful demonstration of how comic Glaucon's imprudent political idealism can be. Socrates is obviously enjoying a joke at Glaucon's expense, since he knows how Glaucon will understand him. But his remark is also a serious demonstration of what would be necessary for the *kallipolis* to be founded in existing cities in the manner Glaucon believes would be most effective. A city that must be founded in this manner cannot be just. True philosophers would not set their city in order in this way. Finally, Socrates' remark is both playful and serious as a demonstration of what would be necessary for the *kallipolis* itself to become a truly just city. When true philosophers come to rule in the *kallipolis*, they will erase the sketch of the *politeia* drawn according to Glaucon's methods and make a new beginning of it with a clean slate (cf. 501a–c, 504a–e). They will make their city truly just and an ikon of the good by eliminating all the injustices of its order that are the result of its improper founding. In particular, they will change the distribution of the *nomos* outlining the guardians' *paideia* and raise all the children in the city according to it. This can be done without warfare or injustice of any kind because the *kallipolis* exists only in speech.

Once all those older than ten have been sent to the country, Socrates says, the philosophers will raise the children in their own ways and laws (*tropois kai nomois*), leading them away from the customs (*ethoi*) of their parents. He reminds Glaucon explicitly that this has been described previously (541a). Glaucon accepts without question the need for a complete reeducation of all children if the *kallipolis* is ever to be established in an existing city. He does not recall the discussion in which Socrates spoke of such things. Had he been reminded of Socrates' story about the adopted child (537e–39d), he might have hesitated a moment and reconsidered his understanding of Socrates' remarks. If the *kallipolis* is to be founded in Glaucon's way and a city's children are to be reeducated by the men he believes are true philosophers, then all of the children will suffer the fate of the adopted child. All will be taught to disdain their adoptive parents' convictions about the beautiful, the just, and the good. All of their parents' *ethoi* and *nomoi* will seem to be equally worthless to them. They will search for their true home, but they will not be able to find it because the men leading them away from their parents' ways are not true philosophers. Eventually, they will become filled with *paranomia* and will be incapable of honoring what is honorable. The *paideia* of Glaucon's guardians is sophistry. True philosophers are not sophistic flatterers who would turn all of a city's children away from what is honorable in order to determine which of them are the most spirited lovers of victory in war and eristic disputation. Their *paideia* is the turning around of souls. They take up the convictions of anyone open to their persuasion and lead them toward the true home: the realm illuminated by *aletheia*, the light of the good. All those educated in this way will not find it difficult to see what is worthy of honor and obedience, nor what is truly lawful and necessary, when they return home from the upward way. And if a sufficient number in a city are open to the ascent, then philosophers—either many or one—will be able to lead the city toward their own *tropoi* and *nomoi* by *paideia* alone.

Socrates brings the discussion to an end by telling Glaucon that the *polis* and *politeia* of which they have been speaking may be established (*katastasan*) quickly and easily in the way he has described. It will be happy (*eudaimonesein*) and will most benefit the people (*ethnos*) among whom it comes to be (*eggentai;* 541a). Glaucon understands this in his own way, and according to his own judgment of who is happy and who pitiable (516c–e). He is certain that the *politeia* of the *kallipolis* can be established quickly and easily in existing *poleis* and that the best of the guardians will be truly happy when they succeed in compelling all those older than ten to leave the city and all the children remaining in the city to leave their parents' ways. There is no need to wonder if the families torn apart in this manner will be happy. Everything they honor is worthless in any case, and few, if any, will ever be truly happy. It would be best for them if the guardians could compel them to abandon all they believe to be just and take their proper place in the new regime. They would then be benefited by their new lives, even though most of them would never understand why their new *polis* and *politeia* are perfectly just.

Once again, Socrates' concluding remarks are both playful and serious. They are playful in bringing out the worst features of Glaucon's imprudent idealism, but they are also serious in indicating how the discussion of political justice may proceed. The *polis* and *politeia* he and Glaucon have been discussing obviously cannot be founded quickly and easily in existing cities. It can only be founded in the soul (592a–b). Furthermore, a soul must come to be (*eggentai*) just. There is no quick and easy way for a proper order to be established (*katastasan*) within it either. It must journey the entire length of the longer way to its end and then return home. Only then can it be said to be truly happy itself and a prudent judge of who among other men is pitiable and who happy in some way. When the just and prudent soul of the true philosopher comes to be among a people (*ethnos*), he will be of most benefit to them. He has seen the good itself and knows that nothing, not even justice, is of any benefit in the absence of the good (505a–b). He knows as well that the good is what every soul pursues and for the sake of which every soul does everything (505d–e). But how will what he knows be of most benefit to his *ethnos*? Through his *paideia*. He benefits every soul open to his persuasion individually by taking up its convictions and leading it toward the good; he benefits the *ethnos* as a whole by taking up its *ethoi* and *nomoi* in his *paideia* and drawing them toward the ways and laws (*tropois kai nomois*) of the true philosophers. The *ethnos* becomes as just as it is possible for it to be in this way.

What are the *nomoi* of the true philosophers to which the *nomoi* of existing cities in Hellas must aspire if the *ethnos* is to be benefited? Glaucon believes that they are the *nomoi* necessary to establish the *politeia* of the *kallipolis* as quickly as possible, but Socrates' remarks suggest something else: they are the *nomoi* that would result from the reordering of the *kallipolis* by true philosophers. The best guardians of Glaucon's city have founded a just city in their own souls, "quickly and easily," as it were, by taking the good as their *paradeigma* in all things. They will most benefit their city through their *paideia*. By eliminating the injustices of Glaucon's city and raising all the children according to the *nomos* describing their own *paideia*, the best guardians will be able to make their city into the *paradeigma* of a just and good city. Socrates does not describe the *nomoi* of such a city for Glaucon. Glaucon has no interest in hearing of them. He has repeatedly refused to leave the cave of the *kallipolis* when Socrates has shown him the way toward the sunlight. And now he is certain that their discussion of justice has reached its end. Socrates does not disagree.

Socrates' several indications of the way toward the sunlight are the only evidence in the *Republic* of the *nomoi* of the true philosophers. The *nomoi* are stated explicitly in the dialogue that takes its name from them: *The Laws*.

II *PHRONESIS* AND THE GOD IN THE *LAWS*

6 THE CITY OF THE *TELOS*

IN THE *POLITICS*, Aristotle says that the *Laws*, like all "discourses of Socrates," is "witty, original and searching." He even goes so far as to say that it is "beyond measure [*peritton*]" (1265a12-14). On the whole, modern scholars do not agree with his assessment. It would be fair to say that many have no idea why Aristotle would praise the *Laws* so highly.

The *Laws* is presently the least well understood of Plato's dialogues. The neglect of the *Laws* has a long history. Plutarch of Chaeronea, who studied at the Academy in the first century, prided himself on knowing of the dialogue's existence, to say nothing of its contents. Its fate did not improve with the rise of Christianity; not only was the dialogue entirely forgotten for centuries, it was almost lost through neglect in the libraries of the Church.[1] Modern scholars have succeeded in preserving the manuscript, but it was only recently that they came to accept the *Laws* as an authentic Platonic dialogue. Since the nineteenth century many scholars have believed it to be a spurious or highly doubtful work, written entirely or in large part by Philippus of Opus, albeit from Plato's notes. As well, many of the few who argued for its authenticity found little to praise in it. Some considered it to be an embarrassing, if not senile, defense of theocracy, and others claimed it was an unimportant, anomalous appendix to Plato's earlier systematic philosophy. In the past several decades, few who have studied the *Laws* have found it unnecessary to criticize or apologize for the dialogue in some similar way.[2]

Most recent studies of the *Laws* have been concerned with analyzing its apparent internal inconsistencies and its discontinuities with Plato's other dialogues, particularly the *Republic*. This type of philological analysis is necessary if the full significance of the *Laws* within the Platonic corpus is ever to be recovered, but it often obscures more than it illuminates. For example, many recent studies have been premised on the assumption that the institutional order of Magnesia is full of puzzling contradictions. Instead

155

of serving as occasions for insight, however, these *aporiai* are generally taken either as indications of the dialogue's unfinished state or as proof of Plato's diminished capacities.[3] Similarly, various recent analyses of the relation between the *Laws* and the *Republic* are premised on the assumption that the discontinuities between the dialogues are problematic and require explanation, but the wide-ranging scholarly disagreements about the nature and significance of the apparent discontinuities have not often led the disputants to question their shared opinion that Plato was a political idealist of some kind.

The two philosophers who have done most to recover something of the Aristotelian understanding of the *Laws* are Leo Strauss and Eric Voegelin. Both would argue that the *Laws* is internally consistent and wholly in accord with Plato's other dialogues. Both would also argue that the *Laws*, like all the dialogues, is intended to lead its readers toward the philosophic life. Indeed, it is likely they would agree that Plato's account of the philosophic life would be fundamentally incomplete without the *Laws*. The reading of the *Laws* presented in this part of my study is in accord with what I understand to be the primary concerns of Strauss's and Voegelin's readings of the dialogue. In many ways, however, it departs from what they have written.

Strauss defends the *Laws* as a mature work of political philosophy. He writes that the *Republic* and the *Statesman* "lay the foundation for answering the question of the best political order, the best order of the city compatible with the nature of man. But they do not set forth that best political order. This task is left for the *Laws*." The *Laws* is thus Plato's "only political work proper." It is his "political work *par excellence*," but it is not merely political, for it also contains "Plato's theological statement *par excellence*."[4] Following Strauss, Thomas Pangle writes that the *Laws* "is far more than a set of speeches about law; through the interaction of the characters Plato intends to show how a philosopher might win the confidence of powerful old political leaders and guide them toward a revolutionary refounding." The drama of the dialogue reveals the "degree to which theory, and the human type that embodies the life of reason, can guide political practice."[5] Voegelin agrees that the *Laws* describes the "embodiment" of the Idea in the city. He writes that it is a compendium of Plato's "mature wisdom on the problems of man in political society" and that it describes a city ordered according to "the quality of men whom

Plato envisage[d] as the vessel of the Idea." Voegelin also agrees that the *Laws* is more than a merely political work. It is "a work of art; and specifically it is a religious poem" in which "every fact and argument adduced serves its purpose in adding to the grand view of human life in its ramifications from birth to death." It is the "*Summa* of Greek life."[6]

It may be better to say that there are two dramas in the *Laws*, both directed toward the same end, and that an understanding of how they are related illuminates what is said in the dialogue about politics and theology. The first drama in the *Laws* is the dialogue between the Athenian, Kleinias, and Megillus; the second emerges from the circumstances of their discussion. The three do not found a city in speech for theoretical or heuristic purposes. It is intended to come into being in deed. At the conclusion of the dialogue, the Athenian and Megillus both offer their assistance in persuading Kleinias's Knossian nomothetic committee that their city should be founded as they have described it. Their city in speech has the best possible regime and laws, and the Knossian committee has the authority to found such a city (702b–e, 968b–69d). The dialogue's second drama is not, however, a turn from theory to an uncertain or imperfect political reality. The Athenian's description of Magnesia assumes that the city's coming into being through the committee's actions will be entirely successful. His apparently theoretical account is also a practical account, but a practical account of a rather unusual nature. It has a dreamlike character. This is in large part because the city takes as its *paradeigma* the *paradeigma* of the cosmos itself. Its order is an image of the order of the cosmos ruled by divine *nous*, described in the theology of book 10. The second drama of the *Laws*, therefore, is the Athenian's demiurgic founding of a city as a "*paradeigma* laid up in heaven" (*Republic* 592b; cf. *Timaeus* 28a–29a). In the first instance, it is a *paradeigma* for all the members of the Knossian nomothetic committee. But since it is assumed that the coming into being of the city through the committee will be successful, the city is most completely a *paradeigma* laid up in heaven for the reader of the dialogue. It remains for the reader to determine not the degree to which Magnesia embodies a theory in political reality, but how closely Magnesia approaches its *telos*, the same *telos* that guides the Athenian in all he says and does. By exercising his judgment in this way, the reader will come to understand how the *Laws* may be said to describe a political order that is the best compatible with human nature, but a political order that, nevertheless, is not a political ideal.

It may be best to describe the *Laws* as a theological poem. Its theology gives an account of the *telos;* its poetry makes one the *telos* of the city and the *telos* of its demiurgic founder. The *telos* has several names. In the *Republic* it is called the good beyond being. In the *Laws* it is called the *arche, nous,* and the god that is the measure of all things. The philosopher's ascent toward the good is also an ascent toward divine *nous* or the god. In the *Theaetetus* (176a–e), Socrates describes the ascent as a flight from the mortal realm: "flight is becoming like the god [*homoiosis theoi*] as far as possible, and becoming like the god is to become just and holy [*hosion*] with prudence [*meta phroneseos*]." Recognition of the god's perfect justice, he says, is wisdom and true virtue. Those who refuse to take flight in any way are "burdens upon the earth" (*Odyssey* 20.379; *Iliad* 18.104; cf. *Apology* 28d). Their ignorance is "folly [*amathia*] and manifest vice [*kakia enarges*]." In the *Laws* the Athenian prevents all such human beings from entering the city. All Magnesians will be persuaded of the god's perfect justice. All will follow their lawgiver's ascent from the mortal realm, as far as they are able, and participate in true virtue to some extent. The theological poetry of the *Laws* thus describes Magnesia as a just and good city, the city of the *telos.*

In this part of my study, I will attempt to demonstrate the dramatic and substantive continuity of the *Republic* and the *Laws* by arguing that Magnesia is the just and good city lacking in the *Republic.* It is the city that is an image of the perfectly just and prudent soul described in Socrates' account of the longer way, the city that could not come into being because of Glaucon's inability or unwillingness to ascend with Socrates beyond geometrical thinking.

It was argued previously that the account of the just soul in the *Republic* is complete, despite Glaucon's inability or unwillingness to follow it completely. A summary of what might be learned from the dialogue between Socrates and Glaucon is given in Aristotle's analysis of the relation between *phronesis* and political *episteme* in the *Nichomachean Ethics:*

> While young men do indeed become good geometricians and mathematicians and become wise [*sophoi*] in such matters, they apparently do not become prudent [*phronimos*]. The reason is that *phronesis* is concerned with particulars, and knowledge of particulars comes

from experience [*ex empeirias*]. But a young man has no experience; for experience is the fruit of time [*plethos . . . chronou*]. (1142a11–17)

It was also argued previously that the account of the just city in the *Republic* is not complete, despite Glaucon's belief that it is. The reason for its incompleteness is not Socrates' reluctance to discuss justice in the city, but Glaucon's inability to experience the vision of the good that is the ground of *phronesis*. Glaucon's lack of the highest type of experience prevents the discussion from proceeding. The city in speech that seems just to Glaucon, therefore, is not truly just. In the imagery of the *Odyssey*, the *kallipolis* is Kalypso's *polis*, a city in which justice is concealed.

There are several indications of the truly just city, the city of the *telos*, concealed throughout the *Republic*. Had Glaucon been able to understand the ikons of Socrates' account of the longer way, he would also have been able to turn away from geometrical thinking and the phantasms of the cave to follow Socrates toward it. He would have learned that the just city is one outside the cave. It exists in the common home, illuminated by the sun and the good, and is inhabited only by those whose souls are open to the transcendent in some way. All those who would live in the cave— the grasping vulgar, the eristic sophists, and the unjust "rival lovers" who form political factions—have no place in it. The distinction between those who live in the common home and those who refuse to do so is described in Hesiod's advice to his imprudent brother Perses:

That man is altogether best [*panaristos*] who understands all things
    himself [*panta noesei*]
And marks what will be better afterwards and in the end [*telos*];
Good also is the man who listens to one who speaks well.
But the one who neither understands by himself nor listens to another
And takes to heart what he hears is an utterly worthless man [*achreios*
    aner].
(Hesiod, *Works and Days* 293–97; cf. *Laws* 718e–19a)

The common home is inhabited by the "altogether best" and those who listen to them and take to heart what they hear. The "utterly worthless" prefer to turn their backs to it. A just city, therefore, would be one in which the *panaristoi*—true philosophers—ruled over the good alone by directing them toward the *telos* in what they say. This describes Magnesia well.

True philosophers understand that the greatest good for a city is what makes it one, and the greatest evil is what splits it apart and makes it many. A city is made one if it is ordered according to "the track of the good": the Pythagorean proverb that friends have all things in common (*Republic* 423e–24a, 462a–b). It is split into factions and made many by the very thing Glaucon believes is justice itself: the opinion that justice is the minding of one's own affairs, which Socrates says is a "track" of justice discovered in the dark by a strange method (432b–33c). A truly just city takes the good itself as its *arche* and *telos*. Glaucon's city does not.[7]

The first thing philosophers must do in ordering a city according to the track of the good is to exclude all lawlessness (*paranomia*) from the souls of the young through proper play (*paidia*) and education (*paideia;* 423e–25c). Socrates describes several features of the rule of philosophers over properly educated adults in his playful testing of Glaucon about the greatest good for the city. He mentions the unity of opinion among the rulers and ruled, an aspect of *sophrosyne* when the rulers possess *phronesis;* the preservation of lawful opinion by the soldiers, an aspect of *andreia* when the soldiers possess *sophrosyne;* and *phronesis* itself, which acquires substance (*enousa*) in the rulers and enables them to rule justly (433c–d). Several other features of their rule are given in Socrates' account of the philosophers' return to the common home. Philosophers rule according to *nomos*. *Nomos* attempts to bring about the well-being of the whole city by harmonizing and adapting the citizens to one another and producing a community (*koinon;* 519e–20a). The members of such a community would be rich in the wealth of a happy man, a good and prudent life. They would all therefore be reluctant to hold office in the city and instead would take their turns drudging in politics from necessity alone. The city would thus be well governed (520d–21b). All would be capable of ruling and being ruled with justice in politics. The permanent rule of true philosophers in the city would be through *paideia* alone.

In order for the city to have proper *nomoi* and the citizens a proper *paideia,* the founding of the city must be an act of true statesmanship. In the *Statesman,* the *techne* of the true statesman is described as the weaving of souls and cities by *paideia.* The first task of the statesman is the testing of all souls by play (*paidia*) in order to exclude those that are uneducable because of their godlessness, pride, and injustice (*atheoteta kai hybrin kai adikia;*

308c-9a). Capable and worthy souls then have their living and eternal parts bound together. The human bonds of appropriate marriages are used to bind the living part, and the divine bond of the eternal part is true and assured opinion (*ontos ousan alethe doxan*) about the beautiful, the just, and the good (309a-10b). The brave and gentle characters of educable souls are made both courageous and moderate by being woven together like warp and woof; and all are drawn together into a common life by like-mindedness or community (*homonoia*) and friendship (*philia*). A city woven together in this manner would lack nothing that makes for happiness (*eudaimonia;* 309a-b, 311b-c). It would be a city that is free (*eleutheran*) and prudent (*emphrona*) and a friend to itself (*heautei philen; Laws* 693b-e).

There is one final indication of the truly just city in the *Republic:* the whole city must take up and honor solid geometry, even be charmed by it, under the guidance of a supervisor of *paideia* like Socrates, ignoring the arrogant opinions of geometrical thinkers and practicing it not for its military usefulness, but because of its ability to turn around the soul (528b-c). If it does, everyone in the city will be able to learn how the city itself "proceeds as if a circle in growth" from its beginning to its end (424a).

The indications of the truly just city concealed in the *Republic* are taken up and brought to light in the *Laws.* The dialogue between the Athenian and two men of experience (*emperia*) sets the city into motion. If Kleinias and Megillus follow his persuasion they may become prudent (*phronimos*) in matters of experience, and if they wish to become wise (*sophoi*), they may study the geometry that the Athenian uses playfully to give order to the city's motion (cf. *Nichomachean Ethics* 1142a11-17). When the city reaches its *telos,* the Athenian says they will have succeeded in constructing a regime that is "an imitation [*mimesis*] of the most beautiful and best life [*kalliston kai ariston bion*]." It would be right to call Magnesia the most beautiful, the best, and the truest (*alethestaten*) tragedy (*Laws* 817b). In comparison, the *kallipolis* is the *mimesis* of a life fit for the comic stage.[8] In tragedy men aspire to be gods and come to recognize the nature of their mortality. Their aspiration is presented as worthy of *mimesis.* In comedy men have baser aspirations that are laughable in themselves and often most laughable when attained. Comedy has its place in a proper *paideia.* The Athenian reminds Kleinias and Megillus that it is not possible to learn the serious without the laughable, nor indeed anything without its opposite, if one is to become prudent (*phronimos*). The comic is necessary for *phronesis*, but it would not be prudent to practice the laughable and serious things equally (816d–e). For Plato what is true of souls is generally true of cities. The *Republic* and the *Laws* describe his comic and tragic cities (cf. *Symposium* 223c–d). If a reader of the dialogues is to become prudent, he must come to understand the different natures of the cities. Once he participates to some degree in virtue, he will know how the things discussed in the *Republic* and the *Laws* should be practiced.

Comedy and tragedy are playful and serious or educative in different ways. The *Republic* and the *Laws* are both intended to educate the reader in serious matters through their unique types of playfulness. The playfulness of the *Laws* is often difficult to see for all its concern with serious political matters. However, the Athenian explicitly describes his discussion with Kleinias and Megillus as a dialogue among three "elderly children" whose "prudent game" about *nomoi* requires them to build a city in speech (685a, 712b, 769a). The largest part of the game for Kleinias and Megillus is to discover the playful way in which the Athenian brings Magnesia into being. The serious purpose of the Athenian's game is to lead his interlocutors—indeed, all those who will inhabit the city they found in speech—toward *phronesis* and the *arche* of all virtue. In order for the game to begin, however, the Athenian tells them they must put aside the usual pastimes of elderly children. They should prefer the Athenian's game to any pleasure they may have in listening to recitations from Homer and Hesiod or in playing draughts.

Kleinias admits to being a lover of recitals. He agrees with the Athenian that puppet shows are preferred by small children, comedies by bigger boys, tragedies by educated women, young men, and the majority of others, and recitals from the epic poets by the elderly. He also agrees that judgment in these matters should not be by pleasure alone, but by the pleasure of the prudent and educated man (658a–59c). If Kleinias is to take pleasure in the Athenian's game of constructing Magnesia as the truest tragedy, he should put aside disputes about the quality of recitations by rhapsodists and study the Athenian's own words as *poiesis* or poetry. The Athenian describes the dialogue itself to him as a kind of poetry in prose form, a well-measured (*metriotatoi*) type of speech that is nonetheless spoken with inspiration from the gods (*epip-*

noias theon). The Athenian even claims there is no better *paradeig-ma* for *paideia*. In order to be certain that this is true, Kleinias should study the dialogue itself, just as the Athenian requires Magnesia's supervisors of *paideia* to study it. He should search through the poetry and prose now said to be the best *paradeig-mata*—Homer and Hesiod in particular—until he comes across speeches that are the "brothers" of the Athenian's speeches. He should then write them down and study all of them together. This type of study is suited not only to the elderly: the Athenian re-quires the Magnesian supervisors of *paideia* to instruct the young who might otherwise prefer comedy and tragedy in the same way (811c–12a).

If Kleinias loves to play draughts (*petteia*) with other old men, he will have to put aside that game as well in order to learn the rules of a far more divine type of draughts playing. The Athenian says the elderly should pass their time gracefully by investigating the relation of commensurables (*metreton*) and incommensura-bles (*ametron*). In order to do this, they must first wonder about "one and two and three" and about the relation of line, surface, and volume. These are two aspects of the study of number. All Magnesian children will begin to learn of these things in their play and in their first reading lessons. The Athenian says there is no part of their *paideia* with as much ability to make them tran-scend their nature by a "divine art [*theiai technei*]" as the study of number (747b). The elderly in Magnesia, in particular those who become members of the city's Nocturnal Council, will be required to study number with greater precision (747b, 817e–20d). Among other things, they will be required to study Pythagorean mathe-matics and number symbolism. The Pythagoreans represented line, surface, and volume playfully with the numbers 2, 3, and 4. The three were related in Pythagorean solid geometry. They repre-sented the *genesis* of all things that have volume from the origin or *arche* of all that *is*. They also called the *arche* the One. The One is the Pythagorean symbol for the divine *arche* of all things, not just all things with volume. It is the origin of *psyche* as well as of *soma*.[9] When the Athenian says that all should wonder about the relation of 1, 2, and 3 and that of 2, 3, and 4, he indicates that the wonder underlying the study of number should draw a soul toward the One. The Athenian calls the One by another name: the god who is the draughts player (*petteutei*) capable of moving all things in the cosmos and is the king (*basileus*) who oversees all virtue in things that have *psyche* (903d–4c).[10] The draughts playing and kingly rule of the god is the *paradeigma* taken by the Athenian for the city he founds in speech. If Kleinias wonders enough to learn of this divine type of draughts playing he will come to understand how Magnesia is second-best only in comparison to the city that is constructed in perfect accord with the divine draughts player's "sacred line" and inhabited by the gods—that is, the cosmos itself (739a–e).

The serious play with number in the *Laws* is another indication of its relation to the *Republic*. The Athenian's references to number throughout the dialogue reveal that the city's *genesis* and order are a *mimesis* of the demiurgic *genesis* and order of the cosmos itself. The city comes into being from the One, as do line, surface, and volume (2, 3, 4). This is one way the whole city may be said to take up solid geometry. Another way it takes up and honors it is through *paideia*. In this context, the Athenian's ordering of the city with Pythagorean mathematics and number symbolism indicates that all Magnesians will be drawn toward the One. What is more, it indicates that the city as a whole exists in the common home illuminated by the good. The good is One for Plato.[11] In other words, the good beyond being and the Pythagorean One beyond all things are two linguistic expressions of comparable experiences of the transcendent.[12] The good beyond being described in the *Republic* is not mentioned in the *Laws*, but it may be said to be the *paradeigma* for all Magnesians. Their institutions and *nomoi* are ordered by it, their *paideia* and piety lead them toward it, and the best Magnesians—those chosen for the Nocturnal Council—provide guidance for the whole city by taking it as the *paradeigma* of their own souls. In short, there is nothing in Magnesia to prevent the turning around (*periagoge*) of any human being's soul toward the good. As Aristotle suggests in the *Politics* (1265a1–5), the Magnesian *politeia* and *nomoi* may be adopted by existing cities, but Plato turns around Magnesia by degrees (*kata mikron periagei*) toward the *Republic*. Plato's serious play with number in describing Magnesia's demiurgic *genesis* and order by means of Pythagorean mathematics and number symbolism reveals it, by degrees, to be the truly just city that remained concealed in the *Republic*.

The Athenian's advice to Kleinias, and through Kleinias to all Magnesians, may be taken as Plato's advice to all readers of the *Laws:* the playful founding of Magnesia in speech can only be

understood if it is approached with a sense of wonder that becomes serious play as the study of the Athenian's speeches proceeds. This process is explained well in Aristotle's *Metaphysics.*
Aristotle writes that all begin by wondering (*thaumazein*) why all
things are as they are, just as they wonder at "puppets, solstices,
or the incommensurability of a hypotenuse." It is through wonder
(*dia . . . to thaumazein*) that a human being begins to philosophize,
first by wondering about obvious perplexities and then, "by
degrees [*kata mikron*]," raising questions about such matters as
astronomy and the genesis of all things. There are accounts of the
things in the cosmos and their genesis in myths. Aristotle goes so
far as to say that the lover of myth is, in a manner, a philosopher,
for myths are composed of wonders (*ek thaumasion;* 982b12–20,
983a13–15).

If the reader of the *Laws* follows the Athenian's advice to study
Homer and Hesiod as well as Pythagorean mathematics and number
symbolism alongside the dialogue, he will discover the myths,
puppets, solstices, and hypotenuses used in it to lead all Magnesians from wonder toward philosophy. In the *Republic* a playful
combination of Homeric and Orphic imagery, together with geometric proportion, was used to compose the three ikons with
which Socrates attempted to lead Glaucon toward the good itself.
Glaucon's geometrical thinking was sufficiently without playfulness and wonder to prevent him from completing the ascent begun
in the cave of sophistic phantasms.[13] In the *Laws,* a playful combination of Homeric imagery and Pythagorean number is used to
compose another three ikons. The Athenian uses them in a comparable way in attempting to lead his interlocutors, and all Magnesians as well, as far as they are able to ascend toward the end
that guides the true philosopher in all he says and does. Magnesians will not encounter Glaucon's difficulties in their ascent. An
indication of this is the absence of any reference to phantasms or
geometry in the *Laws.* The absence of any reference to phantasms
reveals that Magnesia is a city in the common home in which the
sophist has no place; the absence of any reference to geometry
reveals that geometrical thinking has no part in the city's honoring of solid geometry.

The three ikons of the *Laws* are the puppet, the ikon of *nous*,
and the Nocturnal Council. They are the only three images in
speech that are called ikons by the Athenian (644c, 897e, 969b).
The three ikons of the *Republic* are described by Socrates in a

single account. The three of the *Laws* are given at different points in the discussion. Nevertheless, an understanding of their meaning as ikons and their central significance within the dialogue depends as much upon an insight into their relation to one another as does an understanding of the ikons of the longer way. Following the Athenian's advice, a search in poetry for speeches that are the brothers of his own reveals that the imagery used for his three ikons is taken from several related speeches in the *Iliad* and the *Odyssey*. Furthermore, it reveals that the same speeches in Homer are used by Socrates as the basis for the three ikons of the longer way.

The *Odyssey* begins with a theodicy. Homer has Zeus speak to the immortals and say:

Look you now, how ready mortals are to blame [*aitioontai*] the gods.
It is from us, they say, that evils come, but rather it is they
Who through their own blind folly [*atasthaliesin*] have sorrows beyond
    what is given.

(*Odyssey* 1.32–34)[14]

Homer distinguishes between sorrows or evils such as pain and death that are given in mortality and evils that mortals bring upon themselves. The gods are the cause of neither type of evil, but mortals are in the habit of blaming the gods for both. This blind folly undoubtedly allows evil acts to be committed more readily than they might be otherwise. The consequences of the predominance of such folly in a society are easily imaginable. They are described at length by Homer in the *Iliad*.

There are two passages in the *Iliad* comparable to Zeus's announcement of the gods' blamelessness in the *Odyssey*. In the first, Zeus forbids the immortals from aiding either side in the Trojan war. Any of them who attempt to do so risk being hurled down to Tartarus, which is as far below Hades as the earth is below heaven (*ouranos*). The gates and threshold of Tartarus are made of iron and bronze. In order to show that he is the mightiest of all gods, Zeus offers them a test of his strength. If a chain of gold (*seiren chruseien*) is lowered from heaven and they all grasp it, they would never be able to drag Zeus, the highest counsellor, from heaven to earth. When he is strongly minded (*prophron*) to do so, however, Zeus can pull up the chain, drawing with it all the immortals and even the earth and sea themselves (8.5–27). The gods do not test Zeus, but Hera disobeys him. In the second passage, Zeus reminds

Hera, when he learns of her disobedience, of how she had once been punished. Zeus bound her hands with an unbreakable golden chain (*chruseon arrekton*) and suspended her in the air amid the clouds. From her feet he suspended two anvils. None of the gods could loosen the bonds, and any of them who attempted to release her were caught by Zeus and hurled down to earth where they landed with little power (*oligepeleon*). The reminder is sufficient for Hera. She then tells the gods: "Fools [*nepioi*], we who try to work against Zeus thoughtlessly [*aphroneontes*]" (15.14–24, 104; cf. 15.128–29).

In the first passage, a proportion or *analogia* is given for four regions: heaven, earth, Hades, and Tartarus. The distance between the first two is the same as the distance between the second two. The proportion of all four cannot be known as a whole. The immortals inhabit heaven, and the mortals earth. Zeus, however, is beyond heaven and all the regions between heaven and Tartarus. He is able to draw the gods, earth, and sea upward on a golden chain and hurl a god from heaven to Tartarus if he wills it. In the second passage, the upward pull capable of lifting the gods on the golden chain and the downward plunge of a god to Tartarus are combined in a single image. Zeus may punish any immortal by drawing him or her in two directions at once with chains. The chain from which Hera is suspended is again a golden chain, and the two anvils, as well as the chains from which they are suspended, recall the iron and bronze gates and threshold of Tartarus. In the second passage, therefore, the features of the regions from heaven to Tartarus appear in heaven alone and describe the greatness of Zeus in relation to all the immortals. This suggests that something similar may be said of the earth and the greatness of Zeus in relation to all mortals. In the first passage, Zeus is said to be able to hurl a god to Tartarus; in the second, he is said to have punished gods by hurling them to earth, where they landed with little power, if they attempted to undo Hera's chains. Mortals are like the immortals of little power hurled to earth by Zeus. They live the whole of their brief lives in a condition similar to Hera's brief punishment—ever drawn between the downward pulls of the iron and bronze chains and the upward pull on the golden chain. Hera was suspended amid the clouds, drawn between heaven and earth rather than between heaven and Hades or Tartarus. Mortals differ in that they inhabit the earth and experience the downward pulls far more profoundly. There are sorrows in their lives, but they need not live thoughtlessly and in blind folly. If they follow the highest counsellor's pull on the golden chain, they may escape their sorrows for a time and live prudently. They may then even be said to be happy in their lives.

The outlines of the ikons used in the *Republic* and the *Laws* are now apparent. The proportion of the four regions from heaven to Tartarus is similar to the proportion of the four segments of the divided line. Zeus is beyond heaven and is more powerful than the earth and the sea and all the immortals. Similarly, the good transcends all things described in the divided line ikon; it is beyond being, transcending it in dignity and power. The golden chain with which Zeus may draw up the heavenly and earthly things may be found both in the cosmos and within human beings. In the cosmos it is the sun. Indeed, this is made explicit by Socrates in the *Theaetetus* when he says the golden chain is an image "by which Homer means nothing else but the sun" (153c–d). Through his use of the image, "he makes plain that as long as the heavens and the sun go round [*he periphora ei kinoumene kai ho helios*], all things *are* [*panta esti*] and are preserved [*soizetai*] among gods and human beings, but if this should stop as if it were bound, all things would be corrupted, and, as the saying goes, all things would be turned upside down [*ano kato panta*]." The world in which all things are upside down is, of course, the dreamworld of the sophistic cave. The sophists who rule it attempt to bind the souls of all human beings by blocking out the going round of the heavens and the light of the sun and destroying their understanding of all things that *are* and are preserved by the god. They cannot do so, however. The god's golden chain is within every human being. All things that *are* and are preserved by the god's will, therefore, may become evident to them despite the sophists' claims. All live in the common home illuminated by the sun and the good. A life in the common home is not without sorrows, but it is far better than the life of one who refuses to follow the upward pull within his soul and so, through blind folly, has sorrows beyond those given in life.

The three ikons of the *Laws* are the key to understanding the dialogue's account of the best life possible for human beings in the common home. The first is the puppet ikon. According to a myth that has been saved (*sesosmenos*), the Athenian says, every human being is a divine puppet made by the god, either for his play or some serious purpose—we cannot know which. Everyone is pulled in opposite directions by a sacred golden cord and two base, hard, iron cords (*merinthoi*). It can be known, however, that everyone should always follow the sacred upward pull on the cord of *logismos*. In Magnesia all do; the upward pull thus becomes the common law of the city (*tes poleos koinon nomon;* 644e–45b; cf. *Republic* 621b–d). The second ikon is the rotation or going round of the cosmos itself, the motion that is a beautiful ikon of the divine *nous* that guides (*paidagogei*) all things in heaven and earth correctly and eudaimonically. The rotation of the cosmos and the upward pull on the golden cord have the same source. The Athenian makes this evident by recalling the first ikon at the beginning of his account of the second. He says he will begin by holding on to a safe cable (*asphalous peismatos*), a *logos,* and the aid of the god (893b, 897b–e). The golden cord is the safe cable, or more precisely, the safe "ship cable." The *logismos* is more appropriately named the *logos.* The upward pull is more explicitly identified as the aid of the god. The third ikon of the *Laws* makes the account more complete by describing in greater detail how human *nous* may ascend toward divine *nous.* The safe ship cable passes through the Nocturnal Council (*syllogos*). The ship cable is not anchored in the sea. It is anchored in heaven and transmits the upward pull of the god beyond heaven. The ascent of human *nous* may begin in observing the rotation of the cosmos with wonder. Divine *nous* is evident in the cosmos if perception is properly combined with *nous* in the human *psyche.* The proper combination of perception and *nous* makes a human being prudent, the Athenian says. Magnesia's Nocturnal Council is an ikon of how they should be combined. It is thus an ikon of *phronesis* and *nous.* Each of the men who are part of the council may be said to be prudent and wise in some way; together they guide their city as divine *nous* guides the cosmos. They follow the upward pull as far as is possible for mortals and lead all others in the city to the same end. In the Athenian's description they are perfect guardians (*phylakes apotelesthosin*), whose excellence in salvation (*areten soterias*) will really save the whole city (*sozein . . . ontos ten polin holen;* 961c, 962b–c, 965a, 969b–c).

The three ikons of the *Laws* are bound together by Plato's playful use of the imagery of cords and cables. Taken together, they reveal the only salvation (*soteria*) for souls and cities (cf. *Republic* 473c–e, 499b–c, 501e–2c). As well, the three ikons of the *Laws* are bound together with the three of the *Republic* by their common origin in the imagery of Homer's theodicy. Taken together they reveal that Magnesia is the *paradeigma* of a truly just and good city.

My discussion of the *Laws* has three sections, each ordered thematically by one of the dialogue's three ikons. In other words, each of the ikons will be used in turn to illuminate a range of related dramatic features and substantive arguments in the *Laws* and other dialogues. There will be less continuous textual commentary than there was in my discussion of the *Republic*. The richness of the *Republic* is best revealed through the extensive use of such commentary, but the *Republic* and the *Laws* have somewhat different literary characters. The richness of the *Laws* is less in the dialogic relation of its interlocutors than in its composition. There are a great many imaginative associations, suggestive allusions, and puzzling references in the dialogue. The hermeneutical method best suited to following their tracks through the dialogue, and to other dialogues as well, is one that attempts to understand the dialogue's structure and composition. A thematic study ordered by the dialogue's three ikons, therefore, seems most appropriate.

I will first discuss the Athenian's theodicy as it is described in his several accounts of the relation of the god and human beings. All of these accounts are related to one another through the puppet ikon. When taken together, they indicate that the founding of a city governed by the theodicy will begin a new age for mankind, the age of *nous*. I will then discuss the Athenian's arguments against impiety in book 10. The Athenian suggests that the motion of *nous* has three aspects: the unique motion of the demiurgic *genesis* of all things from *nous*, the rotation of the cosmos under the guidance of *nous*, and the noetic ascents and descents of human beings. He says the rotation of the cosmos is an ikon of *nous*, but the same is true of the two other aspects of the motion of *nous*. Finally, I will discuss the Nocturnal Council ikon at some length. The full significance of the Nocturnal Council and its internal composition only becomes apparent when its place in Magnesia's order is made clear. It is difficult to determine because Magnesia is itself an ikon. It is an ikon of the motion of *nous* in all its aspects. Magnesia is not said explicitly to be an ikon of the motion of *nous*. The Athenian's serious play with Pythagorean mathematics and number symbolism suggests this to the reader. Once these things are clarified, the Nocturnal Council is revealed to be an ikon of the *phronesis* and *nous* of the true philosopher.

This in turn is the best evidence that Magnesia is the *paradeigma* of a truly just and good city.

Plato's serious play with ikons and number in the *Laws* is "witty, original and searching." It reveals how the dialogue's city in speech is truly "beyond measure [*peritton:* from *perissoteron*]." It is no wonder, then, that Aristotle praises the *Laws* so highly (*Politics* 1265a12–14).

7 GOD OR SOME HUMAN BEING?

THE FIRST SENTENCE of the *Laws* recalls Homer's theodicy. In the *Odyssey* (1.32–34), Zeus says it is blind folly for mortals to blame (*aitioontai*) the gods for evils they suffer and bring upon themselves. No distinction is made between evils mortals bring upon themselves by acting on their own account or by acting as their *nomoi* direct them. The *Laws'* first sentence is a question about *nomoi*. The Athenian asks his two interlocutors: "God or some human being, strangers—who is the cause [*aitia*] for the arrangement of your *nomoi*?" Kleinias replies it would be most just (*dikaiotaton*) to say a god: the Cretans say Zeus is the *aitia*, and the Lacedaimonians Apollo. He is then reminded that Cretans also say Minos is the cause of their *nomoi*. They do not believe Minos to have been a mere mortal, however. According to Homer, they say, Minos established their *nomoi* with the guidance of his father Zeus. They also say that Minos's brother, Rhadamanthus, became most just (*dikaiotaton gegonenai*). Apparently it is not sufficient to be born of Zeus in order to be a just man (624a–25a).

Kleinias is quite frank in explaining to the Athenian what he understands to have been the result of Zeus's guidance of Minos's lawgiving. Minos ordered all things, public and private, with a view to war, he says. Consequently, all are enemies of all in public and each is an enemy to himself in private (626a–b, d). The Athenian understands Homer far better than does Kleinias. He knows that Kleinias has described the greatest evil mortals may bring upon themselves and has claimed that it is most just for Cretans to say Zeus is its cause. Nevertheless, he does not dismiss Kleinias as a foolish man. Kleinias has sufficient candor, goodwill, and intelligence for the Athenian to take up what he says and lead him to a better understanding of such things (cf. *Gorgias* 487a). The Athenian's better understanding is evident in the theodicy he presents while founding the city of the Magnesians. It is comparable in substance to Homer's theodicy. However, it is given in prose and dialogue, not in poetry or recital, and it is directly associated with

172

lawgiving for a city. At the beginning of the dialogue, Minos's law-giving and Rhadamanthus's justice are thought to be the best standards available to mortals of what is most just. By the end of the dialogue, when the founding of Magnesia is almost complete, a new standard has emerged. The Athenian says, "Rhadamanthus's *techne* would no longer be fitting for the trials of present-day human beings" (948c–d). The same is true of Minos's *techne*. The Athenian's *techne* has surpassed them both, for he has founded a truly just city. What is more, in doing so he has succeeded in persuading Kleinias and Megillus that their city in speech should be founded in accordance with an understanding of the god's blameless justice that neither accepted when the dialogue began.

God is the perfectly just measure of all things, the Athenian says, even of human affairs. Human beings, however, are completely responsible for their own affairs. They are the *aitia* of their own actions; their *nomoi* are their own. But how is it possible for the god to be the measure of things of which he is not the cause and for which he is not responsible? Homer's theodicy has no obvious answer to this question. The Athenian's theodicy answers it explicitly: God is the measure of all human affairs through what is immortal in mortals. Human beings may become divine, not by being born of a god, but by becoming like the god, as far as is possible within the limits of their humanity. Furthermore, human beings may order their *nomoi* to accord with what they learn as a consequence of following the god's upward pull on the golden cord within their souls. In order for this to happen, however, a divine lawgiver is necessary to give the *nomoi* a proper beginning. The Athenian is such a man. The city he founds has *nomoi* that are directed toward the god in all things. His skill in ordering the *nomoi* in this way is most evident in the most important of the city's laws, the ones that speak explicitly of the god. These laws most clearly express the Athenian's theodicy: all that is good in human affairs is attributable to the god in some way, and all that is evil to the blind folly of mortals.

Kleinias is also a lawgiver. It is evident from the beginning of the dialogue that he takes his responsibility seriously. He is following the path from Knossos to the cave of Zeus in imitation of Minos's ascent every ninth year. He intends, therefore, to found the new Knossian colony, for which he is partly responsible, in imitation of Minos's *nomoi*, the *nomoi* he believes to be most just. Kleinias never reaches the cave of Zeus. This is evidence of his skill as a lawgiver. He is persuaded by his dialogue with the Athenian that the Magnesian *nomoi* are the best possible, far better than his own. Kleinias's turning away from the cave to return home to Knossos with the Athenian has epochal significance. The societal order represented by the cave of Zeus is no longer authoritative once the city of the Magnesians has been described. The *telos* toward which the three were walking is superseded by the *telos* toward which they ascended in dialogue. The age of Zeus is thus ended and a new age begun.

The new age is announced at the beginning of the *Laws*, though it does not begin until Magnesia's founding is complete. When the Athenian reveals that Kleinias's account of Minos's lawgiving makes everyone enemies of all in public and each an enemy of himself in private, Kleinias praises the Athenian for taking his *logos* to its *arche*. He then demonstrates that he is willing to turn away from this *arche* by agreeing with the Athenian that the first and best victory is the victory over oneself in the soul that makes all virtue possible. When he agrees, the Athenian suggests: "Let us turn back and reverse the argument [*ton logon anastrepsomen*]." The turning back and reversing of the *logos* that leads to war (*polemos*) and civil strife (*stasis*) in all human affairs must lead to another *arche*. The new *arche* is the *telos* toward which the dialogue between the Athenian, Kleinias, and Megillus ascends. It is a *telos* for the soul, enabling it to win a victory over itself and acquire all virtue. It is also a *telos* for *nomoi*, enabling cities to live in peace and friendliness (626d–27a, 628c–e).

The verb *anatrepho* occurs infrequently in Plato's dialogues. The dramatic significance of its use in the future tense by the Athenian is best understood by reference to the myth of Kronos told by the Eleatic stranger in the *Statesman* (269c–73e). The Eleatic stranger speaks of two fundamentally different times, a golden age of Kronos and the present age of Zeus. In the first age, the god himself guided the circular, revolving course of the all (*to pan*). When the course reached the measure (*metron*) of its time, however, the god released it. It then no longer turned in the same direction. Instead, it turned around (*periagetai*) in the opposite direction. It was able to do this because it had been formed by the god in the beginning (*kat' archas*) as a living being with *phronesis* (269c–d; cf. *Timaeus* 29e–30c, 34a–b). The Eleatic says the cosmos turned back and reversed itself (*anestrephen*), and the age of Zeus began when the helmsman of the all released the rudder. It was an epochal change for all things: the turning-around (*metastrepho-menos*) caused the *arche* and the *telos* to set off in opposite ways (*enantian hormen hormetheis;* 272e–73a; cf. 271a).[1] The age of Zeus must one day run its course and end in another turning around. The Eleatic, however, does not speak of the future—the Athenian does. The turning back and reversing of the *logos* in the *Laws* is an epochal event. It marks the end of the age of Zeus among human beings and the beginning of an age with a new *arche* and *telos*.[2]

The new age is named for the god who rules over all human beings with *nous*. The Athenian answers Kleinias's explicit question "Who is the god?" with his own myth of the age of Kronos (713a–14a). He tells him that Kronos's eudaimonic rule was the cause (*aitia*) of blessed lives for human beings. Kronos did not rule mortal affairs directly. He established a race of daimons more divine than the mortal races as kings and rulers of their cities. Their rule brought peace, awe, good laws (*eunomia*), and justice without envy (*aphthonia*). The mortal races were thus without civil strife (*astasiasta*) and happy (*eudaimona*). In the present age, human beings attempt to rule all things themselves. The Athenian does not call the present the age of Zeus. He says only that it is a time in which there will be no rest from evils and toils for cities while mortals rule rather than the god (cf. *Republic* 473c–e, 499b–c, 502a–c). The god's eudaimonic rule is absent in cities. He seems to have released his guidance of all things, mortal and immortal. However, this is only an appearance. It is mortals who have turned away from the god and all that is immortal. What is more, their turning away leads them to attempt to acquire the god's authority for themselves. The Athenian says human beings become swollen with pride (*hybris*) and injustice (*adikia*) when they assume autocratic authority over everything (*panta*). Instead, they should imitate (*mimeisthai*) life under Kronos by ordering all public and private things in accordance with whatever partakes of immortality (*athanasiai*) within them. Then, he says, the ordering (*dianomen*) by *nous* would be worthy of the name *nomos* (cf. 957c, *Minos* 317d).

The Athenian's city is the first to order its *nomoi* according to *nous*. The founding of the city is not simply a *mimesis* of the age of Kronos in the age of Zeus. It is the beginning of the age of *nous*. The age of *nous* is qualitatively different from the two preceding ones. Human beings ruled by Kronos's daimons could not turn away from the god. Those in the age of Zeus could and did. In the age of *nous*, each human being remains free to turn away but none do. Human beings no longer require the beneficent rule of a race of daimons to live blessed lives. Instead, each lives in accordance with what is immortal within him by turning his *psyche* and *nous* toward the divine *nous* that is the *arche* of all things, and all are governed by those among them who most closely approach the divine.

Once the new age is announced by the turning around of the *logos* of Zeus's age, the Athenian tells Kleinias and Megillus that "it is necessary to start again from the beginning [*ex arches*]" (632d–e). He starts over again by speaking of the *nomoi* said to be from Zeus and Apollo, the laws established by Minos and Lycurgus, in the way he would have liked to hear his two interlocutors speak of them (631b–32c). The refounding of the Cretan and Lacedaimonian *nomoi* according to the *arche* of the new age is playful, but it has a serious purpose as well; it indicates how the Athenian's city in speech will be ordered and ruled.

The *nomoi* should make all those subject to them happy, he says, by providing them with all good things (*panta ta agatha*). Some good things are divine, others human. The human goods are health (*hygeia*), beauty (*kallos*), strength (*ischus*), and wealth (*ploutos*), in descending order of importance. They cannot be acquired alone as goods. Where the divine goods are absent, so too are the human goods (cf. 649d, 661a–c). The divine goods, in ascending order, are *andreia, dikaiosyne, sophrosyne*, and a fourth, the leader (*hegemonoun*) of them all. The Athenian does not complete the list with *sophia*. The most important divine good is given two names, *phronesis* and *nous*. The two names refer to two aspects of the immortal within mortals. When it is turned upward toward the divine *nous*, it is called *nous*. And when it rules over all human and divine goods in accordance with *nous* it is called *phronesis*. The Athenian then says that a lawgiver must first concern himself with the good things and ensure that they are properly ordered. In particular, the citizens must know that the human goods look to the divine for guidance, and the divine to *nous*. They must also know that these goods, as a whole, come before all else. They may learn of these things from the manner in which the lawgiver's *nomoi* apportion honor and dishonor, teach what is noble and ignoble, and regulate all acquisitions and expenditures (cf. 726a–29a). When the lawgiver binds all these matters together in the *nomoi*, the Athenian says he will then set up guards (*phylakas*) for them, some of whom will be guided by *phronesis* and others by true opinion (*alethous doxes*). This is the first description given in the dialogue of the Nocturnal Council, the embodiment of *phronesis* and *nous* in the Athenian's city.

Phronesis and *nous* must have primacy in the city and in the soul. The Athenian says that his *nomoi*, unlike the Cretan and Lacedaimonian, will be established for the sake of virtue as a whole, and especially for the sake of the leader (*hegemona*) of virtue: "*phronesis* and *nous* and opinion [*doxa*], together with the love [*eros*] and desire [*epithumia*] that accompany them" (688a–b). The Magnesian *nomoi*, unlike those of the age of Zeus, will be able to instil *phronesis* regarding the greatest of human affairs and drive out ignorance (*amathia*). In order to do so, they must direct the soul toward the proper objects of love (*eros, philia*). The Athenian says the greatest sort of ignorance is evident when someone hates what is noble and good in his opinion while loving (*philei*) what is wicked (*poneros*) and unjust (689a). The cause of a human being's blindness to the proper objects of love is an excessive love of self (*heauton philian*) that leads him to suppose his ignorance is wisdom. The Athenian goes so far as to say that such excessive love of self is "the cause [*aitia*] of all of everyone's wrongdoing [*hamartematon*] on every occasion" (863c). It does not matter if those who think themselves wise are shrewd at calculating (*logistikoi*) and trained in all things elegant and witty (*panta ta kompsa*); they are to be blamed for their *amathia* and should be given no part of rule in a city. The ruling offices in the Athenian's city will always be in the hands of the prudent (*emphrosi*), who are most properly called wise (*sophous;* 689c–e).

Love of self is the *aitia* of the injustice, insolence (*hybris*), and imprudence (*aphrosyne*) that destroy human beings, no matter how clever they may seem to be. They are saved by justice and moderation together with *phronesis*. They are saved, in other words, by following *phronesis* and *nous* (906a–b), and they must turn around their souls from love of self to a love of all things that share in *phronesis* and *nous*. As the Athenian describes them, the gods in heaven share in them in some way. The greatest object of love for human beings is the divine *nous*, the god beyond the gods in heaven, who is the *arche* and *telos* of all things. Those who think themselves wise deny the divinity of the heavenly gods and attempt to assume for themselves the power of the god beyond heaven. Such sophists believe that they possess the wisest (*sophotaton*) of all

arguments and the greatest prudence (*megiste phronesis*). However, the Athenian says that their arguments only reveal their very
harsh ignorance (*mala chalere amathia*). It is the god who is most
wise (*sophotaton*), not any human being (886b, 888d–e, 902e). The
sophists who claim the god's wisdom for themselves attempt to
draw the divine *nous* into human *nous* (cf. *Philebus* 22c). This is
not simply an error in reasoning or excessive cleverness. It is the
greatest possible *aphrosyne* originating in the greatest possible
love of self.

The Athenian's *nomoi* will lead all those subject to them toward
phronesis and *nous* by directing their love and desires through
paideia. Soon after starting the dialogue over again from the
arche, the Athenian tells Kleinias and Megillus that the *logos* they
have taken up must first define *paideia* if it is to proceed and
arrive at the god (643a). He then suggests a definition that would
not take the *logos* to its proper end, a definition better suited to
Glaucon's *kallipolis* than to the city he will found in speech. The
Athenian suggests that *paideia* is a correct nurture (*orthen trophen*)
that draws the soul of a child at play to a love (*erota*) of what he
must do when he becomes a man who is perfect (*teleion*) in the
virtue of his occupation (*tou pragmatos aretes;* 643c–d). But he
then immediately explains why this is not a definition of *paideia*
at all. It is common at present, he says, to speak of education only
in reference to some trade or occupation. A man who is good at
something, however, is not thereby a good man. *Paideia* must lead
to virtue and goodness in themselves. It must not be directed
toward money or strength or "some sort of wisdom without intelligence and justice [*sophou aneu nou kai dikes*]." This sort of
upbringing is vulgar (*banauson*) and illiberal (*aneleutheron*). In
contrast, the Athenian offers another definition: *paideia* in virtue
from childhood makes one desire and love (*epithumeten te kai
erasten*) to become a perfect citizen (*politen . . . teleon*) who knows
how to rule and be ruled with justice. Men and women educated in
this way generally become virtuous and good, but their *paideia*
must continue throughout the whole of their lives and must always
be set right if it goes astray (643d–44b).

The Athenian's definition is incomplete, but it allows the *logos*
to proceed to its *telos*. The first definition would not. It is evident
from what he says that a differentiation of education by class cannot be a true education in virtue. All must be educated in order to
prevent vulgarity from predominating in the lower classes and an

unjust and thoughtless illiberality from predominating in the upper class. All must become perfect citizens capable of ruling and being ruled in turn. But such citizens require a perfect *polis* in which to be educated in virtue and a perfect *politeia* in which to take their turn ruling. In other words, they require the city and regime the Athenian has yet to describe in speech. If the Athenian is to succeed in describing the *nomoi* of the city, the *logos* should now proceed from the point in his definition of *paideia* that remains to be clarified: how the love and desires of children may be directed toward their proper end.

The Athenian now presents the puppet ikon to his interlocutors in order to clarify matters (644c–45c). He describes the ikon as a myth of virtue, but he adds that the myth must be saved (*sesosmenos*) if it is to save the *logos;* it too is incomplete. Each human being is a puppet of the gods, he says, suspended in the region between virtue and vice. Each has three cords within himself. There are two hard and iron cords that pull the soul downward violently in various ways. They are called pleasure and pain or, in the soul's expectation of the future, boldness and fear. Both are imprudent (*aphrone*) counsellors of the soul. There is also the soft and golden cord of calculation (*logismos*). The *logismos* itself calculates which of the soul's expectations are better and which worse. Calculation of this sort is not virtue. It is cleverness. The cord of calculation alone cannot save the soul from vice. It is saved by the sacred (*hieran*) pull on the cord that draws it upward, away from *aphrosyne* and toward *phronesis* and *nous*. The pull is gentle and requires assistance. Each human being may learn to assist it by acquiring true reasoning (*logon alethe*).[3]

The Athenian's ikon reveals that what is true of souls is also true of cities. It is possible for a city to be clever in calculating which of its expectations of the future are better and which worse and then calling its common opinion—its calculation of which is best—by the name *nomos*. There is no virtue evident in such *nomoi*. Some may seem courageous, but excessive boldness underlies their apparent virtue. It is also possible, however, for a city to assist the upward pull and found its *nomoi* on a *logos* taken either from a god or from some human being who knows of such things. The true reasoning of its *nomoi* would then save the city from *aphrosyne* by assisting all citizens in following the upward pull within their souls and teaching them how to rule and be ruled with justice.

The first task of *paideia* is to enable the soul to resist the violent downward pulls of pleasure and pain, boldness and fear. Once it learns to resist them, it has won the first and best victory, the victory over itself. The victory can be won in childhood if the love and desires of children are properly guided through play. If play (*paidia*) is ordered in a way that leads children to acquire good habits, then *paideia* may succeed in leading them to all of virtue. Only those who are able to rule themselves (*archein hauton*) and are rightly educated throughout the whole of their lives may become good, the Athenian says. A proper education must avoid going astray after the first victory has been won. In particular, it must avoid the great folly and imprudence of mere cleverness in calculation. It must enable the soul to follow the upward pull with true reasoning until it acquires the first and best of the divine goods.

The Athenian calls those who follow the upward pull "the race of gold." The name recalls the use of Hesiod's myth of the ages in the *Republic* to differentiate among the three races or classes of the *kallipolis*. All children born in the *kallipolis* are sorted at birth according to the metal mixed into their souls by the god. It is not explained in the dialogue how the metals in the soul are evident. The children are then directed to the occupation for which they are best suited and the *paideia* appropriate for their function within the city.[4] In contrast, the puppet ikon reveals that the god has mixed all metals into the souls of all human beings. The members of the Athenian's golden race cannot be determined at birth. *Paideia* alone, carried on throughout the whole of life, and not birth or occupation, will indicate who is a member of the golden race. All will therefore have the same *paideia* in the Athenian's city.

The Athenian does not speak explicitly of who may be said to belong to the race of gold. He says only that the upward pull is in need of assistants or "rowers [*hyperaton*]" if the golden race is to be victorious over the other races. This is an ambiguous remark. In the context of the use of Hesiod's myth in the puppet ikon, the other races are comprised of those who follow the downward pulls of the baser metal cords. The golden race, therefore, would seem to include all those who have won the first victory over themselves, the victory over pleasure and pain, by holding on to the golden cord and following its pull in some way. But the Athenian's ikon also refers to cities. In this context, the golden race is comprised of all those fit to rule a city—all those who have lived their lives assisting the upward pull with true reasoning and who have thereby acquired *phronesis* and *nous*. Both contexts are intended by the Athenian's remark, and both must be taken together if it is to be understood. The golden race includes all human beings who have won the first victory and whose lives are guided by the god or divine *nous* in some way. Some are "rowers" and others are skillful pilots. Together they may be victorious over the other races; alone they cannot be (cf. *Republic* 540d–41a). The Athenian's city is founded for the golden race of Hellas. He excludes all who belong to the other races, and he establishes *nomoi* that allow rowers and pilots to sail together toward the end that guides them all. What is more, the city's *paideia* allows all rowers to learn as much of the art of piloting as they wish. This is the best way to ensure that, in time, they will become perfect citizens capable of ruling and being ruled with justice.

Part of the significance of the puppet ikon and the definition of *paideia* it is meant to illustrate emerges more clearly in the Athenian's extensive discussion of *paideia* at the beginning of the second half of the *Laws* (791a–94a). Children experience the violent downward pulls of the baser cords very strongly and require the greatest assistance in following the gentle upward pull. If they are to win the first victory, their frenzied dispositions (*manikon . . . diatheseon*) must be replaced by prudent habits (*hexeis emphronas*) at an early age, when character (*ethos*) is most decisively formed by habit (*ethos;* cf. *Nichomachean Ethics* 1103a14–18). Prudent habits are those of the correct way of life, which neither pursues pleasures nor flees pains entirely. The extreme pursuit of pleasure makes the young ill-humored (*duskola*), irascible (*akrachola*), and easily moved by trifles. Extreme enslavement to painful toils, on the other hand, makes them lowly (*tapeinous*), illiberal (*aneleutherous*), misanthropic, and unsuitable for living in community with others. The correct way of life enjoys the middle (*to meson*). Its prudent habits may be instilled in children through a mixture of persuasion and compulsion. The playful seriousness of games leads them away from enslavement to toils and the compulsion of honorable punishment leads them away from enslavement to pleasure. The middle, however, is not a simple arithmetic mean between extremes. The correct way of life is not lived in accordance with the *logismos* alone. It is lived according to the upward pull that leads to *phronesis* and *nous*. The Athenian says explicitly that

the middle is also the condition of the god. Human beings, therefore, must follow the habit (*hexin*) of the middle way if they are to
become, as far as possible, like the god. They will then be worthy
to be called divine (*theion*).

The Athenian also describes the middle way from prudent habits to the god as a voyage. Newborns are frenzied in body and soul,
he says. So too are Bacchic and Corybantic revellers. Revellers
cure themselves of their frenzy through dance and music. Newborns may be cured in the same way. Nurses should rock and sing
to them continuously in order to still their frenzies and allow
them to embark on the middle way. This is more than homespun
advice about a homeopathic cure. It reveals a fundamental principle: "it is beneficial for all, and not least for the youngest, to
dwell—if it were possible—as if they were always on a ship at sea"
(790c–e). The Athenian explains shortly afterwards that it is indeed
possible. He says that all of life is a voyage (*tou plou*). His discussion of children's *paidia* and *paideia* is similar to what a ship-
wright does in laying down the keels of ships and thus outlining
the shape they will assume when complete. He is laying down
keels for souls in order to outline the passages of life (*ton bion
peiromenos*) that are best (803a–b). The best ways of life may be
known just as the best shapes for ships may be known: by considering the end of the voyage for which they have been made.

Every soul is a ship on a voyage toward the same end. To speak
of it, the Athenian recalls the puppet ikon. In his own words, he
looks toward the god and speaks from the experience (*pathos*).
Human affairs are unworthy of great seriousness (*megala spoudes*),
but it is necessary to be serious about them in some manner. The
Athenian says he speaks of them in a well-measured (*symmetron*)
way, that is, in accordance with the *meson* that is the condition of
the god. By nature (*physei*), he says, the god is worthy of complete
and blessed seriousness. Since human beings are the playthings
(*paignion*) of the god, they should spend their lives playing the
most beautiful games (*kallistas paidias*): sacrificing, singing, and
dancing. The Athenian's *nomoi* describe such games for those who
will live in his city. They will live out their lives in accordance with
the way of nature (*kata ton tropon tes physeos*), being puppets of
the god and sharing in some small portion of the truth (*smikra de
aletheias;* 803b–4c).

If the Athenian is to be able to educate all children born in his
city with serious play directed toward the god, then all their parents must also be open to his persuasion in some way. This means

that they, in turn, must have been fortunate enough to have had good keels laid for them in their childhood and that they will have followed the middle course themselves for some time before coming to colonize the city. In other words, all those who come to colonize the Athenian's city will be good rowers, willing to follow a skillful pilot in search of the best passage through life. The city will be inhabited only by the golden race of Hellas.

The Athenian's discussions of colonization with Kleinias lead to this conclusion as well. He says their city should not be colonized by an overflow mob from some other city arriving in the manner of a bee swarm. Instead, colonists should be drawn from all of Hellas. But the Athenian also insists that not every Greek who wishes to come will be accepted (707e–8b). Just as herds of animals are purged by the removal of the ill-born and unhealthy in body, so too the herd of those who might wish to enter the city must be purged by the removal of all whose souls have been ruined incurably by a corrupt upbringing. The criterion for selection is simple: the bad will be turned away and the good will be given as gracious an invitation as possible. The Athenian neither elaborates further on the difference between the bad and the good nor describes the selection process. He only remarks that it will be possible to tell one from the other by testing them "with every sort of persuasion (*peitho*) over a sufficient period of time" (735a–36c).

The colonists chosen for the Athenian's city will be willing to live by *nomoi*, whose end is to make all subject to them as happy (*eudaimonestatoi*) and as friendly to one another as possible (*malista allelois philoi;* 743c). They will have no hatreds against one another when they arrive (737b), in large part because of the reason for their emigration. The best colonists will probably be those who have been part of an emigration that occurs "when part of a city [is] compelled to move to some foreign place because of civil strife [*stasesi*]" (708b). To use the terms of Socrates' account of the longer way recalled by this passage, the best colonists will be taken from the parts of cities that are threatened with destruction by the civil strife caused by cave-dwelling beggars starved of the good. They will be common-sense souls who refuse to live any longer in cities that have become sophistic dreamworlds. If a sufficient number can be found in Hellas, Magnesia will be entirely a city in the common home, illuminated by the sun and the good, and all the cities left behind will be entirely Hades (cf. *Republic* 520c–21b).

The possibility that Magnesia will be a city in the common

home inhabited by the golden race of Hellas is suggested more explicitly in the Athenian's remark to Kleinias that there have been times "when a whole city went into exile, completely overpowered by an irresistible attack" (708b). This is a reference to myth, not to Greek history. It refers to the emigration of the Phaiakians described in the *Odyssey*. The Phaiakians at one time lived in the spacious land of Hypereia. The name of their land associates them with the sun, Helios Hyperion (12.176); indeed, their own name indicates that they are a "shining" or "brilliant" people. Zeus even describes them as a people "near to the gods in origin" (5.34–36). The Phaiakians were thus godlike mortals. They had the misfortune, however, of living near the Kyklopes in Hypereia. The Kyklopes were a race of cave-dwelling, man-eating giants who had no true knowledge of laws or any good customs because they believed themselves to be better than the gods (9.105–15, 215, 273–98). To escape them, king Nausithoos led all the Phaiakians on a voyage in ships to the island of Scheria. They lived there in peace, for the Kyklopes had no ships nor any builders of ships among them (6.4–12; 9.25–26). The colonists of the Athenian's city are similar. They are human beings near to the gods who long to escape the lawlessness (*paranomia*) of the grotesque, hybristic cave-dwellers who have attacked and overpowered their cities. They have good ships and are willing to follow a kingly pilot to an island in the sun where they will be able to live in peace according to *nomoi* that honor the god above all things. In other words, they are the golden race of Hellas and the city toward which they row together is the only city in Hellas founded entirely in the common home.

The first words to be spoken to the colonists after they "have arrived and are present" give an account of the god that guides both the rowers and pilots of the golden race in all things: "the god (as the ancient saying has it) holding the beginning [*archen*] and end [*teleuten*] and middle [*mesa*] of all things that are [*ton onton hapanton*], completes his straight and revolving course according to nature [*eutheiai perainei kata physin periporeuomenos*]" (715e–16a). The Scholiast writes that the "ancient saying" mentioned is Orphic: "Zeus is the beginning [*arche*], Zeus is the middle [*messa*], from Zeus all things [*panta*] are created, Zeus is the foundation [*puthmen*] of the earth and the starry heaven [*ouranon asteroentos*]." The differences between the Orphic saying and the Athenian's speech announce the end of the age of Zeus and the beginning of the age of *nous* to the assembled colonists. The god of the new age is more than the *arche* of all things in heaven and earth; he is also their *telos*. He is thus both their existence and their excellence. The god is beyond all that he holds, exceeding it in power and dignity (*Republic* 509b). The Athenian's phrasing distinguishes between the *arche* and *telos* of all things and the middle (*mesa*). This suggests that human beings may turn toward the god beyond all things by the middle way leading toward *phronesis* and *nous*, the first of the divine goods.

The Athenian speaks allusively and evocatively in his description of the god who is the guide for all Magnesians. His words might seem paradoxical or even incomprehensible if taken to refer to physical motion alone since a straight course and a circular revolving motion seem irreconcilable.[5] Magnesians, however, will not understand them in this way. They will understand his words to refer to the motion of *nous* in the cosmos and in human beings. Since they are experienced rowers, Magnesians will know how to guide themselves according to the revolution of the cosmic sphere. Their study of number will teach them how the cosmos may also be said to have taken a straight course. Their study of "one and two and three" as well as of the relation of line and surface and volume will instruct them in the Pythagorean account of the demiurgic genesis of all things (817e–20d). Magnesians, therefore, will understand that all things having volume, indeed the cosmos itself, came into being on a straight course from the One. The straight and revolving motion of the cosmos is matched by a comparable motion in human beings. The purpose of studying number, the Athenian says, is to be able to transcend one's nature by a "divine art" (747b). The path of transcending one's nature is ascent and descent along the middle way. One's *psyche* and *nous* may ascend toward the god or divine *nous* beyond the cosmos in loving response to the upward pull on the golden cord, but the ascent must always be followed by a descent or homecoming. If a human being is to become divine, insofar as it is possible for him to do so, he must participate in the ascent and descent as often as possible. The repeated ascent and homecoming of human *psyche* and *nous* necessary for a divine life may thus be said to be a straight and revolving motion comparable to the straight and revolving motion of the cosmos. All these motions together constitute the motion of *nous*.

The words the Athenian chooses to direct the colonists to the god, "*eutheiai perainei . . . periporeuomenos,*" are not only a reference to motion requiring study to be understood. They also refer more immediately to the god. They are an evocative allusion to the good god (*eu-theos*) in the beyond (*peraie*), the god beyond all that has been brought forth (*peri-poreuomenos*).

The Athenian continues the remarks to the assembled colonists by reminding them of what they left behind when they emigrated (716a–b). He says that those who forsake the divine law (*ton theon nomon*)—that is, the *nomos* that accords with *nous*—must pay "blameless penalty" to justice. Anyone who abandons the god, he says, will be abandoned by the god. His catalogue of those who have turned away is rather colorful: those puffed up with boastfulness; those who pride themselves, in mindlessness (*anoia*), on their riches and honors or on their good bodily form; and those who believe themselves to need no ruler (*archontos*) or guide (*hegemonos*) because their souls are inflamed by *hybris*. When human beings abandon the god, they "join with others like themselves" and leap about "overturning everything," each attempting to be great before the others. In the imagery of Socrates' account of the ascent from the cave, those who refuse to ascend toward the sun and the good turn away instead to live together in a Hades of their own creation where they compete against one another in mindless ways for meaningless honors and prizes (*Republic* 514a–17a). The Athenian says that the penalty such human beings pay to justice is the "complete destruction" (*arden anastaton*) of themselves, their households, and their cities. The Magnesian colonists were prudent enough to leave their cities when civil strife and war among such men threatened them. The god abandoned their cities when they emigrated. The Athenian's remarks upon their arrival give them news that the cities they left behind have been completely destroyed by those who remained (cf. *Republic* 521a).

The Athenian's next remarks to the colonists announce the theodicy of the new age. These comments are addressed in part to Kleinias so that he might better understand the differences between human beings who are willing to emigrate to the first city in the age of *nous* and those who will not leave the cities of the age of Zeus. The Athenian says, "The god, for us, is the measure [*metron*] of all things in the highest degree—far more so than, as the others say, some human being." All those who are willing to live in the age of *nous* take the god as their measure and do everything in their power to become like him. The others do the opposite. All those who follow the god may acquire the divine goods. Those who abandon the god in pursuit of the human goods must pay blameless penalty to justice (716c–e; cf. 624a–25a).

The Athenian's contrast of the two measures recalls several things said by Socrates in the *Theaetetus* and the *Republic*. In the *Theaetetus*, Socrates says there are two *paradeigmata* for all human beings: the divine (*theion*), which is most happy (*eudaimonestaton*), and the godless (*atheon*), which is most wretched (*athliotaton;* 176a–77c). If human beings make themselves similar to one (*homoioumenoi*) through their actions, they then become dissimilar to the other (*anomoioumenoi*). Those who have wisdom (*sophia*) and true virtue know that the god is in no way unjust in any respect. They make themselves like their *paradeigma* by fleeing from the mortal realm, in which it is impossible for evils to perish, toward the divine realm, in which it is impossible for evils to exist. Flight (*phyge*) from the mortal realm, Socrates says, is "to become like the god [*homoiosis theoi*] as far as possible." In this way a mortal becomes just and holy (*hosion*) with *phronesis*. But there are also those who are seemingly wise and who commit many injustices and say and do unholy things (*anosia*). Their foolishness and extreme lack of *nous* (*eschates anoias*) make them ignorant of the god's blamelessness and unaware that they cannot avoid paying penalty for their injustices. They pay penalty "by living the life that resembles that to which they make themselves similar," the most wretched *paradeigma*. Socrates does not name the lives that are most like the two *paradeigmata* in the *Theaetetus*. He names them in the *Republic:* the life of the true philosopher and the life of the tyrant. The philosopher takes the good beyond being (*epekeina tes ousias*) as his *paradeigma*. The tyrant, once he has fled law and reason (*phygon nomon te kai logon*), takes as his most wretched *paradeigma* certain slavish pleasures beyond (*epekeina*) the various genuine and bastard pleasures described by Socrates (*Republic* 509b, 587b–c). The tyrant does not even take "some human being" as the measure of all things. For him "the measure of all things is pig- or dog-faced baboon or some still stranger creature" (*Theaetetus* 161c).[6]

Not all human beings are either philosophers or tyrants, but all live their lives between the two *paradeigmata* that philosophers and tyrants most closely approach in their own. All human beings, even philosophers and tyrants, are divine puppets suspended between the cord that transmits the upward pull of the divine *paradeigma* and the cords that transmit the downward pulls of the most wretched *paradeigma*. In other words, all human beings are suspended in the region between virtue and vice. None can escape the region and the tension between the pulls. The pulls demand a response, and all human beings bear the responsibility for the manner in which they respond. The philosopher responds by following the middle, upward way that leads to all virtue. He ascends as far as is possible for a human being, but he cannot escape the downward pulls entirely. The tyrant responds by refusing to follow the upward pull in any way. He descends as far as is possible for a human being, but he cannot escape the upward pull entirely. He pays penalty for his descent by becoming the most vicious possible human being, not simply an animal.

The Athenian tells Kleinias explicitly that his address to the colonists is not intended for the "entirely savage [*panta pasin omais*]." It is intended for those who are "as persuadable as possible to virtue [*eupeithestatous pros areten*]." He intends it for all those who are open to the persuasion of the true philosopher and are willing to follow him upward along the middle way toward all virtue. Those who prefer to follow the tyrant's savage way will not be allowed to enter the city. The Athenian then describes the differences between the two ways and between the human beings who follow them by quoting Hesiod, a poet with whom Kleinias is undoubtedly familiar (718c–19a). He tells Kleinias that Hesiod was wise (*sophon*) to write that the way (*hodos*) to vice is "smooth to travel" and "without sweat" because it is "very short." The longer way is different:

> Before virtue the immortal gods have set sweat
> And a road that is long and steep
> And rough at first. When you reach the end [*akron*],
> Then it's easy to endure, but the ascent is hard.
> (*Works and Days* 289–92)

Few mortals ever reach the end of either way. The lives of most are between the two ways. And what is more, fewer are drawn to the shorter way than its ease of travel would suggest, for all mortals understand what lies at the end of it. The Athenian does not complete Hesiod's verse. He assumes Kleinias will be able to recall the next lines and understand that there are a number of ways to take the long and steep upward road. The verse continues:

That man is altogether best [*panaristos*] who understands all things
   himself [*panta noesei*]
And marks what will be better afterwards and in the end [*telos*];
Good also is the man who listens to one who speaks well [*eiponti pitheta*].
But the one who neither understands by himself nor listens to another
And takes to heart [*en thumoi*] what he hears is an utterly worthless man
   [*achreios aner*].

(Works and Days 293–97)

Hesiod does not simply distinguish between the virtuous and the vicious. He also distinguishes between those good human beings who are willing to follow the upward road with the guidance of someone who has completed the ascent and the utterly worthless ones who refuse all guidance.

The Athenian is as wise as Hesiod, for he uses a similar understanding of the differences among human beings to ensure that the good enter Magnesia and the worthless are turned away (cf. 735a–36c). He intends Magnesia to be the common home of the golden race of Hellas. It will be a city in which the altogether best— those ruled by the divine *nous* in all things—rule the good through *paideia* and persuasion (*peitho*) alone and direct them toward the *telos* they all seek. Those who refuse to take to heart (*en thumoi*) the divine *nous* in any way will have no place in the city.

8 THE MOTION OF *NOUS*

THE PRELUDE TO THE FIRST LAW for Magnesians states that "the human race by nature [*physei*] participates in immortality [*meteilephen athanasias*], and it is the nature [*pephyken*] of all to desire it in every way." The puppet ikon reveals that it is also in the nature of all human beings to be able to turn away from their natural participation in immortality. The Athenian refers to this possibility in the prelude when he adds: "For anyone voluntarily [*hekonta*] to deprive himself of this is never pious [*hosion*]" (721b-c). The first prelude enjoins all Magnesians to do everything in their power to become like the divine measure of all things. Magnesians make the god the mark of all pious reverence (*tes eusebeias skopou*), the target of all their shafts (716c-17a; cf. 962d). But not all human beings are Magnesians. Some attempt to deny that they participate in immortality by nature. They are voluntarily impious. How is this possible? The puppet ikon provides a partial answer to this question. The Athenian's most complete answer is given in his discussion of impious deeds and utterances in book 10 of the *Laws*. This is one reason that the Athenian's discussion of impiety deserves to be called, in Kleinias's words, "the most beautiful and best prelude for all our laws" (887b-c).

The puppet ikon describes human existence in the region of virtue and vice, but it is only a sketch of the human *psyche*. The configuration described by the *logismos* and the cords of pleasure and pain cannot give a complete account of virtue and vice because a human being is more than the relation of calculative reasoning and the bodily affections. The shortfall is made up partly by the Athenian's suggestion of what lies beyond the upward and downward pulls. A more complete account of the pulls is necessary. The Athenian describes the responses of the soul to the pulls as types of love. If a human being is to acquire the divine goods, and particularly *phronesis* and *nous*, then his whole soul must respond to the upward pull; and if he is to turn away from the upward pull toward *aphrosyne* and *anoia*, then his whole soul must turn away

190

and respond to the downward pulls (cf. 886a–b). The soul's turning away is self-love. The Athenian says self-love is "the cause [*aitia*] of everyone's wrongdoing on every occasion" (731e). Similarly, the soul's assisting response to the upward pull on the golden cord may be called love of the god or love of divine *nous*. In book 10 the Athenian expands his account by locating the experiential centers of the two loves within the human *psyche*. Love of self is centered in *thumos* (spirit). The Athenian would agree with Hesiod that the utterly worthless refuse to take the god to heart (*en thumoi*) in any way. The experiential center of what may be called the love of the god, on the other hand, is described in the Athenian's second ikon, his discussion of the motion of *nous* (897e).

The discussion of the law concerning impiety is addressed to all those who deprive themselves voluntarily of their natural participation in immortality. It is the Athenian's intention that no such human being be allowed to colonize Magnesia. The discussion, therefore, may be taken as part of the testing—"with every sort of persuasion over a sufficient period of time" (736b–c)—that the founders of the city will use to purify the herd of colonists of the incurably diseased and to cure all those who are naturally good but drawn toward impiety in some way. This is another reason that it is the best prelude for all the laws (887b–c). After the city has been founded, however, the discussion becomes the lengthy prelude for the Magnesian law concerning impiety. As such, it will be studied by Magnesian children along with all the other speeches in the *Laws* (811c–e). The Athenian intends all his speeches and preludes, not only this one, to lead Magnesians to participate in immortality in every way. Nonetheless, a law for impiety is necessary for the city. Proper *paideia* is not always sufficient. The Athenian explains that "there will always arise people, sometimes more, sometimes less, who have this illness" (888b).

Piety and impiety are not the properties of words or speeches alone. They are rather states of the soul that find expression in words and deeds. In particular, impiety is a diseased state of the soul. In the *Republic*, Socrates calls it "ignorance [*agnoia*] in the soul." Spiritual ignorance, not the ignorance of impious words, is "truly the falsehood [*alethos pseudos*]"; the falsehood in words is only its "after-arising image [*hysteron gegonon eidolon*]" (382b–c). Socrates also agrees when Adeimantus calls all speeches about the god, gods, or the divine "types of theology [*typoi peri theologias*]" (379a). The speeches arising from diseased souls are as much a type of theology as are the speeches arising from healthy souls. Both give evidence in words of possible human responses to the divine.

The speeches that express the soul's turning away from the divine are discussed by the Athenian in the *Laws*, and the speeches that express the soul's long and difficult ascent toward it are discussed by Socrates in the *Republic*. Of the two spiritual states, the former finds a more consistent expression in words. In the *Republic*, Socrates presents two measures for speeches about the divine that allow many different speeches to be considered as instances of the pious type of theology. The first measure is a theodicy. The god is good in reality (*agathos ho ge theos toi onti*). He is not the cause (*aitia*) of all things, but of the good alone. And he is not responsible (*anaitios*) for evil in human affairs; it has other causes (*ta aitia;* 379b–c, 380c). The second measure accounts for the god's unchanging perfection. All things divine are wholly free of falsehood (*apseudos*). The god and all things divine are in every way best. The god, above all, then, does not change; he is one and true (*haploun kai alethes*) and never deceives human beings with phantasms or falsehoods in speech or in deed (381b–c, 382e–83a). The Athenian's discussion of impious theology in book 10 of the *Laws* provides a similar summary. The three propositions he discusses are presented as a paradigmatic account of all expressions of impious spiritual *agnoia*. Its spoken expressions are closely related to the impious deeds that originate in the same spiritual state. The Athenian says that everyone who voluntarily does impious deeds or utters impious speeches suffers (*paschon*) from one of three related affections of the soul: he may not be led to suppose (*ouch hegoumenos*) that the gods *are* (*theous . . . einai*); or he may suppose that they exist, but do not mind or take heed of human beings (*ou phrontizein anthropon*); or he may suppose they take heed of human beings, but are easily appeased (*euparamuthetous*) by sacrifices and prayers (885b; cf. *Republic* 365d–66a).

There is no place for impiety in Magnesia. All Magnesians are pious in a way that accords with Socrates' two measures for piety in the *Republic*. Magnesians are led to suppose (*hegoumenous*) by their *nomoi* that the gods *are* (885b). This does not mean, however, that their *nomoi* require them to accept dogmatically, under threat of punishment, a theology consisting of three propositions contrary to the three negative propositions of impious theology.[1] If it were possible for a city to be founded in this manner, the greatest consequence of its *nomoi* would be the same spiritual *agnoia* that underlies all impious theology.[2] The Magnesian *nomoi* concerning the divine are not a negation of a negation. They affirm what the negative propositions attempt to deny. The *nomoi* accord with divine *nous*, the leader (*hegemon*) of all divine goods for human beings. Therefore, by following where their *nomoi* lead them, Magnesians travel the path of the soul's ascent toward the god and away from the spiritual *agnoia* of the impious. Magnesians accept the two measures of Socrates' pious theology, in speech and in deed, because both are the after-arising images of their own openness to the perfectly good and unchanging god.

The Athenian says there will always be human beings, usually young men, with the illness of voluntary impiety. Their spiritual *agnoia* manifests itself in the contempt (*kataphronesantes*) they have from childhood for all expressions of piety, and it leads in adulthood to the complete corruption of their thinking (*dianoian diephtharmenois*). What is more, there is not one sufficient reason (*henos hikanon logon*), he says, for them to have contempt for those things that are affirmed by anyone with even a small amount of *nous* (*smikrou nou*). Their contempt is against *phronesis* and *nous*, and not according to it. But if not for a reason, then why? The Athenian answers this question when he explains to Kleinias how it would be best for them to reply to such men. They should speak gently, "quelling spiritedness [*sbesantes ton thumon*]" (887c–88c). The spiritual *agnoia* of voluntary impiety originates in *thumos*, and if it is to be cured, the *thumos* must first be brought under control. Those with the disease must first be made as tame (*hemeroun*) as possible by some combination of persuasion and compulsion (890c). The Athenian warns Kleinias that they must be careful to speak without spiritedness (*athumos*) themselves. They do not, however. When the reply to the three propositions of impious theology is complete, the Athenian in particular admits that he has spoken rather vehemently. The reason for the eager spirit (*prothumia*) in his words, he says, is his love of victory (*philonikian*) over evil human beings (*kakon anthropon*). The Athenian's love of victory is not a form of self-love. He does not speak with the intent of simply silencing the impious. The love of victory motivates his words because the impious must first be made to understand that they cannot act as they wish before they may be persuaded to give up their irrational contempt. A degree of compulsion necessarily precedes persuasion in their case. The Athenian tells Kleinias that his words are ultimately directed to persuading (*peithein*) the impious to hate themselves (*heautous men misesai*) as they are and somehow to love an opposite disposition (*enantin pos ethe sterxai;* 907b-d). He intends, in other words, to persuade them to hate the self-love that is based on the thumotic contempt of all things divine, thereby making it possible for them to love the god in some way.

The Athenian understands that it is not always possible to persuade an impious man to hate his self-love. Success or failure in the attempt ultimately depends on the character of the man being addressed. The Athenian describes the differences between the curable and the incurable in his account of the various punishments appropriate for different types of impiety that might arise in the city. He says some men who are not led to suppose that the gods exist have a "naturally just disposition [*ethos physei . . . dikaion*]" and refuse to act unjustly. Others are unjustly disposed by nature and have no such restraint. The spiritual illness of the two types is the same, but the soul of the former is far healthier than that of the latter. In particular, the naturally unjust man— the one who is commonly said to have a "good nature [*euphyges*]"— is full of guile and trickery. This type possesses "all the magical drugs [*pasan ten magganein*]" necessary for his deceits. The two worst of the type are sophists and tyrants. Sophists generally have strong memories and sharp wits. Tyrants generally lack any restraint concerning pleasures and pains. They are similar in using their wits to satisfy their unrestrained desires. But this is not all the Athenian has to say about them. Their natural injustice and their thumotic spiritual ignorance transform these characteristics into a type of madness (*mania*). The Athenian calls it sorcery (908b-d). The magical drugs possessed by sophists and tyrants are poisons, not of the body, but of the soul. They first poison their own souls and then the souls of others using words, "spells and incantations" that persuade all those so disposed to commit acts of great injustice. By poisoning themselves such men become beasts (*theriodeis*) who hold all human beings in contempt (*kataphro-nountes*). Their resentment of anyone superior to them expresses itself in a desire that all should become beasts. For the basest of reasons, therefore, such men "attempt to destroy utterly individuals and whole households and cities." The Athenian says such men should die as animals do (909a-b, 932e-33e, 934c-d). The naturally just, however, need not suffer such punishment. Although they too have become impious through a lack of *nous* (*anoia*), they have become so without "evil anger or disposition." In Magnesia there is a chance that such men might become moderate (*sophronein*). They need only remain open to the persuasion of those, like the Athenian, who know of "the salvation of the soul [*psyches soteria*]" during their five-year imprisonment (908e–9a).

The Athenian's discussion of impiety begins with a description of what one such youth might say out of contempt for the Athenian, Kleinias, and Megillus (885b–e). The youth would first admit that the Athenian's summary of the three propositions of all impious theology is true. However, he does not say that he is not led to suppose (*hegeoumenos*) the gods exist. Instead, he says only that he and his kind do not believe (*nomizomen*) in the gods. His choice of words is significant. Gadamer notes that the verb *nomizo* "is located in the public sphere. It does not relate to the inner experience of holding something to be true . . . but to the palpable publicity of behaviour."[3] When the youth claims the Athenian's words are true, therefore, he is speaking falsely and with a contemptuous voice. The youth would also admit that most of the impious do not refrain from doing unjust things. However, he would explain such behavior by claiming that it accords with what is said to be best by the most honored and perhaps even the majority in society. It seems to him that acting unjustly is only against old conventional beliefs. It is not against the law that the unjust who presently predominate in society take for themselves. In the safety of numbers, the youth can turn the charges around so that it is the Athenian who is speaking and acting unjustly or contrary to present conventional beliefs about justice (cf. *Gorgias* 482e–84c).

The youth has more to say out of contempt for the Athenian, Kleinias, and Megillus. He would mock them by saying that since the three claim to be gentle lawgivers, impious people demand (*axioumen*) that no harsh threats be directed against them. They must be persuaded by words alone. They make this demand, of course, with every intention of refusing to listen (cf. *Republic* 327c). The youth also mockingly sets the terms of the discussion itself. He demands that the Athenian teach (*didaskein*) the impious by "adducing adequate evidence [*tekmeria legontas hikana*]." But what is the measure of adequate evidence and proper demonstration in such matters? The youth demands an apodictic proof (*apodeixis*), a logical demonstration from the things he believes to be true axiomatically. This is impossible. The Athenian can only offer an exhibitive proof (*epideixis;* 892c). He can only point out the reality of the spiritual experience the youth has voluntarily ignored or refused to perceive and invite him to look again.[4] Since the youth believes that the worst of the unjust speak well about the truth (*aletheian*), it is unlikely that he would take up an invitation offered in words alone.

The Athenian's discussion of impiety is not a public speech. His words are meant to be studied, not audited. In particular, they will be studied by all Magnesians, initially as part of the *paideia* of their early youth (809e, 811c–e). The impious who might arise in the city will study them again in a setting better suited than a classroom to focusing their attention. They will study the Athenian's speeches in discussion with members of the Nocturnal Council. This will perhaps enable them to tame their *thumos*. If they become moderate, the *paideia* they have received from their upbringing according to the *nomoi* may then succeed in leading them away from self-love. Schoolchildren without the illness of impiety study the Athenian's speeches for a different reason. They are not drawn toward the impiety described. Their *paideia* draws them toward the highest of the divine goods, *phronesis* and *nous,* and they find nothing attractive in the *aphrosyne* and *anoia* of those who have been abandoned by the god. They study the Athenian's discussion to learn about *nous* itself.

At the beginning of the discussion, the Athenian tells Kleinias and Megillus that he has discovered the source or spring (*pege*) of all the arguments made by the impious young and those who instruct them. They say that fire, water, earth, and air are the first of all things and call them by the name nature (*physis*). A river of arguments flows from this spring. The natural elements mix and combine, the impious contend, to form all existing things: the sun, the moon, all the bodies in the heavens, the earth, and all things on earth. All things that have their genesis from nature, or rather from the chance combinations of natural elements, are completely without *psyche* and *nous*. All things except human beings, that is. The *psyche* and *nous* that humans possess somehow came into being after all body or matter (*soma*) had come to be. The impious do not explain how this happens. They turn instead to *techne*. Human *nous* makes *techne* possible. *Techne* in general is not natural. Particular *technai*, however, do not produce anything that "partake[s] much in truth [*aletheias*]" unless they "have their power [*dynamin*] in common [*ekoinosan*] with nature." This does not mean that *technai* are used to bring about what would happen by nature and chance in any event. *Techne* is "victory by force [*nikai biaxomenos*]" over nature. When human beings have power in common with nature, therefore, they use their cleverness and physical powers to act in the natural realm in order to bring about unnatural but possible ends. This is especially true in politics. What is "most just [*dikaiotaton*]" is whatever enables a man to win victory by force over others. This part of political *techne* is in accord with what is strictly natural and true. All the rest—the greatest part of political *techne*—is legal convention. The whole of legislation is achieved entirely by art, and thus its assumptions (*theseis*) are not true (*ouk aletheis*). The gods too are not natural. Their existence is thus an untrue assumption that itself exists only as a legal convention. The gods are wholly the products of political *techne*. Those unskilled in the *techne* believe in the gods. In other words, they believe that the stones in the heavens—the sun, moon, and stars—are actually gods or divine things when they have only been declared to be so by those skilled in making legal conventions. They may even believe in gods that have no *soma* at all. Those skilled in political *techne*, the impious say, know that all such assumptions are not true, but there is nothing to prevent them from using such beliefs to win victory over others in the *polis* (886d–e, 888e–90a, 891c).

The Athenian says the spring produces a flood of "mindless opinion [*anoeton doxes*]" that threatens to ruin all the young of Hellas through impiety and destroy all the households and cities of Hellas through factional strife. The Athenian's argument in response originates in a different spring and leads all those who wish to escape such ruin and destruction toward Magnesia. He begins by saying that the impious are wrong to believe that *soma* is the first thing that came into being and the "first cause [*proton . . . aition*]" of the genesis and decay of the things in the cosmos. *Psyche* came into being before *soma*. More than anything else, *psyche* is the "ruling cause [*archein*]" of the changes and reorderings of all things, if not simply their first or ruling cause. *Psyche* rules *soma* because it came into being before *soma* and hence is closer in origin to the *arche* from which everything originates. The rule of *psyche* over *soma* is evident in all things, even in human beings and their affairs. All things akin to *psyche* have priority over bodily matters. The most important of the things akin to *psyche* listed by the Athenian are *techne, nomos,* and *nous. Techne* and *nous,* he says, are the "ruling causes [*archomena*]" of the things called nature by the impious. Similarly, *nomos* and *nous* are the ruling causes of the things they say are merely legal convention. The Athenian says the term nature should be used for what is truly first; similarly, the term *nomos* should be used for what is truly in accordance with *nous* (891c–92c; cf. 714a, 957c). Since the Magnesian *nomoi* are truly in accordance with *nous* and honor what is truly first, the city will thus be able to escape the impiety and factional strife that threaten all of Hellas.

The Athenian says his argument demonstrates what follows from the understanding that *psyche* is older than or prior to *soma.* It does more. It leads from the understanding that *psyche* is elder than *soma* to an understanding of what is truly first and is named the *arche,* divine *nous,* or the god. The Athenian chooses his words carefully when he begins his argument in order to lead it toward this end. He says that *psyche* is "among the first things that come into being [*en protois gegenemene*]." It cannot be first without qualification and therefore does not deserve the name nature. The Athenian only says that because *psyche* comes into being before *soma,* it is "in a way by nature [*diapherontos physei*]." It is "by" what is truly first. To say that something is "by nature," therefore, means that it is in accord with the god or divine *nous,* and not in accord with what is somatic. Understanding nature in the light of what is truly first, the Athenian is able to reply to the "mindless opinion [*anoeton doxes*]" of the impious that all things are ruled by art, nature, and chance. He says: "God pilots all things [*panta*], and fortune [*tyche*] and due measure [*kairos*] together with god pilot [*diakybernosi*] all human things. . . . [T]hese are accompanied by a third: *techne.* For the pilot's art [*kybernetiken*] should cooperate with due measure [*kairos*]" (709b–c; cf. *Philebus* 66a–b). The Magnesian *nomoi* are according to *nous* not because the city's lawgiver has the political ability honored by the impious, but because he has some measure of the god's piloting art.

The Athenian presents the arguments that follow from the priority of *psyche* in such a way that anyone taking up the questions that arise from them will be led toward what is first without qualification. Little can be inferred from the priority of *psyche* to *soma* alone. Both *psyche* and *soma* come into being. *Soma* does not have its genesis from *psyche.* The genesis and decay of the things in the cosmos perceivable by human beings are only the changing and reordering of *soma* by *psyche*. The argument obviously cannot proceed without an account of what enables *psyche* to be the ruling cause (*arche*) of all changes and reorderings of things. It must account for the presence of divine *nous* in all *psyche*. What is more, since human being is *nous* within *psyche* and *psyche* within *soma*, the argument must also account for the relation of human *nous* to the divine *nous*, which has no genesis itself but is present in some way in all things that come into being.

The Athenian makes the limitations of the argument about the priority of *psyche* evident at the outset by the imagery he uses to describe it to Kleinias and Megillus. He says his own argument, and not the one originating in the spring of the impious, is a "swift flowing river" that the three of them must cross without becoming dizzy and being swept away (892d–93a). The river is an image representing genesis, or coming into being in all its forms. More precisely, it is an image representing an account of all things given by men thought to be wise. In the *Theaetetus*, Socrates uses the image to represent the arguments of Protagoras, Heraclitus, and others by calling them "the river men" (*tous reontas*). The river men agree that all things are always becoming or are perpetually in motion (*Theaetetus* 152d–e, 181a). The Athenian's warning about the river current, therefore, indicates that unless his argument about the genesis of *psyche* and *soma* is followed carefully, it might cause someone to become dizzy and be swept away toward the impieties of the river men. Protagoras in particular was led from his belief that all things are becoming to the conclusion that man is the measure of all things.

What sort of clearheadedness is required in order not to be swept away? And what does the safe crossing itself indicate? The *Theaetetus*, again, is helpful in clarifying the Athenian's imagery. Socrates hopes to escape the river men, but he also hopes to escape those who argue the opposite. The "arresters of the whole [*tou holou stasiotai*]," as he calls them—Parmenides, Melissus, and their like—insist that nothing becomes. They claim instead that "all things are one [*hen ta panta*]." What is more, Socrates hopes to escape the worst possible fate; if he falls between the two camps, he says, he will be seized by both sides and dragged in opposite directions by their tug-of-war. This would seem to exhaust all possible alternatives: all things are becoming, or being, or some uneasy combination of both. Yet Socrates hopes to escape all these propositional claims. He does so by fleeing the mortal realm altogether. He says that "flight is to become like the god as far as possible" and that becoming like the god is becoming "just and holy [*hosion*] with *phronesis*" (*Theaetetus* 176a–b, 180d–81b). The Athenian's crossing of the river, therefore, does not lead to the argument of the arresters of the whole. He would not wish to arrest moving things any more than he would wish to set immovable things in motion. And a successful crossing does not depend on discovering the correct combination of becoming and being, or motion and rest. It depends on acquiring the clearheadedness of *phronesis* by crossing into the immortal realm and ascending toward the god as far as possible.

The Athenian escapes the river current by ascending. He says three things at the outset that suggest how the ascent is undertaken and how Kleinias and Megillus might follow him (892d–93b). He offers to cross the river alone at first, questioning and answering himself, and then call the others across when the safe way has been discovered. In the *Republic*, this way is a passage (*poreia*) called dialectic. Dialectical questioning is not undertaken alone in order to reach propositional consistency. It is a "test of *ousia* rather than one of *doxa*," and it leads toward the soul's vision of the good itself in *noesis* (*Republic* 532a–b, 534b–c). The Athenian's dialogue with himself, "through the entire argument" if necessary, is an invitation for his interlocutors to follow his guidance in dialectical ascent. Kleinias takes up his offer as soon as the way becomes clear (894b). However, Megillus, who had recently broken a long silence to voice his agreement that arguments should be made against the impious, does not speak again until the very end of the dialogue (cf. 842a, 891a–b, 969c–d). The Athenian also invokes the aid of the gods for the argument. This is the second of the Athenian's two prayers in the *Laws*.[5] The first invoked the aid of the god who is the measure of all things in the founding of the city that begins the age of *nous* for human beings (712b–14a, 715e–16d). The Athenian's "well-measured [*metrion*]" dialogue with himself is thus directed to the same end as his prayer. Finally, the Athenian also tells Kleinias and Megillus that they may "set forth [*epeisbainomen*]" into the argument and escape its current by holding on to a "safe ship cable [*asphalous peismatos*]." His imagery recalls the puppet ikon's description of the soul's ascent toward the god, following his upward pull on the golden cord. By changing the golden cord (*neura*) into a ship cable, however, the Athenian suggests that more will remain to be said after his present argument reaches its end. The ship cable must be anchored properly if it is to be safe. His account of how it is anchored is given in the third ikon of the dialogue, the Nocturnal Council.

The Athenian begins by speaking of things and their appearances. He refers to things in the common sense of the term: things perceived by human beings. The Athenian also refers to the motion of things. The motion of a thing perceived by a human being is an appearance that may reveal something that is not immediately apparent. From this simple beginning, he takes up the argument (893b–e). Things are neither all in motion nor all at rest, he says. Some move and some remain still. Movement and rest take place in locations. A moving thing may move either in one location or in many. The second type of motion, movement in or through many locations, is locomotion. There are two kinds of locomotion: gliding (locomotion in a straight line) and rolling (locomotion in a circular path). The first type of motion, movement in one location, is less straightforward. Indeed, the Athenian's account of it is rather complex. He says it is similar to the turning of a circle's circumference. But there is more to this type of motion than meets the eye. It is not a circular motion. The circumference of a circle only turns when a circular thing rolls, and rolling is a distinct kind of locomotion. The Athenian also says that things that move with the first type of motion obtain the power (*dynamin*) of their movement from something that is still in the middle (*en mesoi*). Again, the circumference of a circle, or even a sphere, receives no power from its middle point. Without explaining how the power of movement is transferred from what is itself unmoving to things that move in this way, the Athenian then says that the first type of motion has a rotation (*periphora*) that turns around (*periagousa*) the largest and smallest circles together, distributing its power to all of them according to reason or proportion (*kata logon*). The accordance (*homologoumena*) of the many circular paths in one *logos* is seemingly impossible (*adynaton*). And since it seems impossible, beholding such motion produces a wonderful effect (*pathos*) in human beings. The Athenian is speaking, of course, of the only thing that moves in this way, the cosmos. He says the cosmos is "the spring [*pege*] of all wonders [*tou thaumaston hapanton*]." More specifically, the accordance of all things within the cosmos that receive the power of their motion from a wondrous unmoving source is the spring of all wonder in human beings. It may even be said to be the spring of all piety, since the experience (*pathos*) of wonder instilled in human beings by the turning around of the cosmos turns around (*periagoge*) their souls as well.

The Athenian's argument has moved rather quickly from a common-sense beginning to an account of the cosmos, the thing that contains all things and the location of all locations and motions. Even the wonder that may occur when a human being beholds the cosmos is itself an event within the cosmos. It would seem possible for the Athenian now to argue that the accordance of all things within the cosmos that gives rise to such an experience in the human soul is the best evidence human beings have of *psyche*'s rule over *soma* in all things. But he does not. Instead, he proceeds by enumerating other types of motion (893e–94a). The third type is splitting, he says. It occurs in the encounter of things in locomotion and things standing still. The fourth is coalescing, which occurs when two things in locomotion encounter one another. The fifth is growth or increase. This is coalescing in which the condition or character (*hexis*) of a thing persists. The sixth is decay or decrease. This is splitting in which the *hexis* of a thing persists. The seventh is destruction. Destruction is either splitting or coalescing in which the *hexis* of a thing is not preserved. What should the next motion be? The Athenian establishes a pattern in the definitions of the second through seventh motions. The next in the sequence should be the motion that preserves the *hexis* of a thing in growth and decay, the motion of genesis within the cosmos. However, the Athenian's eighth motion refers to something else. The sequence of the second through seventh motions makes no reference to the first motion, since all occur within the cosmos. The eighth motion refers directly to the first alone. Although he makes no reference to a demiurge of the sort described in the *Timaeus*, the eighth motion may best be described as the motion of the demiurgic genesis of the cosmos itself. His account of it makes explicit the distinction between the coming into being of *psyche* and *soma* and the coming into being of things through the reordering of *soma* by *psyche* that has so far only been implicit in the argument. His account also gives the name, or rather one of the names, of the unmoving source of all movement that wondrously maintains the accordance of all things in the cosmos.

The Athenian says that the demiurgic genesis of all things (*pantos*) begins when a certain experience (*pathos*) occurs: the *arche* obtains growth (*auxen*). Everything (*pan*) then comes into being through a transformation or change (*metaballon, metakinoumenon*) that is both one and many. It is one because it is a transformation of the *arche;* it is many because it passes through a number of transformations. The Athenian says that after the *arche* obtains growth, it proceeds to the second transformation (*metabasin*), then to the next, and when it arrives at the third it allows of perception by perceivers (*aisthanomenois*). When the cosmos or the all has come into being in this way, it is "really in being [*esti de ontos on*]." It cannot suffer complete destruction (*diephthartai pantelos*) since it cannot pass through a transformation into another character (*hexis*). Its character is preserved by the *arche* from which it originated (894a).

Demiurgic genesis and the genesis of things within the cosmos are different but not unrelated things. It is not possible to give an account of the initial growth (*auxen*) of the *arche* by comparing it to the growth or increase (*sygkrinomena*) of the fifth motion. The opposite is the case, since the growth of the fifth motion must be understood in relation to the growth of the *arche.* Coalescence becomes growth (*auxanetai*) only when the *hexis* of a thing is preserved in the process—in other words, only when something of the *arche*'s initial growth is present to preserve *hexis*.

The most telling indication that the eighth motion is demiurgic genesis is the Athenian's description of its several transformations. He is deliberately ambiguous in numbering them. Including the *arche*'s initial growth, there seem to be either three or four. The ambiguity can be clarified by reference to the Athenian's earlier account of the education of Magnesians in mathematics and solid geometry. All Magnesians will learn of "one and two and three," he says, as well as of the relation between line and surface and volume (818c, 819e). In Pythagorean number symbolism, the tetractys (1, 2, 3, 4) represents, among other things, the demiurgic genesis of all things that have volume from the transcendent One through the geometrical series of line, surface, and volume. There are three transformations of the One and three transformed states, and in the third state of the series, all things that have volume have come into being. The One cannot be considered to be either a transformation or a state or condition. It is beyond motion and rest. The Athenian's account of demiurgic genesis is similar. It is ambiguous because it shifts from numbering transformations to numbering transformed states. This prevents the entire process of the *arche*'s transformation from being understood as a series of motions and stillnesses. The arche is unmoving, but it is not a thing at rest. And yet it remains beyond the motion of its own transformation into the cosmos, just as it remains beyond the motion and rest of the things within the cosmos that came into being from it.[6]

The Athenian's account of the eighth motion is brief as well as ambiguous. Its brevity suits its original purpose of showing the priority of *psyche* to *soma* in demiurgic genesis. *Soma* only becomes evident in the final transformed state. When perception is possible, space, time, motion, and *soma* have all come into being. The Pythagoreans called all these things "volume." The final transformation completes the genesis of the cosmos; the first, therefore, cannot be understood as the motion of a thing in space and time. The growth received by the *arche* is thus appropriately called an experience (*pathos*) to indicate that it occurs before "volume" itself comes into being. But what is the initial growth of the *arche*? It is the transformation of the *arche* in which *psyche* has its genesis (cf. *Timaeus* 34b–35b). *Psyche* is the first thing in genesis, and *soma* among the last (cf. *Laws* 892a). The close relation of *psyche* to the transcendent *arche* of all things enables it to order *soma* when the cosmos is complete. When the things of the cosmos are finally perceived by perceivers, they give evidence of the rule of *psyche* over *soma* and the wondrous preservation of all things by the *arche* through *psyche*. A human being can perceive things and their motions through space and time with his eyes, but he can also perceive *psyche* and the *arche* in the cosmos with the eye of his own *psyche*. The experience (*pathos*) of wonder in the human *psyche* when it "sees" the cosmos is akin to the experience (*pathos*) in which all *psyche* originates. They have the same source, for the *arche* from which all things originate and by which they are preserved is also the source (*pege*) of all wonder for human beings.

Taken together, the Athenian's descriptions of the first and last motions are an account of the genesis and order of the cosmos. It remains only for him to describe more explicitly how the *psyche* and *soma* that come into being from the *arche* are related in the motion of the cosmos. He does this by describing two more motions, which he playfully numbers the ninth and tenth. The ninth and tenth motions are the motions of *soma* and *psyche* respectively. The Athenian does not reveal this immediately. Instead, he names the ninth "other-moving motion" and the tenth "self-and-other-moving motion." He then describes them by reformulating his previous account of the second to the seventh motions. The tenth motion, he says, is always capable of moving itself in "splittings and coalescings, growths and the opposite, generations [*genesisi*] and destructions." It is "one motion among all the motions" because it combines within itself all those listed (894b–c).

The Athenian's new list is odd in several ways. All the motions that are aspects of the tenth motion are given in the plural. This indicates that all occur within the cosmos. Only the demiurgic genesis and the rotation of the cosmos cannot be described in the plural, and neither is described in the list. The Athenian also mentions only one motion in an order other than that of his initial list—generations. And he does not mention decays explicitly. These two oddities together indicate that generations within the cosmos are not to be confused with demiurgic genesis. They should be understood according to the pattern of definitions established by the original list: generations are combinations of growth and decay in which the *hexis* of things is preserved. Finally, locomotion is not mentioned as one of the motions that comprise the tenth. In the Athenian's reformulation, therefore, locomotion is the other-moving motion of *soma*. *Soma* only moves when it is acted upon in some way by the self-and-other-moving motion of *psyche*. The Athenian's reformulation, then, reveals that there are not ten motions. The motions of his initial list can be recategorized as the motions of *psyche* and *soma* within the motion of the cosmos, which received its genesis from and is preserved by the transcendent *arche*.[7]

How should the motions be numbered? The Athenian puzzles over this for a while in order to give Kleinias and Megillus some indication of what has been said. The tenth and ninth motions are obviously ranked first and second relative to each other, but are they truly first and second? They are not. When *psyche* and *soma* and their respective motions are ranked either according to their place in demiurgic genesis or according to their place in the order of the cosmos, they are second and third. The genesis of all things is a single transformation of the *arche* in which *psyche* and *soma* have their place, and the wondrous rotation of the cosmos preserved by the *arche* orders all the motions of *psyche* and *soma* within it. Following Aristotle's suggestion, the first motion evident in both the genesis and the order of the cosmos may be called the motion of the unmoved mover. The unmoved mover is as fitting a name as the *arche*, the One, the divine *nous*, and the god. No matter what its name, the self-and-other-moving motion of *psyche* and the other-moving motion of *soma* are inferior to its own.

Several things said by the Athenian suggest that *psyche* and its motion should be ruled by what is truly first. He says that *psyche* is first in genesis, but adds that it is first "according to reason [*kata logon*]" (894d). He describes *psyche* as the cause (*aitia*) of all transformation and motion in all things, and he once even describes the motion of *psyche* as the "*arche* of all motions," but the Athenian never says that *psyche* is the *arche* of all things (895b, 896b). When he brings this part of his argument to a close by stating that the *psyche*'s priority to and rule of *soma* has been demonstrated, he says that "*psyche* rules [*archouses*] according to nature [*kata physin*]" (896c). Rule according to nature is rule according to what is truly first. When these various hints prove insufficient to prompt either Kleinias or Megillus to ask him what is truly first, the Athenian speaks openly about it.

The Athenian draws several conclusions from the argument for his two interlocutors. *Psyche* leads all things in heaven and on earth, including human beings, by its motions. It is the ruling cause of all motions and thus the cause of all conditions of things. In other words, it is a cause (*aitia*) of all things because it is the cause (*aitia*) of the "good and bad, beautiful and ugly, just and unjust" conditions of all things. The motions by which *psyche* leads things and causes their conditions—its wishing (*boulesthai*), considering (*skopeisthai*), managing (*epimeleisthai*), deliberating (*bouleuesthai*), opining (*doxazein*) and the like—must therefore have a guide or measure. When its motions follow the measure, *psyche* is the cause of good, beautiful, and just things in heaven and on earth. When they do not, it is the cause of bad, ugly and unjust things (896c-97a; cf. 892a-b). The measure is *nous*. It is evident to all reasonable human beings that *psyche* with *nous* guides the cosmos. The Athenian says that when *psyche* takes part in *nous* (*noun . . . proslambousa*) in its rule, "it guides all things rightly and happily" or with a good daimon (*ortha kai eudaimona paidagogei panta;* 897b). He even says that genesis itself was for the sake of this: "that the life of the all (*pantos bioi*) may begin to be [and be ruled by; *hyparousa*] eudaimonic being [*eudaimonon ousia*]" (903c). And since *psyche* with *nous* rules the cosmos that came into being in this way, it is evident that "the whole way [*hodos*] and course [*phora*] of heaven and all the beings in it has the same nature [*physin*] as the motion, rotation, and calculations of *nous* [*nou kinesi kai periphora kai logismois*]" (897b-d).

Human beings may also "take part in *nous*" and thus be ruled by *psyche* that is "full of *phronesis* and *arete*." Unlike the cosmos, however, they may also refuse to take part in *nous*. Their souls may "associate with *anoia*" and become "mad and disordered [*manikos te kai ataktos*]." This is the folly of the worst type of impiety. Those whose souls are ruled by *anoia* cannot perceive the rule of *psyche* with *nous* in the cosmos. They see *anoia* in all things and believe the cosmos itself is nothing but *soma*. They are then mad enough to claim that the eudaimonic "life of the all [*pantos bioi*]" has come into being for their sake alone. The truth is just the opposite. Humans come into being for its sake and must pay penalty if they turn away from it (903b–d).

It would be impossible for the Athenian to convince Kleinias and Megillus immediately of the truth of all he says and suggests. They must think things through for themselves. However, the Athenian tells them that it would be just for them "to take [him] as a helper [*proslambanein*]" in considering what has been said. They should do exactly what *psyche* does when it "takes part in *nous* [*noun proslambousa*]" in order to acquire *phronesis* and rule *soma* according to its guidance. He asks them to begin by considering a question that he admits is difficult to answer prudently (*emphronos*). He inquires what the nature of the motion of *nous* is (897b, d). Kleinias, as always, is open to persuasion. He follows the Athenian attentively as the question is taken up. Megillus, on the other hand, remains silent until the end of the dialogue. He listens for a long while and then tells Kleinias that he will follow the Athenian's guidance as Kleinias himself does. All three then agree to share the risk in founding the city according to the *nomoi* the Athenian has described (969c–d). Had Kleinias not met the Athenian on the road from Knossos, the city he would have founded with Megillus's assistance alone undoubtedly would have been different (cf. 624a–27a).

What then is the nature of the motion of *nous*? It is obviously neither the self-and-other-moving motion of *psyche* nor the other-moving motion of *soma*.[8] It is also not the motion of the demiurgic genesis of all things, for that is a unique event. What is more, it is not the motion of the cosmos either. The Athenian says that *nous* has "motion, rotation, and calculations." The motion of the cosmos is the rotation of *nous*, and not its motion. The Athenian makes this clear in his discussion of "the *eikon* of *nous*" (897e–98b). He recalls the beginning of the argument for Kleinias and Megillus and then playfully tells them that one of the motions he described in his lists resembles a wooden sphere (*sphairas*) turned on a lathe.

That motion, he says, is the ikon of *nous* itself. He does not call it the ikon of the motion of *nous*. The wooden sphere then, is an image of the ikon of *nous;* and the motion of the cosmos, its rotation, is obviously that ikon. When the Athenian says that an object like the sphere has "the greatest possible kinship and similarity to the rotation [*periodoi*] of *nous,*" he is explicitly identifying the motion of the cosmos as the rotation of *nous* and not its motion. *Nous* is evident in the rotation of the cosmos, but it remains beyond the cosmos even while preserving it. The motion of *nous* is not limited to what is evident in the cosmos. The rotation of the cosmos makes it the spring of all wonder and piety for human beings.[9] There is something in the ascent of human *psyche* and *nous*, beginning in wonder, that also takes part in *nous*. It too is a noetic motion.

The Athenian continues to be playful by claiming to be a poor craftsman (*demiurgos*) of ikons in speech. He adds that the motion of a wooden sphere being turned on a lathe may be taken as an original, and the motion of the cosmos as well as of *nous* itself as its two ikons (898a–b). This turns everything upside down, but for a reason. The serious purpose of the Athenian's play with images is to reveal how things appear to the impious. A wooden sphere is a manufactured object that is a false image or *phantasma* of the true image of *nous:* the motion of the cosmos according to reason (*logos*) and order (*taxis*). When the rotation of *nous* is said to be an image of a manufactured sphere, the cosmos appears to be nothing but matter for human production and *nous* itself appears to be nothing but a human capacity for production that lacks all guidance. The fantastic dreamworld that results when such folly comes to predominance among human beings is described in one of the beautiful ikons in speech in the *Republic*, the ascent from the cave.[10]

The Athenian attempts to lead Kleinias and Megillus away from such madness toward a prudent understanding of *nous*. He warns them, however, that they must not look "straight on" at *nous* in considering the nature of its motion. If they turned their eyes to look straight at the sun, he says, they would "bring on night at midday." The same would happen to their *nous* if they looked straight at *nous* (897d–e). The full significance of the Athenian's remarks emerges when they are compared to similar passages in the *Republic* and *Philebus*.

In the *Republic*, Socrates tells Glaucon that eyes become blind when they attempt to see the sun itself. The sun can only be seen by *nous,* the eye of the soul. The *nous* recognizes it as the offspring of the good itself. However, the *nous* can only see the good itself briefly or fleetingly. It too would become blind if it attempted, in the Athenian's words, to look "straight on." The folly is the same in both the visible and the intelligible realms. Eyesight and light are both "sunlike [*helioeide*]," but it would be wrong to believe that either of them is the sun. The blindness of such a belief would be an inability to see either the sun or its light. So too, the human *nous* when it has *episteme* and *aletheia,* the light of the good, are both "goodlike [*agathoeide*]," but it would be wrong to believe that either is the good beyond being. The blindness of such a belief would be the inability of the *nous* to see either the good or its light (*Republic* 508e-9b, 515e-16b). In the *Philebus,* Socrates gives another name to the good beyond being. When Socrates argues that the good life for human beings is one of *phronesis* and *nous* and the pleasures that accord with them, Philebus utters what he believes to be a clear refutation: "your *nous,* Socrates, is not the good." Socrates replies: "My *nous,* perhaps, Philebus, but not so the true and divine nous [*alethinou . . . kai theoion . . . noun*]" (*Philebus* 22c). The good beyond being is the divine *nous.* The same may be said of the relation between human *nous* and divine *nous* as has been said of the relation between human *nous* and the good itself. The Athenian's warning to Kleinias and Megillus distinguishes between human and divine *nous* in the same way that human *nous* and the good are distinguished by Socrates in the *Republic.* The worst type of blindness that may result when human *nous* looks at divine *nous* "straight on" is described as madness in both the *Republic* and the *Laws.* The madness of sophistry and the madness of the worst impiety are the same disease of the soul.

In his warning the Athenian also says that *nous* is not visible or sufficiently knowable (*gnosomenoi hikanos*) with mortal eyes. This remark can be taken in two ways, and he explains both of his meanings in the discussion that follows. In its first sense, the remark indicates that night is brought on at midday by the assumption that *nous* is sufficiently knowable with mortal eyes. Those who see with mortal eyes alone are blind to all evidence of *nous.* They are the ones who believe that a visible and manufactured sphere can be the original of which the cosmos and *nous* itself are only images. The second sense of the Athenian's remark leads in the opposite direction. There is a way that *nous* is visible and even knowable with mortal eyes. The rotation of the cosmos is the ikon of divine *nous* and the spring of all wonders for human beings. If the mortal eyes and immortal *nous* of a human being look together in wonder at the cosmos and recognize it as the ikon of *nous*, it would not be wrong to say that *nous* thereby becomes visible and knowable. Looking at the cosmos in any other way leads to noetic blindness and impiety.

The Athenian's argument, as it now stands, is capable of silencing the curably impious if they have sufficient time and leisure to work through all that has been said with someone capable of directing their studies. The argument has certainly persuaded Kleinias that piety originates in wonder at beholding the cosmos and impiety in the opposite. Yet the Athenian raises one final question. Given that the whole cosmos is turned around (*periagei*) by *psyche* with *nous*, he asks Kleinias to consider if this may be said to be true of any particular thing in heaven (898c–99a). In the manner in which it is presented, it would be a difficult question for anyone to answer prudently, let alone Kleinias. The Athenian intends it to demonstrate how impiety may arise from geometrical thinking. Even though his own argument suggests it is inappropriate, the Athenian uses the relation between universals and particulars that is appropriate for geometrical deductions from axioms or for technical production to speak of the relation between the things in heaven and what transcends them. The Athenian asks Kleinias to consider the sun alone. Every human being sees the *soma* with mortal eyes, he says, but no one sees the *psyche* and the nature of its guidance of *soma*. They are intelligible through *nous* alone. This much has been established. But now, instead of speaking of these matters with *nous*, the Athenian formulates three propositions using "thought [*dianoemati*]." He says *psyche* either resides within the sun's *soma*, just as it does in human beings; or it resides in other bodies and moves the sun's *soma* indirectly; or it is entirely without *soma* and possesses "exceedingly amazing powers [*dynamis . . . hyperballousas thaumati*]" to guide the sun's *soma*. It may be an unfair question for Kleinias, who is too easily persuaded that one of the propositions necessarily must be true. The Athenian prevents him from choosing among them to save him from the consequences of the choice. None of them is true.

The three propositions suggest three other statements that are true only of the cosmos as a whole. All *soma* in the cosmos is ruled by *psyche* with *nous;* the cosmos is thus similar in a way to some human beings. All *soma* in the cosmos is moved by *psyche's* self-and-other-moving motion; *soma* alone has only other-moving motion. And the divine *nous* that is beyond the cosmos but capable of preserving it by ordering *psyche's* motion possesses "exceedingly amazing [*thaumati*] powers." It is thus "the spring of all wonders [*thaumaston*]" for human beings who take *nous* as the guide for their mortal eyes. When these three statements are made to apply to a particular thing in heaven using *dianoia*, they become possible causes of impiety. The second proposition most obviously may be a cause of impiety. If the sun is only *soma* acted upon by other bodies in which *psyche* resides, how is it that *psyche* resides in them and not in the sun? All indwelling of *psyche* within *soma* in the cosmos thus seems to be an unnecessary hypothesis. The first proposition leads to the same conclusion. If the sun's *psyche* resides in its *soma* and exercises autonomous self-and-other-moving motion, then the sun must possess *nous* in the same way human beings do. Since it does not, it seems the sun and all other heavenly bodies are only *soma* without *psyche*. The third proposition is the one the impious themselves would advance in order to contend that there is no *psyche* or *nous* in the cosmos. They would say that a *psyche* independent of human *psyche* and *nous* must have amazing powers to rule *soma* in the cosmos, but since such powers are evident only in the mastery human *nous* has over things, it follows that there is no *psyche* and *nous* in the cosmos independent of human beings.

The best measure for speech about the cosmos and everything within it is the experience (*pathos*) of wonder that occurs when human beings open to the divine *nous* behold the cosmos and its motion. One way the experience may be expressed by human beings is in giving a name to its source. The Athenian names it the *arche* and *nous;* other names are the good and the god. The same is true of all comparable experiences of things in the cosmos that lead to wonder before the whole. The Athenian explains this to Kleinias by telling him everyone should be led to consider the sun a god (*theon hegeisthai;* 899a–b). He does not describe the sun according to one of the three propositional deformations of things known by *nous* to be true of the cosmos as a whole. Instead, he says the sun is a chariot that brings the light of the good *psyche*—the *psyche* that takes part in *nous*—to all human beings. It is fitting to call the sun a god because its illumination is a source of wonder that may lead those who experience it toward the source of all wonders. It is a god ruled by the god. In the *Republic* (508a–9c), Socrates describes it to Glaucon as a god that is the offspring of the good beyond being.

The Athenian continues the explanation by telling Kleinias that the moon and the stars in heaven—even the years, months, and seasons ordered according to the motion of the cosmos—are fittingly called gods. He makes a concession to Kleinias's possible confusion by saying that they are gods because the *psyche* or perhaps *psychai* that are their causes (*aitiai*) are all "good [*agathai*] with all virtue." According to his own argument, however, there is one *psyche* that is the *aitia* of all order because it takes part in *nous* or the good beyond being. The Athenian concludes his argument by citing Thales. Thales' words are often cited by the impious. However, when the Athenian speaks them in openness to the persuasion of what is beyond, they are true. He says: all things are full of gods (cf. *De anima* 411a).

The argument against the worst type of impiety ends without having answered the question, What is the motion of *nous*? The Athenian has described the motion of the cosmos as an ikon of *nous* itself. However, this is the rotation of *nous*, not its motion. He has also distinguished between human and divine *nous* and suggested that their relation is to be understood according to the first ikon of the *Laws*, the divine puppet. By beginning his argument with a warning that those who would follow him must hold on to a safe cable with the aid of the god, the Athenian suggests that human beings may become like the god when human *nous* follows the upward pull on the golden cord, as far as it is able, toward the source of the pull, the divine *nous*. Human beings may escape the mortal realm by ascending along the way of the *logismos*, but they cannot escape it entirely. They remain mortal and are always drawn between the upward and downward pulls to some degree. In other words, the ascent of human *nous* along the way of the *logismos* can never reach the end. Human *nous* is not and cannot become divine *nous*. Its ascent must always be followed by a descent along the way it came. The best life for a human being is one of repeated ascents and descents. These are the *logismoi* of *nous* the Athenian mentions but never explains in his argument against impiety (897c). The *logismoi* of *nous* only become understandable when the Athenian concludes his description of the third ikon of the dialogue, the Nocturnal Council, and it then becomes possible to combine the puppet ikon with the ikon of *phronesis* and *nous* to obtain a complete account of the best possible human being. However, the *logismoi* of *nous* that order the best possible human life are not the motion of *nous* any more than is the rotation of the cosmos. The Athenian states explicitly that *nous* has "motion [*kinesei*], rotation [*periphora*] and *logismoi.*" The *logismoi* of *nous* are an ikon of *nous* itself, but not an ikon of the motion of *nous*.

What, then, is the motion of *nous*? It is both the rotation of the cosmos and the *logismoi* of human beings. All three of the Athenian's ikons thus describe the motion of *nous*. The Athenian also suggests that the demiurgic genesis of the cosmos should be considered together with its rotation as the manifestation of *nous* in all things, just as the ikons of the puppet and the Nocturnal Council may be combined to describe the manifestation of *nous* in human beings. He does not call his account of demiurgic genesis an ikon, however. It cannot be known by any human being in the same way that the other three manifestations of *nous* may be known. The motion of *nous* is one. It moves differently in the cosmos and in human beings. But the two motions may become one when a human being beholds the amazing powers of *nous* in the cosmos with wonder.[11] This in turn may lead to some understanding of demiurgic genesis.

The motion of *nous* in both its aspects is described in Socrates' song of the superheavenly region (*hyperouranion topon*) in the *Phaedrus* (246a–48e). All beings with *psyche* desire to ascend to this region, for *psyche* is immortal and is nourished by the source of all immortality outside of heaven (*exo tou ouranou*). Ascent is only possible on festive occasions; in particular, it is possible upon every completed period (*periodoi*) of the rotation (*periphora*) of the cosmos. On such occasions, human *psyche* is carried aloft on noetic wings. The flight is hampered, however, by the mortal body as well as by those parts of the soul that resist the ascent. Both drag the soul down in various ways. Only the human head (*kephalen*) may be raised into the outer region (*ton exo topon*), and this with great effort. Once outside, it is carried around (*periagei*) by the rotation (*periphora*), but only for a brief time—hardly enough time to behold the things that *are* (*ta onta*). The superheavenly region is the region of "truly existing being [*ousia ontas ousa*] visible only to *nous*, the pilot of the soul [*psyches kybernetei monoi theate noi*]." It is the region in which the noetic wings of the human soul are nourished. They receive little nourishment, however, even on the occasions of successful ascent. Not only does human *nous* hardly behold the things that *are;* it is far less likely ever to behold the source of all things beyond truly existing being. Human *nous* cannot remain in the region for any considerable part of one period of the rotation. That is, it cannot remain on the outside of the rotation of the cosmos for anything but a brief time because the motions of human *soma* and *psyche*, all of which are bound to the motions of cosmic *soma* and *psyche*, inevitably drag it downward as the cosmos rotates. Once the occasion of the ascent passes, the *psyche*, even though it may have failed to reach the superheavenly region, must descend the way it came. And once it has descended through heaven, "it goes home [*oikade elthea*]." Socrates concludes his song with the law of Adrasteia, the "unescapable" Nemesis. He says the *psyche* that follows the god and obtains a view of any of the superheavenly truths is free from harm until the next period (*periodou*) or occasion for ascent.

Magnesians will understand a good deal more than Kleinias and Megillus can be expected to have understood from the Athenian's account of the motion of *nous*. The prelude to their first law enjoins them to participate in immortality in every way, as far as they are able (721c). The god toward which they ascend in all their immortalizing is the divine *nous*. The Athenian describes the god's motion explicitly in his first words to Magnesian colonists: "the god, . . . holding the beginning and end and middle of all things that are [*ton onton panton*], completes his straight and revolving course according to nature [*eutheiai periainei kata physin periporeuomenos*]." Following the god always, the Athenian continues, is Justice, the avenger of those who forsake the divine law (*theiou nomou*). And the messenger of Justice (*Dikes . . . aggelos*) is Nemesis, or Adrasteia (715e–16a, 717d). The Athenian describes the guide for the immortalizing ascent and safe homecoming of all Magnesians in the final ikon of the *Laws*. The Nocturnal Council is the city's head (*kephale;* 961d). Every dawn it is raised into the superheavenly region for a time in order that it might guide all Magnesians that day with *phronesis* and *nous*, according to the god's measure.

9 THE GENESIS AND ORDER OF THE CITY

The Nocturnal Council (I)

THE ATHENIAN BEGINS TO describe Magnesia's offices and institutions near the middle of the dialogue. He tells his two interlocutors that their founding of a city in speech is a mythic discourse (*mythologian*), and he promises to continue recounting the myth in order that it not be left headless (*akephalon*). The mythical city would appear shapeless and would wander (*planomenos*) if it were left headless. It requires an institution to head it that is different from the ones the Athenian first describes (751e–52a). At the end of the dialogue, the Athenian identifies the Nocturnal Council of rulers (*ton archonton nykterinon syllogon*) as the city's head. More precisely, he identifies it is an *eikon* of the "community [*koinonias*] of head and *nous*" that is necessary to prevent the body and soul from wandering in a human being. It will be able to give direction to the city in the same way that head and *nous* together give direction to a human being. The Athenian calls this giving of direction "salvation [*soteria*]." He says the Nocturnal Council will be comprised of "perfected guardians [*phylakes apotelesthosin*]," whose like in "the virtue of salvation [*areten soterias*]" has never before come into being. Indeed, the council is the "perfect perpetual savior [*soterian . . . teleos aei*]" of the city. Its rule is "the salvation of [the city's] regime and laws [*soteria . . . politeia te kai nomois*]" (960b–c,e, 968a, 969b–c; cf. *Republic* 536b).

In the Athenian's myth of salvation, the Nocturnal Council completes Magnesia's genesis and preserves its order in something like the way the three Fates, Lachesis, Klotho, and Atropos, are said to complete and preserve souls. The Athenian's explicit reference to the Fates in his account of the council recalls both Socrates' saving myth in the *Republic* and his song of the superheavenly region in the *Phaedrus*. The similarity of the three mythical discourses illuminates the significance of the council within the city.

215

Socrates' description of the voyage of souls returning to life from death in the saving myth of the *Republic* is comparable to his account in the *Phaedrus* of the ascent to and descent from the superheavenly region by souls during life, according to the law of Adrasteia. The cycle of life, death, and birth described in the *Republic* is comparable to the cycle of celebration, ascent, and homecoming described in the *Phaedrus*. The former spans a whole life; the latter only a part of one day. But Socrates says that human beings are only "souls that live a day" in the *Republic*'s concluding myth. He also says that the Fates order the events experienced by the souls of the dead before they return to mortal life. The Fates are the daughters of Anagke (Necessity), who is also called Adrasteia and Nemesis. Socrates says the rotation of the cosmos itself is spun on Anagke's spindle. She is beyond it, for the spindle turns in her lap. Her three daughters are within the cosmos. They sing in cosmic harmony of what has been, what is, and what will be. After the souls of the dead have seen the turning of the cosmos and heard the singing of the Fates, they are prepared for their return. All souls must choose a *daimon* for themselves and a *paradeigma* for their lives. All may have eudaimonic lives if they choose well. If they choose poorly, "the god is blameless." Lachesis orders the casting of the lots among them, each of which bears a number indicating a soul's turn in choosing. The *paradeigmata* of lives are then displayed. None of them have "an order of the soul [*psyches . . . taxin*]," for a soul necessarily becomes different according to the *paradeigma* it chooses. After all have chosen, Lachesis gives to each the *daimon* that is his life's guardian (*phylaka*). All then go before Klotho, who spins together souls, lives, and daimons, and finally before Atropos, who makes the threads irreversible (*Republic* 616b–19b, 620d–e, 621b–c).

The Athenian's reference to the Fates indicates that the Nocturnal Council is necessary if Magnesia is to come into being. It is the *daimon* for the *psyche* of Magnesia that gives order to the city's life. It is also the *daimon* and order for the *psyche* of every individual Magnesian. The Athenian says the guardians of the council are the salvation both of the city's *nomoi* and of the "good-lawfulness [*eunomia*]" of Magnesia's souls. The council thus makes the *nomoi* "irreversible" and the lives of all who live by them eudaimonic (*Laws* 960c–d).

The Athenian once suggests that the council is the head for which the rest of the city is the trunk (964e). This single use of somatic imagery would seem to indicate a different significance for the council in the city. However, it is intended to be playful. The council is far more than a head. It is the embodiment of *phronesis* and *nous* in the city, ruling all *psyche* and ordering *psyche's* rule over all *soma*. Yet the council may be said to be the head for one particular body. In a way, it is the missing head of the Athenian's puppet ikon. The two ikons complete one another; taken together, they provide a complete account of the best possible human life, a *paradeigma* for all Magnesians throughout their lives. The puppet ikon indicates that every human being must always grasp (*aei xullambanein;* 645a) the golden cord and assist the upward pull. The council ikon describes how this may be done. In the Athenian's words, it describes the pilot's art (*kybernetiken*) that always cooperates (*xullabesthai*) with due measure in human affairs because it is directed by the god who pilots all things (709b–c).

The Nocturnal Council is an ikon of the community of *nous* and the head. It shows how salvation is possible for *psyche* and *soma* by the "blending of *nous* and the finest senses [*kalliston aistheseos*] and their becoming one." Human *nous* and senses are not independent of human *psyche* and *soma*. The *psyche* is the best part of a human being if it takes part in *nous*, and the head is the best part of human *soma* if the senses of sight and hearing are in good condition and are well ruled by *psyche* with *nous*. When *nous* and the senses become one, the ordering of human being by *nous* is complete and both are saved. When they do not become one, both are lost (961d, 969d).

To explain the meaning of these remarks, the Athenian gives a simple example of the piloting art. On a ship, he says, "the pilot and the sailors mix the senses with the *nous* of the piloting art to save themselves and everything about the ship" (961e). The correspondence with a single human being is straightforward: the pilot is *nous*, the sailors *psyche*, and the ship *soma*. The correspondence with a city is more roundabout. If the ship is a city, the pilot is its ruler and the sailors are those ruled. However, the ruler can no more be *nous* alone and the ruled the senses than the opposite can be the case. Every human being in the city must mix *nous* and the senses in some way to save himself, and all must find a way to cooperate in doing so in order to save the city. In other words, the sailors must know something of the piloting art, but they must also recognize who among them is the best pilot and follow his guidance in directing the ship toward its mark (*skopon*) or end (*telos*). The rule of the best pilot is not an end in itself. He is simply the best able to guide the rest in the voyage toward the end they all have in common. Unless a city is ruled in the same way, the Athenian says, it will be without *nous* and senseless (*anous . . . kai anaisthetos*). It will have many aims and its *arche* will wander (*planeo*). In Magnesia the Nocturnal Council will guide all toward the common goal in the best way possible. Its *arche* does not wander, and its aim is one (*hen*). Taking aim carefully, it shoots all things in the city like shafts (*bele*) toward the mark (*skopon;* 962a–e).

The Athenian's example of the piloting art serves as a reminder that Magnesia is to be inhabited by the pilots and rowers of the golden race of Hellas (cf. 645a). In particular, his reference to the shafts shot toward the mark by the Nocturnal Council indicates that the pilots and rowers have the same end in all they do. The Athenian uses the terms *bele* and *skopos* very rarely in the dialogue. The only other time he uses them together in the same way is in describing how the Magnesian colonists may become dear to the god by doing everything in their power to become like him. He says the colonists must shoot their shafts at "the mark of piety [*esebeias skopou*]." The shafts represent various ways that all may participate in immortality. The first of the ones listed, in descending order, is honoring "the gods who keep the city" (716c–d, 717a, 721b–c). This may best be done, he says subsequently, after studying the best prelude to all the laws, the prelude that discusses the motion of *nous*. The Athenian also lists several shafts that the Nocturnal Council will shoot at the mark. The last of the ones he lists, in ascending order, is the same as the first of the first list. No one may be a member of the council, he says, unless he has become divine (*theion*) or as dear to the god as possible and has labored over the prelude discussing the being of the gods. All must learn that *psyche* is the eldest and most divine (*theiotaton*) of all things that have come into being and that *nous* "arranges the all into a cosmos [*to pan diakosmekos*]" and gives order (*taxis*) to the motion of all things over which it has control (*egkrates;* 966c–e). All Magnesians shoot their shafts at the same mark, to the best of their ability, just as all acquire some measure of the piloting art by mixing *nous* and the senses, even though some will be rowers in comparison with others.

The Athenian's shooting and piloting imagery illuminates only part of his account of the genesis and order of Magnesia and the role of the Nocturnal Council in preserving that order. His whole account of the city is best understood by means of another image, the motion of *nous* itself. The Athenian's argument against impiety led to the conclusion that divine *nous* moves the cosmos in one way and human beings in another. The cosmos is moved by *nous* in both its demiurgic genesis and its rotation; of the two, only the rotation of *nous* is evident to human beings. Human beings themselves are moved by *nous* to ascend repeatedly along the way of the *logismos*. The three ikons of the *Laws* are thus ikons of *nous*. Taken together, they reveal the nature of the motion of *nous*. However, there seems to be no single ikon of the motion of *nous* in the dialogue. This is because the Athenian's whole account of Magnesia's genesis and order is his ikon of the motion of *nous* in all its aspects. Magnesia's demiurgic genesis and order is an ikon of the demiurgic genesis and rotation of the cosmos, and the guidance by the Nocturnal Council of the entire city in ascent and homecoming through *paideia* and persuasion is an ikon of the ascent of human *nous* to divine *nous*, as well as its rule over *psyche* with *phronesis*. The Athenian is guided by *nous* in becoming the cause (*aitia*) of Magnesia's genesis and order; the Nocturnal Council is guided by *nous* in preserving the city once it has come into being. The council is the embodiment in the city of the same "amazing powers" that are evident in the city's founder.[1]

The Athenian's play with ikons leads the reader of the dialogue to an understanding of the motion of *nous*, but it is his equally playful references to number and mathematics throughout the dialogue that are the best indication of how his whole account may be understood as an ikon of the motion of *nous* (cf. 746d–47a). Indeed, the full significance of the Nocturnal Council cannot be appreciated without some understanding of how the numerical references in the Athenian's detailed and often puzzling discussion of its composition and organization are related to those he makes in describing all other important Magnesian institutions and offices. The Nocturnal Council is the political end toward which Magnesia's genesis proceeds. And Magnesia's genesis is described in the imagery of a geometric progression. It is one way in which the city may be said to take up and honor solid geometry (cf. *Republic* 528b–c).

Magnesians will learn of these things through their studies. Once the city is founded, the Athenian says, all Magnesians, especially the young, will study three beneficial and relatively easy subjects presently thought to be useless, difficult, or impious by most Greeks. The first is calculation and number, or learning about "one and two and three." The second is the "measurement of length and surface and volume as one." The third is the "revolutions of the divine things" in the heavens or of "the cosmos as a whole [*holon ton kosmon*]." All three studies will have the ability to compel students to surpass their own natures "by a divine art" and become dear to the "greatest god [*megiston theion*]" in every way (747b, 809c–e, 817e–18d, 821a–22c). This is their primary purpose, but they have another purpose as well. They will also teach Magnesians about their city. The third subject, astronomy, will teach Magnesians how their city resembles the cosmic sphere. The first two, taken together, are essentially the study of Pythagorean mathematics and number symbolism. Pythagorean solid geometry will teach Magnesians how their city came into being. In particular, by studying it they will learn how their city, once well started, proceeded, "as if a circle [*kuklos*] in growth [*auxanomeme*]" as it became an ikon of the cosmic sphere (*Republic* 424a).

In the Athenian's argument against impiety, demiurgic genesis is described as a series of transformations originating in the *arche*. He implies that each transformation in the series may be understood as a receiving of growth (*auxe*) by the previous one; the first differs only in that it is a receiving of growth from the *arche* itself (894a). The Pythagoreans described demiurgic genesis similarly as a series of transformations originating in the transcendent One. They formulated the series in several different ways to account for the coming into being of all things. The origin, however, was always the One. The Athenian's brief discussion of solid geometry with Kleinias is based on one of the Pythagorean formulations of the series. He asks Kleinias if he has ever considered how line or length is commensurable with surface, and surface with volume. Kleinias assumes they are all commensurable, but can give no account of his assumption. The Athenian then raises a more difficult matter: "the relation commensurables [*metreton*] and incommensurables [*ametron*] have to one another because of a certain nature [*physei*]." Unfortunately, he says no more about these matters to Kleinias (819e–20c). His remarks suggest two things. Incommensurability is involved in the transformations from line to surface and surface to volume. However, there is a certain nature that explains the relation between commensurability and incommensurability and thus establishes a broader type of commensurability for the whole series of transformations. This suggests that the Athenian has a particular series in mind. Line, surface, and volume are commensurable as radius, circle, and sphere. The transformations from radius to circle and circle to sphere involve the incommensurability that has come to be known today as the "irrational" number π. But π has a certain nature that allows it to bring a type of commensurability to the entire series of transformations because it can be expressed as a relation of radius and circumference. Line or length becomes surface when it receives growth and is transformed into the radius of a circle. Using modern algebraic notation, the circle's surface is calculated through the formula $A = \pi r^2$. Similarly, surface becomes volume when the circle receives growth and is transformed into a sphere. The sphere's volume is calculated through $V = 4\pi r^3/3$. These are the transformations and mathematical calculations that comprise Magnesia's solid geometry. Their evidence throughout the Athenian's account of the genesis and order of Magnesia's institutions and offices indicates one way in which the city may be said to be an ikon of the motion of *nous*. Magnesia's coming into being is an image of the demiurgic genesis of all things that the Athenian describes as a series of transformations originating in the *arche*.

Pythagorean Teachings

A digression is necessary at this point in the discussion. Magnesians will have unique insight into the symbolic significance of their city's genesis and order because of their youthful study of mathematics and astronomy. But modern readers of the *Laws* are not Magnesians. The best way for them to learn of Magnesia's solid geometry and its broader significance is first to study Pythagorean mathematics and number symbolism. And this may not only be true for modern readers. There is some evidence in Plato's letters that his students were expected to have studied Pythagorean treatises before undertaking study of the dialogues themselves (*Letter 12; Letter 13*, 360b).[2] The Pythagoreans played a good deal with number. A study of their treatises would certainly illuminate the number play in the *Laws*. But modern students of the dialogue are confronted by a difficulty not encountered by Plato's own students: the treatises have been lost, and the teachings of the Pythagoreans are difficult to reconstruct accurately from available sources.

Nevertheless, an attempt must be made in order to advance the discussion of the *Laws*. The following summary is my own. It is limited to those teachings that are directly relevant to the dialogue.[3]

A reference to number is not necessarily a mathematical statement. Numbers are ciphers of the science of mathematics, but numbers, and even calculations, may also be used to symbolize or represent nonmathematical things. The Pythagoreans used number in both ways and understood the difference. For example, they used the term "one" in two ways—as the first integer and as a symbol or name for what is also called the god. Their recognition of the difference between the two uses is evident in the teaching that the divine One begat the one along with all other numbers. The two uses are different, but not strictly independent of each other. The significance of a series of calculations does not depend on their accuracy alone, but also on what they are intended to represent. Their mathematical accuracy alone has little or no independent significance. Pythagorean calculations, though almost always accurate mathematically, are often rather unusual for this reason. The Pythagoreans were not poor or confused mathematicians; their calculations were intended to represent something beyond mathematical truth. This is even true of their inaccuracies. They often allowed strict accuracy to give way to approximate accuracy that was better able to convey a symbolic meaning. And frequently such inaccuracies depended on the presence or absence of a single unit, a "one," at a significant point in the calculation.

All things originate in the One, the Pythagoreans say. The One begets the Two from itself, and together they beget all things. The One and Two, or Monad and Dyad, have many other names. In the *Laws*, the Athenian calls them the *arche* and the result of the *arche* receiving growth—in other words, divine *nous* and *psyche*. The Pythagoreans also call them rest and motion, limit and unlimited, odd and even, straight and crooked, and male and female (cf. *Metaphysics* 986a). The many different names serve to illuminate the diversity of all things that have their origin in the One and Two. All numbers from one to ten have similar symbolic significance. Together, they are called the decad. Three is the number of the whole, or of the beginning, middle, and end of all things. Four is the number of justice, or more particularly, of reciprocal equality (4 = 2 × 2). The well-known Pythagorean tetractys 1, 2, 3, 4 thus represents, among other things, the justice of the whole begotten by the Monad and Dyad. Five and Six are both marriage numbers.

The former is the odd or male one, and the latter the even or female one. Five is the hypotenuse of the right-angled triangle with sides of 3, 4, 5; it thus marries or unites the first male and female integers after the One and Two. Six is the area of the same triangle. It is also the only "perfect" number within the decad, a number that is the sum of all its divisors ($1 + 2 + 3 = 1 \times 2 \times 3$). Seven is closely associated with the Monad. It represents both demiurgic genesis from the One and the results of genesis. As the sum of the Three and Four, Seven is the number of the just whole that has come into being. As the number that recurs most frequently in the details of Pythagorean accounts of genesis, it represents the process itself. The Pythagoreans emphasized the Seven's relation to the One by claiming, at times, that it was the only parthenogenetic number within the decad. Eight and Nine both have significance within demiurgic genesis. The Pythagoreans describe genesis, in part, as a process of squaring and cubing, and these two numbers are the first cube ($8 = 2^3$) and square ($9 = 3^2$) outside the tetractys. Ten is the limit and unity of the decad. It is the sum of the tetractys 1, 2, 3, 4.

Plato's Pythagorean account of demiurgic genesis in the *Timaeus* describes an important configuration of seven numbers that came to be known as the *lambda* among the Neoplatonists. In the dialogue, Timaeus speaks of the begetting of all things by the One and Two as the god distributing *psyche* according to a proportion. The seven numbers of the proportion are one, two, and three; the squares of two and three; and the cubes of two and three (*Timaeus* 35b–36a). The numbers can be arranged in the shape of a *lambda* with sides of 2, 4, 8 and 3, 9, 27, united by the one at the point. The *lambda* is a symbol for the harmony and order of all things that have come into being from the One. The Pythagorean number for harmony is thirty-five. It is derived from the tetractys 6, 8, 9, 12 that is used in calculating harmonic intervals. The sum of the tetractys is thirty-five; and the sum of the numbers of the *lambda*, excluding the one, is also thirty-five. The Pythagorean number for order or proportion is thirty-six. It is derived in several ways. It is the sum of the first four odd and even integers; the product of the first even and odd squares ($2^2 \times 3^2$); the sum of the first three cubes ($1^3 + 2^3 + 3^3$); and the square of the perfect six. The sum of the numbers of the *lambda*, including the one, is also thirty-six. The harmony and order of all things is represented by seventy-one, the sum of thirty-five and thirty-six. Seventy-one has special significance because it also represents the relation of the Seven to the One. Like the Seven, it too symbolizes the justice of the whole. The most perfect justice, therefore, may be said to be a result of harmony and proportion.

The significance of the seventy-one can also be seen in a playful series of Pythagorean triangles demonstrating the relation of the things symbolized by thirty-five, thirty-six, seventy-one, and the One. Since $71^2 = 2(35^2 + 36^2) - 1$, it follows that the hypotenuses of two right-angled triangles with sides of 35, 36, and x may themselves be the sides of another such triangle (x, x, 71). What is more, if the sequence is continued, the hypotenuse of the triangle with two sides of 71 is approximately 2x. To the closest whole integer, x = 50, and 2x = 100. The 100, like the ten, is another number symbolically equivalent to the One. The Pythagoreans would accept the mathematical inaccuracy of such triangles in order that the entire series of calculations might demonstrate the complex harmony and proportion of all things that have genesis from the transcendent One.

The tetractys 1, 2, 3, 4 is ubiquitous in Pythagorean teachings. It has significance in harmony, geometry, and astronomy. In harmony it generates the basic intervals as a progressive series of ratios: octave (2:1), fifth (3:2), and fourth (4:3). If the series is continued beyond the tetractys, the major third (5:4), minor third (6:5), and whole tone (9:8) appear. The tempered semitone may then be calculated as $\sqrt{9} : \sqrt{8}$ and the tempered major third as $(9^2:8^2)$. The Pythagoreans preferred a second tetractys of 6, 8, 9, 12 to the first for most harmonic calculations because of its ability to generate all the intervals of the first as well as the whole tone. In geometry the tetractys 1, 2, 3, 4 represents several things. In its simplest meaning, it represents the progression of point, line, triangle (plane), and tetrahedron (solid). Once the most basic solid is generated in this way, the tetractys then represents the various triangular configurations of the four elements of the extended universe. The tetractys of tetrahedron, octahedron, icosahedron, and cube corresponds to the elements of fire, air, water, and earth (*Timaeus* 54d–55c). The tetractys 1, 2, 3, 4 also has a greater significance in geometry. It represents the demiurgic genesis of all things from the One rather than the point. The stages of genesis can be described in several ways: as a series of extensions (One, length, plane, solid); as the mathematical series of the *lambda* (One, number, squaring, cubing); or in the formulation of the *Laws*, as the series (One, radius, circle, sphere). All three of these series are not simply geometrical. They are astronomical as well. The genesis and order of all things in the cosmos can be summarized in a tetractys representing the greater significance of the *lambda:* One, harmony (thirty-five), order and proportion (thirty-six), and the justice of the whole (seventy-one). This is the final determination of the tetractys 1, 2, 3, 4. As such, it is best able to demonstrate the unity of all Pythagorean studies. The Pythagoreans studied the tetractys of number, harmony, geometry, and astronomy. Number was the basis of all their studies just as the One is the origin of all things. And they studied the harmony, order and justice of all things originating in the One by studying harmony, geometry, and astronomy (cf. *Timaeus* 17a).

Astronomy is also theology. As such, it has special significance for justice. The relation between astronomy, theology, and justice is described in perhaps the most important of Pythagorean texts, the *Golden Verses (chrusa epe)*, preserved in the commentary by Hierocles of Alexandria. The verses were most likely the catechism of the Pythagorean school. They may even have been recited collectively every night before retiring. They describe the cosmos as holy nature (*hiera . . . physis*), which makes mortals divine (*theion*) by revealing and bringing everything to light for them if they follow the path of divine virtue (*theies aretes*). If a mortal first honors the immortal gods according to the *nomoi* and practices justice in deeds as in words, Zeus will show him his *daimon.* And if he allows mind (*gnomen*), the divine gift (*kathuperthen aristen*), to be the charioteer (*heniochon*) of his *psyche,* he will leave *soma* behind and soar in the *aither.* He will be a deathless god (*athanatos theos*), divine (*ambrotos*), and no longer mortal (*thnetos;* cf. *Gorgias* 492e–94a, 507a–8a; *Theaetetus* 176a–77a; *Phaedrus* 246a–e). Although a theological poem, the *Golden Verses* are not without reference to number. According to the poem, the initiates say that Pythagoras "instilled in our souls the tetractys, the spring [*pagan*] of ever-flowing nature [*aenaou physeos*]." And in order that the initiates might learn more of the tetractys within their souls, the *Golden Verses* are seventy-one hexameters in length.

Serious Play with Number

The Athenian's playfully Pythagorean account of Magnesia's genesis and order is given as a tetractys with several different formulations. The transformations of the *arche* or divine *nous* are: *psyche, soma,* cosmos; radius, circle, sphere; and harmony, order, justice. All three of these formulations show that the founding of the city is an image of the series of transformations through which the cosmic sphere becomes the spring (*pege*) of all wonder for human beings (*Laws* 893c–94a).

The Athenian's Pythagorean number play is evident both in the drama of the dialogue and in his descriptions of the institutions and offices of Magnesia. The drama of the dialogue is in two parts. It begins with the Athenian's persuasion of Kleinias and Megillus and continues in his account of the successful genesis of his city in speech. The first part of the drama corresponds to the Pythagorean account of the genesis of harmony from the One. The harmony necessary for the founding of Magnesia to proceed is the agreement of all ten members of the Knossian nomothetic committee to follow the Athenian's persuasion in all things. Their agreement is assumed in the second part of the drama, the Athenian's account of Magnesia's successful genesis. The institutions of Magnesia, from the initial Council of Thirty-seven to the Nocturnal Council itself, are an image of the subsequent transformations of the tetractys. These transformations take the harmony of the twelve—the Athenian, Megillus, and the ten Knossians—as a radius and give it growth. The Athenian's references to number throughout his descriptions of Magnesia's institutions and offices are all playfully related to the two calculations ($A = \pi r^2$ and $V = 4\pi r^3/3$) necessary to transform the radius into a sphere. Once the series of transformations is complete, the initial agreement of the twelve has been transformed into a city that is an ikon of the cosmic sphere.

The conclusion of the dialogue is the bridge between its two dramas. The dialogue ends when the three agree to turn back from their ascent toward the cave of Zeus and persuade the Knossian committee that their city in speech should be founded in deed (968b–69d). The Athenian tells Kleinias that he will become his partner (*xulleptor*) with an eager spirit (*prothumos;* cf. 897b). Kleinias agrees that they must all traverse the way along which the god is leading them (cf. 892d, 893b). And when Megillus finally realizes what is at stake and speaks up, Kleinias tells him that he too must assist (*xullambane*). Megillus has the last word in the dialogue: *xullepsomai.* In one laconic utterance, he agrees to assist, grasp, and comprehend (cf. 645a, 752a). The Athenian says "it lies in common [*en koinoi*] and in the middle [*mesoi*] for us" (cf. 739c, 898a). The three "share the risk" in bringing Magnesia into being as an ikon of the cosmos.

It has become apparent by the conclusion of the dialogue that the Athenian's relation to Kleinias and Megillus is comparable to the relation of *nous, psyche,* and *soma.* If the three share the risk together, the Athenian, the personification of *nous,* should then have sufficient persuasion and compulsion to bring the Magnesian *nomoi* into being. However, the Knossian committee is not simply an object of persuasion. It gives an added dimension to the process. The requirement that the Athenian persuade nine other men like Kleinias recalls his own rather playful numbering of the ten or so motions in the argument against impiety. The relation of the twelve, then, recalls the relation of noetic motion, psychic self-and-other-moving motion, and somatic other-moving motion. The committee is thus part of a rather complex image of the rule of *nous* over *psyche.*

The committee has a more important role in the context of the Athenian's account of Magnesia's genesis. Its status as an image of the genesis of harmony from the *arche* also indicates its place in the Athenian's number play. The agreement of the twelve is an image of harmony itself, governed by the tetractys 6, 8, 9, 12. The twelve are an image of the twelve notes of the octave. They may even be said to be an image of the single vibrating string of the monochord, the instrument upon which Pythagoreans calculated the harmonic relations of the twelve notes. This imagery gives further significance to Megillus's last word. Before the Athenian spoke to begin the dialogue, Megillus was ascending with Kleinias to the cave of Zeus and was most likely giving him advice about how to found a new colony. He was, in other words, the eleventh member of the Knossian committee. Eleven is the most dissonant possible number in Pythagorean harmonic calculations. It can generate no harmonic intervals. Any city Megillus and Kleinias might have thought of founding together, therefore, would have been the political equivalent of complete musical dissonance (cf. 625c–26c, 690d–91a). When the Athenian joined them, a twelfth was added. All harmony became possible. In Pythagorean harmonics, however, the eleventh semitone of the octave is the last note to find its place on the scale. This is why Megillus accepts the Athenian's persuasion only after it has been assumed that everyone else will do so. When he does, the perfectly harmonious city becomes possible. The greatest indication of its harmony is the Athenian's remark that its laws (*nomoi*) are songs (*nomoi;* cf. 799e–800a).

If the ten Knossians represent Magnesia's *psyche,* then the 5,040 hearths of Magnesia represent its *soma.* And like the ten Knossians, the 5,040 hearths also have significance in the number play of the dialogue. The Athenian describes the hearths as the city's "numerical mass [*ogkon tou arithmou*]" (737c). The city's *soma* is not meaningless matter, however. It is inalienable, and hence cannot be bought and sold as property. Every hearth must be considered the common property of all. What is more, the division into 5,040 hearths or households is sacred (*heiron*). Every part of the division is "a gift of the god" (741b–c, 771a–b). The number of the division must never be altered. Not one hearth more nor less, the Athenian says. Every household therefore must have only one heir. The Athenian even says that the city's rulers must guard the number throughout the whole of their lives and must study it at leisure until they have firmly understood it and the ways in which it may be preserved (738b, 740a–41a, 929a).

All of these remarks are indications of the number's Pythagorean significance. 5,040 is derived from seven, the number of demiurgic genesis. In particular, it is factorial seven (5,040 = 7!), the product of the integers from one through seven. The 5,040 hearths thus represent the genesis of the city's *soma* from the One. However, genesis itself does not end when the hearths come into being. The 5,040 hearths are also the ever-flowing spring of the city's continued coming into being once it has been founded. They are preserved as such by the Athenian's marriage laws. When the city's guardians study the marriage laws they will discover that they are ordered by the number five, the Pythagorean number for marriage. All Magnesians must be married before they are thirty-five. The Athenian chooses this number both because it is the product of seven (genesis) and five (marriage) and because it represents harmony. In particular, women must marry at some point after they turn sixteen and before they turn twenty-one, while men must marry at some point after they turn thirty and before they turn thirty-five. Both sexes have five years less a day to find mates. The one day may be set aside for the wedding itself. And the average age of all such marriages is twenty-five, which is the square of five (721a–e, 772d–e, 785b).

The Athenian makes several further remarks about the number of hearths that indicate its broader symbolic significance. The number is the first indication of Magnesia's order. The Athenian says 5,040 has "no more than sixty minus one divisors," an odd turn of phrase. Its first divisors are the numbers one through twelve with the exception of eleven (737e–38a, 771c). This is not mentioned simply to demonstrate the number's administrative convenience. It reveals that the city, if properly founded, will exclude all dissonance and will be perfectly just. The number of hearths is the square of the number representing perfect justice, the sovereign number of Magnesia's tetractys, minus one: $5,040 = 71^2 - 1$. The city's 5,041st hearth is the acropolis. If the city is properly founded, the acropolis will not be the hearth of Zeus. The Athenian ends the dialogue by saying that the Nocturnal Council, the embodiment of *phronesis* and *nous*, must dwell in the acropolis. The rule of the city's 5,040 hearths by the Nocturnal Council dwelling in the 5,041st is ultimately what makes Magnesia an ikon of the harmony, order, and justice evident in the cosmos. Its rule brings the age of Zeus to an end and establishes Magnesia as the first city in the age of *nous* (745b, 969b–c).

If the city is to be founded properly, the Athenian and his two interlocutors must find hearths within it. The Athenian will reside in the acropolis with the other members of the Nocturnal Council; Kleinias and Megillus will reside among the citizens. The Athenian suggests this in his remark that the number eleven may become a divisor of 5,040 "if two hearths are set aside" (771c). Kleinias and Megillus are the means of his persuasion. Unless they find hearths in the city, *nous* will not rule it—the city will be dissonant with *anoia*. If they do, however, the Athenian will be able to dwell in the acropolis, his only home in the city (cf. *Meno* 89b).

Once the twelve are in agreement and the 5,040 hearths have been established, the *psyche* and *soma* of Magnesia have come into being from the *arche*. It then becomes possible to join them together "middle to middle [*meson mesoi*]" (*Timaeus* 36e) and set the city in motion "like a circle in growth" (*Republic* 424a). This is done by the first Council of Thirty-seven guardians. The twelve founders of the city give way to the Council of Thirty-seven, whose first task is to order the 5,040 hearths in a circular pattern. The Athenian's description of the council suggests that it has direct continuity with the original twelve founders. It is to consist of eighteen Knossians and nineteen foreign colonists selected for their virtue. The Athenian emphasizes the importance of the first election of guardians by saying that all must be of the highest possible capacity, for "the beginning (*arche*) is half of every deed." Kleinias must be one of the eighteen Knossians. The Athenian and Megillus similarly must be among the foreign members. This should come to pass, for the Athenian says that he and Megillus are both "high-minded" (*phronousin*). Once all three have become members of the council, the Athenian will be able to govern the thirty-six others with *nous* and give proper order to the city. In particular, with the help of Kleinias and Megillus, he will be able to govern the seventeen Knossians and seventeen foreign members of the council effectively through persuasion and compulsion (752d–54a).

The numerical significance of the council is evident in the internal relation of one to thirty-six that allows the council as a whole to bring the order of the One or *nous* to the city. It is also evident in the council's relation to the twelve founders. The increase of twelve to thirty-seven is an increase by approximately the factor of π. Once π has been generated in this way, the city's solid geometry may be set in motion. The progression from the harmony of the radius to the order of the circle requires the formula $A = \pi r^2$. If r is taken to represent the twelve founders and π the relation 37/12, then the order of the city will be the product of thirty-seven and twelve. This may be understood as a symbol of the council's ordering of the city's hearths into twelve sections of a circular pattern. It may also be understood through the calculation $\pi r^2 = 444$. The council's ordering of the city will itself be ordered by the Pythagorean four, the number of reciprocal justice.

The Athenian says the Council of Thirty-seven will arrange the 5,040 hearths in a circle around the acropolis and divide them into twelve equal sections of 420 hearths. The equality of the division will extend to all households. Each will have two land allotments and houses, one in the city and the other in the countryside, arranged in such a way that no household can be said to be superior to another. Each of the twelve sectors will be consecrated to one of the city's twelve gods, and the inhabitants of each sector will be called a tribe. Each tribe is responsible for maintaining the temple and altar of one god. However, all Magnesians honor all twelve of the city's gods, and through honoring them are led to honor the one god beyond the gods whose altar is the acropolis. The Athenian also says the Council of Thirty-seven will arrange the 5,040 hearths into property classes. The number four is significant in three ways in his account of Magnesian property relations, creating a playful correspondence with the calculation $\pi r^2 = 444$. There are to be only four property classes in the city. The first will possess household goods equal to the value of their allotment, and the fourth will be allowed to possess goods of four times the value. All wealth above this limit must be dedicated to the gods. Within these restrictions, changes in a household's wealth do not disrupt the city's harmony, for a movement up or down in property classification produces one of the harmonic intervals generated by the tetractys 1, 2, 3, 4. Furthermore, all exchanges of goods are ordered by the number four, the number of reciprocal justice, since all must be the exchange of equivalents. This is a fitting trade arrangement for Magnesians because the Athenian says they will consider external goods to be the fourth and last of all serious concerns. The gods are first in seriousness; the soul— the first among things human beings possess—is second; the body is third; and external wealth is last. When the Athenian speaks more specifically, he says that wealth is also the last and least noble of the four human goods (726a–29e, 741d–46e; cf. 631b–32b).

After the Council of Thirty-seven has done these things, it will create an institution to preserve the order of the city and harmonize its tribal and class divisions. This is the Council of 360. Its number represents the 360° of the circle. The 360 councillors, who are also called guardians of the laws, are elected in a rather complex way, the intent of which is to ensure mathematically the proportional representation of all 12 tribes and 4 classes. If the tribal and property divisions of the city were distributed to the greatest extent possible, there would be forty-eight subdivisions of 105 hearths having one tribal/class designation. Since forty-eight is the product of the first three even integers ($2 \times 4 \times 6$) and 105 is the product of the first four odd ($1 \times 3 \times 5 \times 7$), this distribution would best correspond with the genesis of all 5,040 hearths from the One (5,040 = 7!). The election process for the Council of 360 is intended to represent all forty-eight subdivisions fairly. It has two stages: a lengthy selection process to arrive at the nomination of 180 candidates per class; and the use of the lot to divide the lists in half. Both stages are necessary because the desideratum is a city council comprised of ninety members per class and thirty per tribe. These two conditions are impossible to meet simultaneously. They would require 7.5 representatives per subdivision. Therefore, fifteen per subdivision are nominated in the first stage, and the lot is then used to overcome impossible fractions. Everyone has a 7:1 chance of being nominated in the first stage. In the second, the odds are even (755e–58e).

Once the Council of Thirty-seven completes the transition from radius to circle by establishing the Council of 360, it no longer has a purpose. The city is now able to undertake the transformation from circle to sphere. However, neither the Council of Thirty-seven, as it was originally organized, nor the Council of 360 has any part in the process. Once the process is complete, the city will be an ikon of the cosmic sphere. Its justice will no longer be merely reciprocal, for the city will be an ikon of the justice of the whole. The geometry of the transformation is summarized in the formula $V = 4\pi r^3/3$. The various terms of the equation are all represented in the Athenian's account by institutions and offices that transform the city into an ikon of the justice of the whole. The first of these institutions is a new Council of Thirty-seven. The initial thirty-seven represented π in the transformation from radius to circle. The new thirty-seven also represents π. It is modified, however, by the fraction 4/3. The fraction is represented institutionally by the changes the Athenian describes for the selection process to the council. The first council had a three-stage process; the new one has four (cf. 752e–53a, 753e–54d, and 753b–d).[4] The Athenian has no place on the new council. His participation on the first allowed him to bring order to the city. Once this has been done, however, he moves to another office. The most important of the thirty-seven new guardians, the supervisor of *paideia*, has a responsibility comparable to the Athenian's on the first council. He must preserve what the Athenian has founded. The Athenian finds a new role in the institutions that represent the cube of the radius in the equation of the transformation to the sphere. In the transformation to the circle, the radius was represented by the city's twelve founders. In the transformation to the sphere, the cube of the radius is represented institutionally by the young agronomists or "country hunters [*agronomoi*]" and the elder directors or "straighteners [*euthunoi*]." The twelve groups of twelve young *agronomoi* set the circle in motion, as it were, by their monthly rotation through all sectors of the city. And the twelve elder directors, chosen by the entire city once its founding is complete, are the most virtuous of all Magnesians. The Athenian is the first among them. Together they preserve the city by straightening all that becomes crooked and directing all things toward their proper end. The directors, therefore, rule and preserve the city just as divine *nous* rules and preserves all things in the cosmos.

The directors straighten the city through their role in the Nocturnal Council. The Nocturnal Council is assembled from the institutions and offices that come into being in the city's transformation from circle to sphere. It will be possible to discuss the details of its composition only when all other aspects of the transformation have been clarified. It is possible, however, to determine how many Magnesians will be members of the Nocturnal Council. At present, the number of the council can be calculated in two ways. Since the council combines harmony and order, it may be taken to represent a Pythagorean triangle with sides of 35, 36, and 50. There should therefore be fifty members of the council. The same number may be derived from the equation of the transformation to the sphere. Given that $\pi = 37/12$ and $r = 12$, the volume of the sphere ($4\pi r^3/3$) is approximately 7,100. This is one hundred times seventy-one, the sovereign number of Magnesia's tetractys. The number reveals that Magnesia's justice is an ikon of the perfect justice evident in the cosmic sphere. The council's role in the city is to preserve its justice. Its relation to the rest of the city is comparable to the relation of 1:100 that is evident in the number of the sphere's volume. Since there are 5,040 Magnesian citizens, the members of the council will be the best one-hundreth part of the citizenry. Again, to the nearest integer, there should be fifty members of the council. In the imagery of another of Plato's dialogues, the members of the Nocturnal Council are thus the fifty true kings and statesmen of all Hellas, more difficult to find than fifty good draughts-players (*Statesman* 292e–93a).

Paideia

The new Council of Thirty-seven guardians is related to the Nocturnal Council in two ways. The ten eldest guardians are to serve on the Nocturnal Council, and so too are the supervisors of *paideia* who have been elected from among the council members (951d–e). The supervisor of *paideia* occupies the office that is the single most important for the preservation of the city's order. The Athenian even describes it as "the greatest of the highest offices in the city." It is so important that the Council of 360 is to have nothing to do with the election of the supervisor every five years

(765e–66c). The supervisor of *paideia* is responsible for educating all Magnesian children in such a way that they might become the best possible human beings. More precisely, he is responsible for leading them with *paideia* from the experiences described by the Athenian's puppet ikon to those described by his ikon of the Nocturnal Council: from their first experiences of pleasure and pain to the first of the divine goods, *phronesis* and *nous.*

The Athenian says *paideia* begins in the correct training of children concerning pleasures and pains in order that they will love (*stergein*) what ought to be loved from the beginning to the end (*ex arches mechri telous;* 653a–c). In specifying the responsibilities of the supervisor, the Athenian describes the way from beginning to end in a manner that recalls Socrates' description of the two *paradeigmata* for all human beings in the *Theaetetus* (176e–77a). He says that the "first coming to light" of human beings must be "set in motion nobly" by an education that will bring about the "perfection in virtue [*pros areten . . . telos*]" that befits their nature (*physeos*). It is in the nature of the human being, he continues, to become the "most divine [*theiotaton*]" creature if properly educated; and if not, it becomes the "most savage [*agriotaton*]" on earth (*Laws* 765e–66a). The way to the end, therefore, is a *paideia* that will lead human beings to become most divine by becoming like the divine *paradeigma*, or the god, as far as they are able. They will then acquire the divine goods and may be called perfect (*teleos*) human beings (631b–d, 653a–c). In Magnesia they may also be called perfect citizens, for their *paideia* also leads each to "desire and love (*erasten*) to become a perfect (*teleon*) citizen who knows how to rule and be ruled with justice" (643e). Magnesia is the city in which it is possible to become both a perfect human being and a perfect citizen (cf. *Politics* 1276b16–77b32). The preservation of the city and its *nomoi*, therefore, cannot be separated from the preservation of its *paideia* (*Laws* 752b–c). It is for this reason that the Athenian says the guardian chosen to fill "the office of the children" (*paidon archen*) must guide their natures on the straight way (*kateuthuneto*) with *paideia*, always turning them toward the good (*pros tagathon*), according to the *nomoi* (808e–9a).

The *paideia* described by the Athenian in the *Laws* turns around and leads all Magnesians toward the good. They follow the same straight ascending way described by Socrates for the guardians of the *Republic's* city in speech. In other words, the *nomoi* of the Athenian's city redistribute the *nomos* describing the education of the guardian class in the *Republic*. All children and youth will be educated in the same way in Magnesia. And all women and men will share in *paideia* and everything else, to the greatest possible extent, in order that the city will not have only half of a "perfectly happy life [*teleos . . . eudaimonos . . . biou*]" (805c–d, 806e). The redistribution signifies that all Magnesians will be open to the good in some way and willing to be led toward it through education; it does not signify that all will be true philosophers and statesmen who have reached the end of the way themselves and are fit to lead others. Indeed, the ratio of rowers to pilots is 100:1. Even so, the rowers and pilots both belong to the golden race of Hellas. Magnesian *paideia* will enable all of them to aspire to the good, as far as they are able. And it will be possible to say that all of them are happy in their lives and conditions. Although their lives will not be free of toils and labors, the life they share will be "perfectly happy" (cf. *Republic* 516c–d, 519e–20d).

In the *Republic*, the guardians are first educated in gymnastic and music to train their bodies and form their souls. They then study the arts founded in number and calculation: geometry, astronomy, and harmony, the advanced study of music. It is also necessary for them to learn of the things pertaining to speech by studying poetry and theology as well as dialectic. By the time they are fifty, they will have completed these preliminary studies and served for several years in the city's minor public offices. Only then will it be possible for them to acquire *phronesis* and become true philosophers by being compelled to see the good itself. In the *Laws*, the supervisor of *paideia* leads all toward the same end with a comparable curriculum.[5]

All Magnesians are first educated in gymnastic and music, the two main branches of the choral art. Their choral education continues throughout their lives. As adults, all must take part in competitive games and celebratory festivals in a manner appropriate for their sex and age. Gymnastics is comprised of physical training and dancing; music is comprised of choral singing dedicated to the gods and the study of harmony. The unique feature of Magnesian gymnastics is that it encourages males and females alike to train the left and right sides of their bodies equally. However, the physical ambidexterity and proportion of Magnesians must be matched by spiritual harmony and proportion. Magnesians will dance only in the Harmonic and Pyrrhic forms. The Pyrrhic imitates warlike postures, and the Harmonic imitates the postures of a virtuous soul at peace. Together they cultivate courage and moderation in due measure. Similarly, it is evident that all Magnesians will sing and play instruments in only the Phrygian and Dorian modes. The Persian Phrygian is warlike and telestic, and the Hellenic Dorian is solemn and stately. Together they also cultivate courage and moderation (*Republic* 399a–c). However, there is another form of dance appropriate to the Phrygian mode besides the Pyrrhic: the ecstatic Bacchic form. All Magnesians will know of it, for all are initiated into the Bacchic and Corybantic mysteries as newborns. The Athenian says the mindless revels that have come to prominence in the cities of Hellas produce sickly souls, cowardly and lacking in self-mastery. Bacchic and Corybantic revellers can find peace only briefly after their ecstasies. Magnesians will be immune to such mindless revelry as youths and adults because of their initiation as children to the homeopathic effects of continuous rocking and singing. Their souls will be at peace; their *paideia*, therefore, will be able to lead them toward justice and wisdom as well as toward courage and moderation (*Laws* 654b–57b, 659d–60d, 672b–73d, 790c–91b, 794c–96e, 814c–16d, 832e–35b). Instead of always hearing the *auloi* of Corybants droning in their ears, Magnesians will hear only their city's *nomoi* (cf. *Crito* 54d).

Magnesia's choruses are the highest form of the choral art. They combine proper posture, rhythm, harmony, melody, and speech about the gods in a joyous celebration of the divine. All children will sing and dance in a chorus dedicated to the Muses. All youths and adults to the age of thirty will do the same in one dedicated to Apollo. Men between the ages of thirty and sixty will comprise a third chorus dedicated to Dionysos. Those above sixty will not sing and dance. Instead, they will present mythologies publicly "with divine, propethic voices [*dia theias phemes*]" (653c–54e, 664b–d). In order that men above thirty are not ashamed to sing and dance publicly, during their first decade as Dionysian choristers they will be introduced to the benefits of wine, the gift of Dionysos bestowed by the god "as a drug that heals the austerity of old age." No Magnesian will drink before the age of eighteen and all will drink in moderation at common meals until they are thirty. At that age Magnesian men will be initiated into the Dionysian mysteries. All Magnesians are Corybants from birth, but middle-aged men apparently require remedial education. If their more than moderate drinking is properly governed, they will be-

come more and not less moderate with age through its homeopathic effect. After twenty years in the Dionysian chorus, all men
will spend a decade perfecting their knowledge of poetry's rhythms
and harmonies. They will become more knowledgeable than most
poets through their studies, for they will also know which speeches
are noble and which ignoble. When they turn sixty they will become the city's mythologues as well as the leaders of the Dionysian
chorus (645d–50b, 664d–66d, 670a–e). As mythologues, they will
present only noble and beautiful poetry to the city—the poetic
speeches that are brothers to their own *nomoi* (811e). As the guardians of the *nomoi* concerning choruses and wine, they will educate
and mold the souls of all men above thirty by instructing them in
the choral art and regulating their drinking. Proper drinking educates men because it leads all to experience, either voluntarily or
involuntarily, "the most noble fear accompanied by justice, the divine fear [*theion phobon*] . . . [named] awe [*aido*] and shame [*aischy-
nen*]." This is the greatest good (*megiston agathon*) brought by the
gift of Dionysos (671d, 672c).

The highest of the Magnesian choruses is not the Dionysian
one, but the Nocturnal Council itself. The best guardians of all the
city's *nomoi* are themselves poets who perform the most beautiful
(*kallistes*), best (*aristes*), and truest (*alethestaten*) tragedy for all
Magnesians. The members of the council are said to have beautiful voices (*kalliphonous*), for when they speak to preserve the
nomoi of the city that is mimetic of the most beautiful and best
life, their voices are more beautiful than those of the tragedians
and poets of Hellas (817a–d). The Nocturnal Council's performance of the truest tragedy recalls the origins of all Greek tragedy
in the dithyrambic celebration of Dionysos. The fifty members of
the council are an image of the fifty celebrants of the dithyrambic
chorus who assemble around the altar dedicated to the god, singing and dancing the "laws [*nomoi*]," guided by the *exarchon* or
"beginner," one of their number who stands atop the altar and
interprets the god's influence in his soul (cf. 700b–d and *Republic*
394c). The Nocturnal Council celebrates the *nomoi* of the most
beautiful and best life, the life governed not by the influence of
Dionysos in the soul, but by the erotic influence of the god beyond
the Muses, Apollo, and Dionysos (cf. *Phaedrus* 265b–c).

All Magnesians, not just council members, celebrate the city's
nomoi. This is the foundation of Magnesian *paideia*. For example,
all Magnesians, for three years from the age of ten, will learn of

the things pertaining to speech by studying the *Laws* itself, as well as all poetry and prose works that contain speeches comparable to those in the *Laws*. They will thereby learn how the founders of their city may be said to be the poets of the most beautiful tragedy. And they will also learn to take the founders' "most well-measured speeches [*metriotatoi logoi*]," spoken with "inspiration from the gods [*epipnoias theon*]," as paradigms for their own speech (809e, 811c–12a; cf. *Republic* 540e–41a). Moreover, all Magnesians will learn of number and calculation, and of harmony, geometry, and astronomy, the highest arts founded on number, by being raised according to *nomoi* that honor them (793e–94b, 817e–22d). The whole city honors harmony in its choral art, geometry in its genesis, and astronomy in its order and piety. When Magnesians study the *Laws*, they will learn of the relation between their city's *nomoi* and the arts founded on number, for they will study the history and order of their city alongside the Athenian's accounts of harmony, geometry, and astronomy. All Magnesians will begin to study these subjects in their childhood games. Only a few, however, will study them to precision (*akribeias;* 818a). Those few will probably become members of the Nocturnal Council. In other words, all Magnesians study the same subjects as the council members. The few who show themselves best in their studies are honored by being elected to offices that entitle them to serve on the council.

Male and female children and youths are educated in all subjects in the same way; yet the few who study these subjects to precision are all men. Indeed, all Magnesian offices and institutions that are in any way associated with the Nocturnal Council are comprised entirely of men. This requires some explanation, for there is no argument made in the *Laws* to suggest that males have an inherently superior ability to be educated. Instead, the Magnesian *nomoi* attempt to make men and women equal in all things, as much as is possible, in order that the city might be an image of the spiritual equality of all human beings. Some allowances must be made for the unique role of the female in the bearing, nurturing, and raising of children, but this neither removes women entirely from the public realm nor suggests that they are in any way less able to study subjects to precision. Concerning the place of women in the public realm, the *nomoi* indicate that family responsibilities are not a sufficient reason to alter the Magnesian practice of common meals for men and women alike. Family responsibilities are also not a sufficient reason to prevent women from holding public office. They are recognized in one minor difference: women may hold office from their fortieth year, while men may do so from their thirtieth (780d–81d, 785b). The female's role as mother, therefore, is not sufficient explanation of why no woman may be a member of the Nocturnal Council. The most convincing explanation is based on the council's significance as the institution that represents the truest tragedy for all Magnesians. Women have no place on it not because it would be immoderate for them to assume such public responsibility, nor because they are by nature incapable of assuming it and completing the studies associated with it, but because the truest tragedy represented by the council is the *mimesis* of the life of one particular man, the Athenian himself. This particularity of the council ikon is emphasized by the drama of the dialogue as well. In the drama of the city's founding, the city cannot be complete until the Athenian himself is elected as the first director of the first Nocturnal Council and the age of *nous* thereby begins.

The list of subjects in which all Magnesians will be instructed under the guidance of the supervisor of *paideia* matches the list of subjects in which all guardians of the *Republic's* city in speech will be instructed. The Magnesian *nomoi* therefore redistribute the *Republic's* *nomos* concerning the guardians' education to everyone in the city. The Athenian does not say that all Magnesians will be instructed in dialectic, but this is not in contradiction to the redistribution. In the *Republic,* Socrates does not describe dialectic as a subject that can be taught and studied like other subjects. He says it is a song (*nomos*) to which all the demonstrable arts are a prelude. It is an ascent from the hypotheses of such arts to the *arche* itself. The ascent begins with a test of being (*ousia*) that measures accounts of things in speech against the *ousia* of the things themselves. But the ascent goes further. Dialectic is the soul's journey (*poreia*) to the good beyond *ousia* (*Republic* 531d, 532b, 533c, 534c). Since dialectic is not a demonstrable art or method, it cannot be taught and studied as one. It can only be exercised. Socrates describes one way of exercising it when he says that thirty-year-old guardians will be tested extensively with dialectic to determine which of them have dialectical natures and how far each of them is willing or able to ascend in the journey toward the good (537c, 539d). In the *Laws,* the Athenian's *nomoi* ensure that all Magnesians will have dialectical natures. All will be open to the good and willing to ascend toward it as far as they are able.

They will be able to meet the test of *ousia* in their practices, for their *nomoi* describe the best way of life. They will be able to meet it in argument as well, to some extent, for all will study the highest things; in particular, all Magnesians will study the Athenian's argument against impiety. And all Magnesians will ascend as far as they are able on the festive occasions when the whole city sets out on the journey to the superheavenly region following the guidance of the Nocturnal Council (cf. *Phaedrus* 247c–48e).

Hunting

The members of the Nocturnal Council are Magnesia's dialecticians not because they spend their council meetings studying it as a subject, but rather because they have ascended to the superheavenly region and returned home on many occasions. They know the way and can guide others along it. The council members do test some Magnesians with dialectic in a manner similar to the testing of guardians in the *Republic*. They speak at length with promising young men under the age of thirty as a way of determining who may attend council meetings after turning thirty to learn what they must know if they are to become leading members of the council themselves in later years. In particular, they test the young *agronomoi* (country hunters). In order to become good dialecticians, the young must first become good hunters. The *agronomoi* are the city's best. They are the ones who will best understand the hunting law that concludes the Athenian's account of Magnesian *paideia*.

In the *Euthydemus* (290b–c), there is a description of the relation between various types of hunting and dialectic, made by one of Socrates' interlocutors and much praised by him, that helps to explain both the Athenian's perplexing hunting law and the significance of the young *agronomoi* in Magnesia's political order. Hunting is the art of capturing prey, it is said. It is not the art of using what has been captured. Hunters must turn over their prey to others who know how to prepare and cook it. Geometry is also a type of hunting. Geometers do not know how to make use of what they capture. They must hand over their prey to dialecticians. And dialecticians in turn cannot exercise their art well unless there has been good hunting beforehand. Geometers capture hypotheses; dialecticians take up what they have captured. Hypotheses are game for the dialectician's skills (*Republic* 510b–11d, 533b–d).

Since dialecticians are also good butchers, the first thing they do with the game is prepare it for cooking by cutting it at the joints. In other words, dialecticians test hypotheses against *ousia* (cf. *Phaedrus* 265; *Statesman* 287c). The Magnesian hunting law describes the best way of capturing the game—the best way of preparing for dialectical ascent. In particular, it describes how the *agronomoi* will hunt and what they will hunt.

The Athenian begins the prelude to the hunting law with a discussion of writing intended to serve as a guide to the study of the *Laws*. Reading and studying the *Laws* is a type of hunting. The Athenian says he has woven things into his account of the *nomoi* that are by nature in between admonition and command, or in between the persuasion of the preludes and the compulsion of the laws. His most perfect praise is reserved for those Magnesians who are willing to hunt through the written record of what he has said and live their lives in obedience with what they discover in between (822d–23a; cf. *Republic* 450b). His account of hunting must also be studied in this manner, for somewhere in between the prelude and the law he describes the way toward the philosophic life.

His brief discussion of hunting (823b–24c) begins with an analytic classification of many of the activities that are named hunting. Hunting may be of things in the water or of things not in the water. The latter may be divided into hunting things with wings and hunting things with feet. The class of footed things that are hunted may be divided into beasts and humans. Beasts may be hunted at night or in daylight in various ways. Humans may be hunted in war or in friendship. Hunting humans in friendship may be done in both praiseworthy or blameworthy ways, but the Athenian gives no explicit criteria for attributing praise or blame. The same is true of hunting in war. Robbery on land and piracy on the seas are always blameworthy, but the Athenian does not discuss explicitly how warfare between cities can be judged either praiseworthy or blameworthy. He does warn Magnesians against the corrupt desire to hunt humans by sea, a type of hunting that he thereby differentiates from piracy. If they hunted in this way, he says, they would be cruel and lawless (*anomous*) hunters. This is an implicit criticism of all human hunting in war, for the activity is no less cruel and lawless when it occurs on land. All such warfare is blameworthy. Only the defense of one's own city when attacked is therefore lawful and praiseworthy.

The Athenian explicitly prohibits or restricts three types of animal hunting: night hunting, bird hunting, and water hunting. There is little in what he says in the law and its prelude to explain why these three types should be so carefully controlled. The Athenian does warn Magnesians against the corrupt desire (*epithumia*) and love (*eros*) that motivate such hunting, but the warning raises more questions than it answers. Magnesians are to desire and love all activities that bring *phronesis* and *nous* (688a–b). How might these three types of hunting lead Magnesians away from *phronesis* and *nous* toward some folly (*aphrosyne; anoia*)? It requires some hunting outside the *Laws* to answer this question. It then becomes evident that the Athenian's discussion of the three prohibited or restricted types of hunting is addressed to all those studying the *Laws* in order to learn of the philosophic life. It is his warning that geometrical thinking and Eleatic idealism may lead away from philosophy toward sophistry.

The Athenian allows bird hunting on land that is not cultivated or sacred, but otherwise it is prohibited as an illiberal activity that demonstrates a corrupt *eros*. The simplest sense of this law is explained in the Athenian's remark that birds are good examples for human beings because they live pious and just lives and are strongly bound by friendship (840d–e). They may be captured only to serve as gifts for the gods, and they are the most divine of such gifts (956b). The illiberal character of bird hunting is explained in the *Theaetetus* (197c–98d). Socrates describes the hunting of knowledge (*episteme*) as bird hunting. There are two types. One is the hunting of birds for the sake of possession. This is the filling of an originally empty "home enclosure" or cage with birds captured in the wild. The other type is the hunting of birds already possessed. This is the search in the home enclosure to lay hands on a bird that has been there for some time. The two types of bird hunting recall Socrates' description in the *Republic* (518b–d) of the difference between geometrical thinking and sophistry on the one hand, and philosophy on the other. Geometrical thinkers and sophists assume that knowledge is acquired when it is placed into a soul in which it is initially lacking. The soul is thus an empty cage for them, and *paideia* is solely possessive bird hunting. True philosophers say that knowledge is acquired when the soul is turned around toward being and the good. The soul, therefore, is not an empty cage. And *paideia* is anamnetic bird hunting, or the recalling of things the soul already knows in some way.

The Athenian prohibits all water hunting in regulated waters: harbors, sacred streams, ponds, and lakes. It is allowed elsewhere if it does not muddy the waters. However, the Athenian explicitly warns Magnesians never to be seized by the corrupt love of such angling. The *agronomoi* are responsible for the sacred streams and waters of Magnesia. They must prevent them from harming the land and regulate them in such a way that the entire city will benefit (760e–61d). The full significance of their activities is revealed when the waters they regulate are understood symbolically. The flow of a river or stream is a Heraclitean or Protagorean image for the growth and decay of all things (*Theaetetus* 152c–e, 180d–81b). The harmony of water and land that brings benefit to all may therefore be understood as an image of the harmony of becoming and being in the order of all things that have come into being from the good. The Athenian also uses the flow of a river as an image for the progress of dialectical argument (*Laws* 892d–93b). The regulation of rivers and streams may therefore also be understood as an image of the proper representation in speech of the relation of becoming, being, and the good. Muddying the waters is confusing the relation in speech. This is done by the Heracliteans and Protagoreans, but it is also done by the Eleatics. Eleatic muddying is discussed at length in the *Parmenides*. Parmenides himself tells a youthful Socrates that philosophers study the forms (*eidoi*) of such seemingly trivial things as mud. Socrates, however, is already wise enough to know that this is a "bottomless pit of nonsense." Although it may seem to be the very embodiment of philosophy, Eleatic idealism is often nothing but trivial and nonsensical speech (*Parmenides* 130c–e; cf. *Theaetetus* 147a–c).

At its worst, Eleatic idealism, like geometrical thinking, may lead to sophistry. Muddying the waters is poor angling, and in the *Sophist* the angler and the sophist are said to be the same type of hunter. Angling is described as the type of water hunting that always strikes its prey around the head and mouth from below with a barbed hook. Sophistry is described as the type of human hunting whose prey is wealthy and prominent young men. It always strikes them from below with a barbed hook by educating them in opinion for money. To complete the comparison, it always strikes its prey around the head and mouth by making them incapable of thinking and speaking properly (*Sophist* 220e–23b).

The Athenian's prohibition of night hunting with nets and traps is succinct: none shall be allowed anywhere. Night hunting with

clever tricks is sophistry itself. The sophist hunts humans by taking refuge "in the darkness of not-being" and setting his traps. He
then attempts to charm others into the darkness where they will
become ensnared. Taking refuge in the darkness of not-being is
the secret of "the magical power of sophistry." It allows the sophist
to claim he is a wizard capable of creating anything from nothing
with clever tricks. If he succeeds in charming others out of the
sunlight and into his dark night, they will believe not only that he
knows everything but also that he has the ability "to make and do
all things by a single art." Those who are charmed believe that
there is nothing the sophist cannot pull out of his hat (*Sophist*
223a–d, 254a–b, 268c–d).

No Magnesian will be allowed to hunt in vicious and blameworthy ways. The Athenian's hunting law allows no human hunting in war and no sophistic human hunting in peace. What is
more, it warns against all activities that may lead to sophistry in
some way. All Magnesians will hunt only in the best way possible,
the way that prepares the soul for dialectical ascent. The Athenian
says the type of hunting "best for everyone" is the hunting of four-
footed prey with horses and dogs, which requires hunters to use
their own bodies in running, striking blows, and throwing shafts.
This cultivates "courage that is divine [*theias*]." The *agronomoi*
are the best and most divine hunters in Magnesia. They most
deserve to be called "truly sacred hunters [*hierous ontos thereu-
tas*]." But what is pursued in the best hunting is the best measure
of whether the hunter is divinely courageous and truly sacred.
Magnesians do not throw their shafts at human beings, for they
know that man is not the measure of all things, as the sophists
claim (716c). Magnesians may hunt boars with shafts when they
hunt animals, but they know that the boar is not the measure of all
things either (*Theaetetus* 161c). All shafts in Magnesia are aimed at
the god (717a, 962d). If the best type of hunting is a preparation for
dialectical ascent, then the target of the soul's ascent with dialectic is the god who is the measure.[6]

The Nocturnal Council (II)

The Athenian's description of the responsibilities of the *agronomoi*
shows that they are the best hunters in the city (760b–63c). They
engage in no warlike human hunting. Although they are called a
"secret service [*krupteia*]," they do not hunt and kill slaves and

domestic servants as did the Spartan *krupteia* (cf. 633b–c, 776c–d). Indeed, they have no slaves or servants themselves. The *agronomoi* have the authority to use those belonging to other Magnesians for public tasks, but they must live by their own efforts alone. Hunting is thus most necessary for them. Although the Athenian encourages everyone to take up the best type of hunting, the requirement that the *agronomoi* live by their own efforts ensures that they will be the best and most courageous Magnesian hunters.

The *agronomoi* may not use their authority freely. In fact, the Athenian says they are themselves slaves. All the *agronomoi* are enslaved to their *nomoi*, "as this is really an enslavement to the gods." They are all therefore courageous in the service of the divine. Furthermore, the young *agronomoi* are enslaved to their elders and all those who have lived honorable lives. The Athenian's description of the second type of enslavement may be taken in several ways. It refers, in the first instance, to the subordination of the twelve younger to the five elder *agronomoi* in each of the twelve groups of seventeen selected by the city's tribes. It also refers to a responsibility specifically given to the younger ones: they are to maintain gymnasia and hot baths for all the old men in Magnesia and welcome graciously (*dechomenous eumenos*) the ill and the weary. This is the most charitable type of human hunting in friendship. And finally, it refers to the enslavement of the best young *agronomoi* to those of their elders who have lived the most honorable lives, the members of the Nocturnal Council and in particular the council's twelve directors or "straighteners [*euthunoi*]." The best of the young *agronomoi* will hunt at the council's bidding after they have completed their service, using their precise knowledge (*akribeias epistasthai*) of the country in whatever way the elders of the council think best.

The relation of the younger *agronomoi* to their elders on the council is symbolically significant in a number of ways. The council is Magnesia's head, an ikon of *phronesis* and *nous*. Within this context, the young *agronomoi* chosen to attend council meetings after their service represent the type of hunting necessary for the dialectical ascent toward divine *nous* that enables a human being to acquire *phronesis* and *nous*. They are the council's anamnetic hunters. To paraphrase the Athenian's own definition of *anamnesis*, they are "the inflow that replenishes *phronesis*" (732b–c). If the order of the whole city is taken as an image of the relation of *nous*, *psyche*, and *soma* in a human being, it may be said that their hunting at the council's bidding represents the purely psychic motion of *anamnesis* directed by *nous*.

The Athenian's entire account of Magnesia is an ikon. It is the ikon of all aspects of the motion of *nous*, including demiurgic genesis. Within this context, the young *agronomoi* are related to the council's directors by means of Pythagorean mathematics and number symbolism. Both represent parts of the city's transformation from circle to sphere, which is summarized in the formula $V = 4\pi r^3/3$. The π in the equation is represented by the new Council of Thirty-seven. And since r = 12 in Magnesian solid geometry, the cube of the radius is represented by the relation between the twelve groups of twelve young *agronomoi* and the twelve directors of the Nocturnal Council. Each of the elder council members must select a young man over thirty to attend council meetings with him. The twelve directors are ultimately responsible for ensuring that only the best are chosen, and the best will undoubtedly be found among the first 144 *agronomoi* to complete their service. The Nocturnal Council is not complete until a number of young men have been chosen in this way, and until the council is complete, it cannot be said that the demiurgic genesis of Magnesia is complete. Within this context the *agronomoi* have a special significance: their activities set the circle in motion and allow the city's transformation into a sphere to reach its end. This is made evident by the references to number in the Athenian's account of their responsibilities.

Every two years, each of Magnesia's twelve tribes elects five elder *agronomoi* who in turn select twelve young ones. The young ones must be between the ages of twenty-five and thirty, and must be able to provide two full years of service prior to marriage and initiation into the Dionysian chorus. The young ones are supervised by the twelve groups of five officers, and beyond them by the thirty-seven guardians of the new council, headed by the supervisor of *paideia*. The corps of sixty officers is a rather ethereal body. Its only apparent function is to act as an intermediary between the supervisor of *paideia* and the young *agronomoi*. Even the number of the officers is ethereal: the twelve groups of five recall the twelve pentagons of the dodecahedron that is said by some to be the shape of the unnamed fifth element the god distributed throughout the cosmos (*Timaeus* 55b).

After all the *agronomoi* have been selected, each of the twelve groups of five officers and twelve young guards is assigned to one of the twelve equal sections of the city; each month all the groups of seventeen move to the immediately adjoining section, rotating in one direction the first year and the other the next. When the city has been set in motion in this way and the young guards have become divinely courageous through their education in the best type of hunting, the Nocturnal Council can be assembled. Those of the thirty-year-olds with "the best natures" chosen for the council will assemble with the elders at the very top of the city. From there, they will be able to "see the whole city in a circle [*kukloi*]" (*Laws* 964e).

The Nocturnal Council also cannot be assembled until the first twelve directors have been elected. The Athenian describes them as divine men who are "in every way amazing [*thaumastous*] in all of virtue [*pasan areten*]." Each is a "ruler of rulers [*archonton archonta*]," superior in virtue and perfectly capable of "applying blameless justice blamelessly" (945c–e). In other words, each always keeps to the upward way toward the god who is blameless in human affairs, and consequently each is able to practice justice with *phronesis* in every way (*Republic* 617e, 621c). The first election of directors brings the demiurgic genesis of Magnesia to an end. The city's recognition of them as the most just and prudent men allows them to preserve the order that has come into being in the city in the same amazing way that divine *nous* preserves the order of all things in the cosmos. Indeed, their role as the saviors of the city and its *nomoi* is celebrated at the same time the new year is celebrated. What is more, their role on the Nocturnal Council enables them to ensure each day that the city never wanders from the "straight and revolving course" of divine *nous* (716a).

The annual election of directors is an image of the cosmic cycle of the year. It takes place on the day that marks the end of the old year and the beginning of the new, the day of the new moon following the summer solstice, when the cycle of seasons and the alignment of the heavenly bodies seem most perfectly harmonious (945e; cf. 767c–d). All Magnesians will then assemble in the part of the city that represents in space what the day represents in time: the sector dedicated to the sun and Apollo. And all will then elect three men from among themselves to replace the three directors that retire every year. The three men chosen for their divine virtue will then be presented to "the god." The god is neither the sun nor Apollo, but the god beyond the visible and intelligible realms represented by the sun and Apollo. The Athenian calls the god by another name when he says that although all twelve of the city's serving directors will be priests of the sun and Apollo, the first among them will also be known as the *archiereus*. The term *archiereus* may be taken to mean both the "ruling priest" and the "priest of the *arche*." The god is thus the *arche* from which all things in the cosmos have come into being.

The Athenian also says that the name of the *archiereus* will be "the measure of the time's number [*metron arithmou tou chronou*]." His use of the term *chronos* is significant. It indicates, first of all, that the election of an *archiereus* will give a name to the year (*eniauton*) in which he rules. However, it also indicates the importance of the election of the first *archiereus* in Magnesia. The annual election of three directors is a recurring event initiated by the first election of twelve directors in the same way that the cosmic cycle of the year is a recurring event initiated by the greater cosmic cycle of "perfect years," or ages, marked at their beginning and end by the perfect harmony and alignment of all heavenly bodies and the reversal of the cosmic rotation. The election of the first twelve directors is comparable to the beginning of a new cosmic age. In the *Timaeus*, the "perfect number of time [*teleos arithmos chronou*]" is said to fulfil the "perfect year [*teleon eniauton*]" of a cosmic age. When the first priest of the *arche* is elected, his name will become the number of time (*chronos*). It will not name the new year, but the new age for human beings that has begun: the age of *nous* (cf. *Timaeus* 39c–e; *Statesman* 269c–73e; *Laws* 626e, 713a–14a).

The first priest of the *arche* is the Athenian himself. His name is never mentioned in the *Laws*. The age begun by his lawgiving therefore takes its name from what he, above all others, is worthy to be called. At the beginning of the dialogue, Kleinias says the Athenian is worthy to be called by the name of the goddess Athena because of his ability to follow the *logos* to its *arche* (626d–e). He is also worthy to be called by the name of the divine *nous* for the same reason. The election of the Athenian as the first *archiereus* is dramatically necessary to complete the dialogue's description of Magnesia as an ikon of the demiurgic genesis of all things from, and preservation of all things by, divine *nous*. In the drama of the dialogue, he must have the double role of being both the source of Magnesia's demiurgic genesis and the source of its preservation. Furthermore, he must be recognized as such by Magnesians. Just as all things that have had genesis are preserved by following the guidance of divine *nous* exercised through "exceedingly amazing [*thaumati*] powers" (899a), so too all those who have their genesis as Magnesians in the Athenian's lawgiving will be preserved only if they follow his guidance in all things once the city is complete. Only if Magnesians honor him as the one man among them who is "in every way amazing [*thaumastous*] in all of virtue" will their city find "salvation under god [*kata theon . . . soterias*]" (945e, 946b).

There is a dreamlike character to the Athenian's double role as the source of Magnesia's genesis and preservation. It results in part from the weaving together of the two dramas of the *Laws*. The drama of the Athenian's dialogue with Kleinias and Megillus is completed by the drama of Magnesia's successful founding in deed, described in the very words the Athenian uses to persuade his interlocutors to begin the city's founding. The dramas themselves are of different characters, and this makes his double role possible. The genesis of Magnesia seems to begin in rather concrete circumstances, but it becomes more like a dream as it nears its end (cf. 969b). The city seems to have a parthenogenetic birth. It emerges fully formed from the Athenian's head, as Athena is said to have been born from Zeus's head. In other words, the Athenian seems able to give birth to a city with the best possible regime and laws through the power of his speech alone. It seems that he need only speak and others listen for Magnesia to come into being; the justice, moderation, and prudence of his "blessed life [*makarios . . . zei*]" will be evident in all he says, and others will wish to become blessed (*makarioi*) themselves when they hear him (711d–12a; cf. 835c). The dreamlike character of the Athenian's double role also results in part from the use of the demiurgic genesis of all things as the *paradeigma* for Magnesia's genesis. The demiurgic genesis of all things does not occur in time. Time itself has genesis and exists only in the completed cosmos (*Timaeus* 38b). Magnesia's genesis is thus a timeless event. The temporal references associated with the Athenian's double role serve to create the impression of timelessness. The Athenian's dialogue with Kleinias and Megillus occurs on a day shortly before the summer solstice, whereas the election of the first twelve directors is to occur on a day shortly following the solstice (683c, 945e). The time between the two events is not the time of most human experience or historical time—it is mythical time. The genesis of Magnesia in deed from the Athenian's speech seems to require only a few days because it occurs in myth.

The Athenian's election as the first *archiereus* on the day that his city celebrates the sun and Apollo recalls a similar event in myth: Odysseus's homecoming to Ithaka shortly before the day the Achaians were all to assemble in the part of the city dedicated to Apollo. Odysseus was brought home by the Phaiakians aboard a magic ship while sleeping the sleep most like death. He presented himself to his countrymen as a nameless old man from Crete until he could find a way to punish the unjust rival lovers who were ruining his home. He revealed himself to them on Apollo's feast day. The first he killed was their leader, Antinoos, whose name means "against mind" (*Odyssey* 13.70–125, 187–202, 16.266–81, 20.276–80). Odysseus's homecoming has a dreamlike and timeless character because it is the myth of his return from the dead to restore order to his city. The Athenian's election as the first *archiereus* has a comparable significance (cf. 865e–66a).

The Athenian's mythical account (*mythologia*) of Magnesia's genesis and order is complete once the directors, the *agronomoi* and the new Council of Thirty-seven, led by the supervisor of *paideia*, have come into being. It remains only to combine the best of the city's institutions and offices to form the Nocturnal Council. Once the Nocturnal Council comes into being, the city will not wander (*planomenos*) without direction as if it were headless (*akephalon*; 751e–52a). The Athenian's account of the council is the third and final ikon of the *Laws*. It completes the *mythologia*. More precisely, it completes the Athenian's account of Magnesia as an ikon of the motion of *nous* in all its aspects. By the conclusion of the dialogue, Magnesia is an ikon of both the demiurgic genesis of the cosmos and the harmonious order and rotation of all things in the cosmos. It remains to be explained how it is an ikon of the ascent and descent of human *psyche* and *nous*, the motion of *nous* in human beings. The Athenian does this by describing the Nocturnal Council's composition and significance.

The council is both the head of the city and the missing head of the puppet ikon. As the head of the city, the council is "the salvation of the regime and laws" (960e). It is not described in this way because it maintains all the particulars of the regime and laws by force, but because it leads the city's ascent toward the super-heavenly region on festive occasions (*Phaedrus* 246d–48c). The most significant of such occasions is the annual election of the directors who will be responsible for leading the council itself in the ascent. However, the city celebrates the divine in a great number and variety of ways. The Athenian says there are to be at least 365 festivals a year, "without any omissions," so that not a day will pass without a festival (828a–b). Not a day will pass without the members of the Nocturnal Council assembling at dawn to provide order and direction for the day's activities and celebrations. Beyond its significance in the city, the Nocturnal Council is also an ikon of "the community of head and *nous*" that prevents the body and soul of a human being from wandering even though they may be well ordered and harmonious (969b). It completes the account of human *psyche* and *nous* begun in the Athenian's puppet ikon. Taken together, the two ikons are an account of the salvation of the soul. Their imagery suggests that, like Magnesia itself, the human soul may be saved through the repeated festive ascents and homecomings that enable it to acquire *phronesis* and *nous*.

The Athenian uses Pythagorean mathematics and number symbolism as well as evocative imagery to describe the Nocturnal Council's composition and significance. It is possible to determine from his references to number that the council is comprised of fifty men: twenty-five elder and twenty-five younger members. There are also an unspecified number of men who are responsible to the council but not counted as members. The relation of the elder members to the younger members and the men responsible to the council, as well as the relations among the elders themselves, make the Nocturnal Council an ikon of the best possible relation of *nous*, *psyche*, and *soma* in a human being. It would not be entirely misleading, therefore, to say that the council is an image of what occurs in the head of the best human being, the true philosopher.

The Nocturnal Council will be comprised of the twelve directors, the ten eldest members of the new Council of Thirty-seven guardians, the present and past supervisors of *paideia*, and an equal number of thirty-year-old men undoubtedly selected by the elders from among those who have been *agronomoi*. All of the council elders must be above the age of fifty, and a man may be a guardian only between the ages of fifty and seventy. The supervisor of *paideia*, therefore, must be at least fifty, and the minimum age for directors is also specified as fifty. The minimum age for these offices is not emphasized to suggest that the council elders will all be close to fifty. It is emphasized to recall something that is said in the *Republic*. When Socrates completes his account of the education of the guardians, he says the best of them will be compelled to see the good itself at the age of fifty in order that they might become true philosophers (*Republic* 540a–c). The minimum age of the council elders indicates that they too will be true philosophers. But the mathematics of the election of directors and the composition of the council itself suggest that they will all be well past fifty.

The Athenian says the directors will serve until they are seventy-five. Since twelve are elected in the first year and three are elected in each subsequent year to replace those who retire, it is evident that the effective minimum age for the office is seventy-one. Indeed, if the first twelve are properly distributed in age, the three elected in each subsequent year will always be seventy-one. In this way, the annual election of directors will always be a celebration of the sovereign number of Magnesia's tetractys, the number of perfect justice. And since the Athenian is to be the first among the first directors, it is safe to conclude, on the basis of his claim to be young for an old man (892d), that his age is seventy-one. The first election of directors, therefore, will be a celebration of the Athenian's perfect justice, and each subsequent one will recall the first. In this way, the Athenian will never grow old in the city (949c), and he will always be the measure of the year's number (947b).

The ten eldest guardians and the supervisor of *paideia* will all be younger than the youngest directors, since guardians may not be older than seventy. All become eligible for election as directors when they complete their service as guardians. The supervisor of *paideia* is first among them. He has the best chance of becoming a director because he will have served for five years in "the greatest of the highest offices in the city" (765e). Since he is responsible for all the city's choruses, including the Dionysian chorus for men between the ages of thirty and sixty, it is evident that the effective minimum age for his office is sixty. If the election of supervisors is understood in the same way as the election of directors, men will be elected to office when sixty and serve until they are sixty-five. And if all are elected as directors sometime after they turn seventy-one, it is safe to conclude that there will always be three past and present supervisors of *paideia* on the Nocturnal Council. There will thus be twenty-five elders in total. Since each of them attends council meetings with a thirty-year-old man of his choice, there will be fifty council members in all.

The significance of the number of council members can be explained by Pythagorean number symbolism. The number fifty represents the unity of harmony (thirty-five) and order (thirty- six) as the hypotenuse of the Pythagorean triangle with sides of 35, 36, and 50. The Nocturnal Council unites harmony and order in two ways: within itself and within the city. It does so within itself by being the ikon of the community of head and *nous*, and it does so within the city by being the institution that ties together the city's choruses and political offices. The council's two ways of uniting harmony and order produce the sovereign number of Magnesia's tetractys, both in the Pythagorean triangle with sides of 50, 50, and 71 and in the more precise calculation $71^2 = 2(35^2 + 36^2) - 1$. The latter equation may be understood as symbolizing the importance of the Athenian in Magnesia. The Athenian is the embodiment of the One or divine *nous* in the city. He is ultimately the difference between Magnesia and all other cities. If Magnesians always honor him in all they do, their city will be perfectly just. When the number of Magnesian hearths is produced by the related calculation $5,040 = 71^2 - 1 = 2([35^2 + 36^2] - 1)$, the Athenian's place in the city becomes evident. All members of the Nocturnal Council except the Athenian will have hearths in the city. The Athenian will reside in the city's 5041st hearth, the acropolis, where the Nocturnal Council assembles every dawn.

The Athenian's use of number in describing the council's composition illuminates the significance of his image of the council as a human head. The relations among the elders indicate the most important things that occur within the head. The relation of the twelve directors to the ten guardians is one of eldest to elder. It represents the relation of *nous* to *psyche*. The number of guardians even recalls the apparent number of *psyche's* motions, mentioned in the Athenian's first argument against impiety (894d). The directors thus rule the guardians as *nous* rules *psyche* and directs its motions. However, the directors are themselves directed by the first among them, the *archiereus*. He is honored with this name, and with the authority to guide the council itself, because he is the best guided by the *arche* of all those serving on the council. The unique role he has among the directors, who as a whole represent *nous*, indicates that human *nous* and divine *nous* are distinct. Human *nous* must allow itself to be guided by divine *nous* in its own rule over human *psyche* and *soma*. The rule of the council as a whole over all Magnesians may be understood as an image of this. Since the directors and the guardians represent *nous* and *psyche* respectively, the council's rule would seem to represent the rule of *psyche* with *nous* over *soma*. But this is somewhat misrepresentative because all Magnesians have *nous, psyche,* and *soma*. A better image of the rule of *psyche* with *nous* in a human being may be derived from the significance of the supervisor of *paideia*. The council as a whole rules over all Magnesians primarily through the activities of the supervisor. He is second in importance only to the *archiereus*. The first priest represents the ascent toward divine *nous;* the supervisor represents the subsequent descent with *phronesis*. The supervisor's main responsibility in the city is to exercise *phronesis* in ensuring that all Magnesians will be able to follow the upward pull on the golden cord within their souls and aspire to the first of the divine goods, *phronesis* and *nous*. In doing so, he teaches them to take the life of the *archiereus* as a *paradeigma* for their own. Therefore, if a human being were to take the Nocturnal Council itself as a *paradeigma* for what should go on in his own head, the relation of the *archiereus* and the supervisor of *paideia* would serve as an image of the repeated ascents and descents of *psyche* with *nous* that are necessary for a human being to live a philosophic life.

The relations of the elder council members to the younger and to those men responsible to the council but not part of its deliberations give a more precise indication of the nature of *noesis* in the human being. The Athenian says the elder and younger members, in common (*koine*), really save the whole city (*sozein . . . ontos ten polin holen*). He likens the elders to *nous* because of their prudent thinking (*diapherontos phronein*) about the things worthy of discussion, and the younger members to the best part of *psyche* because they are capable of keeping watch (*phrourountas*) over all things for the elders. The elders deliberate (*bouleuesthai*) among themselves, using the young as assistants. The young are to learn with all seriousness (*pasi spoudei*) whatever the elders judge approvingly. They will then be able to hand over relevant perceptions (*aistheseis*) to the memories (*mnemais*) as aids for the collective deliberations (*xumboulais*) of the elders (951e–52a, 964e–65a). In the imagery of the Athenian's hunting law, the young are the council's anamnetic hunters, without whom the deliberative or dialectical ascent of the elders would not be possible. They are thus an image of the anamnetic motion of *psyche* necessary for human *nous* to ascend toward divine *nous*.

The men responsible to the council but not members of it are the observers or "spectators [*theoroi*]." The *theoroi* differ from the council's young hunters (*thereutai*). They represent the hunting of *nous* with the best part of *soma*, while the *thereutai* represent the hunting of *nous* with the best part of *psyche*. The Athenian says that no Magnesian man may travel abroad before the age of forty and that no travel is to be for private purposes. Of those allowed to travel, the *theoroi* will be men between the ages of fifty and sixty who are sent abroad by the Nocturnal Council to learn of the *nomoi* and *paideia* of other cities. They are to report to the council immediately upon return and inform it of what they have seen and heard. Their reports will enable the council to ensure that the Magnesian *nomoi* and *paideia* are second to none. The council itself is not bound by their judgment. Indeed, just the opposite is the case. The council judges the worth of their reports without having seen or heard what the *theoroi* have seen and heard. Furthermore, the council judges the *theoroi* themselves to determine if their voyages have made them better or worse or have left them unchanged. If they return worse and claim to have become wise (*sophos*) from their theorizing, they must die. If they return worse but are willing to obey the city's magistrates, they may live, but they are to have no association with Magnesians. If they return the same, they will be honored for their services no matter what they have seen and heard. If they return better, the council will allow them to share what they have learned about other cities with all Magnesians (950d–51d, 952b–53d).

The *theoroi* are obviously the council's eyes and ears. They represent the perceptions associated with theorizing. Such perceptions are not simply stimulations of the sense organs. They are informed. The Athenian says that in each city the *theoroi* visit, they will ask to see something beautiful (*ti kalon*) that differs from beautiful things in other cities (953c). Since beautiful things are evidence of the good in the sensible realm, the observers' search for them on behalf of the council represents the hunting of *nous* in the sensible realm for evidence of the good. It can thus be inferred that perception itself is a seeking out in the sensible realm of things already known in some way by human *nous* and *psyche*. The observers are instructed by the council to go abroad in search of something the council will recognize without perceiving it directly; similarly, particular perceptions originate in the independent ability of *psyche* and *nous* to apperceive the thing being sought through perception. The Athenian suggests that the observers themselves must have some ability to see the good once abroad. He specifies that they too must be above the age of fifty. In other words, their own perceptions must be informed by the good. However, the council is the final judge of whether they have exercised their faculties properly. Similarly, perceptions received by human *psyche* and *nous* as a consequence of seeking out things in the sensible realm must be judged against what is already known in some way. Perceptions need not be accepted blindly or measured against previous perceptions alone. They are measured against *anamnesis* and accepted or rejected accordingly. Even the perceptions that enable a human being to learn and better himself do so through *anamnesis*. This is why the Athenian does not count the *theoroi* as members of the Nocturnal Council. They represent the best part of *soma*, but nothing more. The council is an ikon of the community of *nous* and head because it represents the "blending of *nous* and the finest senses and their becoming one" (961d, 969d). But this does not indicate that the *theoroi* are to be considered council members. It indicates only that *nous* should rule the finest senses just as the council elders rule the *theoroi* responsible to the council as a whole. In general, *nous* rules all *soma* through *psyche*. In the case of the senses that are the best part of *soma*, *nous* rules them by means of the anamnetic motion of *psyche*. This is why the Athenian says that the Nocturnal Council's young hunters, not the *theoroi*, are responsible for handing over perceptions (*aistheseis*) to the memories and thus participating in the collective deliberations of the elders (964e).

The deliberations of the elders make the council an image of *phronesis* and *nous*. The daily council meetings are a simple exercise of *phronesis* in ordering the city's affairs. The council's highest exercise of *phronesis* occurs whenever it judges the Magnesian *nomoi* and *paideia* against those of other cities. For it to make such a judgment, it must first deliberate about the *telos* of *nomos* and *paideia* in general, and this requires it to engage in the dialectical ascent of *nous* through which *phronesis* is acquired. The Athenian's account of the relation between the directors and the council's guardians is an image of dialectical ascent. However, in emphasizing the role played in the ascent by the directors, particularly the *archiereus*, the Athenian does not state explicitly whether the younger council members may be counted among the guardians being led upward. The Athenian uses the term "guardian" in an ambiguous way. It refers specifically to the ten guardians on the council, but it also refers to the council as a whole and thus may be used to refer to all council members, young and old alike (968a; cf. 966b, 969c). If the council is taken as an image of the human head, the twelve directors represent *nous*, and the ten guardians *psyche*. The young council members thus seem to have no part in the ascent of *psyche* with *nous*, even though they are necessary for it to be possible. However, if all council members are understood to possess *psyche* and *nous* themselves and the council as a whole is taken as an image of the best possible *paideia* for human beings, all members will follow the dialectical ascent led by the *archiereus*, and the youngest members may indeed be the most capable and willing to participate in the ascent after the *archiereus* himself. The role of the young may be ambiguous, but the role of the observers is not—they do not participate in the ascent. In the image of the council as a human head, the hunting of the *theoroi* in the sensible realm can only be involved in dialectical ascent indirectly, by way of the anamnetic hunting of the younger members. However, if the *theoroi* are understood to possess *psyche* and *nous* themselves, it is possible for them to participate directly in ascent. They need only do what all Magnesians do: follow the council as a whole in all things.

The Athenian says that all council members must have an education in common for the council as a whole to become the guardian of the city's salvation. All must be compelled to see with precision, he says. This suggests that their common *paideia* will enable all of them to become true philosophers (cf. *Republic* 540a–c). If all are successfully compelled, the council will be divine (*theios*). Moreover, it will be a "perfect and permanent savior" for a "divine regime [*theias politeias*]" (960b–c, 965c, 968a–b, 969b–c). The council's "more precise" education is led by the first of the directors. The Athenian says that the top craftsman (*akron demiourgon*) and guardian in any endeavor must pursue and know (*gnomai*) the One (*to hen*), and once knowing it, order all things with a synoptic view to it (965b). The *archiereus* is the top craftsman and guardian of *paideia* in Magnesia. Indeed, he is the *demiourgos* of all Magnesian *nomoi* and *paideia*. His pursuit of the One is identical with his pursuit of the *arche* because both are names for what is also called divine *nous* or the god. And the manner in which he knows the One or the *arche* is best evident in his *phronesis* and *nous*. He is therefore best qualified to lead the rest of the Nocturnal Council in acquiring an education in common.

The Athenian's account of the council's deliberations indicates that dialectic is a testing of *psyche* and *nous* with argument. In particular, the "more precise" education of each council member is a testing with argument of his ability and willingness to participate in the psychic and noetic ascent toward the end of all things. Argument or dialectic is not strictly necessary for the ascent of *psyche* with *nous*, which may occur on any festive or celebratory occasion. In Magnesia, the daily festivals and the choral performances are just such occasions. Dialectical deliberation, if it is properly directed, is also a celebratory occasion. The ascent in speech complements the ascent in deed. It may even act to bring it about. However, the ascent in speech cannot supplant the ascent in deed. The ability to participate in ascent without any accompanying ability to account for it is evidence of a slavish nature (966b; cf. *Meno* 82b–86c), but the ability to argue without any accompanying ability to ascend in the soul is evidence of an eristic and sophistic nature. Dialectical deliberation is a unique type of ascent capable of making the *paideia* of anyone who practices it more precise in two ways. It compels him to give as accurate an account as possible of what occurs in the *psyche* and *nous* during the ascent and subsequent descent. But more important, it also teaches him how to test others with argument and guide their ascent.

The Athenian says explicitly that all council members must come to know the truth (*aletheian*) of all serious things (*panton ton spoudaion*). They must be capable both of interpreting it in speech (*logoi . . . hermeneuein*) and of following it closely in deed (*ergois xunakolouthein;* 966b). In particular, there are two things they must learn if they are to be capable of giving an account (*logon*) of all serious things that have an account (967e–68a). The two things the Athenian mentions indicate how the ability to interpret the truth of things in speech is founded on the ability to follow their truth in deed. He first says the council members must know how virtue, the beautiful, and the good each may be said to be both many and one (965c–66a; cf. 963a–64a). But this raises the question, How may virtue, the beautiful and the good themselves be said to be both many and one? The second thing the council members must learn suggests an answer. All must labor over the Athenian's arguments against impiety. They will learn from them not only how to speak about the gods, but also how *psyche* may be said to be the eldest and most divine of all things and how *nous* may be said to arrange all things in an order (*to pan diakekosmekos;*

966b–67e). When they have understood the Athenian's account of *nous*, they will know how the gods themselves may be said to be many and one. They will know that the true, the beautiful, the good, and all things divine have a common origin in the god who is also named the One and that the highest virtues of human beings all have their common origin in this knowledge.

The Athenian's concluding account of dialectical ascent in the *Laws* complements Socrates' account of the ascent to the super-heavenly region in the *Phaedrus*. The Athenian emphasizes the importance of deliberation and argument; Socrates, on the other hand, describes it as a festive activity in which no words are spoken. But the two accounts are not at odds. They complement one another perfectly in their use of imagery, and this reveals their substantive agreement. Since the Nocturnal Council is an image of a head, both of the city and of a human being, the council as a whole corresponds to Socrates' image of the head of the best human charioteer raised into the superheavenly region with great effort and maintained there only briefly. The guardians represent *dianoia*. They behold absolute justice, moderation, and knowledge (*episteme*) at the highest point of their ascent. The directors represent *nous*. They behold "truly existing being [*ousia ontos ousa*]." Only the *archiereus* may be said to behold what is beyond being itself, exceeding it in dignity and power (*Phaedrus* 247c–48a; *Republic* 509b). However, if the council is understood as an image of the best possible *paideia* for human beings, the correspondence between the accounts given by the Athenian and Socrates acquires a different and more important significance. All human beings seek the superheavenly "plain of truth [*aletheias . . . pedion*]," even those who fail to reach it. This is because the *psyche* and *nous* are nourished there, and all human beings have some form of erotic longing for such nourishment. Every human being is a charioteer and two winged horses. The charioteer is *nous*, the horse of noble breeding is *psyche*, and the horse of the opposite type, requiring much training, is *soma*. Both horses are winged if they follow the guidance of *nous*, for *nous* is the wing that gives flight to human being itself. It is the part of the human being that most partakes of the nature of the divine (*Phaedrus* 246a–e, 248a–b). All Magnesians have winged horses. Their *paideia* enables them to follow the guidance of *nous* a good part of the way toward the superheavenly region. Human beings who are unable to follow, or who have lost their wings through forgetfulness and evil, have no place in the city. The fifty best Magnesians, the ones best able to raise their own heads into the superheavenly region, comprise the Nocturnal Council. They are the most noetic men in the city. The *archiereus* is first among them, capable of leading all the others. The *archiereus*, of all men, is thus most deserving of the names philosopher, lover of beauty (*philokalou*), and music and erotic man (*musikou . . . kai erotikou; Phaedrus* 248a–b).

10 NAMING THE PARADIGMATIC CITY

SINCE THE CITY of the Magnesians is an ikon of the motion of *nous* in the cosmos and in human beings, it is possible to speak poetically of the original of which it is an image as a city. The cosmos and all things within it may be said to be a city of gods and the children of gods. The Pythagorean proverb that "friends really have all things in common [*ontos esti koina ta philon*]" is most true of the gods who dwell in the cosmic city. It is far less true of the mortals who dwell in earthly cities. The best mortals aspire to godlike immortality. They are worthy to be called children of the gods. A city founded by mortals may also aspire to this end. If it is founded and inhabited by the best mortals, it may take the *politeia* and *nomoi* of the city of the gods as its *paradeigma*. It would then be "nearest to immortality [*athanasias eggutata*]" and "in a way [*pos*] . . . the second one [*he mia deuteros*]" (739c-e).[1]

The city of the Magnesians is "the second one." All other cities founded by mortals are "second [*deutera*]" (951a) in comparison because it is the only city in which all are friends and have all things in common, as much as is possible among human beings. In other words, Magnesia is the only city in which "everyone [lives], as much as possible, collectively [*athroon*], together and in common [*hama kai koinon*], always [*aei*] and in all ways [*pasi panton*]" (942c). The source of the city's unity and salvation (*soterian*) is the first *archiereus*. Of all human beings, he best pursues and knows the One (*to hen;* 965b). As a consequence, he is best able to apply the god's blameless justice blamelessly and remove anarchy (*anarchia*) from the lives of human beings (942c-d, 945d). In other words, he is able to rule all human things as the god rules all things. If all Magnesians follow his guidance, their city will become one from many; if not, it will become "many from one [*pollas ek mias*]." Following his guidance, "the entire country and city [will] flourish and be happy [*eudaimonei*]" (945d-e). The city of the Magnesians, therefore, may be called "the second one" for two reasons. It takes the cosmic city as its *paradeigma*, and it is ordered and preserved

261

by the One (*to hen*), which orders and preserves the cosmic city through the rule of the first *archiereus*.

The cities in speech of the *Laws* and the *Republic* both aspire to the end described in the Pythagorean proverb. Both are thus, in some way, ikons of the city of the gods (739c–e; *Republic* 424a). In Aristotle's terms, both are founded partly on the understanding "that it is best for the city to be as far as possible entirely one [*mian*]." Both are partnerships in many of the things in which partnerships are possible, but neither is an impossible partnership in everything or in all things in which partnership is possible (*Politics* 1260b36–61a17). The end described in the proverb is not attained in either city, but the city of the Magnesians approaches it more closely than does the *kallipolis*. It is more deservedly called "a *paradeigma* in speech of a good city" (*Republic* 472d–e). The *kallipolis* is second to it because it is torn between two conflicting *paradeigmata:* the Pythagorean proverb and the opinion that justice is the minding of one's own affairs (433a–b). The *kallipolis* is made one from many in following the first *paradeigma*, and many from one in following the other. Insofar as it is possible for a city to do so, the city of the Magnesians takes as its *paradeigma* the *paradeigma* of the true philosopher and excludes all things that would "fill it with factions and swiftly destroy it" (*Laws* 945d–e). Since it is most like the cosmic city, it is also most deservedly called "a *paradeigma* laid up in heaven for whomever wants to see" (*Republic* 592a–b).

The city of the Magnesians, like the city of the gods itself, is a *paradeigma* for both cities and human beings. It seems to be a dreamlike city molded from wax, but it could serve as a *paradeigma* for what might be attempted in the cities of Hellas. However, anyone proposing to found a comparable city or reform an existing one according to what he reads in the *Laws* should not read the dialogue dogmatically. He should follow the Athenian's advice to steer away from what cannot be done and always do what is most noble and most true (*Laws* 745e–46d). He should act with *phronesis* in all he does. In order to acquire *phronesis*, he must take the *Laws* itself as the *paradeigma* of his *paideia* (811b–d). He must look to the paradigmatic city of the heavens and "found a city within himself on the basis of what he sees" (*Republic* 592b). When the Nocturnal Council rules in the acropolis of his soul as it rules in the acropolis of the paradigmatic city, he will have acquired the first of the divine goods, *phronesis* and *nous* (*Laws* 969c; *Republic* 566b).

The name of the Athenian's paradigmatic city is "the city of the

Magnesians." It is convenient to call the city Magnesia, as I have done to this point, following scholarly convention. Properly speaking, the city itself has no name. The Athenian only names the inhabitants of the city Magnesians. It would be wrong to assume that the Magnesians are named after their city.

There are only six references to the names of the city and its inhabitants in the dialogue, all made by the Athenian (704a, 848d, 860e, 919d, 946b, 969a). The first occurs immediately after Kleinias tells the Athenian of the responsibilities of the Knossian nomothetic committee. The first thing to enter the Athenian's mind is the name that "it will be necessary to call the city in time to come." For the time being, he suggests that it might be derived in the customary way from some place, or from a river or spring there, or even from a god itself named after the place (704a). All this is said just before the Athenian announces the end of the age of Zeus and describes the god who rules over all those with *nous* (713a–14a, 715e–16d), and well before he gives his account of the spring of all wonders (893c–d). At the end of the dialogue, the Athenian says the city of the Magnesians will be named in a different way. It will be named after someone by the god himself (969a). The penultimate reference to the city of the Magnesians in the dialogue explains who this person will be. The Athenian says the city will find salvation under the god when it elects its directors. The name of the *archiereus* is to be the measure of the year's number (946b, 947a–b). The city, therefore, is best named after the first *archiereus* whose rule will initiate the age of *nous* if the city follows the god in selecting him. The man most worthy to be the first *archiereus*, the Athenian *xenos*, seems to have no name himself. The city he founds in speech must remain nameless until he comes to rule in its highest office and reveals who he is.

The city's inhabitants have a name. The Athenian calls them Magnesians to indicate that they dwell in the paradigmatic city that is an ikon of the motion of *nous* in all its forms. They are called Magnesians after the magnet, which was named the Magnesian stone (*lithos Magnetis*) by Euripides (*Ion* 533d; Euripides frag. 567). The imagery of magnetism underlies two of the most important discussions in the *Laws*. The Athenian's accounts of the amazing powers of *nous* in the cosmos and the celebration of the god in the most beautiful and truest tragedy may both be described in the imagery of magnetism. Taken together, they explain why the inhabitants of the paradigmatic city are best called Magnesians.

The Athenian concludes the first of his arguments against

impiety by referring to Thales' statement that all things are full of gods (899b). It is an appropriate conclusion to his account of how all things in the cosmos that have genesis from the *arche* are comprised of *psyche* and *soma* and are best ruled by *psyche* with *nous*. The Athenian's account suggests that *soma* and *psyche* may be described as other-moving motion and self-and-other-moving motion respectively. The rule of *nous* in the cosmos, therefore, may be described as an amazing type of unmoving motion. According to Aristotle, Anaxagoras was the first to distinguish between *psyche* and *nous* in some way and the first to name *nous* as the *arche*. However, he also said that *psyche* and *nous* are of the same nature, and thus concluded that *nous* sets all things in motion. Thales, on the other hand, said that *psyche* is the cause of all motion. He even went so far as to say that the magnet has *psyche* because it causes motion in iron (*De anima* 405a13–22). The Athenian's account of these matters differs in several ways.

In the *Phaedo*, Socrates praises Anaxagoras for having said that *nous* is the order and cause of all things (*diakosmon te kai panton aition*) but then criticizes him for the many absurd things (*polla . . . atopa*) he then went on to say instead of explaining how *nous* causes all things to be the best they can be. Anaxagoras does not explain what is best for each thing and what is good for all in common. In other words, he does not explain how *nous* preserves or saves all things (*Phaedo* 97b–98c). The Athenian would agree with this criticism. Furthermore, he would argue that Thales is right to say *psyche*, not *nous* is the cause of motion in all things. But he would add that Thales also says many absurd things. For example, Thales claims that water rather than *nous* is the *arche* (*Metaphysics* 983b19–28). On this matter, Anaxagoras's account is obviously preferable. As well, Thales attempts to support his otherwise praiseworthy understanding that all things are full of gods with a propositional statement about the relation of magnets and iron. Propositional statements of this type cannot be true. Statements about the relation of *nous*, *psyche* and *soma* in all things can only be true of the cosmos as a whole. If applied to particular motions or events within the cosmos, they become misleading and even false. At best, such statements might serve as heuristic images. Thales' understanding of the magnet is misleading and false because the motion it causes in iron resembles the motion of *psyche* far less than it does the motion of *nous*. According to the Athenian's account, magnetism is neither other-moving motion, since a magnet does not act through *soma,* nor self-and-other-moving motion, since a magnet cannot move itself. It most resembles the motion of the unmoved mover.

The Athenian says that *nous* is the *arche* of all things and that *psyche* sets all things in motion. He also says that *nous* exercises its amazing powers in preserving or saving all things in the cosmos. The rule of *nous,* therefore, brings about the good for all things in common. All things in the cosmos are moved by it, or move toward it as their end, in a manner somewhat similar to the movement of iron toward a magnet. Since the order of the Athenian's city in speech is an ikon of the order of the cosmos, it is only fitting that its inhabitants should be called Magnesians.

The motion of *nous* in human beings is comparable to the motion of *nous* in the cosmos, but the two occur differently. The motion of *nous* in human beings is an ascent of human *nous* toward divine *nous* and a subsequent descent or homecoming. It may occur within the soul at any time, but it may also occur collectively or publicly on festive occasions. Two such festive occasions are the Dionysian celebration of the dithyramb and the public performance of a tragedy. The two are directly related because tragedy originated in the dithyramb. The Athenian describes the motion of *nous* in human beings in his ikons of the divine puppet and the Nocturnal Council. When the two ikons are taken together, they provide a complete account of the motion of *nous* in human beings. They describe both how it occurs discretely within a soul and how it occurs publicly on a festive occasion. To indicate that his ikons describe the collective or public manifestation of the motion of *nous,* the Athenian compares the Nocturnal Council's role within the city to the performance of a tragedy and the singing of a dithyramb (817a–d; cf. 700b–701a).

When the Athenian's account of the most beautiful and truest tragedy is understood in the light of Socrates' discussion of rhapsody in the *Ion,* the reasons that the Athenian names the inhabitants Magnesians become clearer. Rhapsodes recite epic poetry publicly. According to Socrates' account, such performances are essentially the same as performances of tragedies. The effects that all such performances have on the souls of those who participate in them may be compared to the motion caused in iron by the Magnesian stone.

Socrates says rhapsodes do two things: they recite the words of poets in performance, and they interpret or explain the poetry in their own words. Socrates uses the imagery of magnetism to describe the public performance of poetry. He says that when rhapsodes recite, they convey the words of the god to the audience in a manner similar to the transmission of a magnet's power through several rings formed of pieces of iron. The god is the Magnesian stone. Poets are the first ring of pieces of iron, transformed into magnets themselves by the power of the Magnesian stone. Rhapsodes and similar performers, especially tragic actors, are the second ring, transformed into magnets through contact with the first. The audience is the third and final ring (*Ion* 533d–e, 535e–36a). Socrates' account suggests a circular arrangement, since the god usually inspires a poet through a particular muse and a rhapsode generally finds himself inspired by only one poet. Members of the audience, however, are not similarly bound to the works of one poet or the performances of one rhapsode. What is more, poets need not be inspired by one muse alone. They may be moved directly by the god. This is most true of Homer, whom Socrates says is "the best [*aristoi*] and most divine [*theiotatoi*] of poets" (530b). Socrates says the god's power draws (*helkei;* 536a) the souls of all human beings. The god can draw souls directly or through the power of the words of poets. The words of poets who are inspired (*entheos*) by the god are not the products of *techne* and *episteme*. The god takes for himself (*exairoumenos*) the *nous* of poets when he uses them as his servants (*hyperetais*). Their words are not their own; it is the god who speaks them (533e–34c). This accounts for the power of the words to move human beings distant in time and place from the poet's inspiration. According to Aristotle, "Words spoken are symbols of affections [*pathemata*] of the *psyche;* written words are the signs of words spoken" (*On Interpretation* 16a). The poet's words are symbols of the *pathemata* produced in his *psyche* by the god's influence. When performed or recited by a rhapsode, they are capable of producing the same *pathemata* in the souls of others who are open to the god's influence.

The *pathemata* produced in the soul through the god's influence may have a lasting effect in enabling the soul to become virtuous. In other words, just as the pieces of iron affected by the magnet's power are transformed into magnets themselves, so too human beings affected by the god's power become divine in some way. But human beings, unlike pieces of iron, may become permanent magnets. The magnetism of the human soul is virtue. The study of poetry is one way a soul may be led to virtue because the study of poetry requires the proper interpretation of the god's words.

The poets themselves must be interpreters. Socrates says they are "interpreters of the gods [*hermenes . . . ton theon*]" (534e). Poets must possess some part of the daimonic power of Eros to interpret (*hermeneuon*) and convey things between the mortal and immortal realms (*Symposium* 202d–e). If they do, they will be able to interpret the immortal realm for human beings by giving words to the erotic affections in their souls. Their poetry will then be able to produce a comparable erotic response in the souls of those who hear it. This requires a degree of *techne* and *episteme* no doubt, but any degree of *techne* and *episteme* without the god's influence is worthless.

The interpretation of words inspired by the god requires different skills. Not all rhapsodes are erotic or divinely inspired men capable of proper interpretation. Socrates suggests that most, if not all, rhapsodes are like Ion, his interlocutor. Ion does not interpret poetry with *techne* and *episteme*, but he believes that he does (536c). His mistaken belief results from his assumption that the ability of the poet's words to move others when he recites them is an indication that he understands what they mean and is able to explain them to others. Ion is moved by "divine power [*theia . . . dynamis*]" in recital alone (533d). The poetry itself does not affect his *psyche* and *nous* in any lasting way. No matter how often he recites the words with which the poet interprets the god, he remains a base piece of iron. Therefore, whenever he speaks publicly as one of "the interpreters of the interpreters [*hermeneon hermenes*]," his words are without any guidance from the god (535a). As an interpreter of poetry, he is nothing but a sophist. Those who follow his persuasion may be no better. If they too are unaffected in any lasting, beneficial way by the god's words, their preference for one rhapsode's explanation over another's will be nothing but an interpretation of an interpretation of an interpretation—that is, a phantasm at three removes from the truth.

Ion's failings notwithstanding, it is possible to interpret the poets, even Homer, with *techne* and *episteme* (541e–42b).[2] In the Athenian's city, all will be instructed in the erotics of the proper interpretation of poetry for their lasting benefit. The instruction will turn them into permanent magnets. It is only fitting, therefore, that they be named Magnesians.

The city of the Magnesians is the best and most beautiful tragedy, and the Athenian, inspired by the god himself, is its poet. He has composed it as the *mimesis* of the best and most beautiful life—his own. The Athenian's own life is the truest tragedy because he, above all other human beings, aspires to immortality within the limits of mortality in all that he says and does (817b). If Magnesians are to be worthy of their name, they too must always aspire to this end in all that they say and do, individually and in common. If they follow the guidance of the Athenian's *paideia* and *nomoi,* they will become as much like the god as they are able. When all those in the city are truly Magnesians, their city will be a perfect ikon of the motion of *nous.* It will then be the *paradeigma* of a perfectly just and good city, in which friends, as far as possible, have all things in common. It will then be a city second only to the city of gods ruled by the god himself.

CONCLUSION

The True *Mythologia* of Socratic *Phronesis*

Plato is no idealist. The city of the Magnesians is no more a political ideal than is Glaucon's beautiful city. Plato wrote the *Republic* and the *Laws* in order to lead his readers past the follies of sophistry and idealism toward the truly philosophical life. The philosophical life is one dedicated to acquiring the virtues of *sophia* and *phronesis*. In the Athenian's words, it is the life dedicated to acquiring the first of the divine goods, *phronesis* and *nous*. This does not mean that the *Republic* and *Laws* have no political relevance. It means that they are not intended to have direct and immediate political relevance in the sense of being programs for action or abstract political blueprints to be implemented unthinkingly in the political realm. The conviction that it is possible to apply the methods of geometrical deduction or technical production to the political realm is, for Plato, evidence of a pathology in the human *psyche* that would have grotesque consequences if it ever became predominant in a society. The political relevance of the *Republic* and the *Laws* is perhaps best summarized in this one statement: human beings should be ruled by *phronesis* and *nous* in all they say and do in both the personal and public realms.

The dialogues have indirect political relevance in all societies, and Plato addresses them to all human beings willing to study them. If his readers succeed in acquiring *phronesis* and *nous*, circumstances will then determine what consequences their practice of justice with *phronesis* in all things may have in the public realm. Plato also addresses the dialogues to his contemporaries in a different way. They are full of prudential advice about what should be done in the cities of Hellas. But without *phronesis*, Plato's advice about practical political matters could not have been understood by his contemporaries any more than his understanding of matters not limited to his time can be understood by a modern reader without *phronesis*. The *Republic* and *Laws* are not limited in their relevance to Plato's own time and society. Anyone

269

who studies them seriously, now as then, may become a Magnesian. The city of the Magnesians is not bound by historical time and geometrical space.

Plato's political philosophy is founded on an understanding of the virtues comparable in its main features to the account of the virtues given in Aristotle's writings on ethics. Plato understands that human beings, in all likelihood, will become vicious and calculating if their souls are not properly trained to follow the middle way of moral virtue and their minds are not properly guided from childhood to follow the upward pull on the golden cord. A morally virtuous upbringing and a sound education can enable most human beings to acquire some part of the higher virtues. The highest are *sophia* and *phronesis*. The few human beings who become true philosophers possess these virtues in the most perfect way. In the Athenian's words, these virtues are both many and one. They are many because they may be distinguished: *sophia* is theoretical wisdom and *phronesis* is practical wisdom and deliberative judgment. In this sense, there is no common ground between them. There is no theoretical wisdom of practical matters and no practical wisdom of theoretical matters. Nevertheless, the two virtues are also one. Both are excellences of the *nous* and thus have *noesis* in common. *Noesis* is the motion of *nous* in human beings. It is the ascent of human *nous* toward what may be called by many names: the *arche* and *telos* of all things, the One, the good beyond being, the divine *nous,* and the god. Without *noesis*, neither *sophia* nor *phronesis* is possible. It is the difference on the one hand between *sophia* and *episteme,* and on the other between *phronesis* and simple cleverness.

Although *sophia* and *phronesis* are one as well as many, it is possible to say that *phronesis* is the more important of the two virtues. Plato indicates as much in his description of *phronesis* and *nous* as the first of the divine goods for human beings. *Sophia* is the virtue that governs reasoning about certain theoretical matters. *Phronesis* is the virtue that governs all aspects of living one's life. *Sophia* has no ability to govern life itself. The attempt to subordinate the living of one's life to theoretical reasoning leads to idealism, not wisdom. At best, it is evidence of geometrical thinking; at worst, of sophistry. *Phronesis* is the virtue *par excellence* of the philosophical life. It most distinguishes the true philosopher from other human beings. The true philosopher is not someone who knows many different accounts of justice. He is someone who always practices justice with *phronesis* in everything he says and does. This is what makes him the most divine or godlike of human beings.

Plato's account of *sophia, phronesis,* and *nous* in the *Republic* and *Laws* is not an esoteric doctrine. It is simply difficult to understand. There are several reasons for this. The difficulty of Plato's account is in large part deliberate. Plato places a unique hermeneutical problem before every reader of the dialogues by writing them in such a way that the reader must acquire some part of the virtues he describes in order to be able to understand his account of them. In particular, the dialogues are an exercise in *phronesis.* The reader is continually asked to judge the words and deeds of the speakers and the drama of the dialogues. The better his judgment becomes, the more he is able to make *phronesis* his own. This in turn allows him a better interpretation of the dialogues.

The hermeneutical difficulty of the dialogues is made truly problematic by a philological difficulty. Plato's dialogues are great works of literature or poetry (*poiesis*), comparable to the writings of Homer and the best of the tragedians. Indeed, Plato himself presents them as the culmination of Greek *paideia.* In the Athenian's words, the dialogues are the "most well-measured [*metriotatoi*]" of all Greek poetry and prose. There are no better *paradeigmata* for *paideia* and *poiesis.* Of course, this does not mean that nothing else should be studied. The dialogues cannot be understood as texts without context, in abstract hermeneutical isolation. They can only be understood through direct comparison to the best of all previous writings. Again in the Athenian's words, the speeches in the dialogues should be studied alongside their "brothers" in other works (*Laws* 811c-e). To guide the reader's search for these brothers, Plato fills the dialogues with literary references. However, the modern reader faces a difficulty in his search that Plato did not anticipate in composing the dialogues: many of the brothers to his own accounts have disappeared. For example, although Homer's epic poetry has been preserved, there is almost no textual evidence available to the modern reader of the many commentaries on the *Iliad* and the *Odyssey* that were written in the centuries before Plato. Furthermore, there is very little textual evidence of the school founded by Pythagoras, the man who is said to have coined the term *philosophia.* The "quarrel between philosophy and poetry" (*Republic* 607b) most likely originated in disputes between the Pythagoreans and those who wrote commentaries on Homer's poetry, but their disputes are now inaccessible to us. Little is known of the ways in which poetic commentators and the first philosophers praised or blamed Homer with what they thought was *techne* and *episteme*. Consequently, the ability of the modern reader to understand how Plato himself praises or criticizes the praisers and criticizers of Homer with *techne* and *episteme* is limited (*Ion* 541e; *Republic* 595b-c, 600a-b).

The philological problems in studying the dialogues heighten their hermeneutical difficulty by limiting the reader's ability to follow both the arguments and the dramas of the dialogues, thereby making Plato's account of Socrates more difficult to understand. Plato's dialogues are nothing if not a eulogy for Socrates, "the best [*aristou*], most prudent [*phronimatou*] and most just [*dikaiotatou*]" of all human beings (*Phaedo* 118a). Their form and substance are perfectly matched, and both direct the reader to the same end. They are written in the form best suited to enable the reader to confront Socrates directly; and the account of the highest virtues in the dialogues is a description of the virtues most evident in Socrates' life. The dialogues are not empirical reports of Socrates' actual words and deeds. They are unique works of literature or *poiesis*. They describe the significance of Socrates' life, not the facts of it.

The arguments and dramas of the dialogues are best understood within the context of Plato's intention to compose written works that are able to assist any serious reader in living a Socratic life. All those who are not Socrates but wish to live Socratic lives must make their lives into a *mimesis* of Socrates' own. Given the differences in human circumstances, a life lived in imitation of the particular facts of Socrates' own would be a false *mimesis*. Therefore, only a poetic account of Socrates' life, requiring interpretation, can enable others to lead truly Socratic lives.[1]

Plato's dialogues are a unique type of *poiesis* for another reason as well. They are unique in their poetic use of previous writings. By means of explicit literary references to the most important works of Greek *paideia*, Plato's dialogues describe Socrates' life as the *telos*, or end, of Greek civilization. The arguments and dramas of the dialogues are all somehow part of the greater argument or drama presented in Plato's true *mythologia* of Socrates' life and its significance. Plato's *mythologia* is a hermeneutic whole, even though it extends through seemingly disparate and dissimilar dialogues. The deliberate hermeneutical difficulty of each of the dialogues would make it challenging enough in the best of circumstances for a reader to see the unity of the whole. The philological difficulty of understanding Plato's literary references makes a vision of the whole all the more distant.

No two dialogues seem more disparate or dissimilar to modern readers than the *Republic* and the *Laws*. Throughout my study, I have argued for their substantive and dramatic continuity. Their substantive continuity is evident in Plato's account of *sophia, phronesis,* and *nous*. Their dramatic continuity is evident in Plato's use of Homeric imagery in composing the three ikons of the longer way and the three of the paradigmatic city. The dramatic continuity complements the substantive. Taken together, the ikons reveal that the city of the Magnesians is the city in the common home of all human beings that is most like the city of the gods. Insofar as it is possible for a city to do so, it takes the *paradeigma* of the true philosopher as its own. The true philosopher and the paradigmatic city are both governed by *nous*. One argument for the continuity of the *Republic* and the *Laws* remains to be made: the argument that shows how they are related in Plato's true *mythologia* of Socrates' life. The argument is easily summarized. Its premises are straightforward, if not uncontroversial.

Socrates is the Athenian. Aristotle makes no error in describing the *Laws* as one of the "discourses of Socrates" (*Politics* 1265a10). Plato's *mythologia* uses the imagery of Homer's *Odyssey* to compare Socrates with Odysseus and present him as the greatest Greek hero.[2] The *Republic* and the *Laws* are the two most important parts of Plato's mythical account of Socrates' wanderings and homecoming. They are no more at odds with one another than the first half of the *Odyssey* is at odds with the second. Odysseus's wanderings came to an end when he arrived at the land of the Phaiakians. Their magic ships ensured his homecoming. In the *Republic*, Socrates' wanderings in argument are directed toward a similar end, the *paradeigma* of a perfectly just and good city. The land of the Phaiakians for Socrates is the city of the Magnesians. Odysseus was unrecognized by his countrymen after his homecoming. He appeared to them in disguise as a nameless stranger. In the *Laws*, Socrates also appears in disguise as a nameless stranger. In Homer's *mythologia*, Odysseus's homecoming is a return from the dead to punish the unjust suitors and restore order in his home and kingdom. He returns from a land ruled by Alkinoos (meaning "strength of *nous*") and Arete (meaning "prayed for," and later "virtue") and brings their justice to his homeland. In Plato's *mythologia*, there is no comparable homecoming for Socrates from the city of the Magnesians. He stays to rule the city as its first director even though Odysseus did not stay among the Phaiakians to receive similar honors.

Plato deliberately reformulates Homer's imagery to give it new meaning. He separates the imagery of Odysseus's nameless disguise from the punishment of the unjust suitors and combines it with the imagery of the Phaiakians' honoring of Odysseus. The unjust suitors or rival lovers ruining Socrates' homeland are the four types of inferior souls and factional regimes described in the *Republic*. The perfectly just and good city ruled by *phronesis* and *arete* in which the disguised and nameless Socrates receives the highest honors is described in the *Laws*. At the conclusion of the *Laws*, the dreamlike city has been founded in speech alone. It remains only for Socrates to awaken from the dream and discover that he has returned to his homeland, just as Odysseus awoke on Ithaka after having been brought home aboard one of the Phaiakians' magic ships. However, Socrates never awakens in Plato's *mythologia*.

The meaning of this reformulation of Homer's *mythologia* is complex. It reveals that Socrates, unlike Odysseus, is not a lover of honor (*Republic* 620c). He does not awaken to punish the unjust suitors and restore order because the perfect justice of the paradigmatic city cannot be brought to the unjust regimes that have destroyed his homeland through civil war. The perfect justice of the paradigmatic city appears on earth only in Socrates' soul (592a–b). Socrates' own city could have become an image of the paradigmatic city if it had honored him and followed his persuasion in all things. Instead, it executed him. This is the final reason that Socrates does not awaken in Plato's *mythologia*. Socrates ascended toward the paradigmatic city and returned home from the ascent many times in his life. He finally reached his destination when he was executed. And there is no awakening from the sleep of the dead.

At various times in my analysis of the *Republic* and *Laws*, I have discussed Plato's particular uses of Homeric imagery to order their dramas and indicate how their arguments should be understood. It is now evident that all of Plato's Homeric images may be considered as parts of the *mythologia* of Socrates' life and death that extends throughout the dialogues. It is well beyond the scope of my study of *phronesis* in Plato's political philosophy to undertake an analysis of how the *mythologia* provides hermeneutical unity for all of Plato's dialogues. I leave that for another book. However, it would be appropriate to discuss briefly the one image in the *mythologia* that best demonstrates the relation of the *Republic* and the *Laws*. In the *Republic*, Socrates leaves Glaucon's *kallipolis* and sets out on a "second sailing" for the paradigmatic city, just as Odysseus left Kalypso's island and set out for the land of the Phaiakians. Plato describes Socrates' difficult voyage in the passages of the *Republic* that have come to be known as the discussion of the three waves. He orders the imagery and substance of the discussion of the three waves so that it corresponds in great detail with Homer's account of Odysseus's difficult voyage between the cavernous island of Ogygia and the shining island of Scheria. Since the three waves are almost universally believed to be the best evidence of Plato's political idealism, let the following summary of Socrates' voyage be a final proof that Plato is no idealist.

The Two Second Sailings of Socrates

Socrates uses the phrase "second sailing [*deuteros ploos*]" only once in the dialogues (*Phaedo* 99d). Shortly before his execution, Socrates describes for Cebes how he had been disappointed as a young man to discover that Anaxagoras's famous book was full of many absurdities. The book was said to be Anaxagoras's account of how *nous* is the cause and order of all things, but Anaxagoras gave "no thought to the *agathon*" that embraces and holds all things together. Socrates then decided that since there was no one who could instruct him in the highest things, he should undertake a "second sailing" alone in search of the cause (97b–99d).

The second sailing Socrates undertook alone is the ascent of his *psyche* and *nous* toward the *agathon* or divine *nous*. The imagery Socrates uses to describe it for Cebes (99d–100a) is the same as the imagery he uses in his account of the longer way. The voyage begins with the recognition that the *psyche* is blinded by looking at practical things (*ta pragmata*) with the senses alone. It must turn around toward the things that *are* (*ta onta*) and the light that illuminates them. Socrates describes the end of his ascent cautiously. He did not wish to be blinded like those who look directly at the sun during an eclipse. It is better to look at its ikon (*eikona*) in water, he says. Since he is not speaking of the visible realm governed by the sun, his words refer to the danger of any attempt to look directly at the good itself with the eye of the soul. Socrates then tells Cebes that, fearing blindness, he took refuge in speeches and examined in them "the truth of the things that *are* [*ton onton ten aletheian*]." The examination of speeches is the beginning of dialectical ascent. However, if the ascent is ever to reach its end—the soul's vision of the *agathon* itself—the examination of speeches must be left behind. At best, speeches are ikons of the things that *are* (*ta onta*). The *psyche* and *nous* know them without sense perception or spoken accounts of any kind. Socrates also tells Cebes that his imagery (*eikazo*) may not be entirely accurate. The truth of what the eye of the soul sees may not even be represented perfectly by speaking in ikons. The soul may begin to approach the vision of the good by looking at the things that *are* in speeches (*logoi*), in ikons (*eikosi*), and in deeds (*ergois*), but the good itself is beheld in silence and in stillness. Socrates came to know these things by completing his second sailing.

Socrates' account of the longer way in the *Republic* is a rather more detailed description, in ikons, of his soul's second sailing. In the context of Socrates' extensive discussion of justice with Glaucon and Adeimantus, the longer way is an account of an original against which any image of a soul in speech that seems just may be measured. More precisely, the longer way is Socrates' account of the perfectly just soul, the soul that has completed the second sailing, against which the account of the just soul that has arisen in conversation with Glaucon and Adeimantus may be seen to be a phantasm. The soul that seems perfectly just to Glaucon because it is an image of the city that seems perfectly just to him is actually unjust. Socrates' account of the longer way, of his soul's second sailing, completes the discussion of the just soul in the *Republic*. However, in order for the whole discussion of justice to be complete, there must be a comparable second sailing from the city in speech that seems just to a city that is an ikon of the perfectly just soul. Socrates begins this second second sailing in the *Republic;* he completes it in the *Laws.*[3]

The second sailing to the city of the Magnesians begins at the point in the discussion of justice when images have been produced in speech of a city and a soul that both seem to be good and right to Glaucon (449a). Socrates then attempts to end the discussion by turning to consider the four types of bad and mistaken cities and souls. He is prevented from doing so, however, and is compelled to defend the city. As it has been constructed, the city in speech cannot withstand a proper test. It has been agreed that the city is ordered according to the opinion that justice is the practice of minding one's own affairs, but it has also been agreed that a just city is one, not many, and is ordered according to the Pythagorean proverb that friends have all things in common. As it stands, therefore, the city is torn between the "track" of justice and the "track" of the good. It cannot have both for its *arche.* The drama of Socrates' account of the three waves is a description of the destruction of the city and regime that seem just to Glaucon.

The three waves are the equality in all things of the male and female guardians of the *kallipolis;* the community of women and children in the guardian class; and the requirement that philosophers rule, or rulers become philosophers, and all those now said to be philosophers and good rulers be excluded from cities if there is to be justice. The significance of the three waves is, to say the least, a subject of great controversy among Plato scholars. It is generally agreed, however, that all three are presented by Plato, in complete seriousness, as necessary features of a just city. It is commonly accepted that all three waves are of the same character and that the best indication of Plato's belief that they were all equally necessary components of an ideally just city is his use of the image of waves to present and discuss them. What has not been noted by scholars is that the dramatic and dialogic structure of Plato's presentation of the three waves is based on the passage in the *Odyssey* (5.233–494) describing Odysseus's voyage from Kalypso's island to the land of the Phaiakians. The main feature of Odysseus's voyage is his encounter with a number of "great waves." Although he undoubtedly encountered many waves during the trip, Homer only describes a certain few as "great [*megas*]" and explains their importance. The "great waves" are not all of the same character or significance. Homer's account of these "great waves" indicates how the discussion of the three waves in the *Republic* is best understood. It reveals that the three waves are not all of the same character or significance. The first and second waves are intended to demonstrate that the city in speech is neither just nor good. Indeed, they are intended to demonstrate how its improper founding will lead to its destruction. The third wave is the only one intended to describe a necessary feature of the truly just city. It gives the reader of the *Republic* a first glimpse of the paradigmatic city of the *Laws.*

Odysseus's voyage began when Zeus sent Hermes to tell Kalypso that Odysseus should have his homecoming. When Kalypso released him from captivity, Odysseus built himself a new ship. His first had been destroyed in reaching Kalypso's island. The new ship is described as a raft, but a very unusual one; it had a deck, a mast, a sail, and a steering oar. Once it was complete, Odysseus set out alone for Scheria. He had no godlike companions for a crew. This may be called Odysseus's second sailing.

When Odysseus came within view of Scheria, Poseidon caught sight of him. Poseidon was angered to think that Odysseus would escape the trial of misery to which he had been condemned for wounding Polyphemos the Kyklops, who was Poseidon's son. He stirred up a storm so violent that Odysseus wished he had died at Troy. Poseidon then sent a "great wave [*mega kuma*]" down on him—the first so described by Homer (5.313). It threw Odysseus into the water, where he was weighed down by his clothes. It almost destroyed the ship completely: the steering oar, the mast, the sail, and the deck were all lost. The ship had thus lost its ability to be directed and was now truly a raft. Odysseus swam back to what was left of it and climbed on. A brilliant goddess, Leukothea, then appeared to him and advised him to abandon the raft, remove his clothes, and swim to shore. To aid him in his escape, she gave him an immortal veil that would keep him afloat as he swam. He was to return it to her, with his face turned away from the sea, sometime after taking hold of land with both hands. Odysseus had his doubts. He decided to stay with the raft.

Poseidon then sent another "great wave," more terrible than the first (5.366). It ended Odysseus's doubts by destroying the raft completely, and he began to swim with the aid of the veil. Poseidon then left, apparently satisfied to know that Odysseus's swim would be a hard one. Athena then stilled the winds and calmed the waters somewhat to aid Odysseus. On the morning of the third day of swimming, Odysseus was lifted high atop another "great wave," the third so described (5.393) and the first not sent by Poseidon. This third wave does not threaten Odysseus. Instead, it allows him to catch sight of the land of the Phaiakians. The sight of it was so dear to him that Homer likens it to the sight of a father to his children when, with the help of the gods, the father rises from his deathbed. Odysseus thanks Zeus for the sight of a land beyond hope. It can be assumed, therefore, that Zeus himself sent the wave.

Odysseus now hears the sound of surf crashing against a rocky shore. It is described as a bursting of waves against cliffs, followed by a return flow that sucks back from the shore. While Odysseus worried about what would happen to him, Athena put a thought in his mind and he braced himself. He was then thrown against the rocks by another "great wave" (5.425). This wave is similar to Poseidon's two great waves in that it is the third to test him, unlike the third wave sent by Zeus. But this third wave is sent neither by Poseidon nor by Zeus. It is a natural occurrence and Odysseus's encounter with it is partly a matter of chance. Odysseus escaped immediate death because Athena's warning allowed him to grasp the face of the rock with both hands. However, the backwash of the same wave caught him, skinned his hands as it pulled him off the rock, and cast him far out into open water again.

Homer now says that Odysseus would have perished had not Athena given him thoughtfulness (*epiphrosynen;* 5.437). In other words, Leukothea's veil would not have been enough to save him; a god-given quality of *nous* resembling *phronesis* was necessary. Odysseus then swam clear of the surf and eventually came to the mouth of a sheltered river. When he prayed to the god of the river as a suppliant—Zeus is the god of suppliants—the river stayed its current, allowing him to swim up the channel unhindered. This is how Odysseus finally reached the land of the people ruled by Alkinoos and Arete. As soon as he was able, he returned the immortal veil to Leukothea, turning his face away from the sea as he did so.

The account of the three waves in the *Republic* follows the path of Odysseus's second sailing. When Socrates attempts to escape the city in speech that appears to be perfectly complete, well founded, good, and right, Polemarchus prevents him. It was Polemarchus, the "warlord," who initially compelled Socrates to undertake his lengthy travels in speech at the beginning of the dialogue, with the cooperation of Glaucon and Adeimantus (*Republic* 327b–28b). It was also Polemarchus who inherited an argument from his father only to bequeath it to Socrates' most frightful opponent, Thrasymachus, the sophist who argued "like a wild beast" (331d, 336b–d). Now Polemarchus prevents Socrates from escaping, again with the assistance of others, by demanding that he and the city he seems to have founded alone be put to the test. This stirs up a great swarm of arguments—in other words, a storm. It is so foreboding that Socrates wishes he had never begun the discussion. The test is simple: since it has been accepted that any city will be just and good when it has been founded according to the proverb that friends have all things in common, Socrates must complete his account of how community (*koinonia*) is evident in the particular city that has been founded in speech. Socrates replies that this sets in motion a discussion which returns to the beginning again (*palin . . . ex arches*). Indeed, the test compels him to leave behind the apparently just city and set out for another that is truly just and good, a city founded on a proper *arche* and ruled by *phronesis* and *nous* (449a–50b; cf. 443b–44a).

The parallels with the *Odyssey* are not difficult to see. The city founded in speech, perhaps according to the proverb concerning friendship and community, corresponds to the elaborate ship built by Odysseus for the purpose of sailing to the land of the Phaiakians. The city in speech is a vehicle for attaining an understanding of justice and goodness, both in cities and in souls, but it is also an unsound vehicle, one that will not withstand a proper test. Polemarchus's role in the drama corresponds with Poseidon's role in the *Odyssey*. And Thrasymachus is, of course, best compared with Polyphemos the Kyklops. But who plays Odysseus's part? Odysseus set out alone, but Socrates and Glaucon set out together to encounter the waves, bound together by the argument itself. As their discussion proceeds, they change their roles several times. At first, Glaucon is only Socrates' companion, but he soon takes Odysseus's role for himself. He plays the part poorly, however, and Socrates must then lead him through it to its end.

Socrates begins the voyage with a prayer: "I prostrate myself before Adrasteia . . . for what I'm going to say" (451a). In other words, he prays his soul will come through the test free of harm. According to the law of Adrasteia, he need only follow the god to remain free of harm (*Phaedrus* 248c). But he fears that what he is going to say in following the argument will bring harm to his soul by preventing it from following the god. He has good reason to be fearful. He is bound to Glaucon by the argument—and Glaucon may not follow the god.

The first great wave is the equality of male and female guardians in all things (451c–57b). Its consequences are devastating, not because the guardians' education in gymnastics and music and their training for war must be changed to accommodate the female guardians, but because this sort of equality makes the city appear unjust and even ridiculous. If the first wave were to have originated solely from the proverb that friends have all things in common, it would represent the spiritual equality of all human beings on which a common *paideia* and *nomoi* may be based. But the argument requires that the first wave conform to the city as it has been founded. As a consequence, a great injustice is introduced into the city: the equality of male and female guardians in training for war. Not only is community (*koinonia*) thereby restricted to the guardian class alone, but it is compelled to appear in a distorted form. Within the guardian class, the family is destroyed and training for war becomes the most important part of *paideia*. Within the soul, spiritedness comes to predominance and courage is associated exclusively with warfare. Glaucon does not find the elevated importance of spiritedness and warfare objectionable. He does find the sight of men and women exercising together in the nude ridiculous, not in small part because of the spiritual equality implied by such physical equality. Socrates persuades him that the sight is not ridiculous because the women are clothing themselves with virtue as they exercise. Glaucon is satisfied in believing that the virtue is courage. He does not ask himself if the guardians clothe themselves with moderation, justice, or prudence as a consequence of the first wave.

In the imagery of the *Odyssey*, the city has lost its steering oar, its mast, and its sail, that is, its sense of direction, and the basis of the city's structure, the guardian class itself, has been severely damaged. At this point in the dialogue, Socrates tells Glaucon that they have fallen in the water. They must swim in order to save themselves from the argument, hoping for some unusual rescue (453d). Should they swim toward land or toward the raft? Glaucon swims toward the raft. He does not wish to be saved from the argument. Indeed, he believes that the consequences of the first wave in the city are further evidence of its justice. Socrates would save himself from the argument, which is proceeding in a way that might appeal to a contentious eristic or a geometrical thinker, but not a philosopher. However, he cannot abandon the argument and the floundering city it has produced. He remains bound to it through Glaucon.

Socrates now discusses dialectic and eristic for the first time (454a–b). The reader of the *Republic* later learns that dialectic is directed toward a transcendent end, the soul's vision of the good itself, and that eristic is merely contentious speech. The dramatic parallel with the *Odyssey* again indicates why Socrates raises the topic at this point in the dialogue. Socrates now begins to speak to

Glaucon in the same way that Leukothea spoke to Odysseus. In contrast to the eristic contentiousness of the argument necessary to defend the city in speech, dialectic is an immortal veil that can enable Glaucon to save himself. But Glaucon, like Odysseus, does not take the advice. He does not put on the veil and begin swimming toward the land of the Phaiakians. Instead, he decides to stay with the directionless raft as long as it holds together.

The second great wave, more terrible than the first, now comes crashing down: the community of women and children in the guardian class (457c–61e). If the city is to survive this wave, Socrates tells Glaucon, geometric and erotic necessities must somehow be brought together in a program of eugenics for the guardians. This is an entirely laughable proposal. If the second wave were to have originated from the proper *arche* for the city, it would represent the familial and social harmony and freedom from faction necessary for community. However, the argument once again compels it to conform to the city as it has been founded. Again a great injustice is introduced into the city as a consequence. The eugenics program confuses psychic and somatic matters, as did the first wave, and it makes as much a mockery of true wisdom as the first wave did of true courage. But Glaucon does not find it laughable. He finds it compelling. His *eros* and his belief that geometrical thinking is wisdom both prevent him from understanding that the second wave destroys the city in speech as completely as Poseidon's second great wave destroyed Odysseus's raft. The eugenics program fails, as it must, and the city breaks up (545e–47b). However, Socrates does not describe the destruction of Glaucon's city by faction until he has repeatedly attempted and failed to lead Glaucon away from it toward the good.

Socrates must now remind Glaucon of how the drama proceeds. He sets out on a swim by himself and hopes that Glaucon will be able to follow him. He speaks of how the cities of Hellas, now torn by war and faction, can be ordered according to the greatest good. The greatest evil for any city is what breaks it up, he tells Glaucon, and the greatest good is what makes it one (462a–b). Throughout the discussion, Socrates swims toward a city free from faction and war, a city that is a community (*koinonia*) because it is ordered by the *arche* expressed in the Pythagorean proverb. Such a city could serve as a *paradeigma* for the cities of Hellas he has left behind, as well as for Glaucon's city in speech.

Glaucon raises the question of the possibility of his city's coming into being. He remains satisfied that the city is perfectly just and that the argument defending it is sound. He even believes that if the city in speech should ever come into being in an existing city, "everything would be good" for it (471c). To lead Glaucon away from such imprudent idealism, Socrates reminds him of the direction the argument would proceed with the aid of dialectic. He warns Glaucon of the approach of an unusual third wave that can be seen and heard (472a). Glaucon does not see the wave. Instead, Socrates lifts him up with words in order that he might catch sight of the end toward which the argument is heading, just as the great wave sent by Zeus allowed Odysseus to catch sight of the land of the Phaiakians. He reminds Glaucon that their lengthy discussion of justice and injustice was for the sake of "a *paradeigma* in speech of a good city" (472d–e).

Socrates now tells Glaucon that he hears the gurgling sound of a wave that might drown him in laughter and ill repute, so he braces himself (473c). When Odysseus was thrown against the rocks by the third great wave to test him, he managed to grasp the land of the Phaiakians briefly before being swept out to sea by its gurgling backwash. Similarly, Socrates' third wave allows a brief grasp of the land in which a truly just and good city can be found. The possibility of justice and goodness in any city depends upon government by philosophic rulers, he says, and the exclusion of all those now in power and all those now said to philosophize (473c–d). How will true philosophers rule? Socrates says nothing about this, but Glaucon undoubtedly assumes they would do everything necessary to bring his city in speech into being. For Socrates, it is sufficient to suggest that the rule of true philosophers is the foundation of justice in any city. Glaucon's city, like all existing cities, is in the dark. It too must be brought into the light by rulers whose souls have seen the good itself. The third wave shocks Glaucon, though Socrates had warned him of it. It also skins his hands by reminding him that he has not yet grasped the truly just city.

The wave's backwash now catches the argument. How can cities be persuaded to accept the rule of true philosophers and recognize its benefits? In the context of Socrates' presentation of the third wave, this question has two parts. How do true philosophers differ from those now said to philosophize? And how can cities be persuaded to accept their rule and recognize its benefits? The second part cannot be answered before the first. Socrates therefore

begins to speak with Glaucon about the nature of the true philosopher.

In the *Odyssey*, Homer says that but for one thing Odysseus
would have perished after being cast out into open water. He was
not saved by Leukothea's veil, but rather by the thoughtfulness
(*epiphrosynen*) given him by Athena. In other words, Athena made
him prudent. He then swam until he found the mouth of a river.
The river stayed its current when he prayed to the god, allowing
him to swim up the channel and come ashore on the land of the
Phaiakians.

In the *Republic*, Socrates begins his account of the true philosopher by saying that he must love all of wisdom and not just a part
of it. That is, he must have an insatiable *eros* for all of wisdom,
theoretical and practical wisdom alike (474c–75c). A true philosopher therefore has *phronesis* as well as *sophia*. If a man attempts
to acquire *sophia* without *phronesis*, his soul is in danger of perish-
ing: he may become a geometrical thinker, a lover of opinion, or
perhaps even a sophist. These are the types of men said to philosophize who will be barred from ruling in a truly just city. The nature
of their *eros* prevents them from becoming true philosophers.

Socrates now tells Glaucon that *eros* is a stream whose flow
can be channeled in different directions (485c–d). When it flows
downstream, a man follows his strongest desires, the desires for
bodily pleasures. However, if he concerns himself with the things
of the soul, that is, with truly erotic things, the downstream flow
weakens. The flow can even be channeled in the opposite direction by the soul's love of the good and the help of the god.

What are the characteristics of the true philosopher who has
managed to swim upstream with the help of the god? Socrates
gives a list of some of his qualities and virtues, and *sophia* is notably absent (485e–87a). He says the man must have courage, moderation, and justice. He must also demonstrate liberality (*eleutheria*)
and magnificence (*megaloprepeia*), and he must be a friend and
kin to the truth (*aletheia*). Furthermore, all of these excellences
must be perfected by education and maturity. This is a description
of a truly prudent and virtuous soul, worthy to rule a city.

There is now a dramatic break in the dialogue. Adeimantus
becomes Socrates' interlocutor. Socrates answers his questions in
ikons. He even says that he has become greedy for ikons (487b–88a).
When Odysseus reached the comparable point in his voyage, he
returned the immortal veil to the goddess, keeping his face turned

away from the sea. In the *Republic*, the veil is dialectic. The dramatic break in the dialogue thus indicates that Socrates turns away from dialectic to take up a different sort of discussion with Adeimantus. Dialectic is a divine aid in the voyage toward an end that dialectic itself cannot explain. It enables the soul to attain a vision of the good, but the vision of the good itself can only be expressed in ikons.

Odysseus's difficult second sailing was over when he returned the veil to the goddess and fell asleep where he came ashore. At the comparable point in the *Republic*, neither of Socrates' two second sailings have reached their end. When Adeimantus becomes his interlocutor, Socrates has not yet completed his answers to either part of the question, How can cities be persuaded to accept the rule of true philosophers and recognize its benefits? The three ikons of the longer way provide an answer for the first part—how the true philosopher differs from those now said to philosophize—by completing Socrates' account of his soul's second sailing. Once the longer way has been described, it becomes possible for Socrates to provide an answer to the second part by completing the account of his second sailing to a city that accepts the rule of true philosophers and recognizes its benefits. However, Glaucon's unwillingness to abandon the city in speech that seems beautiful to him prevents Socrates from reaching the paradigmatic city.

Socrates only succeeds in coming ashore in the *Republic*. He enters the paradigmatic city in the *Laws*. His sleep between the time he comes ashore and the time he sets out on foot for the city that will honor him above all other men begins at the end of the *Phaedo* and ends at the beginning of the *Laws*.

NOTES

Introduction

1. Ronald Beiner, *Political Judgment*, 4.
2. Ibid., 24.
3. Hannah Arendt, "Martin Heidegger at Eighty," 297.
4. Ibid., 299, 301, 303.
5. Martin Heidegger, *An Introduction to Metaphysics*, 50–51, 199; cf. 37–39, 45–46.
6. Arendt, "Martin Heidegger," 303. It is certainly questionable whether Heidegger ever settled in his thinking the significance of his political actions. He is ambiguous and evasive in his *apologia* of sorts, "The Rectorate 1933/34: Facts and Thoughts," 481–502. For further discussion, see Richard Wolin, *The Politics of Being: The Political Thought of Martin Heidegger*.
7. Arendt, "Martin Heidegger," 303. For Arendt's own discussion of the differences between tyrannies and totalitarian movements, see Hannah Arendt, "Ideology and Terror: A Novel Form of Government," in *The Origins of Totalitarianism*, 460–79.
8. Karl R. Popper, *The Open Society and Its Enemies*, 1:87.
9. Ibid., 1:5, 90, 169–75.
10. This summary of Popper's account of social engineering is based on the discussion in George Klosko, *The Development of Plato's Political Theory*, 134–36, 149–50.
11. Hans-Georg Gadamer, *Truth and Method*, 20, 22, 278, 472.
12. Ibid., 489–90.
13. Ibid., 491.
14. Hans-Georg Gadamer, *The Idea of the Good in Platonic-Aristotelian Philosophy*, 5, 21–22.
15. Ibid., 34.
16. Ibid., 9, 33–34, 46–47, 60–61.
17. Ibid., 35, 46–47, 60, 64, 132, 138–39, 160–61.
18. Ibid., 144–45, 174. Gadamer's argument is similar to the one presented by Harold Cherniss in *The Riddle of the Early Academy*.
19. Gadamer, *The Idea of the Good*, 177.
20. Eric Voegelin, *Order and History*, 3:273–75, 277–78.
21. Eric Voegelin, *Anamnesis*, 65–69.
22. Stylometric analysis studies the changes in an author's linguistic usages, grammar, and syntax from work to work, and then attempts to make inferences from any patterns that are noticeable. The following summary is based on Klosko, *The Development of Plato's Political Theory*, 15–21.
23. Gadamer, *The Idea of the Good*, 8, 21.
24. Gadamer, *Truth and Method*, 487–88.
25. See Leo Strauss, "On Plato's *Republic*," in *City and Man*, especially 50–62.

26. Jacob Klein, *Plato's Trilogy*, 1-2.
27. Allan Bloom, *The Republic of Plato*, xv-xviii. Cf. Thomas Pangle, *The Laws of Plato*, 376.
28. Stanley Rosen, "Book Reviews," 113-14.
29. Stanley Rosen, *Plato's Sophist: The Drama of Original and Image*, 1-4.
30. Ibid., 12-13.
31. Stanley Rosen, "Platonic Hermeneutics: On the Interpretation of a Platonic Dialogue," 271-72, 285-86.
32. Ibid., 275, 288.

Chapter 1. The Cave and the Ideas

1. The following summary is based on J. E. Raven, "Sun, Divided Line and Cave," 22-23, 27.
2. Bloom, *The Republic of Plato*, xviii.
3. Glaucon's nature has been discussed at length by Leon Craig in "The War Lover: A Study of Plato's *Republic*."
4. It would not be possible to summarize or even list the many articles and books presenting some variation of the argument defended by Raven. Two examples will suffice for the purposes of discussion. The most ambitious interpretation of the importance of the divided line I have encountered is given in Robert S. Brumbaugh, "The Divided Line and the Direction of Inquiry." Brumbaugh claims that all aspects of the *Republic*, even the drama of the dialogue, can be understood by reference to the four segments of the line. The amusing feature of this reading is its failure to hear the irony in Socrates' description of the lesser character of mathematical or geometrical thinking by means of a mathematical or geometrical image. In an equally inventive interpretation, Robert Hahn has noticed this paradox, though he too has overlooked Socrates' irony. He claims the divided line as a whole is "located . . . at the *dianoetic* level of 'Thought'"; that is, it corresponds to *dianoia*, but not to *noesis*. Robert Hahn, "A Note on Plato's Divided Line," 235-37.
5. A. S. Ferguson, "Plato's Simile of the Light Again," 190.
6. The strongest arguments in favor of the central importance of the sun image are given in Voegelin, *Order and History*, especially 3:112-17; Stanley Rosen, *Nihilism: A Philosophical Essay*, especially 174-93; Gadamer, *The Idea of the Good*, 63-103; George Grant, *Technology and Justice*, especially 71-75; and Edward Andrew, "Descent to the Cave."
7. Martin Heidegger gives a third alternative. He claims that Plato understands *ousia* (being, essence) as *idea*, and the *agathon* as the *idea* of all the *ideai*. See Heidegger, "Plato's Doctrine of Truth," and *Nietzsche*, 4:162-69. Good criticisms of Heidegger's presentation of Plato's understanding of *ousia* idea, and *agathon* are given in Robert J. Dostal, "Beyond Being: Heidegger's Plato," and in Carol A. Kates, "Heidegger and the Myth of the Cave." Hans-Georg Gadamer's interpretation of the ascent from the cave is based on Heidegger's understanding of Plato, his criticisms of Heidegger notwithstanding. See Gadamer, "Plato and Heidegger."
8. Stanley Rosen has only a few lines about the cave image (see *Nihilism*, 191-93). An interpretation of the cave compatible with Rosen's reading of the *Republic* has been published recently by Jacob Howland in "The Cave Image and the Problem of Place: The Sophist, the Poet and the Philosopher." Although George Grant has written nothing about the cave, Edward Andrew's

"Descent to the Cave" is a recent interpretation consonant with Grant's understanding of the *Republic*. Gadamer's account of the cave is brief and is found in the context of an ambitious reading of the *Republic* as a "grand dialectical myth" (see *The Idea of the Good*, 70, 74–80). Voegelin's summary of the ascent from and return to the cave as "an allegory of the philosopher's education" (*Order and History*, 3:114–16) is also too brief to serve as the basis for a criticism of idealistic epistemological reconstructions of the cave image.

9. John H. Wright, "The Origin of Plato's Cave," 137–42.

10. The following summary is taken from Dale Hall, "Interpreting Plato's Cave as an Allegory of the Human Condition," 74–75, 83–84.

11. Hall claims the main proponents of the epistemological interpretation are R. L. Nettleship, N. R. Murphy, and J. E. Raven. See Nettleship, *Lectures on the Republic of Plato*; Murphy, "The 'Simile of Light' in Plato's *Republic*" and *The Interpretation of Plato's Republic*; and Raven, "Sun, Divided Line and Cave" and *Plato's Thought in the Making*. Hall claims the main proponent of the political interpretation of the cave is A. S. Ferguson. See Ferguson, "Plato's Simile of Light Again." Colin Strang has defended Ferguson's reading in "Plato's Analogy of the Cave."

12. Allan Bloom, "Response to Hall," 315, 317, 320–21.

13. Ibid., 319, 321–22, 329.

14. Bloom, *The Republic of Plato*, 410.

15. The following discussion is based on *The Republic of Plato*, 397–413, which presents Bloom's reading of *Republic* 503b–40c.

16. Bloom, *The Republic of Plato*, 402. Bloom bases his reading of the *Republic* on the work of Leo Strauss, and in particular on Strauss's essay, "On Plato's *Republic*," in *City and Man*. Strauss's discussion of the good and the ideas is brief and cautious. He writes: "No one has ever succeeded in giving a satisfactory or clear account of this doctrine of ideas." Nowhere does Strauss write that the good is the "*idea* of *ideas*." Martin Heidegger, however, does describe the good in this way.

17. Bloom, *The Republic of Plato*, 402.

18. In his translation of *Republic* 511b, Bloom renders *ten tou pantos archen* as "the beginning of the whole." In a footnote to the text he suggests an alternative rendering: "the beginning which is the whole." Both translations are misleading, but consistent with his interpretation. Cf. Leo Strauss, *What Is Political Philosophy?*, 11.

19. Bloom, *The Republic of Plato*, 409, 403, 402, 409. The transformation of the love of wisdom into sagacity is described by Hegel: "The true shape in which truth exists can only be the scientific system of such truth. To help bring philosophy closer to the form of Science, to the goal where it can lay aside the title of '*love* of knowing' and be *actual* knowing—that is what I have set myself to do" (G. W. F. Hegel, *The Phenomenology of Spirit*, 3). The *Phenomenology* describes this transformation as a process of the development of *Geist* (spirit, mind) from the sense-certainty of consciousness to the attainment of Absolute Knowledge. One well-known interpretation of the *Phenomenology* claims that, in principle, all modern men can attain the Absolute Knowledge of a Hegelian wise man, and that the history of modernity is best understood as the extension of Hegelian sagacity to all men through the rise of the universal and homogeneous state (see Alexandre Kojeve, *Introduction to the Reading of Hegel*).

20. Bloom, *The Republic of Plato*, 408.

21. Ibid., 403, 402, 404, 404, 404, 407, 407.
22. Ibid., 410, 409, 407, 409, 412.
23. Gadamer, *The Idea of the Good*, 68-71.
24. Ibid., 75-77, 100.
25. Ibid., 71, 78-79.
26. Ibid., 64-67, 96, 99.
27. Ibid., 86-87, 89-90.
28. Ibid., 81. I have corrected the second Stephanus number given in Gadamer's text.
29. Voegelin, *Order and History*, 3:112-13.
30. Ibid., 3:115.
31. D. W. Hamlyn, "*Eikasia* in Plato's *Republic*," 14-23.

Chapter 2. The Search for Justice and the Good

1. See the Introduction for a discussion of the significance of this traditional list of cardinal virtues often thought to represent a summary of Plato's moral philosophy. The discussion is based on Gadamer, *The Idea of the Good*, 35, 46-47, 64, and Voegelin, *Anamnesis*, 65-66. The traditional list of cardinal virtues has its origins in Pythagorean doctrines (see David R. Fideler, ed., *The Pythagorean Sourcebook and Library*, 30-33).

Chapter 3. Educating Glaucon about the Good

1. There is no other instance of the term *agathoeide*, not only in the dialogues, but in all of Greek literature. It was coined to emphasize, within the terms set by the image, that knowledge and truth are good-formed, just as sight is sun-formed, and that they are not the good, just as sight is not the sun.

2. *Pistis* is often translated as "faith." Hans-Georg Gadamer has criticized this translation for its inappropriate religious implications. He writes that *pistis* "never occurs in Classical Greek in the context of man's relation to the divine or of the supposition of the gods' existence" ("Religion and Religiosity in Socrates," 55).

3. By "common sense" I mean something comparable to Thomas Reid's understanding of the term. Voegelin has described Reid's common sense as "a compact type of rationality." Common sense "does not connote a social deadweight of vulgar ideas, . . . rather it is the habit of judgment and conduct of a man formed by *ratio:* one could say, the habit of an Aristotelian *spoudaios* minus the luminosity of his knowledge of the *ratio* as the source of his rational judgment and conduct. Common sense is a civilizational habit that presupposes noetic experience, without the man of this habit having himself a differentiated knowledge of *noesis*" (*Anamnesis*, 211-12). Cf. Gadamer, *Truth and Method*, 19-28.

4. Voegelin is one of the few commentators to note that the prisoners themselves cast shadows. He draws no conclusions from this observation, however, except to say, somewhat misleadingly: "To the prisoners truth would be nothing but the shadows of themselves and the objects" (*Order and History*, 3:114).

5. Thomas West has argued that "Socrates' image is purposely incomplete" in order to suggest to his audience that artifact-carriers and artifact-makers are two distinct groups of cave dwellers. "Hence there are four groups or

kinds of cave dwellers: prisoners, artifact-carriers, artisans, and philosopher" (*Plato's "Apology of Socrates": An Interpretation, with a New Translation*, 120–21). It would be possible to think of West's interpretation of Socrates' initial description of the cave as a fanciful excess if it did not also obscure the nature of the carriers' sophistry and hence the nature of the difference between sophistry and philosophy.

6. Bloom's translation of this passage and its immediate context is misleading. When Socrates speaks of the *phantasmata*, Bloom has him refer simply to "appearances," but when Socrates speaks of the *eidola* of human beings in the water, Bloom has him refer to "phantoms" (*The Republic of Plato*, 195).

7. The Alexandrian division of the *Republic* into ten books is generally in accord with the drama of the dialogue. However, the division between books 6 and 7 is somewhat unfortunate, since it disrupts the continuity of Socrates' account of the longer way and gives disproportionate and even central importance to the discussion of the divided line. There is no ideal place in the text at which to divide Socrates' discussion of the longer way with Glaucon. It is best to consider it as a whole and determine its most significant points by following the dialogue itself.

8. Cf. Seth Benardete, "On Wisdom and Philosophy: The First Two Chapters of Aristotle's *Metaphysics* A," 206.

9. Compare what Machiavelli has to say about the "effectual truth" of things, particularly political things and the imagination of them, in chapter 15 of *The Prince*.

10. Cf. Robert Axelrod, *The Evolution of Cooperation*, in which a game called the "iterated Prisoner's Dilemma" is used to show how cooperation can emerge in all conflicts among selfish rational persons, corporations, parties, or superpowers where there is no apparent authority present to police them.

11. Diogenes Laertius is obviously incorrect when he writes that 281 more votes were cast against Socrates than for him in determining his guilt or innocence and that 80 more votes were cast for the death sentence than were for his guilt (*The Lives of Eminent Philosophers*, 2.41–42). Thomas West reports Diogenes Laertius's remarks without criticism in his commentary on the *Apology*. West also interprets the results of the two votes in a surprising and ultimately unpersuasive manner. He implies that Socrates would have preferred a greater number to vote for his guilt than did so, for this would be evidence of the health, if not the justice, of "the city." West also writes that Socrates' remarks after the second vote reveal that Socrates "silently agreed with the judgment of guilty," and that he "speaks more truthfully to those who voted against him than to those who voted for him." West is silent about the fact that Socrates speaks to those who voted for his acquittal—not simply for a fine—as his friends (West, *Plato's "Apology of Socrates*," 209, 222–27).

12. Cf. Bloom, "Response to Hall," 319. Hall had criticized Bloom's interpretation of the *Republic* for divorcing theoretical and practical wisdom in a way that Plato does not and then claiming that Plato believed the philosopher's well-being to consist exclusively in theoretical reflection. Bloom writes in response: "The only authentic virtue is that of mind contemplating its proper objects [i.e., the ideas]. It is not I who Aristotelianize. The *Republic* is not the *Ethics*; there are no moral virtues in it."

13. For a study of twentieth-century totalitarianism along these lines, see

Ernst Nolte, "Fascism as a Metapolitical Phenomenon," in *The Three Faces of Fascism*, 535–67.

14. Bloom translates *eidola* in this passage as "phantoms," thus giving the impression that all such images are *phantasmata*. The descent into the common home of the others, the nonphilosophers, is thereby made to seem as if it were a descent into the sophists' dreamworld.

Chapter 4. Educating the Guardians about the Good

1. When the city in speech receives its name (527c), Socrates explicitly refers to it as "your city" in speaking with Glaucon. From the beginning of book 5 (449a), Socrates almost always identifies the city in speech with his two interlocutors, particularly with Glaucon. He does not consider the city his own. See 458c, 461e, 470a, 470e, 497d, 521a, 527c, 534d, 537c, 539e, and 546b.

2. There are many scholarly opinions about Socrates' reference to an ascent from Hades to the gods. It is generally taken as a reference to some mortal who died and later became a god. Amphiaraus, Asclepius, Heracles, and Pollux are frequently mentioned. Odysseus's travels while alive to Hades, Kalypso's island, and the land of the Phaiakians, and all similar accounts of shamanistic journeys are not considered. In the context of the dialogue, however, it is evident that Socrates is referring to Odysseus.

3. The Pythagoreans considered arithmetic, geometry, music or harmonics, and astronomy to be the four branches of the study of number. See Fideler, *The Pythagorean Sourcebook and Library*, 20–30, 33–36.

4. The verb *anaipeo* may be translated in a number of ways: "to take up," "to answer or respond," "to bear away or carry off," "to take away," or "to destroy." Bloom translates the cited passage as "destroying the hypotheses." The reasons this translation is inappropriate are given in Socrates' account of the difference between dialectical inquiry and the madness (*mania*) of eristical argument (539b–d).

5. Some scholars insist that the equality of the two middle line segments is an unintended or unnoticed consequence of the divided line's geometry; others insist that it is not, but cannot find any proof that Plato was aware of it (see J. S. Morrison, "Two Unresolved Difficulties in the Line and the Cave," especially 212–13). Still others do not understand the proof when they stumble upon it (see L. E. Rose, "Plato's Divided Line," 425–35).

Chapter 6. The City of the *Telos*

1. In *The Vatican Plato and Its Relations*, L. A. Post demonstrates that all existing manuscripts of the *Laws* can be traced to a single Byzantine archetype of the ninth century.

2. For brief discussions of the recent history of interpretations of the *Laws*, see W. K. C. Guthrie, *A History of Greek Philosophy*, 5:321–23; Werner Jaeger, *Paideia: The Ideals of Greek Culture*, 3:213; and Glenn Morrow, *Plato's Cretan City: A Historical Interpretation of the Laws*, 515–18. The most complete bibliography of recent work on the *Laws* is Trevor J. Saunders, *Bibliography on Plato's Laws, 1920–1970, with Additional Citations through May 1975*.

3. The most discussed of these institutional *aporiai* are the apparent double versions of both the Council of Thirty-seven and the Nocturnal Council. For examples, see Morrow, *Plato's Cretan City*, 238–40, 500–515; Trevor J.

Saunders, "The Alleged Double Version in the Sixth Book of the *Laws*," 230–36; Pangle, *The Laws of Plato*, 504–10; and George Klosko, "The Nocturnal Council in Plato's *Laws*," 74–88.

4. Leo Strauss, "Plato," 78, *What Is Political Philosophy?* 29–31, 134, and *The Argument and the Action of Plato's Laws*, 1.

5. Pangle, *The Laws of Plato*, xi; cf. 377.

6. Voegelin, *Order and History*, 3:216, 219, 222, 228.

7. There are only two prayers in the *Republic* besides Socrates' prayer at the festival of Bendis (327a–b). The first is Socrates' prayer before catching sight of justice itself and then stumbling upon the "track" of justice in the dark with Glaucon. The second is a reference to Homer's prayers to the Muses in discussing how "faction first attacked" within the *kallipolis* and caused it to be moved in the wrong way (545d; *Iliad* 16.112). Taken together, the two prayers directly associate Glaucon's opinion about justice with the destruction of his city through faction. See Darrell Jackson, "The Prayers of Socrates," 15–16.

8. The similarity between the *Republic* and the comedies of Aristophanes has been noted frequently. The *kallipolis* seems to be woven together from strands found in the *Birds*, *Lysistrata*, and *Ecclesiazusae*. See Leo Strauss, *Socrates and Aristophanes* and *The City and Man*, 50–138; Dale Hall, "The *Republic* and the 'Limits of Politics,'" 293–313; Bloom, "Response to Hall," 315–30; and Arlene W. Saxonhouse, "Comedy in Callipolis: Animal Imagery in the *Republic*," 888–901.

9. There is as yet no definitive study of pre-Socratic Pythagorean mathematics and number symbolism, and perhaps one cannot be written for lack of materials. My understanding of it is based on a number of different sources: Fideler, *The Pythagorean Sourcebook and Library*; W. Burkert, *Lore and Science in Ancient Pythagoreanism*; V. F. Hopper, *Medieval Number Symbolism*; and S. K. Heninger, Jr., *Touches of Sweet Harmony*.

10. Cf. Heraclitus: "Time is a child playing, playing draughts; the kingly power is a child's [*aion pais esti paizon pesseuon. paidos he basileie*]" (frag. 52).

11. Aristoxenus's account of Plato's lecture "On the Good" has often puzzled scholars. He writes that Aristotle frequently told the story of how those who attended the lecture expected to hear a discussion of human happiness but were surprised to hear Plato speak of mathematics and astronomy instead (Aristoxenus, *Harmonica* 2, 30 Meibom.). Nevertheless, Aristotle, Speusippus, and Xenocrates, among others, took careful notes, according to Simplicius (*Physica* 151.6). The use of number in the *Laws* may help to explain why they did. For recent discussions of the lecture and the tradition of esoteric "unwritten doctrines" it is said to have originated, see Cherniss, *The Riddle of the Early Academy*, and Hans-Georg Gadamer, *Dialogue and Dialectic: Eight Hermeneutical Studies on Plato*, 124–55.

12. See Eric Voegelin, "Immortality: Experience and Symbol," especially 235–41, and "Equivalences of Experience and Symbolization in History," 215–34.

13. In the *Metaphysics* Aristotle states that, while all human beings might wonder at the incommensurability of the hypotenuse, the geometer would wonder at nothing so much as if the hypotenuse were to become commensurable. The geometer's *episteme* is thus in some way preferable to simple wonder (983a19–23). However, there is no *episteme* of the good. If a geometer is ever to acquire *sophia* and *phronesis*, he must turn away from deductions

from axioms and discover—perhaps it would be better to say rediscover—
something of the wonder in which philosophy begins (cf. 982b5–20).

14. The translation, with minor changes of my own, is from A. T. Murray's
Loeb Classical Library edition (Harvard University Press).

Chapter 7. God or Some Human Being?

1. A good summary of Plato's sources in composing this myth and of the
features that are unique to Plato's playful Eleatic presentation can be found
in Guthrie, *A History of Greek Philosophy*, 5:193–96.

2. See Thomas Alan Sinclair, "Myth and Politics in the *Laws*," 274–76.

3. Eric Voegelin gives several comparable analyses of the puppet ikon in
Order and History, 3:230–36; "The Gospel and Culture," 71–76; and "Wisdom
and the Magic of the Extreme: A Meditation," 253–56.

4. For an insightful discussion of the *Republic*'s Phoenician tale, see
Voegelin, *Order and History*, 3:104–8

5. See the discussion of this passage in E. B. England, *The Laws of Plato*,
1:447–48.

6. Philological arguments may be adduced in support of this interpretation of the *Theaetetus* and *Republic* and their relation to the *Laws*. The
passages in the *Republic* describing the *paradeigmata* of the philosopher and
the tyrant are directly related because they give the only two uses of the term
epekeina (beyond) in Plato's dialogues. They are both related to Socrates'
theodicy in the *Theaetetus* in a similar way. The *Theaetetus* describes the
flight (*phyge*) of the human being who makes himself like the divine *paradeigma*, but not the flight of the other. The *Republic*, on the other hand,
describes the flight (*phyge*) of the tyrant from *nomos* and *logos* to something
beyond even bastard pleasures, but it does not describe the philosopher's
ascent to the good beyond being as a flight. The two texts complete one
another. To give as accurate a description as possible of the tyrant's most
wretched *paradeigma*, the texts' relation to the account of the two measures
in the *Laws* is indicated by the unique reformulation in the *Theaetetus* of
Protagoras's dictum about the measure of all things.

Chapter 8. The Motion of *Nous*

1. This is a commonplace in modern interpretations of the *Laws* and is
usually associated with criticisms of Plato's late theocratic dogmatism or
even totalitarianism. One of the most recent examples is R. F. Stalley, *An
Introduction to Plato's Laws*, 166–78.

Thomas Pangle's interpretation of book 10 of the *Laws* is similar, though
he does not bring charges against Plato for religious dogmatism. Pangle
contends that book 10 is a "civil religion" for Magnesia. He takes the term
and the concept from Rousseau's *Social Contract* (4.8). It is appropriate for
analyzing the *Laws*, he writes, because Rousseau's account of civil religion is
based on "the classical understanding." Rousseau "sees the need for divine
support for laws and duties." The "primary function" of the Athenian's civil
religion is the maintenance of civil order through "support of the penal
code." It is necessary to have a civil religion, for "unless men are persuaded
that unseen gods protect them in this life and provide a bearable life after
death, they may feel so threatened that they will be unable to sacrifice their
own safety for the common good." The belief in the three "proofs" of the
Magnesian civil religion is "not rational." Pangle states that "the piety and

belief [the Athenian's] laws call for are not, in general, to be based on the results of rational investigation by the citizens." The religious dogmatism of the citizenry may not be rational, but it is "an absolutely necessary dimension of political life." See "Politics and Religion in Plato's *Laws:* Some Preliminary Reflections," 22-23, and "The Political Psychology of Religion in Plato's *Laws,*" 1060-61. For a study of ancient Greek accounts of piety that is implicitly critical of Pangle's interpretation, see Gadamer, "Religion and Religiosity in Socrates," especially 53-60.

2. See Blair Campbell, "Deity and Human Agency in Plato's *Laws,*" 417-46. Campbell accepts the conventional understanding of book 10 as a civil religion for Magnesia, but claims that "there is no necessity that belief in gods such as those described in Book X . . . should result in a scheme of life which reduces man to submissive passivity." Campbell's conclusion reveals the nihilism underlying civil religion itself. He claims that instead of having "repudiated Protagoras," Plato's civil religion "seems to confirm, even to surpass, Protagoras in practice. Man appears to be the measure not only of all 'things,' but of divinity as well" (418, 420).

3. Gadamer, "Religion and Religiosity in Socrates," 56.

4. This discussion of the difference between *apodeixis* and *epideixis* is based on Eric Voegelin, "Quod Deus dicitur," 578-79.

5. Jackson, "The Prayers of Socrates," 15-16.

6. England addresses the similarity of the Athenian's account of genesis and Pythagorean geometry in his discussion of 894a (*The Laws of Plato,* 2:465-68). He concludes that the *arche* "would seem to be thought of as an invisible point," despite the evidence he himself cites that the Neoplatonists compared the Pythagorean tetractys (1, 2, 3, 4) to *nous, episteme, dianoia,* and *aisthesis. Nous* or the *arche* is not a point for Plato, not even an Archidemian point. Indeed, Aristotle writes explicitly that Plato rejected points as a "geometrical dogma [*geometrikoi dogmati*]" (*Metaphysics* 992a22). The Neoplatonists understood this, even though their insightful attempt to combine the account of the genesis and order of the cosmos in the *Laws* with the account of the divided line in the *Republic* by means of Pythagorean number symbolism was somewhat misguided.

7. The Scholiast is aware of the Athenian's reformulation, but mistakes it in its details. He writes that the ninth and tenth motions are those of *psyche* and the other eight are those of *soma.* Modern scholars generally are not aware of the reformulation and fashion elaborate theories to explain how Plato's ten motions form a systematic whole. An extensive analysis of this type, along with a competent review of the scholarly literature on the topic, can be found in J. B. Skemp, *The Theory of Motion in Plato's Later Dialogues,* especially 96-115, 157-64.

8. R. Hackforth argues convincingly against all those who equate the motions of *psyche* and *nous:* "Plato's Theism," 4-9. Unfortunately, his argument is cast in the mold of modern Christian theological speculation and his presentation of what he takes to be Plato's theism is often less than convincing.

9. The *Timaeus* (28a-29a) gives a more Pythagorean formulation: the cosmos is a beautiful *eikon* of the eternal *paradeigma,* the most beautiful of all things that have come into being (cf. *Laws* 897e). For a good discussion of the relation between *eikon* and *paradeigma* in the *Timaeus,* see Voegelin, *Order and History,* 3:194-203.

10. Plato continues his serious play with wooden spheres in what has come to be called the "philosophical digression" of the *Seventh Letter* (340a–44d; especially 342a–43b). These few pages, addressed to whoever has "followed along" with Plato's "myth and voyage" (*toi mythoi te kai planoi ho xunepispomenos;* 344d), are perhaps the best hermeneutical key available for unlocking the meaning of Plato's dialogues. For an interesting study of the *Seventh Letter,* see Gadamer, *Dialogue and Dialectic,* 93–123.

11. In the third of the Athenian's propositions about the sun, he says its *psyche* might possess exceedingly amazing powers to guide (*podegei*) it—literally, to guide its feet. The only other use of *podegei* in Plato's writings occurs in the *Seventh Letter* (340c). The context of its occurrence is a description by Plato of how to determine if someone's soul has become enflamed by philosophy. The best test, he says, is to indicate the difficulty of the studies leading to it. If a pupil is philosophic and divine (*theios*), he will be led to suppose that he has been shown an amazing way (*hodon . . . thaumasten*) upon which he must set out at once. He will not let go of the way until he and the one leading him (*hegoumenon*) have reached its *telos,* or until he has gained the power (*dynamin*) to guide his own feet (*podegein;* 340b–c). Taken together, Plato's two uses of *podegei* indicate a number of things. The amazing powers mentioned in the Athenian's third proposition are the powers of *nous,* not those of *psyche. Nous's* amazing powers illuminate both the cosmos and the way toward the philosophic life. They are manifest both in cosmic *psyche's* power to move *soma* in an amazing way and in human *psyche's* power to move the feet along an amazing way. The *nous* that possesses these powers is divine. The *psyche* and *soma* of the cosmos and of human beings are moved differently by its powers, but toward the same end. And the "amazing way" toward the philosophic life may begin in and be sustained by the evidence of *nous's* amazing powers in the cosmos.

Chapter 9. The Genesis and Order of the City

1. This may explain why modern scholars have been unable to agree about the relation of the Nocturnal Council and the other institutions and offices of Magnesia. Without an understanding of the council's significance as part of a complex ikon of *nous* and its motion, the council appears to be an anomalous political institution. Scholarly explanations of Plato's apparent anomalies are often rather arbitrary. For a discussion of recent studies, see Klosko, "The Nocturnal Council in Plato's *Laws.*"

2. Perhaps this accounts for Socrates' failure in the *Republic* to ask the Pythagoreans about their understanding of astronomy, harmony, and other forms of motion, though he said he would. Instead, he only implies that the Pythagoreans "rise to problems" in such studies, in particular to the problem "of which numbers are concordant and which not, and why in each case." This way of inquiry, he says, is "useful . . . in the search for the beautiful and the good" (*Republic* 530c–31d; cf. 600a–e). The reader of the dialogue is expected to question the Pythagorean account of such matters and to consider what significance it might have in the context of Socrates' ongoing dialogue with Glaucon.

3. The modern studies of Pythagorean doctrines used for the following summary are listed in note 9 of chapter 6. The most important ancient sources are Plato, *Timaeus;* Aristotle, *Metaphysics;* Proclus, *In Euclidis elementorum librum primum commentaria;* and Iamblichus, *Vita Pythagorae.* The place of

Pythagorean mathematics in Plato's dialogues is discussed in Erich Frank, *Plato und die Sogenannten Pythagoreer;* Harold Cherniss, "Plato as Mathematician," 395-425; and Jacob Klein, *Greek Mathematical Thought and the Origin of Algebra,* 61-99. Rather ambitious attempts to interpret Plato's use of Pythagorean doctrines as evidence of his own Pythagoreanism are found in Robert S. Brumbaugh, *Plato's Mathematical Imagination,* and Ernest G. McClain, *The Pythagorean Plato: Prelude to the Song Itself.*

4. The two Councils of Thirty-seven are often assumed to indicate that Plato left the manuscript of the *Laws* in an unfinished state at his death or that Philippus of Opus was a poor editor. For discussions of such scholarly readings, see Morrow, *Plato's Cretan City,* 204-6, 238-40, and Saunders, "The Alleged Double Version," 230-36.

5. For an extensive discussion of *paideia* in the *Republic* and the *Laws,* see Warren D. Anderson, *Ethos and Education in Greek Music,* 64-110.

6. Jose Ortega y Gasset writes that sportive hunting "submerges man deliberately in that formidable mystery [of Nature] and therefore contains something of religious rite and emotion in which homage is paid to what is divine, transcendent, in the laws of Nature." The "supremely free renunciation by man of the supremacy of his humanity" in hunting makes it possible to compare hunting both with religious rite and with philosophy, as did the ancient Greeks. See *Meditations on Hunting,* 51, 97-98, 131.

Chapter 10. Naming the Paradigmatic City

1. For a discussion of the emendations suggested for the text, *he mia deuteros,* see England's commentary on 739e, *The Laws of Plato,* 1:516-17. My translation of the text as "the second one" would be more appropriate for *mia deutera* or *eis deuteros,* but I believe it better captures the meaning of the Athenian's ambiguous remark than would a more circuitous translation such as "second in point of unity." The Athenian's apparent mixing of genders may have Pythagorean significance. Since the One from which all things originate is beyond distinctions of gender, it is generally given in the neuter, *to hen.* Perhaps the Athenian uses gender playfully in his remark to suggest that the relation of the god, the cosmic city of the gods, and the best possible earthly city corresponds to the relation of the One, the female and the male in demiurgic genesis, which is expressed in speech as a relation of neuter, feminine, and masculine genders. The god, the city of the gods, and the best earthly city are ranked first, second, and third in relation to one another. However, the Athenian's remark suggests that each deserves to be called the one in some way. After the One (*hen*), the cosmic city is the first one (*mia*); after the first one, the best possible earthly city is "the second one," that is, second to none.

2. For a different reading, see Allan Bloom, "An Interpretation of Plato's *Ion.*" Bloom does not find that Socrates distinguishes between performance and interpretation, poetic and rhapsodic inspiration, or poetic and rhapsodic interpretation. In his analysis, poetry is presented as an essentially incorrect account of "the world" and an essentially incomplete account of "the whole." The empirical and rational truths of both are only grasped correctly and completely through philosophy. The greatness of Homeric poetry, for example, would not be the result of its ability to move the *psyche* and *nous* toward some worthy end through persuasion and interpretation, but the result of its ability to persuade many human beings to accept dog-

matically a mythological or irrational account of gods not evident in the sensible realm. This is, for Bloom, how cultures and traditions, if not even civilizations, are begun.

Conclusion

1. Cf. Stanley Rosen, *The Quarrel between Philosophy and Poetry: Studies in Ancient Thought*, 1–26.

2. Two good studies of Plato's use of Homeric imagery are Robert Eisner, "Socrates as Hero," and Charles Segal, " 'The Myth Was Saved': Reflections on Homer and the Mythology of Plato's *Republic*." For comparable studies of Homer's presentation of Odysseus, see Norman Austin, *Archery at the Dark of the Moon: Poetic Problems in Homer's Odyssey;* George Dimock, *The Unity of the Odyssey;* and Mera J. Flaumenhaft, "The Undercover Hero: Odysseus from Dark to Daylight." Two esoteric readings of the *Odyssey* that misconstrue Odysseus in the same way that Leo Strauss misunderstands Socrates and the Athenian are David Bolotin, "The Concerns of Odysseus: An Introduction to the *Odyssey*," and Jenny Strauss Clay, *The Wrath of Athena*.

3. The title of Seth Benardete's study of the *Republic, Socrates' Second Sailing*, reveals that he understands the relation between Socrates' use of the phrase "second sailing" in the *Phaedo* and his account of the longer way. Benardete says nothing to suggest there is a second "second sailing." When the significance of the second "second sailing" is missed, the *Republic* seems to present a stark antithesis between the philosopher and the city. The *Laws* then becomes a curiosity requiring elaborate invention in order to be reconciled with the *Republic*. This is, in short, how Benardete's mentor, Leo Strauss, reads Plato.

BIBLIOGRAPHY

Classical Texts and Translations

All translations from the Greek are my own, unless otherwise indicated. I have used the Loeb Classical Library (Harvard University Press) for the Greek texts. I have also frequently consulted the translations and commentaries listed below. In the case of Aristotle's *Politics*, I have used Carnes Lord's translation throughout.

Aristotle, *The Politics*. Translated by Carnes Lord. Chicago: University of Chicago Press, 1985.

The Laws of Plato. Edited by E. B. England. Manchester: Manchester University Press, 1921.

The Laws of Plato. Translated by Thomas Pangle. New York: Basic Books, 1980.

The Republic of Plato. Translated by Allan Bloom. New York: Basic Books, 1976.

Books and Essays

Anderson, Warren D. *Ethos and Education in Greek Music*. Cambridge, Mass.: Harvard University Press, 1968.

Andrew, Edward. "Descent to the Cave." *Review of Politics* 45 (1983): 510–35.

Arendt, Hannah. "Martin Heidegger at Eighty." In *Heidegger and Modern Philosophy*, edited by Michael Murray. New Haven: Yale University Press, 1978.

———. *The Origins of Totalitarianism*. New York: Harcourt Brace, 1973.

Austin, Norman. *Archery at the Dark of the Moon: Poetic Problems in Homer's Odyssey*. Berkeley: University of California Press, 1975.

Axelrod, Robert. *The Evolution of Cooperation*. New York: Basic Books, 1984.

Beiner, Ronald. *Political Judgment*. Chicago: University of Chicago Press, 1983.

Benardete, Seth. "On Wisdom and Philosophy: The First Two Chapters of Aristotle's *Metaphysics* A." *Review of Metaphysics* 32 (1978): 205-15.

―――. *Socrates' Second Sailing*. Chicago: University of Chicago Press, 1989.

Bloom, Allan. "An Interpretation of Plato's *Ion*." *Interpretation* 1 (1970): 43-62.

―――. "Interpretive Essay." In *The Republic of Plato*. New York: Basic Books, 1978.

―――. "Response to Hall." *Political Theory* 5 (1977): 315-30.

Bolotin, David. "The Concerns of Odysseus: An Introduction to the *Odyssey*." *Interpretation* 17 (1989): 41-57.

Brumbaugh, Robert S. "The Divided Line and the Direction of Inquiry." *Philosophical Forum* 2 (1970-1971): 172-99.

―――. *Plato's Mathematical Imagination: The Mathematical Passages in the Dialogues and Their Interpretation*. Bloomington: University of Indiana Press, 1954.

Burkert, W. *Lore and Science in Ancient Pythagoreanism*. Cambridge, Mass.: Harvard University Press, 1972.

Campbell, Blair. "Deity and Human Agency in Plato's *Laws*." *History of Political Thought* 2 (1981): 417-46.

Cherniss, Harold. "Plato as Mathematician." *Review of Metaphysics* 4 (1951): 395-425.

―――. *The Riddle of the Early Academy*. Berkeley: University of California Press, 1945.

Clay, Jenny Strauss. *The Wrath of Athena*. Princeton: Princeton University Press, 1983.

Cooper, Barry. "'A Lump Bred Up in Darkness': Two Tellurian Themes of the *Republic*." Paper presented at the Canadian Political Science Association Annual Meeting, Ottawa, June 1982.

Craig, Leon. "The War Lover: A Study of Plato's *Republic*." Paper presented at the Canadian Political Science Association Annual Meeting, Winnipeg, June 1986.

Dimock, George. *The Unity of the Odyssey*. Amherst: University of Massachusetts Press, 1989.

Dostal, Robert J. "Beyond Being: Heidegger's Plato." *Journal of the History of Philosophy* 23 (1985): 71-98.

Eisner, Robert. "Socrates as Hero." *Philosophy and Literature* 6 (1982): 106-18.

Ferguson, A. S. "Plato's Simile of the Light Again." *Classical Quarterly* 28 (1934): 190–210.

Fideler, David R., ed. *The Pythagorean Sourcebook and Library.* Translated by K. S. Guthrie. Grand Rapids, Mich.: Phanes, 1987.

Flaumenhaft, Mera J. "The Undercover Hero: Odysseus from Dark to Daylight." *Interpretation* 10 (1982): 9–41.

Frank, Erich. *Plato und die Sogenannten Pythagoreer.* Holle: Verlag von Max Niemeyer, 1923.

Friedlander, Paul. *Plato.* Princeton: Bollingen, 1973.

Gadamer, Hans-Georg. *Dialogue and Dialectic: Eight Hermeneutical Studies on Plato.* Translated by P. C. Smith. New Haven: Yale University Press, 1980.

———. *The Idea of the Good in Platonic-Aristotelian Philosophy.* Translated by P. C. Smith. New Haven: Yale University Press, 1986.

———. "Plato and Heidegger." In *The Question of Being,* edited by M. Sprung. University Park: Pennsylvania State University Press, 1978.

———. "Religion and Religiosity in Socrates." Translated by R. Velkley. In *Proceedings of the Boston Area Colloquium in Ancient Philosophy,* vol. 1, edited by J. J. Cleary. Lanham, Md.: University Press of America, 1985.

———. *Truth and Method.* Translated by G. Barrett and J. Cumming. New York: Crossroads, 1982.

Grant, George. *Technology and Justice.* Toronto: Anansi, 1986.

Guthrie, W. K. C. *A History of Greek Philosophy.* Cambridge: Cambridge University Press, 1978.

Hackforth, R. "Plato's Theism." *Classical Quarterly* 30 (1936): 4–9.

Hahn, Robert. "A Note on Plato's Divided Line." *Journal of the History of Philosophy* 21 (1983): 235–37.

Hall, Dale. "Interpreting Plato's Cave as an Allegory of the Human Condition." *Apeiron* 14 (1980): 74–86.

———. "The *Republic* and the 'Limits of Politics.'" *Political Theory* 5 (1977): 293–313.

Hamlyn, D. W. "*Eikasia* in Plato's *Republic.*" *Philosophical Quarterly* 8 (1958): 14–23.

Hegel, G. W. F. *The Phenomenology of Spirit.* Translated by A. V. Miller. New York: Oxford University Press, 1979.

Heidegger, Martin. *An Introduction to Metaphysics.* Translated by R. Manheim. New Haven: Yale University Press, 1976.

————. *Nietzsche*, vol. 4. Translated by F. A. Capuzzi. San Francisco: Harper and Row, 1982.

————. "Plato's Doctrine of Truth." Translated by J. Barlow. In *Philosophy in the Twentieth Century*, edited by W. Barrett and H. Aiken. New York: Random House, 1962.

————. "The Rectorate 1933/34: Facts and Thoughts." Translated by K. Harris. *Review of Metaphysics* 38 (1985), 467–502.

Heninger, S. K., Jr. *Touches of Sweet Harmony*. San Marino, Calif.: Huntington, 1974.

Hopper, V. F. *Medieval Number Symbolism*. New York: Columbia University Press, 1938.

Howland, Jacob. "The Cave Image and the Problem of Place: The Sophist, the Poet and the Philosopher." *Dionysius* 10 (1986): 21–55.

Jackson, B. Darrell. "The Prayers of Socrates." *Phronesis* 16 (1971): 14–37.

Jaeger, Werner. *Paideia: The Ideals of Greek Culture*. Translated by G. Highet. New York: Oxford University Press, 1969.

Kates, Carol A. "Heidegger and the Myth of the Cave." *Personalist* 50 (1969): 532–48.

Klein, Jacob. *Greek Mathematical Thought and the Origin of Algebra*. Translated by E. Brann. Cambridge, Mass.: MIT Press, 1968.

————. *Plato's Trilogy*. Chicago: University of Chicago Press, 1980.

Klosko, George. *The Development of Plato's Political Theory*. New York: Methuen, 1986.

————. "The Nocturnal Council in Plato's *Laws*." *Political Studies* 36 (1988): 74–88.

Kojève, Alexandre. *Introduction to the Reading of Hegel*. Translated by J. H. Nichols, Jr. New York: Basic Books, 1969.

McClain, Ernest G. *The Pythagorean Plato: Prelude to the Song Itself*. Stony Brook: Nicolas Hayes, 1978.

Machiavelli, Niccolo. *The Prince*. Translated by Harvey C. Mansfield, Jr. Chicago: University of Chicago Press, 1985.

Morrison, J. S. "Two Unresolved Difficulties in the Line and the Cave." *Phronesis* 22 (1977): 212–23.

Morrow, Glenn. *Plato's Cretan City: A Historical Interpretation of the Laws*. Princeton: Princeton University Press, 1960.

Murphy, N. R. *The Interpretation of Plato's Republic*. Oxford: Clarendon Press, 1951.

————. "The 'Simile of Light' in Plato's *Republic*." *Classical Quarterly* 26 (1932): 93–102.

Nettleship, R. L. *Lectures on the Republic of Plato.* 2d ed. London: Macmillan, 1901.

Nolte, Ernst. *The Three Faces of Fascism.* New York: New American Library, 1969.

Ortega y Gasset, Jose. *Meditations on Hunting.* Translated by H. B. Wescott. New York: Scribner's, 1972.

Pangle, Thomas. "Interpretive Essay." In *The Laws of Plato.* New York: Basic Books, 1980.

———. "The Political Psychology of Religion in Plato's *Laws.*" *American Political Science Review* 70 (1976): 1059–77.

———. "Politics and Religion in Plato's *Laws:* Some Preliminary Reflections." *Essays in Arts and Sciences* 3 (1974): 19–28.

Popper, Karl R. *The Open Society and Its Enemies.* Princeton: Princeton University Press, 1962.

Post, L. A. *The Vatican Plato and Its Relations.* Middletown, Conn.: American Philological Association, 1934.

Raven, J. E. *Plato's Thought in the Making.* Cambridge: Cambridge University Press, 1965.

———. "Sun, Divided Line and Cave." *Classical Quarterly,* n.s. 3 (1953): 22–32.

Rose, L. E. "Plato's Divided Line." *Review of Metaphysics* 17 (1964): 425–35.

Rosen, Stanley. "Book Reviews." *Philosophy and Rhetoric* 14 (1981): 112–17.

———. *The Limits of Analysis.* New York: Basic Books, 1980.

———. *Nihilism: A Philosophical Essay.* New Haven: Yale University Press, 1974.

———. "Platonic Hermeneutics: On the Interpretation of a Platonic Dialogue." In *Proceedings of the Boston Area Colloquium in Ancient Philosophy,* vol. 1, edited by J. J. Cleary. Lanham, Md.: University Press of America, 1985.

———. *Plato's Sophist: The Drama of Original and Image.* New Haven: Yale University Press, 1983.

———. *The Quarrel between Philosophy and Poetry: Studies in Ancient Thought.* New York: Routledge, 1988.

———. "The Role of Eros in Plato's *Republic.*" *Review of Metaphysics* 18 (1964–1965): 452–75.

Saunders, Trevor J. "The Alleged Double Version in the Sixth Book of the *Laws.*" *Classical Quarterly* n.s. 20 (1970): 230–36.

———. *Bibliography on Plato's Laws, 1920–1970, with Additional Citations through May 1975.* New York: Arno, 1976.

Saxonhouse, Arlene W. "Comedy in Callipolis: Animal Imagery in the *Republic.*" *American Political Science Review* 72 (1978): 888–901.

Segal, Charles. " 'The Myth was Saved': Reflections on Homer and the Mythology of Plato's *Republic.*" *Hermes* 106 (1978): 315–36.

Sinclair, Thomas Alan. "Myth and Politics in the *Laws* of Plato." *Proceedings: Première Congrès des études classiques: Les mythes grecs dans l'art et la littérature*, Paris, n.d.

Skemp, J. B. *The Theory of Motion in Plato's Later Dialogues.* Amsterdam: Hakkert, 1967.

Stalley, R. F. *An Introduction to Plato's Laws.* Indianapolis: Hackett, 1983.

Strang, Colin. "Plato's Analogy of the Cave." *Oxford Studies in Ancient Philosophy* 4 (1986): 19–34.

Strauss, Leo. *The Argument and the Action of Plato's Laws.* Chicago: University of Chicago Press, 1975.

———. *The City and Man.* Chicago: University of Chicago Press, 1978.

———. "Plato." In *History of Political Philosophy*, edited by L. Strauss and J. Cropsey. Chicago: University of Chicago Press, 1987.

———. *Socrates and Aristophanes.* Chicago: University of Chicago Press, 1966.

———. *What Is Political Philosophy?* Westport: Greenwood, 1973.

Stridbeck, Carl Gustaf. *Raphael Studies.* Uppsala: Almqvist and Wiksell, 1960.

Voegelin, Eric. *Anamnesis.* Translated by G. Niemeyer. Notre Dame: University of Notre Dame Press, 1978.

———. "Equivalences of Experience and Symbolization in History." In *Eternità e Storia.* Firenze: Valecchi, 1970.

———. "The Gospel and Culture." In *Jesus and Man's Hope*, vol. 2, edited by D. Miller and D. G. Hadidian. Pittsburgh Theological Seminary Press, 1971.

———. "Immortality: Experience and Symbol." *Harvard Theological Review* 60 (1967): 235–79.

———. *Order and History.* Baton Rouge: Louisiana State University Press, 1957.

———. "Quod Deus Dicitur." *Journal of the American Academy of Religion* 53 (1985): 569–84.

———. "Wisdom and the Magic of the Extreme: A Meditation." *Southern Review* (Spring 1981): 235–87.

West, Thomas G. *Plato's "Apology of Socrates": An Interpretation, with a New Translation.* Ithaca: Cornell University Press, 1979.

Wolin, Richard. *The Politics of Being: The Political Thought of Martin Heidegger.* New York: Columbia University Press, 1990.

Wright, John H. "The Origin of Plato's Cave." *Harvard Studies in Classical Philology* 17 (1906): 131–42.

INDEX